2 CORINTHIANS

WISDOM COMMENTARY

Volume 48

2 Corinthians

Antoinette Clark Wire

Mary Ann Beavis
Volume Editor

Barbara E. Reid, OP
General Editor

A Michael Glazier Book

LITURGICAL PRESS
Collegeville, Minnesota

www.litpress.org

A Michael Glazier Book published by Liturgical Press

1   2   3   4   5   6   7   8   9

Library of Congress Cataloging-in-Publication Data

Names: Wire, Antoinette Clark, author.
Title: 2 Corinthians / Antoinette Clark Wire ; Mary Ann Beavis, volume editor ;
    Barbara E. Reid, OP, general editor.
Other titles: Second Corinthians
Description: Collegeville : Liturgical Press, 2019. | Series: Wisdom
    commentary ; Volume 48 | "A Michael Glazier book." | Includes
    bibliographical references and index. |
Identifiers: LCCN 2018057550 (print) | LCCN 2019000793 (ebook) | ISBN
    9780814681978 (eBook) | ISBN 9780814681725 (hardcover)
Subjects: LCSH: Bible. Corinthians, 2nd—Commentaries. | Bible. Corinthians,
    2nd—Feminist criticism.
Classification: LCC BS2675.53 (ebook) | LCC BS2675.53 .W57 2019 (print) |
    DDC 227/.306082—dc23
LC record available at https://lccn.loc.gov/2018057550

Contents

Acknowledgments

M y work here goes back to Pomona College philosophy seminars with Gordon Kaufman and Fred Sontag, to Yale Divinity study of Paul's letters with Paul Minear and Paul Schubert, and to Claremont Graduate School work in biblical theologies with James Robinson and in 2 Corinthians itself with Hans Dieter Betz. Only later did I learn how social structures and oral traditions shape biblical texts from colleagues Marvin Chaney, Robert and Polly Coote, Eugene Park and Herman Waetjen at San Francisco Theological Seminary, Norman Gottwald at the Graduate Theological Union and Daniel Boyarin at University of California in Berkeley. Last but not least I met myself in working with feminist writers and co-teachers including Elisabeth Schüssler Fiorenza, Rosemary Ruether, Cynthia Kittredge, Holly Hearon, Linda Maloney, Luise Schottroff, and Carol Robb.

Working on this book I have depended on the libraries at the Graduate Theological Union and at Claremont School of Theology for years of welcome, light and books, and for the CST staff Elaine Walker, Koala Jones, and Ann Hidalgo's tracking down of sources. For help in translating I turned to Bob and Polly Coote and Tom and Jean Roth, for computer rescues to Hugh Wire, Lenore Brashler, and Tim Tipping. A special windfall came from writing within Liturgical Press's Wisdom Commentary series—the stimulating interaction with those who wrote short contributing pieces, both interpreters of 2 Corinthians whom I could convince to offer their own views (see Contributors) and ancient writers whose work I gleaned to set off Paul's speech and thought. Many thanks to the volume editor Mary Ann Beavis and the series editor Barbara Reid for their longstanding patience and careful reading. For help through the maze of permissions and proofs I thank Liturgical Press, its publisher Hans Christoffersen, and Tara Durheim, Stephanie Lancour, Lauren Murphy, Colleen Stiller, and Julie Surma.

But when it comes down to writing, what matters at the desk is the subject, the resource books, and the setting. So praise goes to Paul for writing a letter that has absorbed me for so many years—and to the Corinthians for provoking him to write it. And thanks to the authors whose books on my desk you will see in the notes, my companions on the way toward understanding this interaction. And blessings on Hugh and our circle of family and friends for the time and space and good life in which to write.

The following permissions have been granted to cite copyrighted materials:

"Memory's Mercies" from HAMMER IS THE PRAYER: SELECTED POEMS by Christian Wiman. Copyright © 2016 by Christian Wiman. Reprinted by permission of Farrar, Straus and Giroux.

Richard S. Ascough, Philip A. Harland and John S. Kloppenborg, "Regulations of the Sacrificing Associates of the Mother of the Gods," "Membership List of an Association of Banqueters," and "Honors by Dyers for a Priestess of the Augusti," *Associations in the Greco-Roman World: A Sourcebook*, 28–29, 35, 87. © 2012. Reprinted by permission of Baylor University Press.

Selections from the following volumes are cited from the Loeb Classical Library ®, a registered trademark of the President and Fellows of Harvard College, with permission from Harvard University Press:

Alciphron, Aelian, and Philostratus, translated by Allen Rogers Benner and Francis H. Fobes, Loeb Classical Library Volume 383, Cambridge, MA: Harvard University Press, First published 1949.

Arrian, Vol. 2, translated by E. Iliff Robson, B.D., Loeb Classical Library Volume 269, Cambridge, MA: Harvard University Press, First published 1933.

Dio Chrysostom, Vol. 1, translated by J. W. Cohoon, Loeb Classical Library Volume 257, Cambridge, MA: Harvard University Press, First published 1932.

Dio Chrysostom, Vol. 3, translated by J. W. Cohoon and H. Lamar Crosby, Loeb Classical Library Volume 358, Cambridge, MA: Harvard University Press, First published 1940.

Josephus, Vol. 13, translated by Louis H. Feldman, Loeb Classical Library Volume 456, Cambridge, MA: Harvard University Press, Copyright 1965 by the President and Fellows of Harvard College.

Lucian, Vol. 4, translated by A. M. Harmon, Loeb Classical Library Volume 162, Cambridge, MA: Harvard University Press, First published 1925.

Philo, Vol. 1, translated by F. H. Colson and G. H. Whitaker, Loeb Classical Library Volume 226, Cambridge, MA: Harvard University Press, First published 1929.

Philo, Vol. 4, translated by F. H. Colson and G. H. Whitaker, Loeb Classical Library Volume 261, Cambridge, MA: Harvard University Press, First published 1932.

Strabo, Vol. 4, translated by Horace Leonard Jones, Loeb Classical Library Volume 196, Cambridge, MA: Harvard University Press, First published 1927.

Panel from the Imperial Reliefs at the Sebasteion in Aphrodisias. Photograph by the New York University Excavation at Aphrodisias (G. Petruccioli) from the Faculty of Classics, University of Oxford.

Bas Relief of Saturnia or Tellus on the *Ara Pacis* in Rome, 9–13 CE. Photograph from Archivi Alinari, Firenze (Fratelli Alinari).

Abbreviations

3 Cor.	Third Corinthians (pseudonymous Pauline letter)
AB	Anchor Bible
AJ	*Antiquities of the Jews*
Ant.	*Jewish Antiquities*
ArBib	The Aramaic Bible
BCE	Before the Common Era
BDAG	Danker, Frederick W., Walter Bauer, William F. Arndt, and F. Wilbur Gingrich. *Greek-English Lexicon of the New Testament and Other Early Christian Literature.* 3rd ed. Chicago: University of Chicago Press, 2000 (Bauer-Danker-Arndt-Gingrich)
BETL	Bibliotheca Ephemeridum Theologicarum Lovaniensium
BHT	*Beiträge zur historischen Theologie*
BiBh	*Bible Bhashyam*
BibInt	Biblical Interpretation series
BibLeb	*Bibel und Leben*
BSac	*Bibliotheca sacra*
BTB	*Biblical Theology Bulletin*
BTS	Biblical Tools and Studies
BZ	*Biblische Zeitschrift*

BZNW	Beihefte zur Zeitschrift für die neutestamentliche Wissenschaft
CBQ	*Catholic Biblical Quarterly*
CE	Common Era
Co	Corinthiens (French for Corinthians)
ESV	English Standard Version
FCB	Feminist Companion to the Bible
FCNTECW	Feminist Companion to the New Testament and Early Christian Writings
GBS	Guides to Biblical Scholarship
Hist. Eccl.	*Historia Ecclesiastica* (Eusebius' *History of the Christian Church)*
Hor	*Horizons*
HTR	*Harvard Theological Review*
ICC	International Critical Commentary
IFT	Introductions in Feminist Theology
JB	Jerusalem Bible
JBL	*Journal of Biblical Literature*
JPS	Jewish Publication Society
JSNT	*Journal for the Study of the New Testament*
JSOT	*Journal for the Study of the Old Testament*
JOSTSup	Journal for the Study of the Old Testament Supplement series
JTS	*Journal of Theological Studies*
KJV	King James Version
Kor	Korintherbrief (German for Corinthian letter)
LCL	Loeb Classical Library
LXX	Septuagint (an early Greek translation of the Hebrew Bible)
NABRE	New American Bible Revised Edition
NASB	New American Standard Bible
NEB	New English Bible

Neot	*Neotestamentica*
NIV	New International Version
NJB	New Jerusalem Bible
NovT	*Novum Testamentum*
NovTSup	Novum Testamentum Supplements
NRSV	New Revised Standard Version
NTS	*New Testament Studies*
OBT	Overtures to Biblical Theology
REB	Revised English Bible
RHPR	*Revue d'histoire et de philosophie religieuses*
RSV	Revised Standard Version
SBL	Society of Biblical Literature
SemeiaSt	Semeia Studies
SP	Sacra Pagina
Spec. Leg.	*De Specialibus Legibus* (Philo's *On the Special Laws*)
ST	*Studia Theologica*
Syms	Symposium Series
TDNT	*Theological Dictionary of the New Testament*
TZ	*Theologische Zeitschrift*
WBC	Word Biblical Commentary
WD	*Wort und Dienst*
WUNT	Wissenschaftliche Untersuchungen zum Neuen Testament
ZNW	*Zeitschrift für die neutestamentliche Wissenschaft und die Kunde der älteren Kirche*
ZTK	*Zeitschrift für Theologie und Kirche*

Contributors

Naim Ateek was born in the Palestinian village of Beisan in 1937. He is a Palestinian Anglican priest and former Canon of St. George's Cathedral in Jerusalem. An active leader in shaping Palestinian liberation theology, he founded the Sabeel Ecumenical Liberation Theology Center in Jerusalem. His *Justice, and Only Justice: A Palestinian Theology of Liberation* (Maryknoll, NY: Orbis Books, 1989) explores the foundation of a theology and politics to address the conflict over Palestine. His recent books include *A Palestinian Christian Cry for Reconciliation* (Orbis Books, 2008) and *A Palestinian Theology of Liberation* (Orbis Books, 2017).

Kuanrong Chen is an ordained minister and professor of New Testament Studies at Anhui Theological Seminary in Hefei, Anhui Province, China. She received her master's degree in New Testament in 1995 and is now in full-time study for a doctor of ministry in pastoral theology at Nanjing Union Theological Seminary with a focus on Christian marriage counseling and its contribution to society at large. In addition to teaching New Testament theology, exegesis of John and of Acts, and pastoral counseling, she has published articles including "God's Love Is Greater than Father Love," "Women Disciples of Jesus," and "A Preliminary Study of Women's Theology" in the *Chinese Theological Review* (English) and the *Nanjing Theological Review* (Chinese).

Marlene Crüsemann is an independent scholar in Bielefeld, Germany, with a doctorate in New Testament exegesis who practices feminist and social-historical interpretation of the Bible. A co-editor and a translator of the *Bibel in gerechter Sprache,* she is writing the Kohlhammer commentary on 2 Corinthians. In 2015 her major essays were published by Gütersloher Verlagshaus as *Gott ist Beziehung: Beiträge zur biblischen Rede von Gott,* edited by Claudia Janssen and Luise Schottroff. Her *Pseudepigraphical Letters to the Thessalonians* is translated by Linda M. Maloney and due from T & T Clark in 2019.

Holly E. Hearon is T. J. and Virginia Liggett Professor of Christian Traditions and professor emerita of New Testament at Christian Theological Seminary (Indianapolis). Her writings include *The Mary Magdalene Tradition: Witness and Counter-Witness in Early Christian Communities* (Collegeville, MN: Liturgical Press, 2004); "1 and 2 Corinthians" in *Queer Bible Commentary* (London: SCM, 2006); and "Communication in Context: Jesus Movements and the Construction of Meaning in the Media World of the First Century" in *Bridges in New Testament Interpretation,* ed. Neil Elliott and Werner Kelber (Lanham, MD: Lexington/Fortress, 2018).

Ma. Marilou S. Ibita is an assistant professor in the theology department at Ateneo de Manila University, Philippines, and a visiting professor at the University of Leuven. Her dissertation at the Katholieke Universiteit Leuven is titled " 'If Anyone Hungers, He/She Must Eat in the House' (1 Cor 11:34): A Narrative-Critical, Socio-Historical and Grammatical-Philological Analysis of the Story of the Lord's Supper in Corinth (1 Cor 11:17-34)." Among her recent publications are "Exploring the (In)Visibility of the Christ-Believers' Trans-Ethnicity: A Lowland Filipina Catholic's Perspective" in *Ethnicity, Race, Religion,* ed. Katherine Hockey and David Horrell (London: T & T Clark, 2018); and "Losing and Restoring the *adelphoi* Relationship at the Corinthian *kyriakon deipnon* (1 Cor 11:17-34)" in *Exploring Biblical Kinship: Festschrift in Honor of John J. Pilch,* ed. J. Campbell and P. Hartin (Washington, DC: Catholic Biblical Association, 2016).

Laura Salah Nasrallah is professor of New Testament and early Christianity at Harvard Divinity School. She is author of *Christian Responses to Roman Art and Architecture: The Second-Century Church amid the Spaces of Empire* (Cambridge: Cambridge University Press, 2010) and *Archaeology and the Letters of Paul* (New York: Oxford University Press, forthcoming).

Angela Standhartinger has been professor of New Testament at Philipps University Marburg since 2000. Her dissertation was published as *Das*

Frauenbild im Judentum der hellenistischen Zeit. Ein Beitrag anhand "Joseph und Aseneth" (Leiden: Brill, 1995), followed by *Studien zur Entstehungsgeschichte und Intention des Kolosserbriefs* (Leiden: Brill, 1999). Since then she has co-edited eight anthologies and written over a hundred articles, including, recently in English, "Bringing Back to Life: Laments and the Origin of the So-Called Words of Institution," in *Coming Back to Life*, ed. F. S. Tappenden and C. Daniel-Hughes (Montreal: McGill University Library, 2017 [online]); and "Letter from Prison as Hidden Transcript: What It Tells Us about the People at Philippi," in *The People Beside Paul: The Philippian Assembly and History from Below*, ed. Joseph Marchal (Atlanta: SBL Press, 2015).

Cynthia R. Wallace is assistant professor of English at St. Thomas More College, University of Saskatchewan, where her teaching and research center on the intersections of gender, race, and religion in contemporary literature and theory. Her book *Of Women Borne: A Literary Ethics of Suffering* was published in 2016 by Columbia University Press.

Christian Wiman is a poet from West Texas. He was editor of *Poetry* magazine in Chicago from 2003 to 2013 and is now professor in the practice of religion and literature at Yale University's Institute of Sacred Music. His interests include modern poetry, Russian literature, the language of faith, and theology conducted by unexpected means. His recent books of poetry include *Every Riven Thing* (2010), *Once in the West* (2014), and a book of selected poems, *Hammer Is the Prayer* (2016), all with Farrar, Straus and Giroux.

Foreword

"Come Eat of My Bread . . . and Walk in the Ways of Wisdom"

Elisabeth Schüssler Fiorenza

Harvard University Divinity School

Jewish feminist writer Asphodel Long has likened the Bible to

> a magnificent garden of brilliant plants, some flowering, some fruiting, some in seed, some in bud, shaded by trees of age old, luxurious growth. Yet in the very soil which gives it life the poison has been inserted. . . . This poison is that of misogyny, the hatred of women, half the human race.[1]

To see Scripture as such a beautiful garden containing poisonous ivy requires that one identify and name this poison and place on all biblical texts the label "Caution! Could be dangerous to your health and survival!" As critical feminist interpretation for well-being this Wisdom Commentary seeks to elaborate the beauty and fecundity of this

---

1. Asphodel Long, *In a Chariot Drawn by Lions: The Search for the Female in the Deity* (London: Women's Press, 1992), 195.

Scripture-garden and at the same time points to the harm it can do when one submits to its world of vision. Thus, feminist biblical interpretation engages two seemingly contradictory insights: The Bible is written in kyriocentric (i.e., lord/master/father/husband-elite male) language, originated in the patri-kyriarchal cultures of antiquity, and has functioned to inculcate misogynist mind-sets and oppressive values. At the same time it also asserts that the Bible as Sacred Scripture has functioned to inspire and authorize wo/men[2] in our struggles against dehumanizing oppression. The hermeneutical lens of wisdom/Wisdom empowers the commentary writers to do so.

In biblical as well as in contemporary religious discourse the word *wisdom* has a double meaning: It can either refer to the quality of life and of people and/or it can refer to a figuration of the Divine. Wisdom in both senses of the word is not a prerogative of the biblical traditions but is found in the imagination and writings of all known religions. Wisdom is transcultural, international, and interreligious. Wisdom is practical knowledge gained through experience and daily living as well as through the study of creation and human nature. Both word meanings, that of capability (wisdom) and that of female personification (Wisdom), are crucial for this Wisdom Commentary series that seeks to enable biblical readers to become critical subjects of interpretation.

Wisdom is a state of the human mind and spirit characterized by deep understanding and profound insight. It is elaborated as a quality possessed by the sages but also treasured as folk wisdom and wit. Wisdom is the power of discernment, deeper understanding, and creativity; it is the ability to move and to dance, to make the connections, to savor life, and to learn from experience. Wisdom is intelligence shaped by experience and sharpened by critical analysis. It is the ability to make sound choices and incisive decisions. Its root meaning comes to the fore in its Latin form *sapientia*, which is derived from the verb *sapere*, to taste and to savor something. Hence, this series of commentaries invites readers to taste, to evaluate, and to imagine. In the figure of *Chokmah-Sophia-Sapientia-Wisdom*, ancient Jewish scriptures seek to hold together belief in the "one" G*d[3] of Israel with both masculine and feminine language and metaphors of the Divine.

---

2. I use wo/man, s/he, fe/male and not the grammatical standard "man" as inclusive terms and make this visible by adding /.

3. I use the * asterisk in order to alert readers to a problem to explore and think about.

In distinction to traditional Scripture reading, which is often individualistic and privatized, the practice and space of Wisdom commentary is public. Wisdom's spiraling presence (*Shekhinah*) is global, embracing all creation. Her voice is a public, radical democratic voice rather than a "feminine," privatized one. To become one of Her justice-seeking friends, one needs to imagine the work of this feminist commentary series as the spiraling circle dance of wisdom/Wisdom,[4] as a Spirit/spiritual intellectual movement in the open space of wisdom/Wisdom who calls readers to critically analyze, debate, and reimagine biblical texts and their commentaries as wisdom/Wisdom texts inspired by visions of justice and well-being for everyone and everything. Wisdom-Sophia-imagination engenders a different understanding of Jesus and the movement around him. It understands him as the child and prophet of Divine Wisdom and as Wisdom herself instead of imagining him as ruling King and Lord who has only subalterns but not friends. To approach the N*T[5] and the whole Bible as Wisdom's invitation of cosmic dimensions means to acknowledge its multivalence and its openness to change. As bread—not stone.

In short, this commentary series is inspired by the feminist vision of the open cosmic house of Divine Wisdom-Sophia as it is found in biblical Wisdom literatures, which include the N*T:

> Wisdom has built Her house
> She has set up Her seven pillars . . .
> She has mixed Her wine,
> She also has set Her table.
> She has sent out Her wo/men ministers
> to call from the highest places in the town . . .
> "Come eat of my bread
> and drink of the wine I have mixed.
> Leave immaturity, and live,
> And walk in the way of Wisdom." (Prov 9:1-3, 5-6)

---

4. I have elaborated such a Wisdom dance in terms of biblical hermeneutics in my book *Wisdom Ways: Introducing Feminist Biblical Interpretation* (Maryknoll, NY: Orbis Books, 2001). Its seven steps are a hermeneutics of experience, of domination, of suspicion, of evaluation, of remembering or historical reconstruction, of imagination, and of transformation. However, such Wisdom strategies of meaning making are not restricted to the Bible. Rather, I have used them in workshops in Brazil and Ecuador to explore the workings of power, Condomblé, Christology, imagining a the*logical wo/men's center, or engaging the national icon of Mary.

5. See the discussion about nomenclature of the two testaments in the editor's introduction, page xliii.

Editor's Introduction to Wisdom Commentary

"She Is a Breath of the Power of God" (Wis 7:25)

Barbara E. Reid, OP

General Editor

Wisdom Commentary is the first series to offer detailed feminist interpretation of every book of the Bible. The fruit of collaborative work by an ecumenical and interreligious team of scholars, the volumes provide serious, scholarly engagement with the whole biblical text, not only those texts that explicitly mention women. The series is intended for clergy, teachers, ministers, and all serious students of the Bible. Designed to be both accessible and informed by the various approaches of biblical scholarship, it pays particular attention to the world in front of the text, that is, how the text is heard and appropriated. At the same time, this series aims to be faithful to the ancient text and its earliest audiences; thus the volumes also explicate the worlds behind the text and within it. While issues of gender are primary in this project, the volumes also address the intersecting issues of power, authority, ethnicity, race, class, and religious belief and practice. The fifty-eight volumes include the books regarded as canonical by Jews (i.e., the Tanakh); Protestants (the "Hebrew Bible" and the New Testament); and Roman Catholic, Anglican, and Eastern Orthodox

Communions (i.e., Tobit, Judith, 1 and 2 Maccabees, Wisdom of Solomon, Sirach/Ecclesiasticus, Baruch, including the Letter of Jeremiah, the additions to Esther, and Susanna and Bel and the Dragon in Daniel).

A Symphony of Diverse Voices

Included in the Wisdom Commentary series are voices from scholars of many different religious traditions, of diverse ages, differing sexual identities, and varying cultural, racial, ethnic, and social contexts. Some have been pioneers in feminist biblical interpretation; others are newer contributors from a younger generation. A further distinctive feature of this series is that each volume incorporates voices other than that of the lead author(s). These voices appear alongside the commentary of the lead author(s), in the grayscale inserts. At times, a contributor may offer an alternative interpretation or a critique of the position taken by the lead author(s). At other times, she or he may offer a complementary interpretation from a different cultural context or subject position. Occasionally, portions of previously published material bring in other views. The diverse voices are not intended to be contestants in a debate or a cacophony of discordant notes. The multiple voices reflect that there is no single definitive feminist interpretation of a text. In addition, they show the importance of subject position in the process of interpretation. In this regard, the Wisdom Commentary series takes inspiration from the Talmud and from *The Torah: A Women's Commentary* (ed. Tamara Cohn Eskenazi and Andrea L. Weiss; New York: Women of Reform Judaism, Federation of Temple Sisterhood, 2008), in which many voices, even conflicting ones, are included and not harmonized.

Contributors include biblical scholars, theologians, and readers of Scripture from outside the scholarly and religious guilds. At times, their comments pertain to a particular text. In some instances they address a theme or topic that arises from the text.

Another feature that highlights the collaborative nature of feminist biblical interpretation is that a number of the volumes have two lead authors who have worked in tandem from the inception of the project and whose voices interweave throughout the commentary.

Woman Wisdom

The title, Wisdom Commentary, reflects both the importance to feminists of the figure of Woman Wisdom in the Scriptures and the distinct wisdom that feminist women and men bring to the interpretive process. In the Scriptures, Woman Wisdom appears as "a breath of the power of God, and a pure emanation of the glory of the Almighty" (Wis 7:25), who was present and active in fashioning all that exists (Prov 8:22-31; Wis 8:6). She is a spirit who pervades and penetrates all things (Wis 7:22-23), and she provides guidance and nourishment at her all-inclusive table (Prov 9:1-5). In both postexilic biblical and nonbiblical Jewish sources, Woman Wisdom is often equated with Torah, e.g., Sirach 24:23-34; Baruch 3:9–4:4; 38:2; 46:4-5; 2 Baruch 48:33, 36; 4 Ezra 5:9-10; 13:55; 14:40; 1 Enoch 42.

The New Testament frequently portrays Jesus as Wisdom incarnate. He invites his followers, "take my yoke upon you and learn from me" (Matt 11:29), just as Ben Sira advises, "put your neck under her [Wisdom's] yoke and let your souls receive instruction" (Sir 51:26). Just as Wisdom experiences rejection (Prov 1:23-25; Sir 15:7-8; Wis 10:3; Bar 3:12), so too does Jesus (Mark 8:31; John 1:10-11). Only some accept his invitation to his all-inclusive banquet (Matt 22:1-14; Luke 14:15-24; compare Prov 1:20-21; 9:3-5). Yet, "wisdom is vindicated by her deeds" (Matt 11:19, speaking of Jesus and John the Baptist; in the Lucan parallel at 7:35 they are called "wisdom's children"). There are numerous parallels between what is said of Wisdom and of the *Logos* in the Prologue of the Fourth Gospel (John 1:1-18). These are only a few of many examples. This female embodiment of divine presence and power is an apt image to guide the work of this series.

Feminism

There are many different understandings of the term "feminism." The various meanings, aims, and methods have developed exponentially in recent decades. Feminism is a perspective and a movement that springs from a recognition of inequities toward women, and it advocates for changes in whatever structures prevent full flourishing of human beings and all creation. Three waves of feminism in the United States are commonly recognized. The first, arising in the mid-nineteenth century and lasting into the early twentieth, was sparked by women's efforts to be involved in the public sphere and to win the right to vote. In the 1960s and 1970s, the second wave focused on civil rights and equality for women. With the third wave, from the 1980s forward, came global feminism and the emphasis on the contextual nature of interpretation. Now a fourth wave may be emerging, with a stronger emphasis on the intersectionality of women's concerns with those of other marginalized groups and the increased use of the internet as a platform for discussion and activism.[1] As feminism has matured, it has recognized that inequities based on gender are interwoven with power imbalances based on race, class, ethnicity, religion, sexual identity, physical ability, and a host of other social markers.

Feminist Women and Men

Men who choose to identify with and partner with feminist women in the work of deconstructing systems of domination and building structures of equality are rightly regarded as feminists. Some men readily identify with experiences of women who are discriminated against on the basis of sex/gender, having themselves had comparable experiences; others who may not have faced direct discrimination or stereotyping recognize that inequity and problematic characterization still occur, and they seek correction. This series is pleased to include feminist men both as lead authors and as contributing voices.

Feminist Biblical Interpretation

Women interpreting the Bible from the lenses of their own experience is nothing new. Throughout the ages women have recounted the biblical stories, teaching them to their children and others, all the while interpreting them afresh for their time and circumstances.[2] Following is a very brief sketch of select foremothers who laid the groundwork for contemporary feminist biblical interpretation.

One of the earliest known Christian women who challenged patriarchal interpretations of Scripture was a consecrated virgin named Helie, who lived in the second century CE. When she refused to marry, her

1. See Martha Rampton, "Four Waves of Feminism" (October 25, 2015), at http://www.pacificu.edu/about-us/news-events/four-waves-feminism; and Ealasaid Munro, "Feminism: A Fourth Wave?," https://www.psa.ac.uk/insight-plus/feminism-fourth-wave.

2. For fuller treatments of this history, see chap. 7, "One Thousand Years of Feminist Bible Criticism," in Gerda Lerner, *Creation of Feminist Consciousness: From the Middle Ages to Eighteen-Seventy* (New York: Oxford University Press, 1993), 138–66; Susanne Scholz, "From the 'Woman's Bible' to the 'Women's Bible,' The History of Feminist Approaches to the Hebrew Bible," in *Introducing the Women's Hebrew Bible*, IFT 13 (New York: T&T Clark, 2007), 12–32; Marion Ann Taylor and Agnes Choi, eds., *Handbook of Women Biblical Interpreters: A Historical and Biographical Guide* (Grand Rapids: Baker Academic, 2012).

parents brought her before a judge, who quoted to her Paul's admonition, "It is better to marry than to be aflame with passion" (1 Cor 7:9). In response, Helie first acknowledges that this is what Scripture says, but then she retorts, "but not for everyone, that is, not for holy virgins."[3] She is one of the first to question the notion that a text has one meaning that is applicable in all situations.

A Jewish woman who also lived in the second century CE, Beruriah, is said to have had "profound knowledge of biblical exegesis and outstanding intelligence."[4] One story preserved in the Talmud (b. Berakot 10a) tells of how she challenged her husband, Rabbi Meir, when he prayed for the destruction of a sinner. Proffering an alternate interpretation, she argued that Psalm 104:35 advocated praying for the destruction of sin, not the sinner.

In medieval times the first written commentaries on Scripture from a critical feminist point of view emerge. While others may have been produced and passed on orally, they are for the most part lost to us now. Among the earliest preserved feminist writings are those of Hildegard of Bingen (1098–1179), German writer, mystic, and abbess of a Benedictine monastery. She reinterpreted the Genesis narratives in a way that presented women and men as complementary and interdependent. She frequently wrote about feminine aspects of the Divine.[5] Along with other women mystics of the time, such as Julian of Norwich (1342–ca. 1416), she spoke authoritatively from her personal experiences of God's revelation in prayer.

In this era, women were also among the scribes who copied biblical manuscripts. Notable among them is Paula Dei Mansi of Verona, from a distinguished family of Jewish scribes. In 1288, she translated from Hebrew into Italian a collection of Bible commentaries written by her father and added her own explanations.[6]

Another pioneer, Christine de Pizan (1365–ca. 1430), was a French court writer and prolific poet. She used allegory and common sense

3. Madrid, Escorial MS, a II 9, f. 90 v., as cited in Lerner, *Feminist Consciousness*, 140.

4. See Judith R. Baskin, "Women and Post-Biblical Commentary," in *The Torah: A Women's Commentary*, ed. Tamara Cohn Eskenazi and Andrea L. Weiss (New York: Women of Reform Judaism, Federation of Temple Sisterhood, 2008), xlix–lv, at lii.

5. Hildegard of Bingen, *De Operatione Dei*, 1.4.100; PL 197:885bc, as cited in Lerner, *Feminist Consciousness*, 142–43. See also Barbara Newman, *Sister of Wisdom: St. Hildegard's Theology of the Feminine* (Berkeley: University of California Press, 1987).

6. Emily Taitz, Sondra Henry, Cheryl Tallan, eds., *JPS Guide to Jewish Women 600 B.C.E.–1900 C.E.* (Philadelphia: Jewish Publication Society of America, 2003), 110–11.

to subvert misogynist readings of Scripture and celebrated the accomplishments of female biblical figures to argue for women's active roles in building society.[7]

By the seventeenth century, there were women who asserted that the biblical text needs to be understood and interpreted in its historical context. For example, Rachel Speght (1597–ca. 1630), a Calvinist English poet, elaborates on the historical situation in first-century Corinth that prompted Paul to say, "It is well for a man not to touch a woman" (1 Cor 7:1). Her aim was to show that the biblical texts should not be applied in a literal fashion to all times and circumstances. Similarly, Margaret Fell (1614–1702), one of the founders of the Religious Society of Friends (Quakers) in Britain, addressed the Pauline prohibitions against women speaking in church by insisting that they do not have universal validity. Rather, they need to be understood in their historical context, as addressed to a local church in particular time-bound circumstances.[8]

Along with analyzing the historical context of the biblical writings, women in the eighteenth and nineteenth centuries began to attend to misogynistic interpretations based on faulty translations. One of the first to do so was British feminist Mary Astell (1666–1731).[9] In the United States, the Grimké sisters, Sarah (1792–1873) and Angelina (1805–1879), Quaker women from a slaveholding family in South Carolina, learned biblical Greek and Hebrew so that they could interpret the Bible for themselves. They were prompted to do so after men sought to silence them from speaking out against slavery and for women's rights by claiming that the Bible (e.g., 1 Cor 14:34) prevented women from speaking in public.[10] Another prominent abolitionist, Sojourner Truth (ca. 1797–1883), a former slave, quoted the Bible liberally in her speeches[11] and in so doing challenged cultural assumptions and biblical interpretations that undergird gender inequities.

---

7. See further Taylor and Choi, *Handbook of Women Biblical Interpreters*, 127–32.

8. Her major work, *Women's Speaking Justified, Proved and Allowed by the Scriptures*, published in London in 1667, gave a systematic feminist reading of all biblical texts pertaining to women.

9. Mary Astell, *Some Reflections upon Marriage* (New York: Source Book Press, 1970, reprint of the 1730 edition; earliest edition of this work is 1700), 103–4.

10. See further Sarah Grimké, *Letters on the Equality of the Sexes and the Condition of Woman* (Boston: Isaac Knapp, 1838).

11. See, for example, her most famous speech, "Ain't I a Woman?," delivered in 1851 at the Ohio Women's Rights Convention in Akron, OH; http://www.fordham.edu/halsall/mod/sojtruth-woman.asp.

Another monumental work that emerged in nineteenth-century England was that of Jewish theologian Grace Aguilar (1816–1847), *The Women of Israel*,[12] published in 1845. Aguilar's approach was to make connections between the biblical women and contemporary Jewish women's concerns. She aimed to counter the widespread notion that women were degraded in Jewish law and that only in Christianity were women's dignity and value upheld. Her intent was to help Jewish women find strength and encouragement by seeing the evidence of God's compassionate love in the history of every woman in the Bible. While not a full commentary on the Bible, Aguilar's work stands out for its comprehensive treatment of every female biblical character, including even the most obscure references.[13]

The first person to produce a full-blown feminist commentary on the Bible was Elizabeth Cady Stanton (1815–1902). A leading proponent in the United States for women's right to vote, she found that whenever women tried to make inroads into politics, education, or the work world, the Bible was quoted against them. Along with a team of like-minded women, she produced her own commentary on every text of the Bible that concerned women. Her pioneering two-volume project, *The Woman's Bible*, published in 1895 and 1898, urges women to recognize that texts that degrade women come from the men who wrote the texts, not from God, and to use their common sense to rethink what has been presented to them as sacred.

Nearly a century later, *The Women's Bible Commentary*, edited by Carol Newsom and Sharon Ringe (Louisville: Westminster John Knox, 1992), appeared. This one-volume commentary features North American feminist scholarship on each book of the Protestant canon. Like Cady Stanton's commentary, it does not contain comments on every section of the biblical text but only on those passages deemed relevant to women. It was revised and expanded in 1998 to include the Apocrypha/Deuterocanonical books, and the contributors to this new volume reflect the global face of contemporary feminist scholarship. The revisions made in the third edition, which appeared in 2012, represent the profound advances in feminist biblical scholarship and include newer voices. In both the second and third editions, *The* has been dropped from the title.

---

12. The full title is *The Women of Israel or Characters and Sketches from the Holy Scriptures and Jewish History Illustrative of the Past History, Present Duty, and Future Destiny of the Hebrew Females, as Based on the Word of God.*

13. See further Eskenazi and Weiss, *The Torah: A Women's Commentary*, xxxviii; Taylor and Choi, *Handbook of Women Biblical Interpreters*, 31–37.

Also appearing at the centennial of Cady Stanton's *The Woman's Bible* were two volumes edited by Elisabeth Schüssler Fiorenza with the assistance of Shelly Matthews. The first, *Searching the Scriptures: A Feminist Introduction* (New York: Crossroad, 1993), charts a comprehensive approach to feminist interpretation from ecumenical, interreligious, and multicultural perspectives. The second volume, published in 1994, provides critical feminist commentary on each book of the New Testament as well as on three books of Jewish Pseudepigrapha and eleven other early Christian writings.

In Europe, similar endeavors have been undertaken, such as the one-volume *Kompendium Feministische Bibelauslegung*, edited by Luise Schottroff and Marie-Theres Wacker (Gütersloh: Gütersloher Verlagshaus, 2007), featuring German feminist biblical interpretation of each book of the Bible, along with apocryphal books, and several extrabiblical writings. This work, now in its third edition, has recently been translated into English.[14] A multivolume project, *The Bible and Women: An Encylopaedia of Exegesis and Cultural History*, edited by Irmtraud Fischer, Adriana Valerio, Mercedes Navarro Puerto, and Christiana de Groot, is currently in production. This project presents a history of the reception of the Bible as embedded in Western cultural history and focuses particularly on gender-relevant biblical themes, biblical female characters, and women recipients of the Bible. The volumes are published in English, Spanish, Italian, and German.[15]

Another groundbreaking work is the collection The Feminist Companion to the Bible Series, edited by Athalya Brenner (Sheffield: Sheffield Academic, 1993–2015), which comprises twenty volumes of commentaries on the Old Testament. The parallel series, Feminist Companion

14. *Feminist Biblical Interpretation: A Compendium of Critical Commentary on the Books of the Bible and Related Literature*, trans. Lisa E. Dahill, Everett R. Kalin, Nancy Lukens, Linda M. Maloney, Barbara Rumscheidt, Martin Rumscheidt, and Tina Steiner (Grand Rapids: Eerdmans, 2012). Another notable collection is the three volumes edited by Susanne Scholz, *Feminist Interpretation of the Hebrew Bible in Retrospect*, Recent Research in Biblical Studies 7, 8, 9 (Sheffield: Sheffield Phoenix, 2013, 2014, 2016).

15. The first volume, on the Torah, appeared in Spanish in 2009, in German and Italian in 2010, and in English in 2011 (Atlanta: SBL Press). Five more volumes are now available: *Feminist Biblical Studies in the Twentieth Century*, ed. Elisabeth Schüssler Fiorenza (2014); *The Writings and Later Wisdom Books*, ed. Christl M. Maier and Nuria Calduch-Benages (2014); *Gospels: Narrative and History*, ed. Mercedes Navarro Puerto and Marinella Perroni; English translation ed. Amy-Jill Levine (2015); *The High Middle Ages*, ed. Kari Elisabeth Børresen and Adriana Valerio (2015); and *Early Jewish Writings*, ed. Eileen Schuller and Marie-Theres Wacker (2017). For further information, see http://www.bibleandwomen.org.

to the New Testament and Early Christian Writings, edited by Amy-Jill Levine with Marianne Blickenstaff and Maria Mayo Robbins (Sheffield: Sheffield Academic, 2001–2009), contains thirteen volumes with one more planned. These two series are not full commentaries on the biblical books but comprise collected essays on discrete biblical texts.

Works by individual feminist biblical scholars in all parts of the world abound, and they are now too numerous to list in this introduction. Feminist biblical interpretation has reached a level of maturity that now makes possible a commentary series on every book of the Bible. In recent decades, women have had greater access to formal theological education, have been able to learn critical analytical tools, have put their own interpretations into writing, and have developed new methods of biblical interpretation. Until recent decades the work of feminist biblical interpreters was largely unknown, both to other women and to their brothers in the synagogue, church, and academy. Feminists now have taken their place in the professional world of biblical scholars, where they build on the work of their foremothers and connect with one another across the globe in ways not previously possible. In a few short decades, feminist biblical criticism has become an integral part of the academy.

Methodologies

Feminist biblical scholars use a variety of methods and often employ a number of them together.[16] In the Wisdom Commentary series, the authors will explain their understanding of feminism and the feminist reading strategies used in their commentary. Each volume treats the biblical text in blocks of material, not an analysis verse by verse. The entire text is considered, not only those passages that feature female characters or that speak specifically about women. When women are not apparent in the narrative, feminist lenses are used to analyze the dynamics in the text between male characters, the models of power, binary ways of thinking, and the dynamics of imperialism. Attention is given to how the whole text functions and how it was and is heard, both in its original context and today. Issues of particular concern to women—e.g., poverty, food, health, the environment, water—come to the fore.

---

16. See the seventeen essays in Caroline Vander Stichele and Todd Penner, eds., *Her Master's Tools? Feminist and Postcolonial Engagements of Historical-Critical Discourse* (Atlanta: Society of Biblical Literature, 2005), which show the complementarity of various approaches.

One of the approaches used by early feminists and still popular today is to lift up the overlooked and forgotten stories of women in the Bible. Studies of women in each of the Testaments have been done, and there are also studies on women in particular biblical books.[17] Feminists recognize that the examples of biblical characters can be both empowering and problematic. The point of the feminist enterprise is not to serve as an apologetic for women; it is rather, in part, to recover women's history and literary roles in all their complexity and to learn from that recovery.

Retrieving the submerged history of biblical women is a crucial step for constructing the story of the past so as to lead to liberative possibilities for the present and future. There are, however, some pitfalls to this approach. Sometimes depictions of biblical women have been naïve and romantic. Some commentators exalt the virtues of both biblical and contemporary women and paint women as superior to men. Such reverse discrimination inhibits movement toward equality for all. In addition, some feminists challenge the idea that one can "pluck positive images out of an admittedly androcentric text, separating literary characterizations from the androcentric interests they were created to serve."[18] Still other feminists find these images to have enormous value.

One other danger with seeking the submerged history of women is the tendency for Christian feminists to paint Jesus and even Paul as liberators of women in a way that demonizes Judaism.[19] Wisdom Commentary aims to enhance understanding of Jesus as well as Paul as Jews of their day and to forge solidarity among Jewish and Christian feminists.

---

17. See, e.g., Alice Bach, ed., *Women in the Hebrew Bible: A Reader* (New York: Routledge, 1998); Tikva Frymer-Kensky, *Reading the Women of the Bible* (New York: Schocken Books, 2002); Carol Meyers, Toni Craven, and Ross S. Kraemer, *Women in Scripture* (Grand Rapids: Eerdmans, 2000); Irene Nowell, *Women in the Old Testament* (Collegeville, MN: Liturgical Press, 1997); Katharine Doob Sakenfeld, *Just Wives? Stories of Power and Survival in the Old Testament and Today* (Louisville: Westminster John Knox, 2003); Mary Ann Getty-Sullivan, *Women in the New Testament* (Collegeville, MN: Liturgical Press, 2001); Bonnie Thurston, *Women in the New Testament: Questions and Commentary*, Companions to the New Testament (New York: Crossroad, 1998).

18. Cheryl Exum, "Second Thoughts about Secondary Characters: Women in Exodus 1.8–2.10," in *A Feminist Companion to Exodus to Deuteronomy*, FCB 6, ed. Athalya Brenner (Sheffield: Sheffield Academic, 1994), 75–97, at 76.

19. See Judith Plaskow, "Anti-Judaism in Feminist Christian Interpretation," in *Searching the Scriptures: A Feminist Introduction*, ed. Elisabeth Schüssler Fiorenza (New York: Crossroad, 1993), 1:117–29; Amy-Jill Levine, "The New Testament and Anti-Judaism," in *The Misunderstood Jew: The Church and the Scandal of the Jewish Jesus* (San Francisco: HarperSanFrancisco, 2006), 87–117.

Feminist scholars who use historical-critical methods analyze the world behind the text; they seek to understand the historical context from which the text emerged and the circumstances of the communities to whom it was addressed. In bringing feminist lenses to this approach, the aim is not to impose modern expectations on ancient cultures but to unmask the ways that ideologically problematic mind-sets that produced the ancient texts are still promulgated through the text. Feminist biblical scholars aim not only to deconstruct but also to reclaim and reconstruct biblical history as women's history, in which women were central and active agents in creating religious heritage.[20] A further step is to construct meaning for contemporary women and men in a liberative movement toward transformation of social, political, economic, and religious structures.[21] In recent years, some feminists have embraced new historicism, which accents the creative role of the interpreter in any construction of history and exposes the power struggles to which the text witnesses.[22]

Literary critics analyze the world of the text: its form, language patterns, and rhetorical function.[23] They do not attempt to separate layers of tradition and redaction but focus on the text holistically, as it is in

20. See, for example, Phyllis A. Bird, *Missing Persons and Mistaken Identities: Women and Gender in Ancient Israel* (Minneapolis: Fortress, 1997); Elisabeth Schüssler Fiorenza, *In Memory of Her: A Feminist Theological Reconstruction of Christian Origins* (New York: Crossroad, 1984); Ross Shepard Kraemer and Mary Rose D'Angelo, eds., *Women and Christian Origins* (New York: Oxford University Press, 1999).

21. See, e.g., Sandra M. Schneiders, *The Revelatory Text: Interpreting the New Testament as Sacred Scripture*, rev. ed. (Collegeville, MN: Liturgical Press, 1999), whose aim is to engage in biblical interpretation not only for intellectual enlightenment but, even more important, for personal and communal transformation. Elisabeth Schüssler Fiorenza (*Wisdom Ways: Introducing Feminist Biblical Interpretation* [Maryknoll, NY: Orbis Books, 2001]) envisions the work of feminist biblical interpretation as a dance of Wisdom that consists of seven steps that interweave in spiral movements toward liberation, the final one being transformative action for change.

22. See Gina Hens-Piazza, *The New Historicism*, GBS, Old Testament Series (Minneapolis: Fortress, 2002).

23. Phyllis Trible was among the first to employ this method with texts from Genesis and Ruth in her groundbreaking book *God and the Rhetoric of Sexuality*, OBT (Philadelphia: Fortress, 1978). Another pioneer in feminist literary criticism is Mieke Bal (*Lethal Love: Feminist Literary Readings of Biblical Love Stories* [Bloomington: Indiana University Press, 1987]). For surveys of recent developments in literary methods, see Terry Eagleton, *Literary Theory: An Introduction*, 3rd ed. (Minneapolis: University of Minnesota Press, 2008); Janice Capel Anderson and Stephen D. Moore, eds., *Mark and Method: New Approaches in Biblical Studies*, 2nd ed. (Minneapolis: Fortress, 2008).

its present form. They examine how meaning is created in the interaction between the text and its reader in multiple contexts. Within the arena of literary approaches are reader-oriented approaches, narrative, rhetorical, structuralist, post-structuralist, deconstructive, ideological, autobiographical, and performance criticism.[24] Narrative critics study the interrelation among author, text, and audience through investigation of settings, both spatial and temporal; characters; plot; and narrative techniques (e.g., irony, parody, intertextual allusions). Reader-response critics attend to the impact that the text has on the reader or hearer. They recognize that when a text is detrimental toward women there is the choice either to affirm the text or to read against the grain toward a liberative end. Rhetorical criticism analyzes the style of argumentation and attends to how the author is attempting to shape the thinking or actions of the hearer. Structuralist critics analyze the complex patterns of binary oppositions in the text to derive its meaning.[25] Post-structuralist approaches challenge the notion that there are fixed meanings to any biblical text or that there is one universal truth. They engage in close readings of the text and often engage in intertextual analysis.[26] Within this approach is deconstructionist criticism, which views the text as a site of conflict, with competing narratives. The interpreter aims to expose the fault lines and overturn and reconfigure binaries by elevating the underling of a pair and foregrounding it.[27] Feminists also use other postmodern approaches, such as ideological and autobiographical criticism. The former analyzes the system of ideas that underlies the power and

24. See, e.g., J. Cheryl Exum and David J. A. Clines, eds., *The New Literary Criticism and the Hebrew Bible* (Valley Forge, PA: Trinity Press International, 1993); Edgar V. McKnight and Elizabeth Struthers Malbon, eds., *The New Literary Criticism and the New Testament* (Valley Forge, PA: Trinity Press International, 1994).

25. See, e.g., David Jobling, *The Sense of Biblical Narrative: Three Structural Analyses in the Old Testament*, JSOTSup 7 (Sheffield: University of Sheffield, 1978).

26. See, e.g., Stephen D. Moore, *Poststructuralism and the New Testament: Derrida and Foucault at the Foot of the Cross* (Minneapolis: Fortress, 1994); *The Bible in Theory: Critical and Postcritical Essays* (Atlanta: Society of Biblical Literature, 2010); Yvonne Sherwood, *A Biblical Text and Its Afterlives: The Survival of Jonah in Western Culture* (Cambridge: Cambridge University Press, 2000).

27. David Penchansky, "Deconstruction," in *The Oxford Encyclopedia of Biblical Interpretation*, ed. Steven McKenzie (New York: Oxford University Press, 2013), 196–205. See, for example, Danna Nolan Fewell and David M. Gunn, *Gender, Power, and Promise: The Subject of the Bible's First Story* (Nashville: Abingdon, 1993); David Rutledge, *Reading Marginally: Feminism, Deconstruction and the Bible*, BibInt 21 (Leiden: Brill, 1996).

values concealed in the text as well as that of the interpreter.[28] The latter involves deliberate self-disclosure while reading the text as a critical exegete.[29] Performance criticism attends to how the text was passed on orally, usually in communal settings, and to the verbal and nonverbal interactions between the performer and the audience.[30]

From the beginning, feminists have understood that interpreting the Bible is an act of power. In recent decades, feminist biblical scholars have developed hermeneutical theories of the ethics and politics of biblical interpretation to challenge the claims to value neutrality of most academic biblical scholarship. Feminist biblical scholars have also turned their attention to how some biblical writings were shaped by the power of empire and how this still shapes readers' self-understandings today. They have developed hermeneutical approaches that reveal, critique, and evaluate the interactions depicted in the text against the context of empire, and they consider implications for contemporary contexts.[31] Feminists also analyze the dynamics of colonization and the mentalities of colonized peoples in the exercise of biblical interpretation. As Kwok Pui-lan explains, "A postcolonial feminist interpretation of the Bible needs to investigate the deployment of gender in the narration of identity, the negotiation of power differentials between the colonizers and the colonized, and the reinforcement of patriarchal control over spheres where these elites could exercise control."[32] Methods and models from sociology and cultural anthropology are used by feminists to investigate

28. See Tina Pippin, ed., *Ideological Criticism of Biblical Texts: Semeia* 59 (1992); Terry Eagleton, *Ideology: An Introduction* (London: Verso, 2007).

29. See, e.g., Ingrid Rosa Kitzberger, ed., *Autobiographical Biblical Interpretation: Between Text and Self* (Leiden: Deo, 2002); P. J. W. Schutte, "When *They*, *We*, and the Passive Become *I*—Introducing Autobiographical Biblical Criticism," *HTS Teologiese Studies / Theological Studies* 61 (2005): 401–16.

30. See, e.g., Holly Hearon and Philip Ruge-Jones, eds., *The Bible in Ancient and Modern Media: Story and Performance* (Eugene, OR: Cascade, 2009).

31. E.g., Gale Yee, ed., *Judges and Method: New Approaches in Biblical Studies* (Minneapolis: Fortress, 1995); Warren Carter, *The Gospel of Matthew in Its Roman Imperial Context* (London: T&T Clark, 2005); *The Roman Empire and the New Testament: An Essential Guide* (Nashville: Abingdon, 2006); Elisabeth Schüssler Fiorenza, *The Power of the Word: Scripture and the Rhetoric of Empire* (Minneapolis: Fortress, 2007); Judith E. McKinlay, *Reframing Her: Biblical Women in Postcolonial Focus* (Sheffield: Sheffield Phoenix, 2004).

32. Kwok Pui-lan, *Postcolonial Imagination and Feminist Theology* (Louisville: Westminster John Knox, 2005), 9. See also, Musa W. Dube, ed., *Postcolonial Feminist Interpretation of the Bible* (St. Louis: Chalice, 2000); Cristl M. Maier and Carolyn J. Sharp,

women's everyday lives, their experiences of marriage, childrearing, labor, money, illness, etc.[33]

As feminists have examined the construction of gender from varying cultural perspectives, they have become ever more cognizant that the way gender roles are defined within differing cultures varies radically. As Mary Ann Tolbert observes, "Attempts to isolate some universal role that cross-culturally defines 'woman' have run into contradictory evidence at every turn."[34] Some women have coined new terms to highlight the particularities of their socio-cultural context. Many African American feminists, for example, call themselves *womanists* to draw attention to the double oppression of racism and sexism they experience.[35] Similarly, many US Hispanic feminists speak of themselves as *mujeristas* (*mujer* is Spanish for "woman").[36] Others prefer to be called "Latina feminists."[37] Both groups emphasize that the context for their theologizing is *mestizaje* and *mulatez* (racial and cultural mixture), done *en conjunto* (in community), with *lo cotidiano* (everyday lived experience) of Hispanic women as starting points for theological reflection and the encounter with the divine. Intercultural analysis has become an indispensable tool for working toward justice for women at the global level.[38]

Prophecy and Power: Jeremiah in Feminist and Postcolonial Perspective (London: Bloomsbury, 2013).

33. See, for example, Carol Meyers, *Discovering Eve: Ancient Israelite Women in Context* (New York: Oxford University Press, 1991); Luise Schottroff, *Lydia's Impatient Sisters: A Feminist Social History of Early Christianity*, trans. Barbara and Martin Rumscheidt (Louisville: Westminster John Knox, 1995); Susan Niditch, *"My Brother Esau Is a Hairy Man": Hair and Identity in Ancient Israel* (Oxford: Oxford University Press, 2008).

34. Mary Ann Tolbert, "Social, Sociological, and Anthropological Methods," in *Searching the Scriptures*, 1:255–71, at 265.

35. Alice Walker coined the term (*In Search of Our Mothers' Gardens: Womanist Prose* [New York: Harcourt Brace Jovanovich, 1967, 1983]). See also Katie G. Cannon, "The Emergence of Black Feminist Consciousness," in *Feminist Interpretation of the Bible*, ed. Letty M. Russell (Philadelphia: Westminster, 1985), 30–40; Renita Weems, *Just a Sister Away: A Womanist Vision of Women's Relationships in the Bible* (San Diego: Lura Media, 1988); Nyasha Junior, *An Introduction to Womanist Biblical Interpretation* (Louisville: Westminster John Knox, 2015).

36. Ada María Isasi-Díaz (*Mujerista Theology: A Theology for the Twenty-First Century* [Maryknoll, NY: Orbis Books, 1996]) is credited with coining the term.

37. E.g., María Pilar Aquino, Daisy L. Machado, and Jeanette Rodríguez, eds., *A Reader in Latina Feminist Theology* (Austin: University of Texas Press, 2002).

38. See, e.g., María Pilar Aquino and María José Rosado-Nunes, eds., *Feminist Intercultural Theology: Latina Explorations for a Just World*, Studies in Latino/a Catholicism (Maryknoll, NY: Orbis Books, 2007).

Some feminists are among those who have developed lesbian, gay, bisexual, and transgender (LGBT) interpretation. This approach focuses on issues of sexual identity and uses various reading strategies. Some point out the ways in which categories that emerged in recent centuries are applied anachronistically to biblical texts to make modern-day judgments. Others show how the Bible is silent on contemporary issues about sexual identity. Still others examine same-sex relationships in the Bible by figures such as Ruth and Naomi or David and Jonathan. In recent years, queer theory has emerged; it emphasizes the blurriness of boundaries not just of sexual identity but also of gender roles. Queer critics often focus on texts in which figures transgress what is traditionally considered proper gender behavior.[39]

Feminists also recognize that the struggle for women's equality and dignity is intimately connected with the struggle for respect for Earth and for the whole of the cosmos. Ecofeminists interpret Scripture in ways that highlight the link between human domination of nature and male subjugation of women. They show how anthropocentric ways of interpreting the Bible have overlooked or dismissed Earth and Earth community. They invite readers to identify not only with human characters in the biblical narrative but also with other Earth creatures and domains of nature, especially those that are the object of injustice. Some use creative imagination to retrieve the interests of Earth implicit in the narrative and enable Earth to speak.[40]

Biblical Authority

By the late nineteenth century, some feminists, such as Elizabeth Cady Stanton, began to question openly whether the Bible could continue to be regarded as authoritative for women. They viewed the Bible itself as

39. See, e.g., Bernadette J. Brooten, *Love between Women: Early Christian Responses to Female Homoeroticism* (Chicago and London: University of Chicago Press, 1996); Mary Rose D'Angelo, "Women Partners in the New Testament," *JFSR* 6 (1990): 65–86; Deirdre J. Good, "Reading Strategies for Biblical Passages on Same-Sex Relations," *Theology and Sexuality* 7 (1997): 70–82; Deryn Guest, *When Deborah Met Jael: Lesbian Feminist Hermeneutics* (London: SCM, 2011); Teresa Hornsby and Ken Stone, eds., *Bible Trouble: Queer Readings at the Boundaries of Biblical Scholarship* (Atlanta: Society of Biblical Literature, 2011).

40. E.g., Norman C. Habel and Peter Trudinger, *Exploring Ecological Hermeneutics*, SymS 46 (Atlanta: Society of Biblical Literature, 2008); Mary Judith Ress, *Ecofeminism in Latin America*, Women from the Margins (Maryknoll, NY: Orbis Books, 2006).

the source of women's oppression, and some rejected its sacred origin and saving claims. Some decided that the Bible and the religious traditions that enshrine it are too thoroughly saturated with androcentrism and patriarchy to be redeemable.[41]

In the Wisdom Commentary series, questions such as these may be raised, but the aim of this series is not to lead readers to reject the authority of the biblical text. Rather, the aim is to promote better understanding of the contexts from which the text arose and of the rhetorical effects it has on women and men in contemporary contexts. Such understanding can lead to a deepening of faith, with the Bible serving as an aid to bring flourishing of life.

Language for God

Because of the ways in which the term "God" has been used to symbolize the divine in predominantly male, patriarchal, and monarchical modes, feminists have designed new ways of speaking of the divine. Some have called attention to the inadequacy of the term *God* by trying to visually destabilize our ways of thinking and speaking of the divine. Rosemary Radford Ruether proposed *God/ess*, as an unpronounceable term pointing to the unnameable understanding of the divine that transcends patriarchal limitations.[42] Some have followed traditional Jewish practice, writing *G-d*. Elisabeth Schüssler Fiorenza has adopted *G*d*.[43] Others draw on the biblical tradition to mine female and non-gender-specific metaphors and symbols.[44] In Wisdom Commentary, there is not one standard way of expressing the divine; each author will use her or his preferred ways. The one exception is that when the tetragrammaton, YHWH, the name revealed to Moses in Exodus 3:14, is used, it will be without vowels, respecting the Jewish custom of avoiding pronouncing the divine name out of reverence.

---

41. E.g., Mary Daly, *Beyond God the Father: A Philosophy of Women's Liberation* (Boston: Beacon, 1973).

42. Rosemary Radford Ruether, *Sexism and God-Talk: Toward a Feminist Theology* (Boston: Beacon, 1983).

43. Elisabeth Schüssler Fiorenza, *Jesus: Miriam's Child, Sophia's Prophet; Critical Issues in Feminist Christology* (New York: Continuum, 1994), 191 n. 3.

44. E.g., Sallie McFague, *Models of God: Theology for an Ecological, Nuclear Age* (Philadelphia: Fortress, 1987); Catherine LaCugna, *God for Us: The Trinity and Christian Life* (San Francisco: Harper Collins, 1991); Elizabeth A. Johnson, *She Who Is: The Mystery of God in Feminist Theological Discourse* (New York: Crossroad, 1992). See further Elizabeth A. Johnson, "God," in *Dictionary of Feminist Theologies*, 128–30.

Nomenclature for the Two Testaments

In recent decades, some biblical scholars have begun to call the two Testaments of the Bible by names other than the traditional nomenclature: Old and New Testament. Some regard "Old" as derogatory, implying that it is no longer relevant or that it has been superseded. Consequently, terms like Hebrew Bible, First Testament, and Jewish Scriptures and, correspondingly, Christian Scriptures or Second Testament have come into use. There are a number of difficulties with these designations. The term "Hebrew Bible" does not take into account that parts of the Old Testament are written not in Hebrew but in Aramaic.[45] Moreover, for Roman Catholics and Eastern Orthodox believers, the Old Testament includes books written in Greek—the Deuterocanonical books, considered Apocrypha by Protestants.[46] The term "Jewish Scriptures" is inadequate because these books are also sacred to Christians. Conversely, "Christian Scriptures" is not an accurate designation for the New Testament, since the Old Testament is also part of the Christian Scriptures. Using "First and Second Testament" also has difficulties, in that it can imply a hierarchy and a value judgment.[47] Jews generally use the term Tanakh, an acronym for Torah (Pentateuch), Nevi'im (Prophets), and Ketuvim (Writings).

In Wisdom Commentary, if authors choose to use a designation other than Tanakh, Old Testament, and New Testament, they will explain how they mean the term.

Translation

Modern feminist scholars recognize the complexities connected with biblical translation, as they have delved into questions about philosophy of language, how meanings are produced, and how they are culturally situated. Today it is evident that simply translating into gender-neutral formulations cannot address all the challenges presented by androcentric texts. Efforts at feminist translation must also deal with issues around authority and canonicity.[48]

---

45. Gen 31:47; Jer 10:11; Ezra 4:7–6:18; 7:12-26; Dan 2:4–7:28.

46. Representing the *via media* between Catholic and reformed, Anglicans generally consider the Apocrypha to be profitable, if not canonical, and utilize select Wisdom texts liturgically.

47. See Levine, *The Misunderstood Jew*, 193–99.

48. Elizabeth Castelli, "*Les Belles Infidèles*/Fidelity or Feminism? The Meanings of Feminist Biblical Translation," in *Searching the Scriptures*, 1:189–204, here 190.

Because of these complexities, the editors of Wisdom Commentary series have chosen to use an existing translation, the New Revised Standard Version (NRSV), which is provided for easy reference at the top of each page of commentary. The NRSV was produced by a team of ecumenical and interreligious scholars, is a fairly literal translation, and uses inclusive language for human beings. Brief discussions about problematic translations appear in the inserts labeled "Translation Matters." When more detailed discussions are available, these will be indicated in footnotes. In the commentary, wherever Hebrew or Greek words are used, English translation is provided. In cases where a wordplay is involved, transliteration is provided to enable understanding.

Art and Poetry

Artistic expression in poetry, music, sculpture, painting, and various other modes is very important to feminist interpretation. Where possible, art and poetry are included in the print volumes of the series. In a number of instances, these are original works created for this project. Regrettably, copyright and production costs prohibit the inclusion of color photographs and other artistic work. It is our hope that the web version will allow a greater collection of such resources.

Glossary

Because there are a number of excellent readily available resources that provide definitions and concise explanations of terms used in feminist theological and biblical studies, this series will not include a glossary. We refer you to works such as *Dictionary of Feminist Theologies*, edited by Letty M. Russell with J. Shannon Clarkson (Louisville: Westminster John Knox, 1996), and volume 1 of *Searching the Scriptures*, edited by Elisabeth Schüssler Fiorenza with the assistance of Shelly Matthews (New York: Crossroad, 1992). Individual authors in the Wisdom Commentary series will define the way they are using terms that may be unfamiliar.

Bibliography

Because bibliographies are quickly outdated and because the space is limited, only a list of Works Cited is included in the print volumes. A comprehensive bibliography for each volume is posted on a dedicated website and is updated regularly. The link for this volume can be found at wisdomcommentary.org.

A Concluding Word

In just a few short decades, feminist biblical studies has grown exponentially, both in the methods that have been developed and in the number of scholars who have embraced it. We realize that this series is limited and will soon need to be revised and updated. It is our hope that Wisdom Commentary, by making the best of current feminist biblical scholarship available in an accessible format to ministers, preachers, teachers, scholars, and students, will aid all readers in their advancement toward God's vision of dignity, equality, and justice for all.

Acknowledgments

There are a great many people who have made this series possible: first, Peter Dwyer, director of Liturgical Press, and Hans Christoffersen, publisher of the academic market at Liturgical Press, who have believed in this project and have shepherded it since it was conceived in 2008. Editorial consultants Athalya Brenner-Idan and Elisabeth Schüssler Fiorenza have not only been an inspiration with their pioneering work but have encouraged us all along the way with their personal involvement. Volume editors Mary Ann Beavis, Carol J. Dempsey, Gina Hens-Piazza, Amy-Jill Levine, Linda M. Maloney, Ahida Pilarski, Sarah Tanzer, Lauress Wilkins Lawrence, and Seung Ai Yang have lent their extraordinary wisdom to the shaping of the series, have used their extensive networks of relationships to secure authors and contributors, and have worked tirelessly to guide their work to completion. Two others who contributed greatly to the shaping of the project at the outset were Linda M. Day and Mignon Jacobs, as well as Barbara E. Bowe of blessed memory (d. 2010). Editorial and research assistant Susan M. Hickman has provided invaluable support with administrative details and arrangements. I am grateful to Brian Eisenschenk and Christine Henderson who have assisted Susan Hickman with the Wiki. I am especially thankful to Lauren L. Murphy and Justin Howell for their work in copyediting; and to the staff at Liturgical Press, especially Colleen Stiller, production manager; Angie Steffens, production assistant; and Tara Durheim, associate publisher.

Author's Introduction

"Who Is Adequate for These Things?"
(2 Cor 2:16)

A Feminist Commentary?

Commentaries are for people who want informed company when reading a difficult text.[1] A feminist commentary should provide feminist company, dealing especially with questions in the text that arise from women's experience and with challenges faced in a male-oriented world. So I take as my text above Paul's question in the Corinthian situation, "Who is adequate for these things?"[2] To be realistic, I am writing for the small group of people, women and men, who are preparing to teach or preach Paul's 2 Corinthians or who are curious for their own reasons and have sought out a feminist perspective. I assume that you look with your peers from the margin of social power for a fresh grasp of what is happening between Paul and these Corinthians and what might happen in our hearing of them today.

A feminist lens sharpens vision at three different ranges, and I will focus in each way as I look at Paul's letter. After the NRSV text and some words of introduction I begin each chapter with the broad focus favored by both science and philosophy. I ask what the text says about the reality of all bodies or beings in what we now call an ecosystem on this earth within a functioning universe—and here I do not exclude whatever these beings produce, including the speed of light, the webs of spiders, and

---

1. Gerhard Lohfink, "Kommentar als Gattung: Rudolf Schnackenburg zum 60. Geburtstag," *BibLeb* 15 (1974): 1–16.
2. Within my commentary, biblical translations are mostly my own.

the culture of humans, so the broadest focus includes the specific. This focus could be too broad for Paul's letters, blind as he seems to be about where food comes from, why families nurture children, or how water sustains life. Yet he grapples again and again with the limits of his body and the threat of death and finds in Jesus' dying and rising a way out of fear toward what he calls "a new creation." And Paul's upbringing in a largely Gentile world, yet with intense commitment to Israel's role, drives him to communicate to Gentiles his vision of a living Christ who can reconcile all people to God or he himself will utterly lose heart. Giorgio Agamben has named Paul's perceived location as "messianic time," the time that remains for waking up before the impending crisis.[3] Claudia Janssen in her study of 1 Corinthians 15 names this as "body-time/ Körper-Zeit," the time that is the moment of opportunity when bodies reach toward God's righteous presence.[4]

A woman's world in Greece of Paul's time involves long hours in procuring and preparing if not also raising food, fetching water, spinning thread, and making clothing. Women know the human body in its harsh constraints from threat of death at female birth (the ancient birth control method) and death in giving birth to death in poverty as widows. And the mourning rituals that follow all deaths are women's complaints. We do not need to identify this care of the body as essentially feminine to observe it at that time and in modified ways today as an education in this broad vision. We can ask: Is the identification of these Corinthians with Christ's death and raised life different from Paul's because of their sharper material lens? First Corinthians shows that they have gone from restricted lives to expressive living by participation in Christ, while Paul, who was born into significant rights as a free male Jew in a Greek-speaking city, has found himself in Christ multiply restricted.[5] Yet 2 Corinthians suggests that the physical hardships of his itinerant existence may be showing Paul that their rising up in Christ is not a denial of Christ's death but the fruit that comes from it when their shared, if constricted, space and time open up to God's Spirit.

---

3. Giorgio Agamben, *The Time That Remains: A Commentary on the Letter to the Romans* (Stanford, CA: Stanford University Press, 2005), 59–78.

4. Claudia Janssen, *Anders ist die Schönheit der Körper: Paulus und die Auferstehung in 1 Kor 15* (Gütersloh: Gütersloher Verlagshaus GmbH, 2005), 298–306.

5. Antoinette Clark Wire, *The Corinthian Women Prophets: A Reconstruction through Paul's Rhetoric* (Minneapolis: Fortress, 1990; repr. Eugene, OR: Wipf and Stock, 2003), 62–71, 159–76.

Second, we cannot make sense of this broad reality of life and death without focusing in on the specific social, political, and economic world in which it is occurring. For Paul's letters this is the world of Roman imperial rule based on centuries of military conquest, enslavement of resisting populations, efficient economic exploitation through provincial capitals such as Corinth, and a comprehensive ideological imprint in monumental art and the imperial cult. All of these structures functioned to the benefit of some at the expense of others, with almost all women falling in the serving, if not also the enslaved, populations. Two centuries earlier Rome had conquered and destroyed Corinth, then, after a century, "restored" it as a Roman colony on Greek soil. Here the Roman citizens held all administrative positions while local people worked on the land or in labor or trade, and at least a third of all residents were enslaved captives or their progeny. We see Paul expressing in his letters at least two different responses to Roman rule. The first is resistance. If God who raised Christ is the giver of all good, then all praise and glory belong to God, and this directly contests the emperor's claim to be the giver of peace and security. The second response to Rome is imitation, in that all of these claims for God and Christ are made in the language and reflect the power and patronage structures that dominate Roman Corinth. Whoever speaks in Corinth, including the one who reads Paul's letter aloud to its recipients, speaks in this double world and needs to be heard there.

Third, at a close-up range I focus on the letter as a move by Paul to accomplish something that is contested in a specific relationship. Paul writes not to assert timeless truths or to describe a historical situation but to persuade people in Corinth's new messianic sect of Israel and thereby to impact their relationship to him. So I read the letter as an argument provoked by a particular exigency. Questions about this exigency and Paul's stance in it, as far as it can be reconstructed from the argument, are feminist for a number of reasons. First, women and others in marginal social positions know that speaking is not neutral description but doing something that needs to be watched for its impact on us and, if necessary, contested. Second, though very few women were taught reading and writing skills, letters were composed and delivered orally, and women were active in the communities where letters were being heard and discussed. Yet the women in Corinth are not mentioned in 2 Corinthians, and this will not have escaped them. Third, Paul's rhetoric in this letter includes unusual cascades of images, pleas, threats, and caustic role plays that might particularly catch the ear of those whose speech often interrupts from the margin. So my ultimate focus is on the local issue and the power dynamics at work in Paul's writing. I will conclude the analysis of each text with this close-up focus because I find in this interaction of Paul and the Corinthians not only the seed but also the fruit of my feminist exploration.

The three ranges for examining a text sketched above can also be distinguished methodologically. The broadest focus, used by most theologians, philosophers, and scientists, looks at the big picture. They want to know the underlying reality of their subject, considering it either in terms of its origins and ultimate ends (diachronically) or in terms of its structures and functions (synchronically). They are eclectic and speculative in method, proposing and testing theories that hold water in so far as they give a comprehensive explanation of their subject and the way it is known.

The mid-range focus on the political, economic, and social implications of the text applies what can be called a socio-historical method. It draws from all available literary and material remains contemporary with what is being studied to piece together the human activity of which the text is an integral part. Here recent methods developed by people marginalized in modern historical criticism are crucial to get an accurate reading—not only feminist criticism, but also the critique from oppressed racial, religious, and sexual groups and postcolonial nations.

Finally, the close-up focus on a particular interaction of a writer and those to whom a text is addressed employs rhetorical methods, methods most effective where the audience is specific, as in oral speaking and letter writing. My purpose is not to tag each move Paul makes with its appropriate title in ancient rhetorical handbooks but to track how Paul is speaking at each point to persuade others and what this tells in turn about those he wants to persuade. Because his arguments must gauge the perspectives of his interlocutors in order to seek certain responses from them, it is possible to make a tentative reconstruction of the interactions of Paul and the Corinthians in the period around this letter. I take particular interest in the perspectives and actions of women in Corinth's church who are a recurring object of Paul's attention in 1 Corinthians but are not singled out in 2 Corinthians. I ask: What happened to the Corinthian women prophets?

One Letter or Many?

Because of the sharp contrast in tone between Paul's attack in the last four chapters of 2 Corinthians and his encouragement in the framework of the early chapters, this letter has been read for over a century as a collection of several letters that Paul wrote. The dominant theory has been that Paul first attacked his opponents in Corinth (chaps. 10–13) but was then able to achieve reconciliation (1:1–2:13; 7:5–9:15), having made, either before or after the attack, a strong defense of his apostleship (2:14–7:4). One short passage within the latter section is thought not to be written by Paul (6:14–7:1). Other interpreters have simply taken the clear break in tone after chapter 9 as a sign that time passed before Paul wrote the later chapters, and further news from Corinth or Paul's own reconsideration gave the letter(s) a sharpened ending. Recently, many interpreters have returned to taking the letter as a whole, not only because all manuscripts do so, but also because the disruptions within a document may be as important as its consistencies in understanding the situation in which it was written. To show the options for reading 2 Corinthians, I will describe one recent multiletter thesis, one interesting compromise position, and then list the major reasons why I will read the letter as a single communication, drawing on others who are doing so now.

Margaret M. Mitchell in a number of recent publications has explained 2 Corinthians as a series of five letters from Paul to Corinth.[6] Though the five-letter thesis has been standard for a half-century,[7] she has strengthened it in major ways. She proposes that Paul begins the sequence of letters by writing chapter 8 and ends it with chapter 9, two short letters promoting the collection for Jerusalem. In the first of these Paul reverses his promise made in 1 Corinthians 16:4 to allow Corinth's envoy to carry their own gift to Jerusalem, provoking suspicion that he is using the collection to feather his own nest. Paul then writes to defend his integrity as a servant of Christ (2 Cor 2:14–6:13; 7:2-4), and later, when a quick visit goes sour, he sends a sharp and ironic retort asserting his authority as an

6. Margaret M. Mitchell, "The Corinthian Correspondence and the Birth of Pauline Hermeneutics," in *Paul and the Corinthians: Studies of a Community in Conflict*, ed. Trevor J. Burke and J. Keith Elliott, NovTSup 109 (Leiden: Brill, 2003), 20–36; Mitchell, "Paul's Letters to Corinth: The Interpretive Intertwining of Literary and Historical Reconstruction," in *Urban Religion in Roman Corinth: Interdisciplinary Approaches*, ed. Daniel N. Schowalter and Stephen J. Friesen (Cambridge: Harvard University Press, 2005), 317–35.

7. For a history of partition theories, see Hans Dieter Betz, *2 Corinthians 8 and 9: A Commentary on Two Administrative Letters of the Apostle Paul* (Philadelphia: Fortress, 1985), 3–36. For proposals of how the pieces were edited together, see Günter Bornkamm's "The History of the Origin of the So-Called Second Letter to the Corinthians," *NTS* 8 (1962): 258–63; Andreas Lindemann, "'. . . an die Kirche in Korinth samt allen Heiligen in ganz Achaja': Zu Entstehung und Redaktion des '2. Korintherbriefes,'" in *Der zweite Korintherbrief: Literarische Gestalt—historische Situation—theologische Argumentation, Festschrift zum 70. Geburtstag von Dietrich-Alex Koch*, ed. Dieter Sänger (Göttingen: Vandenhoeck und Ruprecht, 2012), 131–59.

apostle (10:1–13:10). After hearing of their regret for offending him, he writes words moving toward reconciliation (1:1–2:13; 7:5-16; 13:11-13), and finally he sends the second collection letter (9:1-15), praising Achaia for their gift and challenging them to fulfill their pledges. In this way the two collection letters are no longer seen as addenda to three theological missives but become the framework for understanding that Paul's whole effort in writing 2 Corinthians is to complete the collection.

It is significant that Mitchell does not get deflected into exploring the identity of the rival itinerants operating in Corinth but keeps her focus on the local believers. These are the ones Paul addresses. Having been educated in Greek, Paul was trained to contend with others, as is evident in the agonistic rhetoric with which he meets each response to his previous letter. By commenting on his own previous statements and the Corinthians' responses to him he enters into the process of interpreting his letters that extends from their first hearers down through church history. At this point Mitchell's focus shifts to the way that late antiquity interprets Paul. I only wish that, since his strategic use of every image and tradition was shaped to persuade a small circle in first-century Corinth, she did more to ferret out these people's apparent stance and behavior, particularly that of the women among them. Yet her penchant to see Paul from the perspective of early Christian writers can help expose the limits of our modern ways of reading Paul. In the early Christian debate over whether Paul is a hard-nosed speaker of plain truths or a visionary of deep meanings, she eliminates neither option. She calls for the interpretive tool of a sliding "veil scale" from the clearest syllogism to the most veiled allusion to God's perfect knowledge.[8] No wonder someone in Corinth claimed that Paul's gospel was veiled (4:3)—and provoked Paul's retort comparing himself with Moses who veiled his face when he had seen God's glory.

An intermediate position on 2 Corinthians assumes it was written in the present sequence but with significant time breaks, at least one before chapter 10 when collegiality suddenly gives way to vituperation.[9] Margaret Thrall's careful commentary notes that Titus and a brother have not yet arrived in Corinth when Paul writes 8:6 but are known there by

8. Margaret M. Mitchell, *Paul, the Corinthians and the Birth of Christian Hermeneutics* (Cambridge: Cambridge University Press, 2010), 77.

9. Victor Paul Furnish, *II Corinthians*, AB 32A (Garden City, NY: Doubleday, 1984), 30–55.

12:18.[10] Others use the break before chapter 10 and Paul's harsh rhetoric that follows as a basis for reversing the order of writing and calling the final chapters the "letter of tears" that Paul says he wrote to Corinth before Titus came back with news of Corinthian reconciliation (2:4; 7:6-7). David Trobisch has argued from a study of ancient letter collections that reordering of letters by an editor is highly unlikely, but he finds authors who join short letters into a single unit for further circulation.[11] He therefore proposes that Paul sent the Corinthians several letters before, during, and after traveling to Macedonia and then joined them himself for wider circulation in the order he wrote them, adjusting only at the seams. Yet would Paul who wrote letters so sharply and distinctively directed to each setting have reorganized letters for more general reading? The first hint of such circulation appears in the Colossians 4:16 note to have that letter read in the neighboring Laodicea, but it could indicate a specific problem common to both cities or a practice after Paul's death.

This commentary will read 2 Corinthians as a single letter of Paul. I follow here a growing number of interpreters who find the partition theories unnecessary and the present format more simply attributed to Paul's situation of writing than to a later editing.[12] I list here my primary

10. Margaret E. Thrall, *A Critical and Exegetical Commentary on the Second Epistle to the Corinthians*, ICC (Edinburgh: T & T Clark, 1994), 3–49, specifically 19. Thrall's commentary is often printed in two volumes but is paginated as one volume and will be so treated.

11. David Trobisch, *Die Entstehung der Paulusbriefsammlung: Studien zu den Anfängen christlicher Publizistik* (Göttingen: Vandenhoeck & Ruprecht, 1989), 120, and more fully 90–97, 119–31.

12. For an early critical defense of literary unity, see Niels Hyldahl, "Die Frage nach der literarischen Einheit des Zweiten Korintherbriefes," *ZNW* 64 (1973): 289–306. Others followed, including Frances Young and David F. Ford with *Meaning and Truth in 2 Corinthians* (London: SPCK, 1987), 28–36; Bärbel Bosenius in *Die Abwesenheit des Apostels als theologisches Programm: Der zweite Korintherbrief als Beispiel für die Brieflichkeit der paulinische Theologie* (Tübingen: Franke, 1994), 97–107; Shelly Matthews, "2 Corinthians," in *Searching the Scriptures*, ed. Elisabeth Schüssler Fiorenza, vol. 2 (New York: Crossroad, 1994), 198–201; and, in greatest detail, R. Bieringer in R. Bieringer and J. Lambrecht, *Studies on 2 Corinthians*, BETL 112 (Leuven: Leuven University Press, 1994), 67–105 on partition theories, 107–79 on 2 Corinthians unity. Others who are now working with a unity hypothesis include the following: Jan Lambrecht, *Second Corinthians*, SP 8 (Collegeville, MN: Liturgical Press, 1999), 7–11; Marlene Crüsemann, "2 Korintherbrief," in *Bibel in gerechter Sprache*, ed. Ulrike Bail et al. (Gütersloh: Gütersloher Verlagshaus, 2006), 2131–32; Crüsemann, *Gott ist Beziehung: Beiträge zur biblischen Rede von Gott*, ed. Claudia Janssen and Luise Schottroff (Gütersloh: Gütersloher Verlagshaus, 2014), 184–85, 206–8; Crüsemann, *2 Corinthians* (Stuttgart:

reasons for this approach, at the same time recognizing that the case is not closed.

1. No manuscript gives evidence of multiple letters. This means any editing of fragments into the present letter must have been in the first century, with all originals lost well before 140 CE, when the letter was known by Marcion. If Trobisch's theory of the author editing his own work is uncharacteristic of Paul, the motivation for anyone else to put fragments together in this order seems even less probable.

2. The break in tone after Paul's call to collect for Jerusalem in chapters 8 and 9 and before his severe retorts in chapters 10–13 is not inexplicable. Günter Bornkamm gives examples of ancient letters that end with warnings when he argues this for the 2 Corinthians' editor's motivation to do so.[13] How much more would it suit Paul, who has made himself vulnerable in intimate pleas (6:11-13; 7:2-16), to stress that he will not tolerate being dismissed when he comes to Corinth (10:1-6; 11:5-6; 13:1-3, 10). Once begun, this warning leads Paul to accuse the Corinthians of favoring others who call themselves apostles and to mock such people by taking on the persona of a fool (11:22–12:10).

3. When Paul's account of travel to Macedonia to find Titus in 2:12-13 is broken off and taken up again only in 7:5, the intervening confessional self-defense is often considered a separate letter fragment. It is more likely a digression evoked by the memory of Titus's good news (yet untold) that inspires Paul's expansive thanks to God (2:14-16) in spite of his own sense of inadequacy. This in turn provokes him to make an extended defense of his work among them (2:17–7:4). Though the length of this digression-turned-defense, like that of the final attack in chapters 10–13, has led to theories of several letters, Paul's prolixity is better seen

---

Kohlhammer, forthcoming); Ivan Vegge, *2 Corinthians: A Letter about Reconciliation; A Psychagogical, Epistologographical and Rhetorical Analysis*, WUNT 2.239 (Tübingen: Mohr Siebeck, 2008), 12–37; Thomas Schmeller, *Der zweite Brief an die Korinther*, Teilband 1: 2 Kor. 1:1–7:4 (Neukirchen-Vluyn: Neukirchener Verlag, 2010), 19–40; Caroline Vander Stichele, "2 Corinthians," in *Feminist Biblical Interpretation: A Compendium of Critical Commentary*, ed. Luise Schottroff and Marie-Theres Wacker, trans. Lisa Dahill et al. (Grand Rapids, MI: Eerdmans, 2012); Thomas Schmeller, "No Bridge over Troubled Water? The Gap between 2 Corinthians 1–9 and 10–13 Revisited," *JSNT* 36 (2013): 73–84; Udo Schnelle, "Der 2. Korintherbrief und die Mission gegen Paulus," in Sänger, *Zweite Korintherbrief*, 303–6, 318–20; Peter Arzt-Grabner, *2. Korinther. Unter Mitarbeit von Ruth E. Kritzer; Papyrologische Kommentare zum Neuen Testament 4* (Göttingen: Vandenhoeck & Ruprecht, 2014), 95–148; Christopher Land, *The Integrity of 2 Corinthians and Paul's Aggravating Absence* (Sheffield: Sheffield Phoenix, 2015).

13. Bornkamm, "History of the Origin," 258–63.

as a sign of the unusual pressure he feels himself under to recover good relations with this community.

4. Paul's call to donate for Jerusalem in chapters 8 and 9—not misplaced, as partition theories claim—comes appropriately after he has pleaded for the Corinthians' support (6:11-13; 7:2-4) and charged them to be devoted to God alone (6:14–7:1). Paul may share the prophets' vision that, when the Gentiles are welcomed into Jerusalem with their offerings, then creation will be renewed as Jew and Greek together glorify God.[14] Paul wants to meet physical needs in Jerusalem (Gal 2:10) and have Jerusalem believers accept the Gentiles he is converting (Rom 15:15-16), both within his ultimate purpose that all people glorify God, the giver of all good (2 Cor 9:11-15).

5. The sequence of events referred to in 2 Corinthians is most simply reconstructed by understanding that Titus, after bringing Paul good news in Macedonia, has already gone back to Corinth as Paul writes this letter (7:5-7; 8:6; 12:18).[15] Paul is confident in Titus's good reception in Corinth and may recognize that Titus can best renew the collection himself (12:17-18). Yet Paul plans to go to Corinth very soon and writes to argue that his own work is integral to the Corinthians' faith and to the collection that Titus is making. Johannes Munck and now Marlene Crüsemann propose the following sequence for the letter: Paul deals first with the past issues in chapters 1–7, then supports the present collection in chapters 8–9, and finally prepares them for his future arrival in Corinth in chapters 10–13.[16] Reimund Bieringer sees Paul praising the Corinthian assembly for their past dealing with a single offender in order to challenge them to be equally effective with the "false apostles" so that he need not discipline them when he comes.[17]

---

14. 2 Cor 9:11-12; Rom 11:25; 15:8, 15-16; Isa 66:18-23. A classic defense of this thesis was made by Johannes Munck in *Paul and the Salvation of Mankind* (Richmond, VA: John Knox, 1959), 297–305. See also Keith F. Nickle, *The Collection: A Study in Paul's Strategy* (Naperville, IL: Allenson, 1966). David J. Downs in *The Offering of the Gentiles* (Tübingen: Mohr Siebeck, 2008), 3–9, 140–65, denies there is sufficient evidence that Paul saw the collection as an eschatological event. Yet he acknowledges that Paul intended the collection not only to meet physical needs but to be a cultic offering uniting all people in returning to God the harvest of God's benefaction (28–29)—something very similar.

15. The verbs about Titus's sending are consistently in the aorist past tense, and only his positive feelings for Corinth are expressed in present tense.

16. Munck, *Paul*, 171; Crüsemann, "2 Korintherbrief," 2131–32.

17. R. Bieringer, *Studies on 2 Corinthians*, 156–75.

6. First Corinthians has been widely ignored in recent interpretation of 2 Corinthians although it provides crucial background in several ways. It shows that the community to which Paul writes tends toward factionalism. The news Titus brings Paul described in 2 Corinthians 7:5-16—that the Corinthians have repented after Paul's reproach—is focused on only one case and is accompanied by further pleas for reconciliation (6:1-13; 7:2-4). Apparently some groups that Paul restricted in the earlier letter, such as women taking speaking roles in the assembly, have not changed their conduct. It is Paul who changes his approach between the letters from giving advice to defending himself. This also raises the likelihood that 1 Corinthians itself was not an answer to respectful community questions but a rebuke of community slogans in the guise of fatherly advice.[18] First Corinthians thus may have been the letter Paul wrote under "much affliction and pressure of heart through many tears" (2 Cor 2:4), whereas in 2 Corinthians Paul acknowledges his own vulnerability.

7. If we could keep in mind that letters were "written" aloud by dictation and "read" aloud as people listened to a single voice, we would not move so quickly to theories of partition when explaining rough seams. A scribe could not be expected to write accurately for long stretches, materials for writing or lighting could run out, the author's voice could tire, not to speak of interruptions in Paul's itinerant artisan life.[19] A great deal would depend on whether there was time to read back what had already been said before continuing or whether the carrier was about to leave. In this case Titus may already be waiting in Corinth for the letter's support. Eve-Marie Becker argues on text-linguistic grounds that coherence in oral communication—here as a letter is dictated and read aloud—is found also where cohesion in the lexical, syntactic, or semantic sense is lacking, since oral comprehension depends most of all on the context and the comprehending voice.[20]

8. A final reason for reading 2 Corinthians as a whole is that partition theories raise more problems than they solve. If Paul wrote multiple letters in the same sequence as we receive them, a partition theory

18. Wire, *Corinthian Women Prophets*, 13–14, 80–83.
19. Pieter J. J. Botha, "Writing in the First Century," in *Orality and Literacy in Early Christianity* (Eugene, OR: Wipf and Stock, 2012), 62–88; E. Randolf Richards, *The Secretary in the Letters of Paul*, WUNT 2.42 (Tübingen: Mohr Siebeck, 1991), 113–14.
20. Eve-Marie Becker, *Letter Hermeneutics in 2 Corinthians: Studies in Literarkritik and Communication Theory*, trans. Helen S. Heron (London: T & T Clark, 2004), 29–38; Schmeller, *Zweite Brief*, 1:29–31.

contributes little to understanding the letter and adds further room for error in proposing what an editor has omitted or added in the process. Most seriously, theories that reorder multiple letters are prone to reshape the letter to fit our image of Paul. So the favored reordering of 2 Corinthians sees Paul having once moved from moderate self-defense (2:14–7:4 without 6:14–7:1) to direct attack (10:1–13:13) and finally into reconciliation (1:1–2:13 and 7:5-16) and request for donation (8:1–9:15), giving us a happy ending. Some argue that Paul's plan soon after to take the collection to Jerusalem on his way to Spain supports this view of his Corinthian success. Paul does tell the Romans that Macedonia and Achaia were glad to provide support for Jerusalem and that he has completed his mission in the East (Rom 15:25-27, 19).[21] But do we expect him to complain to Rome about Corinth's minor contribution or say that he is no longer welcome in this eastern provincial capital? If we recognize Paul's letters as rhetoric aiming to build the relationships he needs to accomplish his goals in specific situations, we require stronger evidence of later tampering with his letters before we begin to tamper ourselves.

Reading 2 Corinthians as a Letter Collection

In my view 2 Corinthians is a collection of letters that originated in the sequence of what we call 2:14–6:13; then 10:1–13:13, and third 1:1–2:13, with chapter 7 split (7:2-4 and 7:5-16) between the first and last of these. The letters document a competition to win over the Corinthians between Paul and other apostles. Did the Christ-event demonstrate God's solidarity with the suffering and crucified people of this world? Or did it show God's resurrection power now visible in Christ's apostles? Apparently Paul, the fool for Christ, failed to win over the Corinthians, though Titus managed to achieve some mediation (7:6-7).

It was not before the second century that the three letters were edited into one, along with Paul's two short efforts to collect funds for Jerusalem (chaps. 8

---

21. Compare the contrasting views of Paul's success in Harrill, who calls Paul's collection "the crowning achievement of his Aegean mission," and Mell, who takes the collection as Paul's final failure: J. Albert Harrill, *Paul the Apostle: His Life and Legacy in Their Roman Context* (Cambridge: Cambridge University Press, 2012), 69; Ulrich Mell, "Paulus: scheiternder Gescheiter: Ein historischer und literarischer Einwurf," in Sänger, *Zweite Korintherbrief*, 199–223.

and 9) and one non-Pauline polemic against lawless people (6:14–7:1). This compilation was likely intended to attack "the heretics," as were the writings of Justin Martyr (Eusebius, *Hist. Eccl.* 4.9.10) and others from the mid-second century onward. Paul had become the legendary champion in the fight against so-called false teachers (2 Thess, Pastoral Epistles, 3 Cor., etc.).

No letters that Paul himself wrote have survived, only copies that other people compiled. While 1 Corinthians was already known in Rome at its century's end (*1 Clement*), the reading of 2 Corinthians is first documented at the end of the second century when Tertullian cites Marcion's use of 2 Corinthians 2:14–6:13 + 7:2-4 several decades earlier (*Against Marcion* 5.11–5.12). The earliest manuscript to contain any of 2 Corinthians is 𝔓[46], written at least 150 years after Paul wrote. How can we know what happened meanwhile?

In antiquity collecting letters involved editing. Archaeological findings of papyri include copybooks with letter collections.[22] Their scribes regularly deleted greetings and quoted other letters or selections.[23] Manuscript evidence of Cicero's correspondence shows selecting and rearranging of individual letters in the process of editing. Scholars count in this correspondence between 846 and 966 letters, suggesting that some letters are shortened or split while others are the postscripts of missing letters.[24]

The best evidence that Cicero's correspondence was edited is that only letters to and from prominent Roman senators survive, none of those written to his many clients. Just as Cicero's image as a prominent politician was being crafted by later editors, so Paul's image as the arch-martyr and guarantor of doctrinal truth was shaped by churches preserving, then circulating, and finally editing and compiling fourteen letters attributed to Paul. The original Paul can, if at all, only be detected in between the lines of that fabric.

Angela Standhartinger

22. John L. White, *Light from Ancient Letters* (Philadelphia: Fortress, 1986), 217–18; also Roger S. Bagnall and Raffaella C. Cribiore, *Women's Letters from Ancient Egypt, 300 BC–AD 800* (Ann Arbor: University of Michigan Press, 2006), 114–25.

23. Brent Nongbri, "2 Corinthians and Possible Material Evidence for Composite Letters in Antiquity," *Collecting Early Christian Letters: From the Apostle Paul to Late Antiquity*, ed. Bronwen Neil and Pauline Allen (Cambridge: Cambridge University Press, 2015), 54–67.

24. Peter White, *Cicero in Letters* (Oxford: Oxford University Press, 2010), 31–61, 171–96; Mary Beard, "Ciceronian Correspondences," in *Classics in Progress: Essays on Ancient Greece and Rome*, ed. T. P. Wiseman (Oxford: Oxford University Press, 2002), 103–44.

Where Are the Women in 2 Corinthians?

In 1 Corinthians Paul tells women who pray and prophesy in common worship to cover their heads because a man is God's image while a woman is man's glory (1 Cor 11:5-7). Later in the same letter he instructs that women be silent in the gatherings and ask their questions at home because it is shameful for a woman to speak in the assembly (1 Cor 14:34-35).[25] These statements raise both literary and historical questions but at least make unmistakable that when Paul was writing 1 Corinthians women in his audience were praying and prophesying publicly (1 Cor 11:5). In 2 Corinthians Paul does not mention women except to cite Scripture concerning God as Father of believing sons and daughters (6:18) and to compare the Corinthian believers to Eve seduced by the snake (11:3). My question is whether the Corinthian women that Paul once reined in are part of the audience to whom Paul directs 2 Corinthians.

Three options suggest themselves: (1) either the prophesying women have left the community, (2) they remain present and have submitted to his restrictions, or (3) they continue to pray and prophesy in worship without covering their heads. Are they gone, silent, or speaking as before? Though a definitive answer is not possible, 2 Corinthians shows that some options are more probable then others.

First, though we might fancy the women have left to establish the Second Church of Christ in Corinth, no exodus of women or any other group from the community is suggested in 2 Corinthians, as is the case, for example, in John 6:66; 1 John 2:19; or Hebrews 10:25. The fact that women are not mentioned in 2 Corinthians cannot be taken as evidence of their absence since Paul does not discuss most of the concrete conflicts in Corinth about which he gave instructions in 1 Corinthians.

Second, there is also no indication in 2 Corinthians that the women have agreed to Paul's stipulations, either to cover their heads when praying or prophesying or to keep silence in the gatherings. Although Paul does say that his anxiety about the Corinthian response to his earlier letter was alleviated by Titus's news from Corinth (2:12-13; 7:5-16), the news apparently concerned one person (2:5-8; 7:12) and Paul is still

---

25. For a defense of these sentences as an integral part of Paul's letter, see Wire, *Corinthian Women Prophets*, 149–52, 229–32; Curt Niccum, "The Voice of the Manuscripts on the Silence of Women: The External Evidence for 1 Corinthians 14:34-35," *NTS* 43 (1997): 342–55; Jorunn Økland, "Paratexts: The 1 Cor 14 Gloss Theory Before and After *The Corinthian Women Prophets*," in *After the Corinthian Women Prophets: Rhetoric, Power, and Possibilities*, ed. Joseph A. Marchal. SemeiaSt (Atlanta: SBL Press, forthcoming).

relentless in calling the Corinthians to reconcile with him (6:11-13; 7:2-4), finally threatening punishment of those who oppose him (10:1-6). Were Paul to have had their support and that of others who received his advice in 1 Corinthians, one would anticipate a much less fraught 2 Corinthians than we read.

Third, the more open tension between Paul and the community in the second of these two letters suggests that the women have continued practices that Paul proscribed. Yet why does he not then repeat or intensify his restrictions? This withholding of instruction in 2 Corinthians is not a matter of one issue but applies also to sacrificed food and marriage and speaking in tongues. The only reference back to his previous instructions concerns a single person whom they have rebuked as he instructed, and he urges them now to forgive him (2:5-11; 7:12). Otherwise Paul has reversed his previous strategy of giving concrete advice. The first imperative verb in 2 Corinthians appears only after five chapters and then is very broad: "Be reconciled to God!" (5:20). Instead of advising them, he apparently recognizes that he is the one on trial and makes a defense of his work among them. This reversal of Paul's approach from advice to defense, from a deliberative to a more forensic rhetoric, is the best evidence of his perception that advice was not working, probably also among women, and that only by shifting from the stance of knowing father to vulnerable brother could he attempt a lasting reconciliation with them.

Of course, caution is called for when we try to read from Paul's rhetoric the historical situation that brought on Paul's change in strategy.[26] It remains possible that his failure in 1 Corinthians to persuade through giving advice occurred in areas other than his instruction about women. Yet it is indicative that when he appeals in 2 Corinthians to the community, he no longer speaks of its women as a special class. Nor does he speak of the male being God's image but reserves this role for God's Spirit and for Christ (1 Cor 11:7; 2 Cor 3:18; 4:4-6). Even the metaphor of Eve seduced by the serpent in 11:3 applies to the community as a whole, though it could suggest that active women are in his mind's eye.

---

26. Yet as Margaret Mitchell has said, a correspondence such as Paul's with Corinth can only be understood as a history of negotiated meanings, requiring efforts at reconstruction of apparent responses from his addressees: "The Corinthian Correspondence," 24–36. See also Elisabeth Schüssler Fiorenza, "Rhetoricity of Historical Knowledge: Pauline Discourse and Its Contextualizations," in *Religious Propaganda and Missionary Competition in the New Testament World: Essays Honoring Dieter Georgi*, ed. Lukas Bormann, Kelly Del Tredici, and Angela Standhartinger (Leiden: Brill, 1994), 443–69, and Cynthia Briggs Kittredge, *Community and Authority: The Rhetoric of Obedience in the Pauline Tradition* (Harrisburg, PA: Trinity Press International, 1998), 99–110, 146–58.

If women have continued as leaders in public prayer and prophecy—the people's address to God and God's address to the people[27]—the question arises how they receive this new approach from Paul. Do they accept this vulnerable brother as a clay pot of the divine treasure in them, or do they take him as a disposable founder of the community seeking a comeback when God's glory in Christ is already at home among them? Whichever way they reacted, the letter's survival in our Scriptures presses us to consider this new Paul and what we want to make of his defense.

What Can 2 Corinthians Mean Today?

Reading someone else's mail is awkward in any case. How much more so at almost two thousand years and thousands more miles of distance? Add to this the challenge of continuous interpretation of this letter since its writing, each effort embedded in its own complex situation, and the task of understanding is overwhelming. Further, of all Paul's letters, this one may be the most contentious, both in the situation that provoked it and in the ways it has been read. Yet rather than give way to despair, I suggest there is reason for hope. A text so rich and multifaceted, born in conflict and likely received in altercation, should have some wisdom for those of us contesting structures in another time.

As a stimulus to its study, I sketch three traits of the interaction of Paul and Corinth shown in 2 Corinthians that might have special relevance for twenty-first-century feminists: facing conflict, accepting difference, and claiming relation.

Facing Conflict

The most striking aspect of 2 Corinthians is that Paul no longer instructs the community by affecting the secure position of father and founder as in 1 Corinthians.[28] He now faces their opposition directly and struggles to defend himself. This is evident not only in the final four chapters, where he cites their attacks against him,[29] defends himself,[30] and charges them and their preferred guides with specific offenses.[31]

27. Wire, *Corinthian Women Prophets*, 140–46.
28. 1 Cor 3:1-3; 4:15; 15:1-2.
29. 2 Cor 10:10; 11:5-6, 11; 12:11, 13.
30. 2 Cor 10:7-8, 13; 11:5, 7-9, 12-13; 12:1-10, 12-13; 13:3-4.
31. 2 Cor 10:12, 15; 11:13, 19-20, 22-23.

Already in the early chapters he defends himself against their claim that he promises to come but does not (1:15-18, 23), that he writes to distress them (2:4; 7:8), that he commends himself but is not recommended by others (3:1; 5:12), that he lacks confidence (3:4; 4:1, 16; 5:6), that his message is obscure (4:3), that he is deceptive, even an imposter (2:17; 4:2; 5:11; 6:8), that he is not charismatic or even successful (4:7-12; 6:4-10), and that he means to gain personally from his collection for Jerusalem (8:20).

It is important not to dismiss Paul's defensive moves as signs of a weak ego or a paranoid mind. They suggest that Paul was far more marginal in Corinth than his rhetoric in 1 Corinthians let on. His measured advice had apparently not achieved compliance. In 2 Corinthians Paul reverses his strategy, concedes his own vulnerability, and defends himself. I propose that this change presents an opportunity for the feminist interpreter to move beyond begrudging admiration for Paul or suppressed resentment against his authority. Our option is to face the conflict. It behooves us to hear Paul's side with care and then to do everything possible, lacking responding letters to Paul from Corinth, to recover the other side of the conversation. This means reconstructing as much as possible from Paul's rhetoric the rhetoric to which he is responding as he writes and the response he receives from Corinth that followed the letter. The aim of this is not to disparage Paul or to extol his opposition but to see in this struggle where women are at work, some issues at stake that we still face, and some insights about what can be done in times of sharp conflict.

Accepting Difference

In 1 Corinthians Paul does not accept the difference between himself and the Corinthians. He concludes several arguments with the words, "Be imitators of me," or, we might translate, "Take me as your model" (1 Cor 4:16; 11:1). Though some believers in Corinth were apparently confident that they could eat sacrificed meat without worshiping idols because the gods represented by the idols didn't exist, Paul insists that they follow his example of giving up their freedom so that a weak believer would not be misled into idol worship (1 Cor 8:1–9:23). Paul thus assumes that they also had social advantages that could be sacrificed for others, yet he had just conceded, "Not many of you were wise by human standards, not many powerful, not many from honored families" (1 Cor 1:26).[32] Paul apparently did not see what it would mean for people who so

---

32. Wire, *Corinthian Women Prophets*, 62–71.

recently had no social influence to give up their new freedoms. He challenges the women to cover their heads when praying and prophesying. Finally, he insists they be silent in the gatherings, using arguments from a narrative of woman's creation after man's to deny them the exercise of gifts they had received in Christ.[33]

In 2 Corinthians there is a shift. Paul's advice has given way to self-defense, and he now wants to show that he measures up to their standards, yet often without accepting those standards. This involves considerable contortions in the argument, but it does require him to concede the differences between himself and them. The demand for them to imitate him is gone. He remains aware that he represents Christ crucified among them (1 Cor 2:2), but now he says, "death is active in us, but life in you" (2 Cor 4:12), and at the letter's end he summarizes, "Since you seek proof that Christ speaks in me, he is not weak toward you but is powerful in you, for he was crucified from weakness, but lives from God's power. Even so we are weak in him, yet we are alive with him from God's power toward you" (13:3-4).[34] Paul thus accepts the difference between himself and them. The Corinthians' gifts of speech and wisdom, which Paul had recognized in 1 Corinthians and yet disparaged and even curtailed,[35] are now affirmed. He claims the Corinthians' faith as the fruit of his ministry, as the letter of Christ that he has delivered, as the treasure in his clay pot.[36] And in persuading them he seems to have found—even in himself—not only weakness and dishonor but also the fragrance and glory that has drawn them to Christ.[37]

Claiming Relation

A third aspect of Paul's interaction with the Corinthians in this letter is the intensity with which he seeks a positive relation with them. He no longer takes their relation with him for granted because he founded this community; nor does he give up on them and move on—at least not yet (Rom 15:23)—but he pleads and explains and threatens, pulling out all the stops to arouse them to take him seriously. One can even argue that it is due to their alienation from him and his desire for reconciliation with them that he is the first among Christ believers to borrow the metaphor

33. Ibid., 116–58.
34. This translation of mine is explained where the text is discussed.
35. 1 Cor 1:5-7; 4:8, 10; 14:26, 34-35.
36. 2 Cor 4:12; 3:3; 4:6-7.
37. 2 Cor 2:15; 3:18.

of reconciliation from military or domestic life in order to express who God is ("God was in Christ reconciling the world to himself" [5:19]), similarly for what Christ does ("Christ's love constrains us, judging this, that Christ died for all" [5:14]). So the relation he seeks with the Corinthians is not simply their reconciliation with himself, or even his own reconciliation with Jerusalem through their collection for the poor, but their acceptance of God's reconciliation with all including themselves. As he puts it, "If anyone is in Christ, there is a new creation" (5:17).

It is out of this vision that he speaks in the first-person plural of a process in which he and the Corinthians can share across their difference, a process begun in Moses' unveiling himself when he approaches God, "We all with unveiled face reflecting the Lord's glory are being transformed into the same image from glory to glory, this from the Lord, the Spirit" (3:15-18). Here the point is no longer that Paul must be imitated, or that the man rather than the woman is God's image (1 Cor 4:16; 11:1, 7), or even that Christ Jesus alone is the image of God, but "It is the God who said, 'Out of darkness let light shine,' who shines to illumine in our hearts the knowledge of God's glory in the face of Christ" (2 Cor 4:6).

Who Is Writing to Whom, When, and Where?[38]

About 30 CE a Galilean village prophet named Jesus of Nazareth who taught and healed and contested religious practices that served the elite was crucified by the Romans. He was hailed by his followers as Israel's Messiah either in his last days or when they declared him risen from the dead and alive among them. A certain devout Jew from Cilicia in Asia Minor joined others in persecuting this growing band of Messiah followers but was himself transformed by God's revealing his Son to him and sending him to proclaim Jesus Christ to the Gentiles (Gal 1:16).

This was Paul, who then traveled with others carrying word of Jesus to cities in Rome's internal, pacified provinces of Asia Minor, Macedonia, Greece, and Italy. The good news that began among rural Jews in Rome's occupied areas and vassal states of Judea and Galilee had to be reshaped for urban people who neither faced the Roman army's violence nor shared Israel's history. In doing this, Paul came into conflict on at least two fronts with others proclaiming Jesus Christ: on one side

---

38. For alternate summaries of the situation of writing 2 Corinthians, see Thrall, *The Second Epistle*, 77; Furnish, *II Corinthians*, 54–55; Schmeller, *Zweite Brief*, 1:38–40.

with those who wanted to make the Gentile believers members of Israel through circumcision, Sabbath, and law-keeping (see Galatians), and on the other side with those who experienced in Christ God's Wisdom and Spirit in ways that he feared might cut off ties with Israel and its Christ followers in Jerusalem. It was on the latter side that he fought in Corinth, as is evident from the arguments in his letters to the Corinthians, his efforts to get their support for the collection for Jerusalem, and the many ways he says, "Give no offense to Jews or to Greeks or to the church of God" (1 Cor 10:32).

Paul, Timothy, and Sylvanus had first gathered the Messianic community in Corinth during a stay of over a year around 51 CE. Apparently Paul then wrote the Corinthians some warnings (1 Cor 5:9), and they wrote back asserting their freedoms in Christ.[39] When Chloe's people brought Paul news from them (1 Cor 1:11), he wrote 1 Corinthians to challenge their factionalism and to counteract the influence of a certain Apollos who had apparently encouraged their interest in wisdom, spiritual practices such as speaking in tongues, and leaving married life for single devotion to Christ in prayer and prophecy. Paul cautioned and even restricted them in many aspects of life in Christ, promising to visit Corinth soon and send their gifts with their envoy to Jerusalem, recommending Timothy to them, and giving excuses for Apollos not coming (1 Cor 16:1-12).

The reaction to Paul's first letter was apparently sharp. He misjudged to think the Corinthians were willing to accept his restrictions and live by his model of sacrificing one's freedom in the Gospel so as not to offend others. Some interpreters think Paul may have reacted by making an interim visit to Corinth, which was a disaster when those he had offended turned against him (2 Cor 2:1). But Paul begins 2 Corinthians on the defensive because he has not come as promised (1:15-19). He did send Titus to Corinth with hopes that he could recover the situation (2:12-13). Now he is writing 2 Corinthians from Macedonia, having heard from Titus on his return that some Corinthians were grieved, have repented, and have disciplined an offender (2:5-11; 7:5-16)—probably referring to the man who was living with his father's wife (1 Cor 5:1-5). Yet Paul is clearly aware that his relation to the Corinthians remains tenuous and requires serious cultivation, both through self-defense and words

---

39. 1 Cor 4:8; 5:6; 6:12; 7:1; 10:23.

of endearment (2 Cor 1–7).[40] He then challenges them to complete the collection for Jerusalem (2 Cor 8–9). Finally, he returns to a sharp tone, not wanting his goodwill to be taken advantage of, and charges them to prepare themselves for his pending arrival (2 Cor 10–13).

40. At least one interpreter reads the epistolary aorist in 2 Corinthians 2:3, 4, and 9, taking "I have written" as referring to the present letter and identifying 2 Corinthians itself as Paul's "letter of tears": Eve-Marie Becker, "Paulus als weinender Briefschreiber (2 Kor 2,4): Epistolare parousia im Zeichen visualisierter Emotionalität," in Sänger, *Zweite Korintherbrief*, 11–26. This can be an alternative to identifying 1 Corinthians as the "letter of tears" for those who see the earlier letter as irenic. Yet note that the anguish and pain that Paul may be associating with the earlier letter is expressed only as Paul writes the later letter when he can remember the pain he felt on hearing how the Corinthians had responded.

2 Corinthians 1:1-11

Paul Greets Corinth and Blesses God

Text and Its Structure (1:1-11)

In 1:1-2 the standard three-part Greek letter salutation—writer, to addressee, greeting—is further specified in each part to stress God's initiative. It is by God's will that Paul writes as Christ's apostle, it is to God's assembly in Corinth that the letter is addressed,[1] and it is both "God our Father and the Lord Jesus Christ" who offer grace and peace. At the same time, Paul broadens the scope of the letter. The writer's name is extended to include with Paul "the brother Timothy."[2] The addressee is extended to include with Corinth's assembly "all the saints throughout Achaia," Rome's Greek province of which Corinth is the capital. And the greeting is extended to include with "grace" Israel's oral greeting of "peace." By these theological claims and relational extensions Paul indicates that this is no ordinary letter but is God's message

---

1. I translate ἐκκλησία as "assembly" or "community" rather than "church" to limit our projecting later meanings back on that time and because the term was used for civic assemblies.

2. The article "the" indicates that they know this person, hence the NRSV "Timothy our brother."

¹:¹Paul, an apostle of Christ Jesus by the will of God, and Timothy our brother,

To the church of God that is in Corinth, including all the saints throughout Achaia:

²Grace to you and peace from God our Father and the Lord Jesus Christ.

³Blessed be the God and Father of our Lord Jesus Christ, the Father of mercies and the God of all consolation, ⁴who consoles us in all our afflic-tion, so that we may be able to console those who are in any affliction with the consolation with which we ourselves are consoled by God. ⁵For just as the sufferings of Christ are abundant for us, so also our consolation is abundant through Christ. ⁶If we are being afflicted, it is for your consolation and salvation; if we are being consoled, it is for your consolation, which you experience when you patiently endure the same sufferings that we are also suf-

through chosen agents of God to a province-wide community that God is assembling.

The salutation is followed by a blessing of God in 1:3-4, a form of praise characteristic of Israel's common speech and psalms[3] and of the Hellenistic synagogue liturgy.[4] A blessing, like its opposite, a curse, is performative speech that is understood to accomplish what it says.[5] In this sense it can be seen as a yet stronger form of the thanks to God that opens all Paul's other unmistakably genuine letters, except the polemical Galatians. It is also distinctive that God is blessed, not for the Corinthians' faith or wisdom in Christ, but for the courage that Paul has himself received that now makes possible his encouraging the Corinthians.[6] When the term παράκλησις is translated with the RSV as "comfort" or with the NRSV and NEB as "consolation," it signifies in contemporary

3. Gen 24:27; 1 Kgs 5:7; Pss 28:6; 124:6; 135:19-21.

4. Margaret E. Thrall, *A Critical and Exegetical Commentary on the Second Epistle to the Corinthians*, ICC (Edinburgh: T & T Clark, 1994), 100–102, who cites R. Deichgräber, *Gotteshymnus und Christus-hymnus in der frühen Christenheit* (Göttingen: Vandenhoeck & Ruprecht, 1967), 37–41, 87.

5. Since the verb is understood rather than expressed, one could read "blessed is God," but the prayer setting suggests "blessed be God."

6. The variety in Greek manuscripts of verse 6 comes from a scribe's eye having skipped from one "our encouragement" to the next (as in manuscripts 81 and 630), followed by other scribes trying to make sense of what was left.

fering. ⁷Our hope for you is unshaken; for we know that as you share in our sufferings, so also you share in our consolation.

⁸We do not want you to be unaware, brothers and sisters, of the affliction we experienced in Asia; for we were so utterly, unbearably crushed that we despaired of life itself. ⁹Indeed, we felt that we had received the sentence of death so that we would rely not on ourselves but on God who raises the dead. ¹⁰He who rescued us from so deadly a peril will continue to rescue us; on him we have set our hope that he will rescue us again, ¹¹as you also join in helping us by your prayers, so that many will give thanks on our behalf for the blessing granted us through the prayers of many.*

* NRSV notes: 1:8, Gk *brothers*; 1:11, Other ancient authorities read *your* for *our*.

English a solace or peace in times of loss.[7] But the point in this context is that confidence and energy are needed to continue in a time of affliction or oppression, a time under external attack and internal pressure. In this context, the παθήματα of Christ are closer to hardships than to sufferings (NRSV), stressing the broad passive sense of bearing or enduring what is not chosen. Paul's rhythmic braiding of the terms "courage" and "hardships" heightens the rhetoric and binds together Paul and the Corinthians with Christ as those who are sustained by God. Consider my alternate translation of 1:3-7:

> Blessed be the God and Father of our Lord Jesus Christ, the father of mercies and the God of all courage who gives us courage in our every affliction so that we are able to encourage those in every affliction through the courage with which we ourselves are encouraged by God. For just as the hardships of Christ increase for us, so also our courage increases through Christ. Yet if we are afflicted, it is for your encouragement and salvation, and if we are given courage, it is to give you courage that becomes active when you endure the same hardships which we also endure. And our hope for you is solid, since we know that as you are our partners in hardships, so also in courage.

7. Compare a German translation and interpretation in Marlene Crüsemann, "Christology der Beziehung," in *Gott ist Beziehung: Beiträge zur biblischen Rede von Gott*, ed. Claudia Janssen and Luise Schottroff (Gütersloh: Gütersloher Verlagshaus, 2014), 186–91.

> ### Courage in Palestine
>
> In the conflict over Palestine, the daily pain and suffering of the Palestinian people, especially that of women and children, is excruciating. Yet despite the agony and oppression, many of them, Muslims and Christians, find comfort, strength, and consolation in God's presence with them. This gives them the courage to continue in resisting the illegal occupation of their country. Many times it is the women, even more than the men, who go out to demonstrate against the infractions of their human rights by the occupying forces of Israel. In one memorable incident, an Israeli soldier caught a small child throwing stones at soldiers and was dragging him off for arrest. Immediately and spontaneously a number of women rushed toward the soldier and clung to the child shouting, "This is my son, let him go!" Every woman claimed the child as her own in order to save him. With unflinching courage, they confronted the soldier and had the boy released. Their faith in God and in the justice of their cause made them fearless and courageous in their resistance to the occupation.
>
> *Naim Ateek*

Next, in 1:8-11, we get the explanation (γὰρ) for why Paul is full of courage and is blessing God—because he has just experienced rescue from a harrowing event, probably in Asia's prime city of Ephesus.[8] Paul gives no details but only the explication that (ὅτι) he was oppressed beyond strength to bear it, with the consequence that (ὥστε) he felt himself under a sentence of death, in order that (ἵνα) he should discover his confidence was strictly in the God who raises the dead. Whether or not Paul's speaking in the first-person plural means that he shared this trauma with Timothy, the cosender of the letter, Paul at least wants to present himself as one representative of Christ among others and not as a sole suffering apostle (1:9, 19).

God's raising the dead is a prominent theme in Paul[9] and in Hellenistic Judaism generally, especially in prayers like the second of the Eighteen Benedictions, "Blessed art thou, O Lord, who makes the dead live."[10]

8. Compare this with descriptions of Paul's conflicts in Ephesus in 1 Cor 15:32 and Acts 19:21-41.

9. Rom 4:17; 6:4; 1 Cor 15:15.

10. On the development of this prayer of Eighteen Benedictions, see Joseph Heinemann, *Prayer in the Talmud: Forms and Patterns* (Berlin: de Gruyter, 1977), 13–36, including an early example (26–29). See also 2 Baruch 48.8.

Also, Jewish martyrdom accounts quote the Hebrew Scriptures to prove that God alone gives life.[11] It is not Jesus' resurrection per se that is said to sustain Paul here but the discovery in his own experience that God brought him back to life. Relative pronouns echo the liturgical tone of the opening blessing of this God who (ὅς) rescued and will rescue Paul, the God in whom (εἰς ὄν) Paul can trust that he will still be kept alive. Here "we trust" is a better translation for ἐλπίκαμεν than "we hope," which in English has become weakened to mean "wish for," so that the NRSV adds two words "set our hope." The final lines suggest that this rescue is not only God's act but the accomplishment of prayers on Paul's behalf. He challenges them to join in praying for him so that many voices will thank God for continuing to save his life. If we grasp why and how this praise of God is so important for Paul, we may come to understand this letter.[12]

A Feminist Lens at Three Ranges on Paul's Opening Greeting and Blessing (1:1-11)

The Broad View of All Bodies in Time and Space, Death and Life

Paul's opening greeting and blessing locate the letter in space and time. It comes to the assembly in Corinth and Achaia from Paul who is, we hear later, in Macedonia, where Titus has brought him word about Corinth (7:5-6). The letter is dated, not by the name of an emperor, governor, or priest, as Luke dates his Gospel and Acts,[13] but by recent acts of God—God's will that made Paul Christ's apostle some two decades before, God's gathering an assembly in Corinth and Achaia a few years earlier, and now God's blessing of grace and peace pronounced by the person reading Paul's letter aloud (1:1-2). Before these came the hardships of Christ and God's raising him from the dead, which for Paul precipitated all of the above (1:5-9). And now there is God's rescuing Paul in Asia, giving him courage through hardships so that he can encourage the Corinthians in their hardships and they in turn can pray to God and thank God for him (1:3-4, 10-11).

---

11. 2 Macc 7:9, 14, 23, 29, 36; 4 Macc 16:25; 18:17-19, 23.
12. On thanksgivings in Paul's letters, see George Henry Boobyer, *"Thanksgiving" and the "Glory of God" in Paul* (Leipzig: Universitätsverlag von Robert Noske, 1929), and Paul Schubert, *Form and Function of the Pauline Thanksgivings*, BZNW 20 (Berlin: Alfred Töpelmann, 1939), 38.
13. Luke 1:5; 3:1; Acts 4:5-6; 12:1-3; 18:12; 24–26.

Yet for Paul this is not a mere sequence in time and space that he is re-counting. He is telling an experience he has had that has taken him from despair into trust, from a verdict of death into rescue and life. The letter that follows will reveal that Paul is beset as he writes by multiple physical problems: some debilitating speech handicap (10:10; 11:6); a chronic ill-ness, pain, or disability (12:7-10); intolerable living and travel conditions (6:4-5; 11:25-27); and a foreboding sense of his mortality (4:16–5:10). He also betrays signs of what we would call depression when he asserts over and over that he is confident and has not lost heart (3:12; 4:1, 16; 5:6). All this is in addition to what faces him as he writes, namely, the apparent defection of this community in Achaia's provincial capital that he and his coworkers founded and nurtured. They are now dubious about him, if not still hostile after his previous letter, and are attracted to other lead-ers who seek to replace him. In this setting he chooses to begin, not by any instructions to them, but by recounting what just happened to him in Asia and blessing God for rescuing him from death.

This both shifts the focus from their problems to his and broadens their attention to matters of life and death. It is when his very life was threatened that he discovered that his courage increased as his hardships increased: "For just as the hardships of Christ are abundant for us, so also our courage becomes abundant through Christ" (1:5). He claims to have received the sentence of death so that he would rely no longer on himself but on the God who raises the dead (1:9). This, he says, is all for the Corinthians' sake, so that he can encourage them to share in these hardships and receive this courage (1:6-7). But it tells us that Jesus' cruci-fixion and resurrection are not, for Paul, past events in a world of magic realism meant to comfort believers concerning the afterlife. He does not tell of seeing an empty tomb, touching wounds, or recognizing Christ by the sea. Rather, it is when Christ's hardships become abundant in present time that endurance produces courage through Christ, and from this Paul says he learns to "rely not on ourselves but on the God who raises the dead." He witnesses resurrection by experiencing Christ's death in the verdict of his own death and discovering God who raises the dead.

We can recognize this as witness to God the Creator who is not only the source of all life but its sustaining foundation and the power draw-ing life toward its goal. For Paul, this is the bottom line in dealing with his own increasing limitations and, as we will see, the limitations of the created world at large. The new creation that Paul affirms in this letter is articulated less as a crisis of all created life, as it is in Romans 8:18-25, than as the crisis of those who are alienated and trapped in "the valley of the shadow of death," where he has just found himself (1:8-11; 5:17-20; see Ps 23:4). Because he has learned in his own body that the courage to live comes with meeting death, he claims to have discovered God's life-giving at work and demonstrated God's raising of the dead.

When Paul then blesses God for bringing him through near-death to life, he is not simply giving vent to his feelings. Nor does the courage that Paul receives designate him the heroic apostle for their admiration. He says, "If we are given courage, it is for your encouragement when you bear up under the same hardships that we also endure" (1:6). It is for them. Yet rather than instructing the Corinthians to risk opposition as he did, Paul encourages them by his own witness of what happened to him at death's door. Paul anticipates that "as the hardships of Christ increase, so does our courage through Christ," and as word of this spreads, God raises afflicted bodies in wider and wider circles. In this way the disheartened can take courage and life can overcome death in the world.

Be a Comforted Comforter

In 1 Corinthians Paul's identity is that of a mentor, but in 2 Corinthians he takes the role of a pastor. Paul experienced a lot of difficulties in the process of evangelism, but he kept working due to the comfort he received from God and he learned to be thankful. So he told the Corinthians, we have a wonderful God, the Father of our Lord Jesus Christ and the Source of all compassion. When we face difficulties and trials, he comforts us and gives us strength. And why does he do that? So that when other people have trials and need our comfort and encouragement, we can comfort them with the help and comfort provided by God. This makes us comforters of others God is comforting. Therefore, the suffering that Christians experience is not in vain.

As Paul experienced trouble in the world, Christians today will also experience difficulties and trials. Churches too face times of testing, such as the Chinese Church experienced in the Cultural Revolution for ten years (1966–1976), a time with some disastrous consequences in cultural, artistic, and religious circles. Many found the suffering unbearable. In those days Christians had no Bibles, no song books, and all the churches and seminaries were closed. The people lost the freedom to practice their faith. But God the Comforter comforted those who were in trouble and many like Paul were able to overcome their sufferings. They liked to sing the twenty-third Psalm, "The LORD is my shepherd, I shall not want. . . . Even though I walk through the valley of the shadow of death, I will fear no evil, for you are with me. Your rod and your staff, they comfort me." This was indeed the experience of the Chinese Church. It can help the Bible reader understand how the gospel spread orally before it was written in the Bible. God does comfort and the Holy Spirit has great power. This witness of the Chinese Church can be a consolation to other people in trouble.

At a meeting in December 1978, the Chinese government promulgated the policy about "freedom of religious belief." Christians have freedom of belief, and the doors of the church are now open. The government helps to reestablish the destroyed churches. As the number of believers has increased rapidly, new churches have been built. Now the government pays more attention to religion, and religious believers are regarded as a positive force in building the motherland. Now the church is working to cultivate theological reflection in order to clarify a set of theological affirmations of Chinese Christianity.

Finally, I want to say that we have tribulations in the world, but in the Lord we have peace because the Lord has overcome the world (John 16:33) and he is a Comforter. When we were in trouble, he comforted us. And Paul teaches us by his example to comfort those who are suffering. We can all be comforted comforters!

Kuanrong Chen

A Mid-Range Focus on the Political, Economic, and Social Context

The Greek city of Corinth was destroyed by Rome two hundred years before Paul's time for opposing the Roman takeover and was left in ruins. A hundred years later it was rebuilt as a Roman colony with Roman civic structure in which only the Roman freedmen and veterans settled there had citizenship. Though official inscriptions at this time were written in Latin, graffiti and many gravestones found in Greek show that some local families survived or moved back to take advantage of service and trade work in what by Paul's time was the capital of the Roman province of Achaia (Greece). When Luke wrote the Acts of the Apostles some decades after this letter, synagogues were known in Corinth that had grown in numbers as Jews were twice expelled from Rome in 19 and 39 CE (Acts 18:2).

It is significant that Paul chose the Roman capital of Corinth to center his work of persuasion in Greece. He had lived there for some time shortly after the mid-century mark, gathering a group of adherents of

Christ and then carrying on an extended conversation with them in messages and letters.[14] Was it because he could better practice his trade there, where raw materials from the occupied provinces of the empire's borders passed through on their way to Rome? Or was the initial response there more positive? Or did the very size of the city allow him to attract a following without stirring up an active opposition until the second year (Acts 18:11-12)? Paul's address to the saints "throughout Achaia," in a letter that also names other regions by their Roman provincial titles (Asia [1:8], Macedonia [1:16; 2:13]), probably refers to the whole province of which Corinth was the Roman capital including the Peloponnese and the mainland north to the Macedonian border.[15]

The address to Achaia raises several questions: Was the letter meant to be circulated for reading aloud? Then which Corinthians would carry, interpret, and return it (compare Phoebe carrying Romans [Rom 16:1-2])? Or was the word of Paul's goodwill and blessing a sufficient message, perhaps carried back home by visitors to Corinth? In any case, when Paul gives Corinth the responsibility to be the center from which Achaia will receive this letter or this blessing, he operates within a Roman system of provincially based status relations shared by the men or women who transmit his message. Even though their message counters the emperor's claim to be the foundation of peace and the giver of all blessings, it nonetheless travels the same roads and arrives with the same capital-city status as the provincial tax collectors and the circulating assize.

When Paul names the Roman province of Asia as the place where he has just undergone some life-threatening experience (2:8-9), this again would not be heard in a vacuum. The major cities of Asia (now western Turkey) were founded many centuries before as colonies of Greek cities and retained the Greek language and culture later infused with local ways. By Paul's time these Asian coastal cities had become more prosperous, and Greece itself had become more depopulated.[16] (Compare

14. 1 Cor 1:11; 2:1; 5:9; 7:1; 2 Cor 1:18; 2:1; Acts 18–19. Others argue for one short interim visit.

15. Ralph P. Martin argues that distances for circulating a letter suggest Paul means only the region around Corinth once called Achaia (*2 Corinthians*, WBC 40 [Waco TX: Word Books, 1983], 3).

16. Alcock's analysis based on recent landscape studies of the remains of Roman Greece puts extreme depopulation in question, yet she concludes that villages became fewer and weaker as estates grew and the extent of cultivation decreased (Susan E. Alcock, *Graecea Capta: The Landscapes of Roman Greece* [Cambridge: Cambridge University Press, 1992], 24–92, esp. 24–32, 40–49, 74–86).

the American colonies and Britain by the late twentieth century.) Paul's tale of woe in Asia may have been intended to play on the competition between the provinces and draw from the Corinthians some sympathy for Paul. Intracity competition can certainly be documented for this period, yet Paul has avoided naming the city in Asia, speaking about the empire's provinces and encouraging an imperial sense of the world as a whole. By naming these provinces as locations of his work, Paul also suggests he has been sent out by a central authority with responsibility for far-flung areas, very much the way Rome's annual consuls were sent out to be governors of senatorial provinces such as Achaia and Asia. Yet Paul claims not a Roman portfolio but to be "apostle of Christ Jesus by God's will" and blesses God for giving him courage so he can encourage the Corinthians when they share Christ's hardships. In this way the exalted rhetoric of this blessing, with its reverberating echoes of encouragement and its final aim to swell the voices returning praise to God, at once depends on and undermines imperial rhetoric.

A Close-Up Focus on the Interaction of Paul and the Corinthians

The words of greeting make clear that what follows is a letter, a communication from certain people to certain other people in a certain time and place. This is perhaps the most difficult thing to keep in mind two thousand years later, considering the intervening roles that this text has played.[17]

Paul introduces himself with a single name, making clear that they know him and that he is not appealing to family connections. Then he identifies himself as "an apostle of Christ Jesus by God's will." What Paul is claiming to be in relation to the Corinthians by the term ἀπόστολος ("apostle," one sent out) needs to be read in the context of Paul's six other recognized letters, half of which begin with this title (1 Cor 1:1; Gal 1:1; Rom 1:1), the other half without it (1 Thess; Phil; and Phlm). Apparently many in his own time did not recognize Paul as an apostle: witness even his biographer Luke who decades later calls him and Barnabas "apostles" only in Acts 13 and 14 when they are "sent out" by the church in Antioch, reserving the title for the twelve and Jesus' brother James, who knew

---

17. Schubert stresses that Paul's thanksgivings are structurally epistolary in form and function, "characterized—as far as finite verb form and personal pronouns are concerned—by the first and second persons" (*Form and Function*, 38). See also Christine Gerber's *Paulus, Apostolat und Autorität, oder vom Lesen fremder Briefe* (Zürich: Theologischer Verlag Zürich, 2012), 9–15.

Jesus during his lifetime. And Paul consistently deflates references to himself as apostle by calling himself a slave of Jesus Christ (Rom 1:1; Phil 1:1), a miscarriage (1 Cor 15:8), one not authorized by others (Gal 1:1), one like an infant's wet-nurse (1 Thess 2:7), and last of all and sentenced to death (1 Cor 4:9). Yet 1 Corinthians shows that he considers himself to have seen the Lord and therefore to be an apostle (1 Cor 9:1; 15:7-9), though he uses the title for himself in 2 Corinthians only in his opening greeting and in his closing efforts to dissociate himself from others who claim to be apostles (1:1; 11:5; 12:11-13).[18] Has the title become debased from its use by those he calls "false apostles"? Or is he avoiding the title because of the Corinthians' reaction to his claims in the previous letter?

The primary force of this opening greeting is that everything that has happened is attributed to God's action. It is God's will that makes Paul Christ's apostle; God has called the Corinthians out (ἐκκλησία from ἐκ καλέω, "I call out," hence a gathered body, assembly; NRSV: "church") and made them holy (ἅγιοι; NRSV: "saints"); and God gives the grace and peace that Paul pronounces. Because the Lord Jesus Christ is also named as a giver of this grace and peace that Paul pronounces, the opening words "Paul, apostle of Christ Jesus" probably do not indicate simply that Jesus is the content of Paul's message but that Paul is sent out by Jesus according to God's will. This double source of sending out and of blessing with peace could be difficult in the monotheistic context of Judaism in which this assembly was a small, if contentious, sect. It is clarified by God being named "Father" and by Christ being named "Lord" or "Master," one suggesting an originating or ultimate source, the other a more immediate or functional source. Paul makes a point of using the first-person plural pronoun, "our" (ἡμῶν)—"Grace to you and peace from God our Father and the Lord Jesus Christ"—explicitly binding together the letter senders with the receivers as the people of this God and Christ.

How the Corinthians heard this greeting when the letter was first read to the gathered community we do not know, but there were likely no surprises from a formal opening so similar to Paul's 1 Corinthians. Probably the terms "Father" and "Lord" would not have carried the

---

18. Christine Gerber notes that in spite of headings inserted in many translations of 2 Corinthians that identify its first half as a defense of his apostleship, the word "apostle" plays no part in his defense here. He assumes it, and elsewhere he defends it when his role as community founder is questioned or his right to financial support (though he refuses to take it in 1 Corinthians 9), but here he calls himself διάκονος (courier, servant, agent) (*Apostolat und Autorität*, 35–43).

weight they do for feminists today, but the Corinthians may be brac-
ing themselves for Paul's consequent demands. Their surprise would
have come at Paul's blessing of God that follows the salutation, which
is distinctive among Paul's recognized letters (though followed later in
Ephesians and 1 Peter). Paul, who normally begins by thanking God for
his hearers and their particular gifts,[19] here begins by blessing God in
an almost liturgical rapture for giving himself and Timothy "courage in
our every crisis so that we can encourage those in any crisis through the
courage with which we ourselves are encouraged by God" (1:4). This
praise to God for sustaining "us" might well be heard to include Corinthian listeners as an instruction that they encourage others. But Paul
goes on to speak of how courage increases when experience of Christ's
hardships increase and is finally explicit that they are the ones he can
encourage because God gives him courage. So Paul is focused initially on
the courage God gives him and Timothy and only then on encouraging
the Corinthians to share in the hardships that bring courage.

This is confirmed by Paul's explanation to them: "For we want you to
know, brothers and sisters,[20] about the crisis we experienced in Asia," in
which he (and Timothy?) came close to death and was delivered by the
God who raises the dead, assuring him of God's future care for which
they can thank God. What we have here is not just a reversal of Paul's
usual order so that an opening thanks for God's blessings becomes a
blessing of God finally thanked for.[21] Paul's normal practice of thanking
God for gifts to them has been reversed into a challenge that they thank
God for blessing him. This gets the letter off to a very different start,
giving the first clear indication that Paul is approaching them in a new
way, not with attention on their practice of life in Christ, but by draw-

19. 1 Thess 1:2-3; Phil 1:3-5; 1 Cor 1:4-7; Rom 1:8; Phlm 4-6.
20. I hesitate to make explicit with the NRSV the "sisters" that Paul probably assumes in the collective masculine ἀδελφοί. Until recent changes in English usage,
"brothers" was a more accurate English translation, being a masculine collective used
for everyone but without thinking of women. Yet now the English word "brothers"
refers strictly to males, so Paul's possible inclusion is made explicit by the NRSV's
"brothers and sisters," even if the "sisters" stands out inappropriately for Paul. Note
that when the context suggests that women are not intended the NRSV shifts to "my
friends" rather than making the "brothers" explicit (1 Cor 14:39). Yet on what basis,
then, does the NRSV revert to "brothers and sisters" immediately (1 Cor 15:1) and
by the end of that chapter evade "brothers and sisters" altogether (1 Cor 15:58)? Do
we go back to the archaic "brethren"?
21. Paul Schubert points out the inversion of Paul's normal syntax in his 2 Corinthians thanksgiving (*Form and Function*, 50, 54–55, 61).

ing them into his harsh experience with its challenges and benefits for himself and only consequently for them.

We find out that this letter will be about him, not them. Having apparently not been able to reach them effectively in 1 Corinthians by assuming their support of him, he will now use the relative lull in their long-strained relationship recently achieved by Titus (7:5-16) to face their opposition, expose his vulnerability, and defend his shifting travel plans and unusual financial expectations. He risks being open toward them to get them to be open toward him in order to pave a way for reconciliation. Though he begins by blessing God for his recent Asian rescue, claiming to be confident in God and not discouraged, later he shows that in fact he has a thin skin, is easily offended, and has come near to "losing heart" and being reduced to threats and curses. Yet he begins with his newfound courage, which does dominate the tone of this letter, blessing God for the gift (χάρισμα, 1:11) that has brought him through death threats so that he can encourage others, including the Corinthians, as he writes.

Thinking of the Corinthian women prophets, we wonder how those Paul has offended in the past will take this change in Paul. He is not canceling any previous instructions he has made, and these can—and still do—rise up to shape his memory. Is the present move to be taken as a mere change of strategy in an old battle for control? Or do they see in him some genuine openness to difference that might leave space for the Spirit of God to be recognized in them? How much should be risked to find this out? The Corinthians, and especially women in leadership among them, will have been at least as hesitant about this as any modern reader. Perhaps their response can be traced in part and ours reconsidered.

How Words Shape Relations between People

The words we use to negotiate relationships between ourselves and others are imperfect tools. They sometimes produce unintended consequences when our skill falls short, or we have been overly hasty in our design. They also produce unintended consequences because the hearer filters them through experiences of which we are unaware.

While words may succeed in building bridges that lead to understanding, the moment will be fleeting if the words are not supported by actions.

In 2 Corinthians 1:1-11 Paul is trying, as Anne Wire describes, to salvage his relationship with the Corinthians. The relationship has become fraught as a result of words and actions that have created a distance perhaps too wide to be bridged. In her comments, Wire wonders how the Corinthians might hear Paul's words: "Are they merely a change of strategy in an old battle for control? Or do they demonstrate genuine openness to difference, creating room for the Spirit of God to be recognized in the Corinthians themselves?"

The questions that Wire raises are questions I share. As I listen to Paul's words, I filter them through my experiences as a cisgender, lesbian, feminist woman of faith. I am keenly aware of times when the church and others have spoken words that created hopes that remained unsupported by actions, or have questioned whether or not the Spirit of God resides in me. The deep chasms created by these words have been difficult to bridge.

My experience leads me to examine with care how Paul attempts to rebuild his relationship with the Corinthians in his opening words. My purpose here is not to take sides but to reflect on how language is used and how it may be heard. What can we learn from this attempt to mediate sharp conflict?

I note first Paul's use of pronouns. He begins with what appears to be inclusive language—*our, us, we* (1:3-5)— describing a shared experience. A shift takes place at verse 6 with the introduction of *your*. Now *we* clearly refers to Paul (and Timothy?). As he continues, Paul tries to build points of connection with the Corinthians: "*we* are being consoled, for *your* consolation . . . when *you* endure the *same* suffering *we* are suffering. *Our* hope for *you* is unshaken; as *you* share in *our* suffering, *you* share in *our* consolation" (vv. 6-7). After describing his perils in Asia, Paul returns to challenge the Corinthians: "*you* help *us* by *your* prayers" (v. 11).

Paul's use of pronouns calls to my attention that the hardships described here are entirely Paul's. The Corinthians experience consolation/ encouragement when they endure the *same* suffering as Paul. But do they? In particular, do the women endure the *same* hardships or are theirs different? And if different, can they expect to receive encouragement? Or is it only as they share in the *same* hardships as Paul that they receive encouragement? Further, can the Corinthians offer *Paul* encouragement gained through their hardships? Or, as Paul seems to say, are they able to offer support only through their prayers?

Holly E. Hearon

2 Corinthians 1:12–2:11

Paul Explains His Long Absence

Text and Its Structure (1:12–2:11)

After greeting the Corinthians and blessing God for his rescue (1:1-11), Paul immediately begins to defend himself by calling witnesses and explaining his past conduct. First, he claims he has been open and above board—holy and transparent to God—in all he has done (1:12-14).[1] Second, he claims he has meant only the best for them in his travel plans (1:15–2:4). He wanted to visit Corinth both on the way to Macedonia and on the return before going to Judea, giving them a double benefit, and when he dropped this plan it was only to spare them further hurt. Third, he asks them to forgive a person they had disciplined, apparently on his behalf (2:5-11).

Because we do not know all that Paul can assume they know about his conduct and travel and the offender he mentions here, modern reconstructions of these past events differ significantly. A key problem is that

---

1. The manuscript evidence is too weak to follow the Greek Nestle-Aland twenty-eighth edition and the NRSV, which replace "holiness" (ἁγιότητι) with "frankness" or "singleness of mind" (ἁπλότητι) on the basis that the latter is common in Paul's writing and suits the context well. More likely, in the early centuries when all texts were written in capital letters, this word "singleness" (ΑΠΛΟΤΗΤΙ) arose when a scribe misread the similar letters in "holiness" (ΑΓΙΟΤΗΤΙ).

¹:¹²Indeed, this is our boast, the testimony of our conscience: we have behaved in the world with frankness and godly sincerity, not by earthly wisdom but by the grace of God—and all the more toward you. ¹³For we write you nothing other than what you can read and also understand; I hope you will understand until the end—¹⁴as you have already understood us in part—that on the day of the Lord Jesus we are your boast even as you are our boast.

¹⁵Since I was sure of this, I wanted to come to you first, so that you might have a double favor; ¹⁶I wanted to visit you on my way to Macedonia, and to come back to you from Macedonia and have you send me on to Judea. ¹⁷Was I vacillating when I wanted to do this? Do I make my plans according to ordinary human standards, ready to say "Yes, yes" and "No, no" at the same time? ¹⁸As surely as God is faithful, our word to you has not been "Yes and No." ¹⁹For the Son of God, Jesus Christ, whom we proclaimed among you, Silvanus and Timothy and I, was not "Yes and No"; but in him it is always "Yes." ²⁰For in him every one of God's promises is a "Yes." For this reason it is through him that we say the "Amen," to the glory of God. ²¹But it is God who establishes us with you in Christ and has anointed us, ²²by putting his seal on us and giving us his Spirit in our hearts as a first installment.

²³But I call on God as witness against me: it was to spare you that I did not come again to Corinth. ²⁴I do not mean to imply that we lord it over your faith;

the Greek language can refer to a present act of writing with a completed past tense called an epistolary aorist. Therefore, when Paul speaks of his writing (ἔγραψα, 2:3, 4, 9) in tears he may be saying, "I have written just now" (i.e., "I am writing"), or he may be saying, "I have written some time ago." A few interpreters say that Paul is speaking of his present writing,[2] and this could help explain the convoluted structure and extreme outbursts of 2 Corinthians that have led to partition theories. Then the translation could read:

2. This is the conclusion of Eva-Marie Becker ("Paulus als weinender Briefschreiber [2 Kor 2,4]: Epistolare *Parousia* im Zeichen visualisierter Emotionalität," in *Der zweite Korintherbrief: Literarische Gestalt—historische Situation—theologische Argumentation. Festschrift zum 70. Geburtstag von Dietrich-Alex Koch,* ed. Dieter Sänger [Göttingen: Vandenhoeck & Ruprecht, 2012], 11–26). Pseudo Callisthenes 2.19.2 is evidence that the epistolary aorist can also be used at the opening of a text (BDAG, 207).

rather, we are workers with you for your joy, because you stand firm in the faith. ²⋅¹So I made up my mind not to make you another painful visit. ²For if I cause you pain, who is there to make me glad but the one whom I have pained? ³And I wrote as I did, so that when I came, I might not suffer pain from those who should have made me rejoice; for I am confident about all of you, that my joy would be the joy of all of you. ⁴For I wrote you out of much distress and anguish of heart and with many tears, not to cause you pain, but to let you know the abundant love that I have for you.

⁵But if anyone has caused pain, he has caused it not to me, but to some extent—not to exaggerate it—to all of you. ⁶This punishment by the majority is enough for such a person; ⁷so now instead you should forgive and console him, so that he may not be overwhelmed by excessive sorrow. ⁸So I urge you to reaffirm your love for him. ⁹I wrote for this reason: to test you and to know whether you are obedient in everything. ¹⁰Anyone whom you forgive, I also forgive. What I have forgiven, if I have forgiven anything, has been for your sake in the presence of Christ. ¹¹And we do this so that we may not be outwitted by Satan; for we are not ignorant of his designs.*

* NRSV notes: 1:12, Other ancient authorities read *holiness* for *frankness*; 1:15, Other ancient authorities read *pleasure* for *favor*; 1:17, Gk *according to the flesh*.

> I am writing this very letter in order that I not be hurt when I come by those who ought to make me glad, since I am confident in you all that my joy is all of yours as well. For I am writing you in much affliction and pressure of heart through many tears, not that you should be hurt, but that you should know the love I have for you more and more. . . . I am writing for this very reason, so that I can know that you stand the test, if indeed your conduct shows that you are listening. (2:3-4, 9)

Yet when Paul returns to this issue of a painful letter in 7:8-13, he unmistakably is speaking with ἔγραψα (7:12) about a letter he wrote in the past. If the ἔγραψα of the first chapter is read in the past tense as in the NRSV, Paul is claiming to already have written them a letter in a great struggle, intending not to cause them pain but to spare them a painful conflict on his arrival, and apparently they have disciplined someone in response. From this, most modern interpreters have accepted the hypothesis that Paul made an interim visit to Corinth, left quickly after some humiliating incident, and wrote an anguished letter accusing the person involved. But the invention of a sudden visit and lost letter is unnecessary if 1 Corinthians can be the letter to which he refers.[3] This makes sense if 1 Corinthians is read, not as Paul's answer to respectful questions about sexuality, sacrificed meat, and worship, but as his intense effort to undermine their bold slogans and practices and to restore order of a kind that he can respect and they—he hopes—can tolerate.[4] If so, writing 1 Corinthians could have caused Paul significant anguish and at the same time met opposition from the Corinthians (2 Cor 2:3-4) in spite of their willingness to discipline one person (2:5-9). Now Paul is seeking to resolve the conflict. He claims to be speaking frankly and clearly, justifies his absence as sparing them pain, and asks them to forgive the person they punished on his behalf.

I take ἔγραψα ("I have written") as a past-tense reference back to 1 Corinthians and see Paul beginning 2 Corinthians hopeful about reconciliation with the Corinthians, defending himself with the aim of recovering their affection and their participation in the Jerusalem gift. At the same time he is defensive about their charges against him[5] and struggles with discouragement,[6] reverting occasionally and in conclusion to strict warnings.[7]

A Feminist Lens at Three Ranges on Paul's Defense of His Past Actions (1:12–2:11)

A Broad Focus on All Bodies in Space and Time, Flesh and Spirit

Though not named as analytical terms, space and time are very much at play in Paul's defense of his travel plans and his appeal for Corinthian understanding. Paul writes because of the space between himself and those he addresses, and this in two senses. The geographical distance, he says, is a result of the personal distance—"it was to spare you that I haven't come back to Corinth" (1:23). He writes now to ask them to reinstate someone they had disciplined, perhaps on his instruction (2:7; 7:11-12). He implies that once this is done, he will be able to come to them without increasing the pain and alienation. They will share space again, physically and personally.

---

3. See Niels Hyldahl, "Die Frage nach der literarischen Einheit des Zweiten Korintherbriefes," *ZNW* 64 (1973): 299–300, 305–6.

4. 1 Cor 6:12-13; 7:1; 8:1, 8; 10:23.

5. 2 Cor 1:12; 10:10.

6. 2 Cor 2:3-9; 4:1, 16.

7. 2 Cor 6:14–7:1; 10:1-6; 13:1-10.

He makes clear his desire for this by defending his shifting travel plans over time in terms of his concern for them, speaking of his love and of his desire that they share not pain but joy. Because he makes explicit in this way the personal distance that stands behind the geographical distance, what happens after this time of separation can be taken as a gauge of whether the letter succeeds or not. When Paul gets back to Corinth, is there a reconciliation? Although Paul has set up the spatial and temporal scene in this way, the rest of the letter puts the likelihood of such reconciliation in doubt. Will their one act of forgiveness be enough to satisfy Paul? Will this letter from Paul satisfy their grave doubts about him (10:10; 12:16-17; 13:3)? Some interpreters reorder the different parts of the letter so that it ends in reconciliation (see my introduction, One Letter or Many?), but the letter read in sequence, as I read it, ends with its most harsh chapters. Finally, the letter's survival as Scripture in a continuing community creates a third space beyond the geographical and personal gaps between Paul and the Corinthians, a gaping space between their inconclusive relationship and each group of interpreters, including our feminist selves.

Because Paul is reviewing his conduct here, we would expect a focus on past time. He does defend how he has acted in public and private (1:12) and how he has made his travel plans (1:15-17, 23; 2:1-2). Even his past letter writing is evaluated[8]—they have at least partially understood it (1:14). But his attention is anchored firmly in the present: "We write you nothing except what you can read and also understand" (1:13). And when he culminates this argument with confidence in the future—"and I trust that you will understand completely . . . in the day of our Lord Jesus" (1:14)—even this is supporting his initial point that they can at present read and understand him.

Again in reference to past travel plans, where someone has mocked his "yes, yes," and "no, no," Paul reminds them that in Jesus "all has become 'yes'" (1:19). Here the perfect tense γέγονεν, "has become," states that something begun in the past has present force. And when Paul goes on

---

8. Margaret Mitchell in her 2008 Oxford lectures takes 2 Corinthians as a series of letters and reads Paul's recurring reference back to his own correspondence with the Corinthians as the beginning of the long and contentious process since that time of interpreting his letters (*Paul, the Birth of Christian Hermeneutics* [Cambridge: Cambridge University Press, 2010], 58–115; "The Corinthian Correspondence and the Birth of Pauline Hermeneutics," in *Paul and the Corinthians: Studies of a Community in Conflict*, ed. Trevor J. Burke and J. Keith Elliott, NovTSup 109 [Leiden: Brill, 2003], 24–36, 47–49).

to explain that "all God's promises find their 'yes' in him and through him we say amen to the glory of God" (1:20), both God's past promises and God's ultimate glory are seen to be realized in the present common life, quite a claim considering the fragile present relation of Paul to the Corinthians. A final sentence identifies this God as the one who continues to establish or imbed them all in Christ through the past events of their anointing, sealing, and receiving the confirming gift of the Spirit (1:21-22).

Paul could not evoke more sharply than he does in these passages the present communal experience of spiritual life, and this without the recurring "yes, but" qualifications and restrictions we find in 1 Corinthians.[9] Even the final warning here—that he is testing whether they will listen and carry out the forgiveness he has enacted on their behalf (2:9; see 1 Cor 5:3-5)—itself challenges them to exercise a present spiritual power. For Paul, the time that matters is the present. The past is demonstrated in the common present and the future confirms it.

Twice in this section Paul seems to speak negatively of the flesh. Are we to take this as his rejection of the human body and the material world it represents? First, he claims to have acted in the world and toward them "with the holiness and transparency of God and not by wisdom oriented on the flesh but by God's grace" (1:12). I take these closing phrases as instrumental: it is not by the intelligence that serves human needs and desires but by the free generosity and openness of God that he claims he can be transparent. A few lines later he is speaking of having wanted to visit them twice, both in going to Macedonia and on return. He asks, "In wanting this, was I taking you lightly? Or did I want what I wanted according to the flesh so that with me it was 'yes, yes' and 'no, no'? God is faithful that our message to you is not 'yes and no'" (1:17-18). This "wanting according to the flesh" seems to mean following one's own desires and taking others lightly (NRSV: "making plans according to ordinary human standards"), and Paul contrasts this with God's faithfulness that realizes all past promises in the "yes" that is Jesus.

Clearly, Paul's point here is that he came to them impelled by God's promises of good for them realized in Jesus, not by his shifting needs or desires. Yet because human desire is expressed in terms of "flesh," the question is raised whether Paul assumes that humans are by nature torn between flesh and spirit. Pointing against this may be Paul's reference to Satan here, not in terms of physical desire, but of mental strategy (2:11).

9. 1 Cor 6:12; 7:2; 10:12-15, 23; 11:3; 12:3; 13:1; 14:2, 32-36.

And "spirit" appears not as a higher human nature but as a divine gift (1:21). If there is dualism here, it differentiates human flesh (and blood) from divine Spirit and glory, with the understanding that this separation has been overcome by God's grace in Jesus now speaking to all nations through Paul, Timothy, and Sylvanus the "yes" promised to Israel.[10]

And what can a feminist make of this? Do we read it postcolonially as Paul's universalizing his people's ideology to compete in the imperial age? Or do we read it from a liberal perspective as Paul's extending his people's vision to liberate other nations among whom he was raised? Or possibly we read it from within Israel as Paul's announcing the Messianic age when God's righteousness is confessed by all nations as they bring their thank offerings to God. Our reading is our task as we seek to shape our world and meet its needs.[11] But Paul, as an early Western interpreter of Israel's tradition and a formulator of the "yes" to the nations in Jesus, is a forerunner not to be ignored.

A Mid-Range Focus on Social, Political, and Geographical Aspects of Paul's Defense

The long opening sentence here (1:12-14) is framed in terms of Paul's boast (καύχησις). Because "boast" is a pejorative word in English, this is better translated as "pride." Paul moves from "what we are proud of is this" (1:12) to "we are your pride as you are ours" (1:14). This identifies Paul's defense as agonistic rhetoric (ἀγωνίζομαι, "I contest, struggle") and locates it within a culture of male competition for recognition. Though Paul is closer to Israel's prophets, speaking against false prophets and deferring judgment to the righteous God, he is also speaking in Greek to people in a Roman colony where higher education was shaped to train men for contesting cases in court.[12] For example, a common practice was to require students to give speeches either to accuse or to defend the protagonist in a hypothetical case, using a format much like our

---

10. In her analysis of 1 Corinthians 15 Claudia Janssen interprets Paul's "flesh and blood cannot inherit the kingdom of God" (15:50) to refer to those who are unjust (1 Cor 6:9-11) and live by the flesh rather than the Spirit, not to all living people (*Anders ist die Schönheit der Körper: Paulus und die Auferstehung in 1 Kor 15* [Gütersloh: Gütersloher Verlagshaus, 2005], 228–33).

11. Christine Gerber, *Paulus, Apostolat und Autorität, oder vom Lesen fremder Briefe* (Zürich: Theologischer Verlag Zürich, 2012), 14–15.

12. Mitchell, *Birth of Christian Hermeneutics*, 18–27.

debates.[13] Everything depended on effective persuasion. Both Paul's task to carry news of Jesus to the nations and his setting in Roman Greece geared him to compete with other voices. Here he speaks of his pride in having expressed himself clearly and without deception so the Corinthians can be proud of him, and if they are persuaded they become his pride as well. The focus is not on Paul's competitors for the Corinthians' attention, figures who begin to surface only in later chapters of the letter. Paul's bottom line is recovering his own good relationship with the Corinthians, and to do so he must face their criticisms because his authority is contested, both within and outside the news about Jesus, and his arguments are shaped to work in that agonistic world.

Paul's travel talk (1:15-22) plays out within his specific social, political, and geographical world in at least four ways.[14] As an itinerant he operates in harsh physical conditions and with unreliable communications systems. Second, he must contend with prejudice against traveling teachers for being lightweights or charlatans. Third, he deals with different regions of the empire that compete for respect and imperial favors. And fourth, he operates within the imperial ideology of a unified inhabited world in which people receive benefits in different ways according to their relation to the center.

First, the harsh physical conditions of Paul's itinerant work are better documented later in this letter[15] but what is striking in this opening defense is his ability to make travel choices and carry them out and his willingness to do so in spite of difficulties. Note that he does not attribute his erratic travel plans to bad roads, lack of a ship, political or military obstructions, or even harsh weather. He had relative freedom to travel, and when he did not travel he could send and receive messages with coworkers who did.[16] It is to this slow and inexact practice of

---

13. Ronald F. Hock and Edward N. O'Neil, *The* Chreia *in Ancient Rhetoric*, vol. 1: *The Progymnasmata* (Atlanta: Scholars Press, 1986), 10–22; Burton L. Mack, "Elaboration of the *Chreia* in the Hellenistic School," in *Patterns of Persuasion in the Gospels*, ed. Burton L. Mack and Vernon K. Robbins (Sonoma, CA: Polebridge Press, 1989), 31–67; Ronald F. Hock and Edward N. O'Neil, *The* Chreia *and Ancient Rhetoric*, vol. 2: *Classroom Exercises* (Atlanta: Society of Biblical Literature, 2002), 79–354.

14. On the many possible implications of Paul's itinerancy, see Timothy Luckritz Marquis, *Transient Apostle: Paul, Travel, and the Rhetoric of Empire* (New Haven: Yale University Press, 2013).

15. 2 Cor 4:8-9; 6:4-10; 11:23-27.

16. Ulrich Mell notes that Paul handled his many defeats by staying flexible, not changing his values but his routes and times, and working to stabilize crises through

letter writing—Paul's dictating and his colleagues' writing and carrying and reading aloud—that we owe our remarkable, yet strictly limited, access to the communication that did take place. Though the public post was restricted to military and government use, Roman roads were adequate so that people could travel and carry letters for others, and in this sense the Pax Romana was a condition for the spread of news about Jesus.[17]

Second, beyond the proverbial "high mountains and wide rivers" Paul had to contend with widespread prejudice against any itinerant seeking adherents. His opening claim to have acted transparently in public and toward them (1:12) counters the stereotype of the peripatetic swindler.[18] And his rhetorical questions pose the charge that some in Corinth had likely made: "In wanting this was I acting flippantly [ἐλαφρός, 'light in weight'; ἐλαφρία, 'levity']? Or was I wanting what the flesh wants [κατὰ σάρκα βουλεύομαι]?" (1:17). Paul thus surfaces and denies the accusation that he fits the image of the philosopher as snake-oil dealer. Timothy Luckritz Marquis has recently proposed that Paul also plays on positive images of ancient figures such as Odysseus and Aeneas who traveled west from Asia through many trials to carry out a divine vision.[19] Paul's vision is evident not only in Jesus Christ as God's "yes" that overcomes all his "yes yes" and "no no" but also in God's continued faithfulness that will make them proud of Paul and him proud of them on the Lord's day.

Third, Paul speaks in a world where different regions compete for respect and imperial favors. The very fact that Paul does not name Philippi and Corinth, two Roman colonies where he had close ties, but instead names the broader Roman provinces of Macedonia and Achaia, could be an effort to diffuse competition between two cities. Yet each time Paul justifies his changing travel plans he indicates that the plan is made particularly to favor Corinth, in this case twice over Macedonia.[20] Is this simply Paul's way of cultivating his ties with whatever

---

intense correspondence ("Paulus: scheiternder Gescheiter: Ein historischer und literarischer Einwurf," in Sänger, *Zweite Korintherbrief*, 215–23).

17. In addition to Paul's and other New Testament letters, the Acts of the Apostles attests a number of letters between first-century synagogues, assemblies in Christ, and officials (Acts 9:1-2; 15:22-32; 16:4; 23:25-30, 33-35; 25:26-27).

18. Hans Dieter Betz, *Lukian von Samosata und das Neue Testament: Religionsgeschichtliche und paränetische Parallelen* (Berlin: Akademie-Verlag, 1961), 112–14.

19. Marquis, *Transient Apostle*, 22–46, 67–69.

20. 1 Cor 16:5-7; 2 Cor 1:15-16, 23.

community he is addressing, so also with Philippi in Philippians 4:10-20? Or is he dealing with a particular objection in Corinth about his close ties to Macedonia?

The political setting stimulated this interprovincial competition in several ways. Greek city-states were more powerful than Macedonian towns until Philip of Macedon and his son Alexander conquered Greece in the late fourth century BCE, reversing the power scale. Since the rise of Rome in the third century BCE and Rome's defeat of both Macedonia and Greece in the second century, these two regions no longer operated independently as city-states, as leagues of cities, or, in Macedon's case, as a kingdom, free to set their own political and military polities. Rome designated a few cities, such as Athens, Sparta, and Thessalonica, as "free cities," but most others owed tribute, and none could make decisions about external affairs.[21] The favored cities were the Roman colonies, such as Corinth and Philippi, ruled in Latin by imported Roman colonists according to Roman systems. Also favored were the capitals of Roman provinces where regional administration was exercised, so in Achaia at Corinth and in Macedonia at Thessalonica. These were doubtless chosen for their thriving commercial activity and convenient access from Rome by sea or land, Corinth at the isthmus and Thessalonica on the Aegean Sea and at the Via Egnatia, which stretched westward to the Adriatic Sea. Corinth's advantage was increased by the use of wooden platforms that carried cargo and even small ships on a stone slipway (δίολκος) from one gulf to the other across the isthmus.[22] All this served Rome's interest in turning the face of Greece toward the west, as also did Augustus's founding the new cities of Nikopolis and Patrae on Greece's west coast. Corinth as a Roman colony and provincial capital would have been intent on negotiating its own interests in relation to these other centers of the Greek-speaking Roman Empire.

21. J. A. O. Larsen, "Roman Greece: Greece and Macedonia from Augustus to Gallienus," in *An Economic Survey of Ancient Rome*, ed. Tenney Frank (Baltimore: Johns Hopkins University Press, 1938), 436–98; Susan E. Alcock, "Regional Development in the Roman Empire: The Eastern Mediterranean," in *The Cambridge Economic History of the Greco-Roman World*, ed. Walter Scheidel, Jan Morris, and Richard Saller (Cambridge: Cambridge University Press, 2007), 671–97.

22. James Wisemann, *The Land of the Ancient Corinthians* (Göteborg: Paul Aströms, 1978), 45–50.

The Context of Roman Corinth

Feminist scholarship has pushed biblical interpreters not only to understand the ancient rhetorical forms deployed by those who wrote the text—in this case, Paul and Silvanus (1 Cor) or Paul and Timothy (2 Cor)—but also to consider the responses of those who first received, interpreted, resisted, and embodied the ethical, social, political, and theological exhortations of these letters. Rhetoric is the art of persuasion, and persuasion is a means of exercising power. Thus, looking closely at the rhetoric of the letters of Paul means investigating how they engage with power, as scholars Antoinette Clark Wire, Elisabeth Schüssler Fiorenza, and Delores Williams, among others, have taught us.

The use of the term ἐκκλησία to describe those to whom Paul wrote seems to be a practice that predates him—that is, he reflects back the language of community that they use for themselves. As Anna C. Miller has shown, Greek cities under the Roman Empire still had active political ἐκκλησίαι or assemblies, which engaged in democratic, deliberative discourse and civic debate. The use of the term ἐκκλησία as a term of address in the Corinthian correspondence implies that the Christ followers who were addressed in the letters thought of themselves in light of the practices of civic assembly. They were accustomed to practices of democratic debate, including the use and adjudication of persuasive rhetoric.

To reconstruct the ἐκκλησία or assembly at Roman Corinth that first received these letters, we should have two contexts in mind. First, Corinth was a city characterized as having experienced grief, due to its destruction in 146 BCE under the Roman general Mummius. This grief was mentioned in an epigram and by philosophical voices as found in Cicero's correspondence and his *Tusculan Disputations*, and the topic of grief also arises in 1 Corinthians 7:29-31. Other kinds of grief are also found throughout the city, in its sites and archaeological evidence: the story of Medea's murder of her children is memorialized in the Fountain of Glauke in the town center, and Pausanias describes how the inhabitants of Corinth continued to remember that legend. Grief is also instantiated in the Fountain of Peirene, said to be produced by the tears of a mother for her dead son. Bioarchaeological evidence indicates an elevated death rate for children at Roman Corinth; we can reasonably conclude that this would lead to grief. A grievous story is found in nearby Isthmia, as the body of the child Melikertes-Palaimon is carried to shore by a dolphin before his heroization.

The second context to keep in mind as one reconstructs the ἐκκλησία that Paul addresses is that of slavery. Roman Corinth, which Julius Caesar established in 44 BCE as *Colonia Laus Iulia Corinthiensis*, was a city of freed persons, or former slaves. Some of these gained leadership in civic administration, an unusual procedure since former slaves did not usually qualify for civic magistracies, as Anthony Spawforth has discussed. Caesar made an exception for this city. It is not coincidental that it is only in 1 Corinthians that we find the word ἀπελεύθερος, "freed person," in the New Testament. The work of reconstructing the impact of the words of Paul and his cowriters must extend to considering the listening ears of slaves and former slaves. Not everyone had the material freedom to care for his or her purity and body, as the work of Jennifer Glancy, Katherine Shaner, and Joseph Marchal, among others, reminds us. For references and further discussion, see chapters 2 and 5 in my *Archaeology and the Letters of Paul* (Oxford: Oxford University Press, 2019).

Laura Salah Nasrallah

Specific events intensified competition between the provinces of Achaia (Greece) and Macedonia. After the Roman civil wars of the first century BCE, which left the whole peninsula devastated by battling armies, Augustus in 27 BCE organized the empire into two parts,[23] claiming for himself as military commander-in-chief or imperator all the outlying provinces recently conquered or prone to revolt, including most of what is now Spain, France, and Germany; the Alpine and Balkan areas as far as the Danube reaches; Syria and several vassal kingdoms on the east; and Egypt on the south. He then restored to the civil rule of Rome's Senate the internal provinces of the empire, including Achaia and Macedonia on the Greek peninsula; Asia, Bithynia, and later Cilicia in what is now costal Turkey; also Cyrene and North Africa to the south; the major Mediterranean islands and southernmost Spain and France.

The impact of this division on daily lives in these two major regions of the empire is not exaggerated by speaking of occupied provinces

---

23. Dio Cassius, *Roman History* 52.1.1–41.2; 53.12.1–16.3; Frank Burr Marsh, *The Reign of Tiberius* (New York: Barnes & Noble, 1959, repr. 1993), 28–30. Tenney Frank calls this division of rule the diarchy (*A History of Rome* [New York: Henry Holt, 1923], 350). Though emperors encroached more and more on the Senate's rights over internal provinces, the respect for Augustus Caesar kept the system intact into the second century CE.

and pacified provinces.[24] All legions were stationed in the outer imperial provinces and could march through internal senatorial provinces only if their commanders were celebrating a triumph in Rome by vote of Rome's Senate. In the outlying occupied provinces Rome appropriated all kinds of natural resources, above all human beings through slavery, whereas in the pacified provinces Rome largely restricted itself to fiscal exploitation of commercial and agricultural production through regular tribute and other taxes. No question in earliest Christian history is more interesting than how a movement begun in rural areas of an occupied vassal kingdom first came to flourish in the cities of Rome's pacified provinces around the Aegean Sea. Paul's role in this transition cannot be contested.

By the first century CE the pacified provinces around the Aegean had become the centers of commerce in the Roman east. But revolts were taking place in occupied areas toward the north in Illyricum, and then in Moesia and Thrace, and sometime between 15 and 19 CE the emperor Tiberius assimilated Achaia and Macedonia into the occupied province of Moesia,[25] probably to give the imperial legate Poppeaus Sabinus more flexibility to recruit, provender, and lead legions in putting down the revolts. Though this surely increased imperial investment in the area, the resources would have gone into roads and supplies for the armies in the north and not into building up local production or trade. And agricultural produce would have been confiscated from across the area for military use. It was not until 44 CE, under Claudius, a decade before Paul wrote 2 Corinthians, that Macedonia and Achaia regained their status as independent senatorial provinces free of military rule.[26]

How this recent history impacted the relation between Macedonia and Greece in the 50s CE is hard to determine, but it certainly made both of them aware of their dependence on decisions occurring elsewhere and their vulnerability to forces beyond their control. Because it was not possible for cities even to debate the wisdom of such decisions as these, let alone to change policies or prosecute any abuses that occurred,

---

24. For the history of research on the impact of this division, see my "Women in Early Christian Stories: Serving and Served, Rural and Urban, in Occupied and Pacified Provinces," in *Bridges in New Testament Interpretation: Interdisciplinary Advances,* ed. Neil Elliott and Werner Kelber (Lanham, MD: Lexington Books/Fortress Academic, 2018), 23–25.

25. Tacitus, *Annals* 1.76.4; 1.80.1; Dio Cassius, *Roman History* 58.25.5; Theodore Mommsen, *The Provinces of the Roman Empire from Caesar to Diocletian,* vol. 1 (Chicago: Ares, 1909, repr. 1974), 283–302; Marsh, *Reign of Tiberius,* 146.

26. Suetonius, *Claudius* 25.3; Dio Cassius, *Roman History* 60.24.1.

deliberative and judicial rhetoric had largely atrophied in Greek city assemblies by Paul's time, or at least had been limited to local and personal issues. This left public gatherings focused on epideictic or celebrative discourse—on declarations honoring donors to the city, dedications of temples to the gods or the emperors, the giving and receiving of titles and priesthoods, and the announcements of games and their victors. Cities competed with each other for permission from the emperor to build temples to the imperial family or establish major games.

When Paul claims that he is coming through Macedonia in order to have more time in Achaia (1 Cor 16:5-6), or that he is coming through Achaia to Macedonia in order to give Corinth the benefit of a second visit on his return (2 Cor 1:15-16), and finally that he is not coming back in order to spare the Corinthians (2:1), he claims to favor Corinth in negotiating the rivalry between Corinth, a Roman colony and provincial capital in Achaia, and Philippi, a Roman colony, and/or Thessalonica, a Roman capital, in Macedonia. Also one can see behind Paul's honoring of those to whom he speaks the persona of a traveling dignitary, welcomed everywhere but always unfortunately short of time. Recent postcolonial interpretation has highlighted the ambiguous, often exploitative, role of this kind of itinerant who has an agenda for the local people in the many places he alights.[27] Paul's rhetoric is fraught with questions about his wider role and the Corinthians' relation to it.

In a fourth and final way, the imperial world sets the scene for the scope of Paul's plans. By the time that Paul writes to Rome, probably from Corinth on his last stay, Paul's travel plans seem to have a worldwide scope. He says in Romans 15:19, 23-24: "From Jerusalem and around as far as Illyricum I have completed preaching the gospel of Christ . . . and now I have no further scope for work in these parts and . . . I am hoping to come through to see you and be sent on by you [to Spain]." Before and after these words Paul stresses his aim not to preach where others have already brought the news, but this seems hardly enough reason for leaving the Roman east for the west. Illyricum was initially Augustus Caesar's name for a Roman administrative district that stretched from what is now Switzerland and the Croatian coast all the way east to

---

27. Christopher Stanley, *The Colonized Apostle: Paul through Postcolonial Eyes* (Minneapolis: Fortress, 2011); Marquis, *Transient Apostle*; Musa W. Dube, *Postcolonial Feminist Interpretation of the Bible* (St. Louis, MO: Chalice, 2000); Musa W. Dube Shomanah, Andrew Mütüa Mbuvi, and Dora R. Mbuwayesango, eds., *Postcolonial Perspectives in African Biblical Interpretation* (Atlanta: Society of Biblical Literature Press, 2012).

the Black Sea along the south side of the Danube, but it was later separated into the five imperial provinces of Ratia, Norica, Dalmatia, Pannonia, and Moesia.[28] Since Paul is not attested to have been in Illyricum (as Dalmatia then came to be called),[29] it is possible that Illyricum could still signify for Paul the entire northern border area that he has moved along in Macedonia.

Because Paul says he went "from Jerusalem right around as far as Illyricum," some interpreters see in this Paul's plan to circle the Mediterranean world through Rome, Spain, North Africa, and Egypt in order to bring the nations to worship God in Jerusalem according to ancient Israel's prophecies (Isa 56:6-8; 66:18-23).[30] This need not exclude another proposal that he aims to circle the empire as the forerunner of the universal news he carries.[31] We can marvel at the light footprint of such a mission strategy, never to settle down and dominate any community (1 Cor 1:13),[32] though his letters show he does not let go easily, and at the same time we can be appalled by the imperial nature of an ambition that assumes one message fits all, though he claims he adapts himself to fit each group (1 Cor 9:19-23). Even in his own urban Greek-speaking context, has he been able to negotiate the tensions between the major cities that compete for his time? If not, how does he think he will manage in the Latin-speaking cities of Spain, let alone among rural tribes there?

A Sharp Focus on the Interaction of Paul and the Corinthians

1:12-14. If we focus our feminist lens on Paul's persuasion of the Corinthians, including whatever we can ferret out of the ways they have provoked what he says or might react to it, this review of his past should be particularly rich. His self-defense will respond to what he at least assumes are their objections within the general patterns of argument at the time. He first claims to have acted in the world and especially toward

---

28. Mommsen, *The Provinces*, 1, 21.

29. Yet Paul's coworker Titus is associated with Dalmatia in 2 Timothy 4:9.

30. Johannes Munck, *Paul and the Salvation of Mankind* (Richmond, VA: John Knox, 1959), 303–8.

31. David J. Downs, *The Offering of the Gentiles* (Tübingen: Mohr Siebeck, 2008), 28–29.

32. This strategy was advocated in African missions by Roland Allen and later adapted in China as the Three-Self Movement of self-governing, self-propagating, and self-supporting: Roland Allen, *Missionary Methods: St. Paul's or Ours?* (Chicago: Moody Press, 1959); Philip Wickeri, *Seeking the Common Ground: Protestant Christianity, the Three-Self Movement, and China's United Front* (Maryknoll, NY: Orbis Books, 1988), 36–42.

them not in fleshly wisdom but in God's holiness, transparency, and grace. He repeats this kind of assertion regularly in the letter, insisting he is not like the many who peddle God's word, dilute what they offer to their advantage, and seduce others with their cunning.[33] This image of the itinerant shyster in philosopher's robes is a typical motif in anti-sophistic rhetoric and in slurs against traveling teachers with whom Paul might contrast himself.[34] Yet there are some indications that Paul is also reacting to Corinthian charges here.

He rejects wisdom oriented on the flesh. The flesh in Greek literature and Jewish Hellenism could signify not simply physical desire but more broadly manipulation for personal gain. Paul claims instead to be acting with God's transparency and holiness and according to God's grace, which seems to mean with openness and integrity. Paul's evidence for this is that the Corinthians can read and come to understand what he writes, or, he assures them, what they don't understand will be completely clear on the Lord's Day when "we are your pride and you are ours." So God is both the source of his openness and its ultimate measure on the Lord's Day, envisioned by Paul as the time of God's final redress of all wrongs at the appearing (παρουσία) of the Lord Jesus. And Paul is convinced that, whether proud or ashamed, they will stand or fall together.

Margaret Mitchell has named these words (1:12-14), a single sentence in Greek, as the thesis statement of this letter that is Paul's final effort to reconcile with the Corinthians.[35] It not only states in broad terms how Paul defends his work in Corinth but also suggests that the Corinthians have resisted understanding his letters, apparently considering him either obscure or deceptive. He has now determined not to ignore the alienation or to explode in response. Instead he acknowledges the issue by claiming that because he has been open and above board throughout, saying nothing they cannot understand, they will finally come to understand him and be proud of him—and he of them—as soon as everything is made clear.

When we ask how this was received by those being addressed, we can only say that, if Paul gauged them well, the lector was willing to keep reading and the others to keep listening. Yet we can expect there was more of what Paul called "understanding in part," or "half-understanding,"

---

33. 2 Cor 2:17; 4:2; 11:2-4.

34. Hans Dieter Betz, *Der Apostel Paulus und die sokratische Tradition: Eine exegetische Untersuchung zu seiner "Apologie" 2 Korinther 10–13*, BHT 45 (Tübingen: J. C. B. Mohr [Paul Siebeck], 1972), 50–55, 112–15; Marquis, *Transient Apostle*, 99–103.

35. Mitchell, *Birth of Christian Hermeneutics*, 96–97.

which by them might be expressed in anything from shrugs, looks at each other, and questions to vocal objections, counterargument, and noncompliance. If 2 Corinthians is a single letter following 1 Corinthians with one yet previous letter from Paul (1 Cor 5:9) and no letters lost between—the simplest projection of the evidence—Paul is probably referring back to the Corinthians' response to 1 Corinthians, which is itself hardly obscure, suggesting they have made some objections to his advice about sex, food, and worship.

1:15–2:4. Paul next addresses a specific complaint about his changing travel plans. We see at the end of 1 Corinthians that Paul said he would come to Corinth via Macedonia in order to be able to stay a longer time; that is, he justified an initial quick visit to Macedonia by his eagerness to get to Corinth (1 Cor 16:5-7). Now he says his more recent plan was to come through Corinth on the way to Macedonia and again on the way back before heading to Judea with the collection (2 Cor 1:15-16), and this time he justifies the plan by wanting to make Corinth a double visit. Yet again he disappointed them and now writes from Macedonia on his way to Corinth and justifies this by saying he wanted to avoid hurting them or dominating their faith (1:23–2:2). Does this denial of domination suggest some have made this charge concerning his earlier letter? Or do they just consider him mercurial and arbitrary? Will they now be convinced by his attributing the three different changes in his travel plans to his particular concern about them? All this shows that he at least doubts they will be ready to send him on with gifts to Judea any time soon.

Paul defends himself against charges of vacillation not only by showing how each travel plan was motivated to benefit them but by arguing that the message he and Sylvanus and Timothy first brought to Corinth has not changed (1:19-20). If they mock his "yes yes" and "no no"—and he would not speak this way except to echo them—he insists instead on the blanket affirmation that all God's promises find their "yes" in Jesus. This in turn evokes his "Amen" to God's glory. It could recall to Paul the "Amen" in his common worship with them and his joy in their common faith. Paul may be referring to their baptisms when he identifies God as the one who imbeds them into Christ, anoints them, and seals them with the Spirit.[36] But James D. G. Dunn argues that this language is not found

---

36. Erich Dinkler, "Die Taufterminologie in 2 Cor. I 21f," in *Neotestamentica et Patristica* (Leiden: Brill, 1962), 173–91; Margaret E. Thrall, *A Critical and Exegetical Commentary on the Second Epistle to the Corinthians*, ICC (Edinburgh: T & T Clark, 1994), 151–55; Victor Paul Furnish, *II Corinthians*, AB 32A (Garden City, NY: Doubleday, 1984), 147–50.

in baptismal texts until the second century. He claims Paul is pointing to the yet more basic gift of God's Spirit that alone makes the security of human faith possible.[37] If so, Paul could be seeking common ground with those in Corinth who claim God's Spirit, which would include the women prophets.

2:5-11. The third issue that Paul raises concerns a particular individual in Corinth. Eve-Marie Becker argues that Paul not only is in tears as he writes but tells them so (see p. 16, n. 2), apparently in order to move his hearers toward him and soften their feelings toward this person. Becker has compared this letter with those Cicero wrote from exile to his family members in which he speaks of weeping when thinking of them.[38] But if, as I hold, Paul is referring to his anguish when writing his earlier letter as he sought to correct their conduct before he came, now he says he did not want to hurt anyone or dominate them (1:23–2:4) but only to share their joy. Paul's allusion to his tears may be meant to rekindle their pity for him, which he has just evoked by his story of terror barely survived in Asia (1:8-11). He now wants them to reverse a previous judgment that they made on his instruction. The person's offense seems to have been some time back, something Paul addressed in 1 Corinthians that did receive community action, possibly that of the man "living with his father's wife" (1 Cor 5:1-5).

Two objections to this identification are not definitive. Many commentators judge that Paul was so appalled by the case of incest in 1 Corinthians 5:1-5 that he could not be speaking here of forgiving the man. But Paul was quite capable of making conflicting arguments about the same matter, for example, on eating sacrificed meat.[39] And the man's situation or Paul's understanding of it may well have changed. Patristic interpreters, closer than we are to Paul in time and culture, assume the forgiveness is intended for this man.[40] This suggests that our surprise

---

37. James D. G. Dunn, *Baptism in the Spirit* (Naperville, IL: Allenson, 1970), 133; *The Theology of Paul the Apostle* (Grand Rapids, MI: Eerdmans, 1998), 453.

38. Cicero, *Letters to His Friends* 14.1.5; 2.1; *Letters to His Brother Quintus* 1.3.10; Becker, "Weinender Briefschreiber," 22–26.

39. In 8:8 and 9:9-10 he defends eating sacrificed meat; in 8:7 and 13; 10:7, 14, 20-21 he opposes it. See Antoinette Clark Wire, *The Corinthian Women Prophets: A Reconstruction through Paul's Rhetoric* (Minneapolis: Fortress, 1990; repr., Eugene, OR: Wipf and Stock, 2003), 98–101.

40. See, for example, John Chrysostom, *Homilies on Second Corinthians* 4.4-5 in *Nicene and Post-Nicene Fathers*, vol. 12, ed. Philip Schaff (Peabody, MA: Hendrickson, 1995, repr. of Christian Literature Publishing Company's 1889 edition).

at Paul's forgiveness may come from our calling the conduct "incest" whereas sexual relations with a father's wife could mean something else at that time when elderly men often chose young women for remarriages before their own deaths. Paul's referring to Satan in this case (2 Cor 2:11) could be an effort to relieve fears he had earlier stoked (1 Cor 5:5).

A second objection is that Paul implies this person caused him pain (2:5) whereas such pain would not have been personal. But Paul's denial that he was the one hurt could be his way to stress that the person's conduct put them all in jeopardy. We should also ask if Paul was referring instead to a certain woman's conduct in worship. Though Paul's pronouns for the individual after the initial generic τις (anyone) are masculine (2:5-10), it is conceivable that a generic allusion to an unnamed person by Paul has become masculine through interpreters and scribes who assumed it applied to the man in 1 Corinthians 5:1-5. Or Paul's reference could be to a man who has been an advocate for the women, as may be the associates of Euodia and Syntyche in Philippians 4:2-3. In any case, this effort by Paul to improve relations with the Corinthians by making up with one person they have disciplined has broader implications. If women are still praying and prophesying uncovered in the Corinthian assembly, as Paul's defensiveness while writing might suggest, his asking the Corinthians to forgive a more severely chastised offender while making no reference to others could itself be heard as a concession.

I raise these possibilities not to suggest that Paul's greater openness in this letter resolves the differences between him and the Corinthian women or relieves us of the weight of a patriarchal ancestry. The shifts in Paul's arguments from chapter to chapter and letter to letter show us, rather, that he was negotiating living relationships in which he did not hold all the cards, not even most of them. Because two letters of Paul to one community survive, we do get a glimpse of these dynamics. What we see is that he is no longer talking about their conduct, as in 1 Corinthians, and giving them advice on a string of topics in response to their assertions.[41] Instead, he is talking about his own conduct and giving explanations for it in response to their critiques. In this passage we learn that some Corinthians consider his letters obscure and self-serving. Others fault him for being long absent, unreliable in his promises to come to them, and yet trying to dominate them from afar. Still others resent his restrictions, which in the one case that provoked their discipline has led

---

41. Wire, *Corinthian Women Prophets*, 13–15, 80, 94.

to alienation, and now he wants that reversed. It appears that the scene is anything but stable, let alone oppressive. Instead communication has begun at key points of tension and there appears to be space for further negotiation. Paul invokes God, not as their judge, but as the source and witness of his transparent conduct, the one who has imbedded them into Christ with the seal of the Spirit and the one whose glory will be magnified when they are proud of him and he of them on the day of the Lord Jesus.

2 Corinthians 2:12–3:3

Paul Begins His Defense

Text and Its Structure (2:12–3:3)

It is within this brief section that Paul shifts from reporting his travel to defending his life work. This shift has been treated in at least three different ways. Some find the break after 2:13 so sharp that they argue two letters of Paul were later joined at this point, the travel report continuing in 7:5-16 (see the introduction: "One Letter or Many?"). Others see Paul's attention shifting here as he slips into a digression that ends only when he returns to his travel narrative in 7:5. This assumes that Paul, like most letter writers, is writing primarily to arrange practical matters and that his broader reflections and interpretations are best seen as digressions. The third, and perhaps best, option is to see that Paul chooses, if at the last minute, to delay until later his account of arriving in Macedonia. This allows him to develop first and at length (2:14–7:4) his reasons for being encouraged even in the worst times—which he senses are not over. Once they have heard his defense and come to understand him, he will tell them that Titus met him in Macedonia with good news about them (7:5-16), and this may inspire them to return his love and be open to supporting the collection for Jerusalem (8:1–9:15). However we understand this shift, Paul's mention of leaving Troas to find Titus in 2:12-13 does remind him of what happened next in Macedonia and

2:12When I came to Troas to proclaim the good news of Christ, a door was opened for me in the Lord; 13but my mind could not rest because I did not find my brother Titus there. So I said farewell to them and went on to Macedonia.

14But thanks be to God, who in Christ always leads us in triumphal procession, and through us spreads in every place the fragrance that comes from knowing him. 15For we are the aroma of Christ to God among those who are being saved and among those who are perishing; 16to the one a fragrance from death to death, to the other a fragrance from life to life. Who is sufficient for these things? 17For we are not peddlers of God's word like so

provokes an exclamation of thanks to God for a place in God's triumph (2:14-16), then a defense to charges against him (2:17–3:1), and finally a flurry of images that affirm his relation to them (3:2-3).

In this short section we see Paul beginning his juxtaposition of the two realities that absorb him and shape the extended defense of his work in Corinth that follows (3:1–7:16): his trials and inadequacy that tempt him to lose heart[1] and God's all-sufficiency. On the one hand, he is frustrated and defensive at their suspicions about him. On the other hand, he marvels at God's power that nevertheless has worked through him. He begins concretely: a door was open for proclaiming the good news in Troas, but he was unable to go through it because he was waiting anxiously for Titus to come back with news from Corinth. But as he recollects the good news that he finally heard from Titus in Macedonia, the news yet untold (7:5-16), he marvels at how God has been leading him in triumph and spreading the scent of knowing God everywhere. This raises for him the question of who can be adequate to spread this news. He does contrast himself to those who peddle news for a profit, whereas he speaks as one transparent before God. And to those who hear this as self-commendation he claims that he needs no letters of recommendation because they themselves are his letter and show what he has accomplished. Finally, he rephrases this to say that they are Christ's letter, which he has delivered, not one written with ink that fades or even on stone like the commandments, but one written with God's Spirit on

---

1. Stanley Norris Olson, "Confidence Expressions in Paul: Epistolary Conventions and the Purpose of 2 Corinthians" (PhD diss., Yale University, 1976).

many; but in Christ we speak as persons of sincerity, as persons sent from God and standing in his presence.

³:¹Are we beginning to commend ourselves again? Surely we do not need, as some do, letters of recommendation to you or from you, do we? ²You yourselves are our letter, written on our hearts, to be known and read by all; ³and you show that you are a letter of Christ, prepared by us, written not with ink but with the Spirit of the living God, not on tablets of stone but on tablets of human hearts.*

* NRSV notes: 2:17, Other ancient authorities read *like the others*; 3:2, Other ancient authorities read *your hearts*.

his heart.² In the following chapters he keeps up this juxtaposing of his own defensiveness and God's abundant accomplishments through him, seeking every possible way to persuade them—and, the repetition hints, also to persuade himself—that his inadequacy and God's sufficiency are compatible with, or even necessary to, each other.

Many English Bibles insert the heading "An Apostolic Defense" before the chapters that begin here, but Paul does not use the word "apostle" for himself after the first sentence of the letter until its closing chapters, where he says he is not inferior to others who call themselves apostles (11:5-6; 12:11-12).³ In fact, Paul opens 2 Corinthians in the first-person plural, speaking to the Corinthians with coauthor Timothy, also noting Sylvanus as another partner in their first preaching in Corinth (1:1-13, 18-22). He does switch into the first-person singular to speak of his travel plans and how to resolve them in 1:15–2:13, yet reverting in this three times to the plural (1:18-22; 2:4, 11). And he returns to the first-person plural in order to describe a collective participation in God's triumph and the spread of the scent of knowing God. The plural "we" dominates

2. Most early manuscripts read "our hearts" here, referring to Paul and his colleagues, but one fourth-century codex and a few minuscules read "your," probably either by an accident of the codex's scribe or under influence of the following verse. See Margaret E. Thrall, *A Critical and Exegetical Commentary on the Second Epistle to the Corinthians*, ICC (Edinburgh: T & T Clark, 1994), 223–24. I use the singular here to reflect Paul's first-person rather than second-person focus, though he includes his coworkers.

3. Christine Gerber, *Paulus, Apostolat und Autorität, oder vom Lesen fremder Briefe* (Zürich: Theologischer Verlag Zürich, 2012), 42.

the chapters that follow, in contrast to the "I" that reappears strongly in chapters 10–13.[4]

Christine Gerber argues that Paul does not assume a given view of apostolic authority but works to shape the meaning of "apostle" so as to include himself among the apostles as original witnesses to Jesus because he founded the Corinthian community.[5] I find this to be true in 1 Corinthians, but in the present passage he returns quickly to the first-person plural. Both his speaking as "we" and his avoiding the word "apostle" signal that the following chapters are not a defense of one person as worthy of a certain title but the defense of a way of representing Christ that Paul wants to defend in concert with his colleagues. He calls what they do a serving, forwarding, mediating, or ministering (διακονία) of a letter that comes from Christ, the letter that the Corinthian believers themselves are. And he asserts that this letter is not written with ink or on stone but by God's Spirit on hearts of flesh (3:1-3).

A Feminist Lens at Three Different Ranges (2:12–3:3)

Paul's Persuasion within an Ecosystem of Time and Space, Life and Death

The opening travel report reveals that Paul is spread thin, that the limits on a human life keep catching up with him. He can only be in one place at a time, and as with all people whose aims are large, his time is always tight. In addition, he mentions close calls with death, both in the Asia incident (1:8-11) and in the rigors of his travels and provocations (4:8-9; 7:5; 11:23-29). This has rhetorical force as a sign of his commitment (witness heroes under great stress like Odysseus and Hercules),[6] but it also shows the practical limits of one human body. We can ask how serious he is in developing a cohort that can carry the load when

---

4. In line with reading this part of 2 Corinthians as an apostolic self-defense, most interpreters take Paul's first-person plural as a reference to himself alone except where he incorporates all believers, as in 3:18, so Thrall, *Second Epistle*, 195–96, and Victor Paul Furnish, *II Corinthians*, AB 32A (Garden City, NY: Doubleday, 1984), 102–4. M. Carrez stresses Paul's flexibility in shifting between the "we" of the community, of the coworkers, of the apostles, and of himself personally in "Le 'Nous' en 2 Corinthiens," *NTS* 26 (1980): 474–86.

5. Gerber, *Apostolat und Autorität*, 16–17, 35–51.

6. Timothy Luckritz Marquis, *Transient Apostle: Paul, Travel, and the Rhetoric of Empire* (New Haven: Yale University Press, 2013), 22–46.

we see he was not able to take the "open door" in Troas and let Titus handle the Corinthian situation. The problem may be that he now wants to go beyond his stated aim of opening up new ground for the gospel (10:14-16; Rom 15:20) in order to maintain good relations with groups once established, since we find him here giving up new opportunities in Troas to recover old in Corinth. Is he thinking of how much more Corinth can contribute than Assos or Troas toward the Jerusalem collection? Or are his ties in Corinth too deep to let slip? Nonetheless, it may be this overextending of himself that leads Paul to decide soon after to wind up his work in the east with the collection and go west (Rom 15:23-28).

Yet the urgency Paul expresses may be due less to the limitations of space and time in a human life span, let alone to his inability to let colleagues take over. Paul is convinced, as he says to the unmarried in his earlier letter to Corinth, "I think it good in the stress of present circumstances—that it is good for a man to stay as he is. Are you bound to a wife, do not seek release. Are you free from a wife, do not seek a wife. . . . I am saying, brothers, that the time left is shortened. . . . The form of this world is passing away" (1 Cor 7:26-31). Apparently Paul anticipates God's victory procession soon reaching its culmination, and he tells the Corinthians, "we are your boast as you are ours on the day of the Lord Jesus" (2 Cor 1:14).The post-Marxist philosopher Giorgio Agamben sees Paul living in what he calls "messianic time" when the ultimate transformations are in process, when "the time that remains" is radically opening up because it is radically closing in.[7] Or one might say that Paul sees Christ is executed in one world order and is being raised in another. Yet the communal enactment of this messianic event that has caught Paul up with the Corinthians now finds itself derailed in alienation and accusation.

It is in this charged time that Paul comes to the threshold of telling how he met Titus and got his first hopeful news from Corinth since his long letter. But the thought propels him instead into thanking God for this potential breakthrough with images of being bound in God's triumphal procession and spreading everywhere a fragrance of knowing God that attracts some and repels others. This allows him to pick up their debate over whether he is adequate to represent God and challenge them to see that they are his recommendation letter or, better, Christ's letter written by

---

7. Giorgio Agamben, *The Time That Remains: A Commentary on the Letter to the Romans* (Stanford, CA: Stanford University Press, 2005), 62–64.

God's Spirit on his heart. As Christ's letter, they communicate knowledge of God not in ink or on stone but in speech that comes from hearts of flesh, thereby fulfilling the prophecies of Jeremiah and Ezekiel.

Written on the Heart

This is the covenant that I will make with the house of Israel after those days, says the LORD: I will put my law within them, and I will write it on their hearts; and I will be their God, and they shall be my people. No longer shall they teach one another, or say to each other, "Know the LORD," for they shall all know me, from the least of them to the greatest, says the LORD; for I will forgive their iniquity, and remember their sin no more. (Jer 31:33-34)

A new heart I will give you, and a new spirit I will put within you; and I will remove from your body the heart of stone and give you a heart of flesh. (Ezek 36:26)

And what of the stark dualism in Paul's calling those who bring this news "the fragrance of Christ to God," which is "a scent from death to death" to people dying and "a scent from life to life" to those coming to life? At least he sees that "the fragrance from Christ to God" that attracts and repels is the same for all. And the extent of its reach is not divinely set but has no limit other than the reach of voices that carry the news and ears that receive it. And he includes his hearers in Corinth not just as ears and voices in this image but in the additional image as Christ's letter. Thus they are the ultimate exhibit of the transformation process from life to life that confirms Paul's work. But he takes for granted, as we would not, that those who are repelled by the Christ he preaches forfeit life and fall into corruption and death. He ignores at this point the fact that not each voice is tuned for each ear and that God is not restricted to one channel of communication.[8] Yet within the conflict that provokes this letter about whether the Corinthian assembly can recognize Paul's beleaguered work as valid if he recognizes "the Spirit of the living God" in them, the dualism here functions inclusively to reconcile the alienated as channels of the life that is God's in them both.

8. Elsewhere he does see the challenge of meeting different people where they are (1 Cor 9:19-23) and the implication that if God is One, no group can have exclusive knowledge of God (Rom 3:29-30).

A Mid-Range Focus on the Social and Political World of Paul's Persuasion

Here Paul speaks of how he got to Macedonia, where he is apparently writing this letter. At this time the ancient city of Troy in the northwest corner of the Roman province of Asia (now western Turkey) had long been eclipsed by larger Troad towns along the coast, especially Alexander Troas from which Paul may have sailed to Macedonia. Because Paul speaks here of entering "the Troad," rather than the cities of Assos or Alexander Troas within that region,[9] it is unclear whether the "open door" he finds is not strictly urban but regional and rural. Archaeological studies of this area do note that in the early Roman period the number of rural villages diminished as the land was absorbed into larger estates, pressing local people who do not become serfs alongside imported slaves to go into the cities as laborers or small traders.[10] So Paul's "Troad" may be a broad term that encompasses several cities as do the provincial titles of Galatia, Macedonia, and Achaia.

The urban or rural location of Paul's work is a significant question. The early account of Jesus' life in Mark shows him entering no city before his final week, whereas Paul's letters are largely directed toward cities. Apparently the story about Jesus generated in rural areas of an occupied province spread not only into the pacified provinces (see commentary on the political context of 1:12–2:11 above) but specifically into the cities there that benefit from the wealth generated by surrounding farm labor and by the trade that brings resources from occupied to pacified provinces. Even when Paul goes to a port city like the Roman colony of Alexander Troas, his "open door" may well be among marginal people of rural origin without urban citizenship or respect.[11] Yet in spite of the "open door," Paul abandons Troas for Macedonia in hopes of finding Titus and getting news from Corinth. Would Paul tell the story differently in a letter to Troas? Or can we infer that Paul gives priority to the large

---

9. 2 Cor 2:12; see Acts 16:8, 11; 20:5, 6, 13-14; 2 Tim 4:13.

10. John M. Cook, *The Troad: An Archaeological and Topographical Study* (Oxford: Clarendon Press, 1973), 368. The same process of small farmers pushed off the land was also taking place in the Corinthia: Susan E. Alcock, *Graecea Capta: The Landscapes of Roman Greece* (Cambridge: Cambridge University Press, 1992), 105–18.

11. On the urban poor: Dio Chrysostom, "The Euboean Discourse," in *Discourses*, vol. 1: 1–11, ed. and trans. J. W. Cohoon, LCL (Cambridge, MA: Harvard University Press, 1961), 103–26, 133–52; Philostratus, *Life of Apollonius of Tyana* 1.15; Alciphron, *Letters of Parasites* 24 (3.60).

commercial and service hubs like Corinth and Thessalonica,[12] particularly if his work there is in jeopardy?

When Paul thanks God who leads him in a triumphal procession and spreads the fragrance of knowing God everywhere so that the Corinthians become Paul's letter of recommendation, he is using a rush of metaphors from his social world that may be as obscure for us as they were clear for those who listened to his letter being read.[13] At one time modern interpreters looked for handy synonyms to replace the metaphors, hence Bultmann said, "ὀσμή [aroma] is a paled figure for 'effect.'"[14] But we now recognize that metaphors, as Christine Gerber explains it, are not just images standing for abstract words but whole expressions that juxtapose two areas of meaning not otherwise related, sometimes involving multiple points of comparison and evoking far more than is made explicit.[15] So Paul's image of God's triumph here indicates not only that God, like recent emperors on return to Rome after military victories, is being hailed as conqueror but also that God displays Paul and his colleagues as captives in the procession, since θριαμβεύομαι ("I celebrate a triumph") with either a prepositional phrase, a second verb, or direct object always means to demonstrate a triumph over others, not to celebrate with one's own generals or soldiers.[16]

This meaning is then further complicated by Paul's second metaphor: "revealing through us the fragrance of knowing him in every place, for we are the fragrance of Christ to God" (2:14-15). This could suggest that the triumph referred to is less a military victory parade than a religious

---

12. M. P. Charlesworth, *Trade Routes and Commerce of the Roman Empire* (Chicago: Ares, 1974), 114–29; Donald Engels, *Roman Corinth: An Alternative Model for the Classical City* (Chicago: University of Chicago Press, 1990).

13. Marquis sees in this excess of images Paul's new strategy in 2 Corinthians to meet the demands of a great diversity of marginal people. The images represent all that the empire excludes them from (*Transient Apostle*, 18–21).

14. Rudolph Bultmann, *The Second Letter to the Corinthians* (Minneapolis: Augsburg, 1985 [German, 1976]), 68.

15. Christine Gerber, *Paulus und seine "Kinder": Studien zur Beziehungsmetaphorik der paulinischen Briefe* (Berlin: de Gruyter, 2005), 81–111; *Apostolat und Autorität*, 53–62.

16. Strabo, *Geography* 12.3.35.6; Col 2:15; Cilliers Breytenbach, "Paul's Proclamation and God's 'Thriambos' (Notes on 2 Corinthians 2:14-16)," *Neot* 24 (1990): 262; Thrall, *Second Epistle*, 191–96; Scott J. Hafemann, *Suffering and Ministry in the Spirit: Paul's Defense of His Ministry in II Corinthians 2:14–3:3* (Grand Rapids, MI: Eerdmans, 1990), 16–34; Gerber, *Paulus und seine "Kinder,"* 181–87.

procession with incense celebrating the epiphany of a god or goddess.[17] But such a transferred meaning of the verb "to celebrate a triumph" is not attested. Military triumphs were sometimes accompanied by incense at the point where the conqueror appeared, but the incense was not carried by captives.[18] Yet the metaphors of military triumph over captives and the sweet and bitter scent have been integrated by some interpreters who argue that the scent could come from a sacrifice to the gods at a military triumph as suggested by "the fragrance of Christ to God."[19] There was in fact the practice for the supreme captives to be executed at the climax of the triumphal procession, which would evoke the most contrary reactions from the Romans and their defeated foes, though the captives' deaths were not by burning and were not the sacrifices to the gods of unblemished animals that also took place.[20]

The Triumph of Titus in Rome after the Fall of Jerusalem

Not one person stayed at home out of the immense population of the city [of Rome] . . . so that there was barely enough room left for the procession itself to pass. . . . Masses of silver and gold and ivory in every shape known to the craftsman's art could be seen, not as if carried in procession but like a flowing river. . . . And what caused the greatest wonder was the structure of the travelling stages; indeed their immense size caused alarm through mistrust of their stability, as many of them were three or even four stories high. . . . Placed on each stage was the commander of a captured town [in the flesh] just as he had been when captured. A number of ships followed. . . . Simon son of Gioras, who had been marching in the procession

---

17. Paul Duff, "Metaphor, Motif, and Meaning: The Rhetorical Strategy behind the Image 'Led in Triumph' in 2 Corinthians 2:14," *CBQ* 53 (1991): 84–92; Harold W. Attridge, "Making Scents of Paul: The Background and Sense of 2 Cor 2:14-17," in *Early Christianity and Classical Culture: Comparative Studies in Honor of Abraham J. Malherbe*, ed. John T. Fitzgerald, Thomas H. Olbricht, and L. Michael White (Leiden: Brill, 2003), 71–88; George H. Guthrie, "Paul's Triumphal Procession Imagery (2 Cor 2.14-16a): Neglected Points of Background," *NTS* 61 (2015): 79–91.

18. Appian, *Roman History: Punic Wars*, 66.

19. Hafemann, *Suffering and Ministry*, 35–52.

20. Antoinette Clark Wire, "Reconciled to Glory in Corinth? 2 Cor 2:14–7:4," in *Antiquity and Humanity: Essays on Ancient Religion and Philosophy Presented to Hans Dieter Betz on His 70th Birthday*, ed. Adela Yarbro Collins and Margaret M. Mitchell (Tübingen: Mohr Siebeck, 2001), 265–66.

among the prisoners, now with
a noose thrown round him was
being dragged to the usual
spot in the Forum . . . decreed
by the law of Rome for the

execution. . . . When the news
of his end arrived it was received
with universal acclamation and
the sacrifices [to the Gods] were
begun.[21]

That Paul depicts himself as captive in God's triumph seems clear, but that his impending death is a scent of Christ's sacrifice is far less so. Paul in other contexts does occasionally speak of Christ's death as a sacrifice,[22] and in this letter he speaks of his own "carrying around in the body the dying of Jesus" (4:10). Yet can we assume that Paul expected the Corinthians to hear the present thanks to God for leading Paul and his colleagues in triumph as a reference to Christ's sacrifice enacted by Paul's execution so as to attract and repel? When Christine Gerber analyzes the way that Paul uses conflicting metaphors to articulate his role, she shows how aspects come through in each metaphor without shaping one coherent picture.[23] There seems to be a shift here between Paul's thanks for being led in God's victory triumph—though as a one-time enemy persecutor now captured and publicly exhibiting God's power—and his thanks that he can be the fragrance of knowing God in every place, sweet as Christ is to God among those being restored and bitter among those being lost (2:14-16). The "fragrance of Christ to God" does suggest sacrifice in a period when gods were understood to welcome the odor of an animal sacrifice, but attention here is not on Christ's sacrifice, let alone God's expiation of sin, but on the fact that the single aroma of knowing God spread by Paul and his colleagues is absorbed in contrary ways, as death or as life.

This scent image suggests Paul may be drawing on Israel's tradition of personifying God as female Wisdom. Wisdom is described in the Greek Old Testament (LXX) in terms of diffusion, emanation, or penetration. Wisdom is also associated with incense, fragrant plants, and fruits.[24] In Proverbs and 1 Enoch Wisdom appears as a wandering prophet or

21. Josephus, *The Jewish War* 7.122–55, trans. G. A. Williamson (Harmondsworth: Penguin, 1959), 371–73.

22. 1 Cor 5:7; Gal 2:20; Rom 3:25.

23. Gerber, *Apostolat und Authorität*, 54.

24. Sir 24:1, 15, 17-18; Dominika A. Kurek-Chomycz, "The Scent of (Mediated) Revelation? Some Remarks on φανερόω with a Particular Focus on 2 Corinthians," in *Theologizing in the Corinthian Conflict: Studies in the Exegesis and Theology of 2 Corin-*

stranger who continually calls out to people but is ignored and rejected, except by the wise.[25] She is also compared to and contrasted with a prostitute; they both attract others, one to life, the other to death.[26]

Who Is Wisdom?

For wisdom moves more easily than motion itself; she is so pure she pervades and permeates all things. Like a fine mist she rises from the power of God, a clear effluence from the glory of the Almighty; so nothing defiled can enter into her by stealth. She is the radiance that streams from everlasting light, the flawless mirror of the active power of God, and the image of his goodness. She is but one, yet can do all things; herself unchanging, she makes all things new; age after age she enters into holy souls, and makes them friends of God and prophets. (Wis 7:24-27, NEB)

Where Is Wisdom?

Wisdom could not find a place in
    which she could dwell;
but a place was found (for her)
    in the heavens.
Then Wisdom went out to dwell
    with the people,
but she found no dwelling place.
(So) Wisdom returned to her
    place
and she settled permanently
    among the angels.
Then Iniquity went out of her
    rooms,
and found whom she did not
    expect.
And she dwelt with them,
like rain in a desert,
like dew on a thirsty land.
(1 Enoch 42)[27]

The texts that transmit Israel's wisdom tradition to us are written by men for whom the female characterization of Wisdom with its sexual attraction and threat represent the tensive quality of their relation to

thians, ed. Reimund Bieringer, Ma. Marilou S. Ibita, Dominika A. Kurek-Chomycz, and Thomas A. Vollmer, BTS 16 (Leuven: Peeters, 2013), 90–95.

25. Prov 1:20-33; 8:1-36; 1 En. 42.

26. Prov 9:1-6, 13-18.

27. 1 Enoch, trans. E. Isaac [with "children of men" altered to "people"], in vol. 1 of *Old Testament Pseudepigrapha*, 2 vols., ed. James H. Charlesworth (Garden City, NY: Doubleday, 1983 and 1985), 33.

God. Yet if this tradition did not come to Israel strictly as a reflective mythology, borrowed from other cultures by educated men, but came from worship practices in Israel parallel to local religious groups—as the ubiquitous finds of female votive figures suggest—it will have been part of women's experience in ancient Israel.[28] In such worship women may have identified with certain aspects of Wisdom, as men did with the righteousness and mercy of YHWH. Such identification impacts religious self-image and assists people to represent God in outreach to others. In 2 Corinthians Paul, who counted many women among his coworkers,[29] takes himself and his coworkers as "the fragrance of Christ to God" that both attracts and repels others. This may have been intended to appeal to the Corinthians who claimed wisdom through the Spirit.[30]

This image of the fragrance that attracts and repels provokes Paul's question: "Who is adequate for such things?" (2:16b). His rhetorical question indicates the reverse, that no one is adequate to evoke God.[31] Yet Paul claims he is not like most people who profit from God's word because his task comes from God and he is transparent to all. His further rhetorical questions echo the Corinthians' complaint that he is commending himself again (3:1; 5:12), and he asserts in return that he, in contrast to others, does not need letters of recommendation in Corinth, since their own faith is what recommends him. He puts this in a metaphor: they are his letter of recommendation (3:2). In this way he puts them at the center of the identity politics among Corinthian leaders. Then he intensifies the image so that they become Christ's letter, a letter served or forwarded by those who came to them as the fragrance of Christ (3:3). This implies that they recommend Paul whenever they speak out of the Spirit of Christ in them.

All of these images—the triumph, the scent, and the letter—are comprehensible only in Paul's setting as he writes to people in a Roman colony in the pacified province of Achaia. He takes his itinerant life, torn

28. "Göttinnenverhrung im Alten Israel: Eine Kurzenformation (1999)"; "Zum Stand der feministisch-exegetischen Diskussion um die Göttinnen im Alten Israel"; "Der biblische Monotheismus—seine Entstehung und seine Folgen (1999)"; all in Marie-Theres Wacker, *Von Göttinnen, Göttern und dem einzigen Gott: Studien zum biblischen Monotheismus aus feministisch-theologischer Sicht* (Münster: Literatur Verlag, 2004), 48–75, 105–37.

29. Rom 16:1-3, 6-7, 12, 15; 1 Cor 16:15-16, 19; Phil 4:2-3.

30. 1 Cor 1:26–2:5; 3:1; 4:10; 12:4-11; 14:26, 37.

31. See other uses of rhetorical questions by Paul to provoke contrary responses: Gal 2:14; 3:3-5, 21; Rom 2:3; 3:1-6, 9, 27; 6:1-2, 15, 21; 7:7, 13; 8:33, 35; 9:19; 11:1-2, 11.

between opportunity in the Troad and anxiety over Corinth, as reason to thank God when he remembers getting Titus's good news in Macedonia, yet he gives thanks not for his own success in deciding to send Titus but for God's providing a turn in his relations to Corinth that he hopes will lead to reconciliation. It is not a politically neutral act by Paul to apply the triumph-procession metaphor, reserved in his time for emperors and their heirs, to Israel's God revealed in the crucified Christ and—if the images are meant to interpret each other—made known through himself and his colleagues as the procession's aroma. Paul does not stress the execution of Jesus here as he does in 1 Corinthians or his own role as one led captive and threatened with death, although these are inchoate in his metaphors and may be inferred, particularly if he has used them in Corinth before this. Rather, he remains intent on God's glorious triumph among them and on his own effective work of spreading the news.

This affirmative mood that culminates in the aroma of Christ to God in those who are being restored to life presents his hearers' new life as the ultimate positive effect of what God has done through him. From here, after an interlude about who is sufficient to spread this news (his cohort) and who are obsessed with commendations (his competitors who bring letters), he identifies the Corinthian believers in his third metaphor as the letter that commends him and his coworkers, or the letter commending Christ forwarded by himself to them, returning the focus to the Corinthians as the product of his and his colleagues' work. Yet this is because the Corinthians reflect or commend Christ who is thus inscribed, not on stone or with ink but on hearts of flesh, and inscribed by the Spirit of the living God who gives life to all who live.

A Close-Up View of Paul's Persuasion as Shaped by and Shaping the Corinthians

Because Paul did not find Titus, who was to meet him in the Troad after coming through Macedonia with news from Corinth, Paul says that he abandoned the "open door" for work there and hurried on to Macedonia. Or at least Paul tells it this way in order to declare his intense concern to get news from Titus about them. The Corinthians hearing these lines read would already know that their attitude about Paul had been ambiguous, and they would be wondering what Titus told Paul and how he reacted. It seems that Titus had gone to Corinth to mediate between Paul and those alienated by a letter he had written them (7:8). Whether or not the issue is the man severely chastised by Paul in 1 Corinthians

5:1-6 for "living with his father's wife," some restriction in Paul's earlier letter has had repercussions. Paul says he had struggled greatly as he wrote to get them to mend their ways before he came (2 Cor 2:3-4, 9), and now they should forgive the man they punished on his behalf (2:5-11).

When Paul breaks off the travel narrative with a shout of thanks to God (2:14), hearers in Corinth may think that Titus has reassured Paul and he is anticipating a full reconciliation with them. Or do they wonder if he will next lash out because other offenders have not been disciplined? But he delays for almost five chapters before saying how he reacted to Titus's news about them (7:5-16), making them share the tension he felt when waiting for Titus while they listen to his letter being read for most of an hour. One commentator puts it that he encloses his entire self-defense in an account of his tension while waiting for word from Corinth (2:14–7:4).[32] Paul's defensive rhetoric shows, not his centrality to the Corinthians, but his marginality among a swirl of leading voices.[33] He is apparently pressed by the situation in Corinth to meet certain charges that have been made and to reconceive how he and his coworkers are related to them in a way that both he and they can accept.

Except for Paul's letter openings, each outburst of thanks to God in his letters reacts to some aspect of what he has just been speaking about,[34] suggesting here that the thanks is for Titus's news from Corinth yet untold, even though their communication to him did not come through a proper delegation or letter from them but comes solicited by his colleague after tension and losses taken. Paul expresses the crisis of not finding Titus in the Troad in the first-person singular, but his thanks to God are expressed in the plural, showing that Paul conceives of himself working alongside others like Titus: "we are led in triumph," "we are the fragrance of Christ to God" (2:14-15). This means it is not apostleship narrowly defined but service or ministry more broadly that he is describing here. The images Paul uses to project this—the advancing triumph, the spreading scent—provoke his question, "Who is sufficient for these things" (2:16), and raise the presenting issue: can Paul recover his close relation with the Corinthians?

To claim this, Paul creates a new metaphor: "You yourselves are our letter [of recommendation], written on our hearts, to be known and read

---

32. Thomas Schmeller, *Der zweite Brief an die Korinther, Teilband 1: 2 Kor. 1:1–7:4* (Neukirchen-Vluyn: Neukirchener Verlag, 2010), 17, 146.

33. Marquis, *Transient Apostle*, 12–13.

34. Rom 6:17; 7:25; 1 Cor 15:57; 2 Cor 8:16.

by all people" (3:2). Yet Paul is apparently uneasy with this formulation because he clarifies within the same Greek sentence: "You demonstrate that you are Christ's letter delivered by us." Christ has become the source of this letter that they are, with Paul as its deliverer—does he mean speaker, scribe, or courier? Or are they a letter that recommends not Paul and company but Christ? In this case Paul may be seen as its writer. In either case, the verb for the role of Paul and his colleagues is διακονεῖν, meaning to serve or administer or represent someone to others.[35] In its noun forms it becomes the key term in Paul's following comparison of his service or agency with that of Moses. It is critical that it appears here first as a passive participle describing the letter, "served/executed [NRSV: prepared] by us" (3:3), characterizing how Paul and Timothy are related to the letter of Christ that the Corinthian believers are.

Paul's meaning here is often interpreted from 1 Corinthians, "If I am not an apostle to others, surely I am to you, for you are the seal of my apostleship in the Lord" (1 Cor 9:2). This would mean Paul's enabling the Corinthian community to become a recommendation of Christ in the world—or Christ's letter to the world—is to be read as Paul's claim to an apostolic office. But this ignores his change of strategy in 2 Corinthians. The focus here, much more relevant for feminist work, is on whether he and his coworkers can defend their effectiveness for Christ in a context where others are looking for immediate and visible signs of authority. Not that Paul has given up the understanding of himself as apostle and witness to the risen Christ, but his purpose is not claiming this title but proving to the Corinthians that the work he and his colleagues do is effective for their faith. So he presents the Corinthians themselves as the evidence of his work, the letter of Christ that he and Timothy and Sylvanus, and now Titus, have delivered.

Paul then characterizes them—Christ's letter "served by us"— as "written not with ink but with the Spirit of the living God, not on tablets that are stone, but on tablets that are hearts of flesh" (3:3). Here Paul is reaching for traditions already rich from Israel's Scriptures: the God who engenders all life,[36] the tablets of the law given to guide Israel,[37] and the

---

35. John N. Collins, *DIAKONIA: Reinterpreting the Ancient Sources* (New York: Oxford University Press, 1990); Collins, *Diakonia Studies: Critical Issues in Ministry* (Oxford: Oxford Scholarship Online, 2014), parts 1 and 2; Thrall, *Second Epistle*, 225, 231–32; Gerber, *Paulus und seine "Kinder,"* 129–42; *Apostolat und Autorität*, 41–43.

36. Gen 1–2; Deut 32:39; Ps 139:13-16; Ezek 37:1-10.

37. Exod 24:12; 31:18; 32:15, 19; 34:1.

promise that the law will be written on human hearts.[38] All of this, Paul claims, has been realized in them by Christ through the διακονία (agency, ministry, service) of himself and his coworkers.

How might women in Corinth have shaped or been shaped by these words? First, their continuing to lead worship by prayer and prophecy in God's Spirit may have been crucial in Paul's shift from advising them to defending himself. Second, they could in turn be moved by Paul's impatience to meet Titus and get news about them (2:12-13). And as for the triumph, everyone loves a parade. The image of Paul and Timothy as "the fragrance of Christ to God" might have been particularly striking to them from their own burning incense or wearing fragrance or even cooking, though the sweet smell could seem incongruous with Paul who worked in leather. Paul's saying that his news is either sweet or stinking, a smell from death to death or from life to life, could revive their past experience, both of life in the hope Paul brought, and of death in the restrictions he wanted.

And how do they react now that he is shifting his tune from demanding imitation to seeking "mutual joy," from punishment to forgiveness, from advice to encouragement? They will not have missed the fact that Paul is reacting to their response to 1 Corinthians, to their community's continued expressions of the Spirit's work. They may ask themselves about his new tack: Is he simply recruiting us to support him and his friends against competitors, since he has no other letter of recommendation? We do commend Christ and we know that Paul and Timothy and Sylvanus brought the news here, but does that make us their recommendation "to be known and read by all people"? Has he even noticed that most people don't read? And when the Spirit of the living God written on our heart speaks through us, will he listen?

---

38. Jer 31[LXX 38]:33; Ezek 11:19-20.

2 Corinthians 3:4-18

Transformed in God's Glory as Was Moses

Text and Its Structure (3:4-18)

Paul continues here to alternate between conceding his own insufficient qualifications and stating his confidence due to God's effectiveness through him, displaying God's great achievements in fresh images that interpret Israel's traditions. Already in the previous passage Paul swung back and forth between his anxieties that blocked his work in the Troad and God's nonetheless leading him and his coworkers in triumph and spreading the odor of the Gospel in every place (2:12-16). He claimed no qualifications for this but only transparency while others merchandize their wares by presenting letters to recommend themselves. Yet all the while the Spirit of the living God was at work in Corinth through what he and Timothy and Sylvanus had done so that the Corinthians did receive his letter of recommendation, namely, themselves (1:19; 2:17–3:3).

Here in 3:4-18 Paul begins again to assert that he and his colleagues are confident, not in themselves, but before God in Christ, because God made them mediators of a new covenant, a mutually binding relationship with God, fulfilling ancient prophecies that God would give the people a new spirit (Jer 31[LXX 38]:31-34; Ezek 11:19). To demonstrate this, Paul interprets God's glory seen in Corinth through the Exodus story about

3:4Such is the confidence that we have through Christ toward God. 5Not that we are competent of ourselves to claim anything as coming from us; our competence is from God, 6who has made us competent to be ministers of a new covenant, not of letter but of spirit; for the letter kills, but the Spirit gives life.

7Now if the ministry of death, chiseled in letters on stone tablets, came in glory so that the people of Israel could not gaze at Moses' face because of the glory of his face, a glory now set aside, 8how much more will the ministry of the Spirit come in glory? 9For if there was glory in the ministry of condemnation, much more does the ministry of justification abound in glory! 10Indeed, what once had glory has lost its glory because of the greater glory; 11for if what was set aside came through glory, much more has the permanent come in glory!

12Since, then, we have such a hope, we act with great boldness, 13not like

the glory on Moses' face when he received the commandments from God (Exod 32–34). Paul's sharp contrast between letter and spirit, death and life (2 Cor 3:4-7), may be drawing its negative side from the Exodus 32 account of Moses' first descent from Sinai when he threw down and broke the commandments at the sight of the golden calf, leading to the slaughter of thousands by the Levites.[1] The broken law meant death.

But Paul's focus moves on to Moses' second descent from the mountain, which did bring God's glory to Israel (Exod 34:29-32). Here, the argument is carried by a triple a fortiori deduction from God's glory that Moses mediated on Sinai to God's glory in Christ mediated by Paul, Timothy, and Sylvanus in Corinth (2 Cor 3:7-11; 1:19): if the covenant that once brought judgment and death was glorious, how much more so is the one bringing life. The glory of God on Sinai is thus seen as outshone by an overriding glory of God in Christ. I translate these difficult lines:

> But if the mediation of death carved in script on stones was so glorious that the people of Israel could not stare into Moses' face due to the glory of his face that is now being eclipsed, how much more will the mediation of the Spirit be glorious? For if the mediation that condemned had

---

1. Scott J. Hafemann, *Paul, Moses, and the History of Israel: The Letter/Spirit Contrast and the Argument from Scripture in 2 Corinthians 3* (Tübingen: J. C. B. Mohr [Paul Siebeck], 1995), 195–98; Frances Watson, *Paul and the Hermeneutics of Faith* (London: T & T Clark, 2004), 289 and nn. 35–36; Dierk Starnitzke, "Der Dienst des Paulus: Zur Interpretation von Exod 34 in 2 Korintherbrief 3," *WD* 25 (1999): 200–202.

Moses, who put a veil over his face to keep the people of Israel from gazing at the end of the glory that was being set aside. [14]But their minds were hardened. Indeed, to this very day, when they hear the reading of the old covenant, that same veil is still there, since only in Christ is it set aside. [15]Indeed, to this very day whenever Moses is read, a veil lies over their minds; [16]but when one turns to the Lord, the veil is removed. [17]Now the Lord is the Spirit, and where the Spirit of the Lord is, there is freedom. [18]And all of us, with unveiled faces, seeing the glory of the Lord as though reflected in a mirror, are being transformed into the same image from one degree of glory to another; for this comes from the Lord, the Spirit.*

* NRSV notes: 3:7, Gk *on stones*; 3:13, Gk *end of what was.*

> glory, the mediation that vindicates exceeds that much more in glory, since what had glory in this sense has no glory due to the overwhelming glory. So if what is eclipsed shone with glory, how much more what persists shines in glory! (2 Cor 3:7-11)

Next Paul contrasts the veil Moses puts over his shining face (Exod 34:33) with Paul's own forthright manner, claiming that this veil obscures the understanding of Moses' story in Paul's own time, "where it is not revealed that it is eclipsed in Christ" (2 Cor 3:12-15). And finally it is a quotation of Exodus 34:34 LXX (this is obscured in the NRSV)—"Whenever he [Moses] went in before the Lord to speak with him he removed the veil"—that becomes the clue to the way the Spirit works both in Moses' and in Paul's time to overcome the veiling for those who turn to the Lord (2 Cor 3:16-18). This "Lord" in the quotation of Exodus is immediately identified by Paul, not specifically as Christ, but as the Spirit of the Lord who gives freedom. This seems to be a broader name for the divine presence, one perhaps parallel to Wisdom, that can include God's glory on Moses' face. And this leads Paul to the conclusion that "we all," like Moses, with faces uncovered behold the same image of God and are transformed from one degree of glory to another. And, in case we missed the point, he concludes, "just as [I said], from the Lord, the Spirit" (3:16-18). So the passage turns out to be a step-by-step exegesis of Exodus 34:29-35 in light of the tragedy of law-breaking and death in Exodus 32 and since. In this way Paul's claim to be a confident mediator of God's life-giving Spirit, even though he is unqualified, ends with all who respond to God's Spirit being transformed from glory to glory. Therefore I translate:

> Having this sure hope, we act with much boldness, and not like Moses who put a veil on his face so the people of Israel would not stare into the climax of the eclipse. Indeed, their minds were hardened, for the same veil remains to this day on the reading of the old relation with God, it not being uncovered that it is eclipsed in Christ. Even down to today whenever Moses is read, a veil lies on their heart. Yet [Scripture says of Moses] "Whenever he turns back to the Lord, the veil is taken off." Now "the Lord" here is the Spirit. And where the Spirit of the Lord is, there is freedom. And all of us with faces uncovered, beholding the glory of the Lord as in a mirror, are being transformed into that very image from glory to glory, this from the Lord, the Spirit. (3:12-18)

This translation reflects one reading of this text. In what follows I will defend it further and indicate some alternate readings of Paul's argument with the evidence offered. The key questions are: How do we understand καταργεῖν (remove, abolish, set aside, eclipse)? Is Paul's point that Christ's glory cancels out and abolishes—or that it outshines, eclipses, and thus suspends—the glory in Moses' face? That is, does Paul at this point see the new relation to God replacing or amplifying the old? In addition, does Paul's first-person plural pronoun throughout signify himself or does it signify his circle of coworkers, believers in Christ, or all believers? Hence, is the διακονία that Paul is defending his personal apostleship or is it a much wider mediation, ministry, or representation of God?

A further question concerns how all of this is relevant for a feminist practice of life in God's Spirit. How wide is our vision, our task, the work of the Spirit in us? What do we learn from Moses about turning back to the Lord? What do we learn from Paul about confidence in God though we are insufficient to the task? What do we learn from the Corinthian women about persistence in mediating God's glory until Paul recognizes their shared transformation through God's Spirit?

A Feminist Lens at Three Ranges on Being Transformed in God's Glory (3:4-18)

An Ecosystem of Life and Death, Glory and Obscurity, Time and Space

Although Paul is not speaking here of the ecosystem as we might conceive it in which humans are one species in a symbiotic world of other animals and plants and minerals, our modern effort to understand everything on our planet as one or another kind of material involved in a continuing but unrepeating history of lives and deaths is not without parallel in Paul's effort to defend his work in Corinth in terms of the reality of his people's past. He sees there the roots of both the judgment and the blessing that shape his people's world, understood in terms of God's covenant relation with them that brings both justice and glory. When Paul is writing to the Romans the issue of God's justice predominates, but in writing 2 Corinthians Paul conceptualizes the tradition in terms of the experience of God's glory, which the Corinthians most prize, in order to argue that it is consummated in the work he and his coworkers have been doing among them.[2]

First, he follows the prophets Jeremiah and Ezekiel in announcing a new covenant relation to God in the people's hearts, whereby "the Spirit of the living God" gives them life, distinct from the letters carved in stone that have brought death. This is confirmed by the story of Moses, here remembered not so much as the lawgiver but as the man who saw God and lived, who spoke to God and prevailed, whose transformed face so shocked the people that he covered it after communicating God's will to them (Exod 34:33-34). Paul argues that if such glory nonetheless made people afraid of condemnation and death from offending God, how much more glory comes from God's good news of vindication and life in Christ. Though most Christian interpreters think Paul understands Moses' veil as a disguise to hide the fading of God's glory, the verb καταργεῖν means in this context not that the glory is fading or canceled but that it is something like being suspended, as when one brightness eclipses another and makes it no longer separately visible.

Finally, Paul quotes how Moses "whenever he turns to the Lord takes off the veil" (3:16, from Exod 34:34), making Moses, when he talks with God unveiled, the prototype for all others who turn to the Lord. When this "Lord" is explained to be the Spirit of God, Paul anticipates the veil taken off the faces of those reading Moses' story, so that "we all" can freely see God's glory in the Spirit. By a kind of "mirror-seeing" in common (κατοπτριζόμενοι, "seeing reflected," from κάτοπτρον, "mirror") all are transformed (μεταμορφούμεθα from μετά, "[set] aside," and μορφή, "form") "into the same image" of the one seen—not Moses, or Christ in this context, but the Lord who is the Spirit (3:17-18) that both of them

---

2. Antoinette Clark Wire, "Reconciled to Glory in Corinth? 2 Cor 2:14–7:4," in *Antiquity and Humanity: Essays on Ancient Religion and Philosophy Presented to Hans Dieter Betz on His 70th Birthday*, ed. Adela Yarbro Collins and Margaret M. Mitchell (Tübingen: Mohr Siebeck, 2001), 263–75.

turn to and reflect. And this happens, not in a single event, but as a process of taking on and spreading God's glory in being "transformed from glory to glory" (3:18).

Can it be said that an ancient story of the special people of Israel is here opened up to a comprehensive significance? It is in fact seldom read this way because, though Paul is explicit in defining "the Lord" to whom Moses turns as "the Spirit," and in conclusion repeating himself—"this from the Lord, the Spirit" (3:17-18)—Christians who read the passage tend to hear "the Lord" as Christ. We assume that either "the Lord" means "Christ" throughout 3:17-18, or that, although "the Lord" to whom Moses turns is defined as "the Spirit," Paul then interprets this as "the Spirit of the Lord," that is, of Christ, or that Paul at least concludes the passage by reference to Christ, the Spirit—adding to this the complications of trinitarian theology from our minds.[3]

A simple word count shows that Paul's theme here is the work of the Spirit of God, not the work of Christ. The phrase "eclipsed in Christ" is the only place in 2 Corinthians 3:4-18 where Paul mentions Christ after an opening statement of confidence "through Christ toward God" (3:4). In contrast he refers to the Spirit six times in this section, beginning by characterizing his mediation of the new relation with God as "not in script but in spirit, for the script kills but the Spirit gives life" (3:6). His opening a fortiori arguments also highlight the Spirit: if the mediation of death was so glorious, "how much more will the mediation of the Spirit be glorious!" (3:8). Then, finally, after citing the text about Moses removing the veil as the model for whoever turns to the Lord, he defines "the Lord" here as "the Spirit" and this Spirit as the place of freedom where "we all with unveiled faces . . . are being transformed into the same image from glory to glory, this from the Lord, the Spirit" (3:17-18). Even the reference to "the same image" in this context of Moses' glory refers to the "the Lord, the Spirit" seen by all who "turn to the Lord," not yet referring specifically to Christ as it does in 4:4.[4]

---

3. James D. G. Dunn, "2 Corinthians III. 17—'The Lord Is the Spirit,'" *JTS* 21 (1970): 309–20.

4. Here Richard Hays, who maintains a consistent reading of "the Lord" as God's Spirit in this passage, nonetheless brings Christ in as the image of God in anticipation of 4:4, and thereby reads 3:18 strictly as an affirmation about Christian believers: Hays, *Echoes of Scripture in the Letters of Paul* (New Haven: Yale University Press, 1989), 144, yet see 145.

If we read the "we all" here as restricted to Paul's coworkers and the Corinthian believers being transformed into the image of Christ, we project our concept of two religions, Christianity and Judaism, back into Paul's time. Thus Israel is conceived as one exclusive covenant community replaced with another just as exclusive covenant community. But this is the Paul who in Romans 8:18-23 moves even beyond the topic of human redemption to claim God's redemption of the whole creation. And Paul goes on from there in Romans 9–11 to incorporate the good news of life in Christ within the longer story of God's redemption of Israel so that all people might be given justice and God vindicated. Similarly, here in 2 Corinthians 3, when Paul is pressed to speak in the spiritual idiom of the Corinthian believers, he finds in the account of God's glory when Moses uncovers his face a way to speak not only of Israel turning to the Spirit of God but of the Corinthians incorporated through Christ within Israel's experience of God's presence.

In contemporary feminist circles it is not common to make comprehensive claims or pursue universal philosophy, preferring as we do to settle for open debate and difference. But sometimes we are pressed by universal assumptions of our opponents or our own desire for clarity to consider whether their quantifiable explanations of all reality are sufficient. Or to put this into Paul's idiom in Corinth, we ask whether "the Spirit of the living God" has been active among us and requires a defense. Philosophers such as Sarah Coakley, mathematicians such as Martin Nowak, and historians of religion such as Carol Zaleski are talking about "one mind" or an "evolving consciousness ecosystem" that is not simply a product of the physical universe—this in order to help explain what we might call grace, altruism, or revelation experience.[5] There are thinkers who conceive the material world itself animated

5. Sarah Coakley, "Sacrifice Regained: Reconsidering the Rationality of Religious Belief," An Inaugural Lecture by the Norris-Hulse Professor of Divinity given in the University of Cambridge, October 13, 2009 (pamphlet without imprint); Sarah Coakley, ed., *Faith, Rationality and the Passions* (Chichester: Wiley-Blackwell, 2012); Martin A. Nowak and Sarah Coakley, eds., *Evolution, Games, and God: The Principle of Cooperation* (Cambridge, MA: Harvard University Press, 2013); Carol Zaleski, *Otherworld Journeys: Accounts of Near-Death Experience in Medieval and Modern Times* (New York: Oxford University Press, 1987); Robert Traer, "Loving and Evolving Consciousness: A Bigger History," in *Gratitude and Hope: Doing Theology at Pilgrim Place 10*, ed. Paul Kitlass, Pat Patterson, and Connie Kimos (Shelbyville, KY: Wasteland Press, 2015), 50–60.

by life-spirit in an open process of development and decay.[6] Are these people too bold for us?

Our language for comprehensive thought may be less from science than theirs, more like Paul's from the history of our survivals stretching back through time. Yet are there not claims to be made about the terrors and the glories we human women have seen? Here we may be able to learn from Paul. Addressing this Corinthian community that claims a spiritual life, he defends his work in terms of an iconic story of God's glory on the human face. He uses all the arguments that can persuade— appeals to texts, deductions from logic, heroic stories, striking images, and personal revelations—in order to project a vision that might heal their alienation from him and each other. I argue that he does this because the Corinthians have persisted by prophecy and prayer in their witness to the glory of God's Spirit that he can no longer dispute.

The More Specific Social, Political, and Religious Context

Paul's being led in God's triumphal procession in the previous passage (2:14) is blatant in adopting imperial imagery, whereas the present defense of his work for Christ in terms of the glory on Moses' face is not. This use of Scripture to claim all glory to be the work of God's Spirit could be said to mimic the imperial practice of totalizing rhetoric,[7] were the scale of Paul's influence in his time not so small as to turn such a threat comic. The contextual question here is how Paul is using the prophecies of a new covenant and the narrative of Sinai glory to compete for influence in a growing Second Temple sect of Judaism. Is he primarily contrasting his own mediation of glory in Christ with the synagogue's glory of Moses as the comparison at first suggests and most interpret-

---

6. Jane Bennett, *Vibrant Matter: A Political Ecology of Things* (Durham: Duke University Press, 2010). For assistance in reading Alfred North Whitehead's *Process and Reality: An Essay in Cosomology* (c. 1929; repr. New York: Harper, 1960) consider C. Robert Mesle's *Process Theology* (St. Louis: Chalice Press, 1993) and John B. Cobb Jr., *Whitehead Word Book: A Glossary with Alphabetical Index to Technical Terms in* Process and Reality (Claremont: P & F Press, 2008).

7. See Jeremy Punt, "Paul and Postcolonial Hermeneutics: Marginality and/in Early Biblical Interpretation," and other essays in *As It Is Written: Studying Paul's Use of Scripture*, ed. Stanley E. Porter and Christopher D. Stanley, SymS 50 (Leiden: Brill, 2008), 261–90. On Paul's use of Scripture in the Roman context, see also the recent essay collections edited by Christopher Stanley, his *The Colonized Apostle: Paul through Postcolonial Eyes* (Minneapolis: Fortress, 2011), and his *Paul and Scripture: Extending the Conversation* (Atlanta: Society of Biblical Literature, 2012).

2 Corinthians 3:4-18 59

ers hold? Or is he primarily claiming the power and legitimacy of these biblical images to give weight and color to his much contested leadership among Christ followers in Corinth? This is the key social question of whether Paul defends his news about Christ that is transforming the Corinthians over against a recognized religious tradition or as a culmination in that religious tradition.[8] This is for feminists not only an issue of strategy in how to introduce change—whether to present the new from within the old—but also an issue of discipline in knowing our tradition well enough to use it or take it on. Finally it is an issue of integrity in being faithful both to the tradition and to the people in the broadest possible sense to whom it belongs and can yet belong.

The opening section of the chapter (3:1-6), with its sharp dualisms, points toward Paul's defending his work over against another religious community. The Corinthian believers as a letter of Christ are written not with ink and not on stone but with the Spirit of the living God on hearts of flesh (1:3). This in turn qualifies Paul and his colleagues to be διάκονοι ("agents, mediators, ministers") of a new covenant, secured not by the script that puts to death but by the breath/spirit that brings to life (3:5-6). This contrast is then specified as that between an old and a new διαθήκη ("covenant, relationship, bond"; 3:6, 14) and their respective διακονίαι ("mediations, ministries"; 3:7-9), producing contrary results, represented here by Moses and Paul. It seems that God's written covenant with Israel is being disqualified by a new relation with God in Christ.

But several aspects of Paul's argument point the other way, suggesting that the Scriptures are being drawn on primarily to support Paul rather than to provide a contrasting foil. First, the term from Israel's Greek Scripture, διαθήκη ("covenant, relation"), is being interpreted by the more widespread Greek term διακονία ("service, mediation, ministry").[9] The effect is to focus on the mediators being compared and the different

---

8. Hays takes a mediating position, seeing Paul arguing by dissimile, "suggestive denials," which are so evocative that they finally spill over into positive comparison (Hays, *Echoes of Scripture*, 140–49).

9. Διακονία appears in the Greek Old Testament called the Septuagint (LXX) only once in Proverbs before the late text of Esther. Though the term could be used for table and other manual service, by Paul's time it signified any kind of representation of one person to another by a third party functioning as an agent or messenger. See John N. Collins, *DIAKONIA: Reinterpreting the Ancient Sources* (New York: Oxford University Press, 1990).

effects of their mediation rather than on any conflict between God's covenants. Even the contrast of Paul's and Moses' individual mediations is overdrawn when interpreters assume that Paul is here defending his personal apostleship. This ignores the plural authorship of the letter (1:1), his explicit reference to Timothy and Sylvanus as coworkers in Corinth (1:19), and his first-person plural speech throughout defending their ministry (3:4, 5, 6, 12, 18).[10]

Second, both terms Paul is contrasting are drawn from Scripture prophecies so that his announcement of a new covenant confirms rather than undermines the authority of Israel's tradition. It is Jeremiah who speaks for God: "I will make a new covenant . . . not like the one they broke. I will put my law within them and I will write it on their hearts" (Jer 31:31-33; LXX 38:31-33). And Ezekiel tells God's promise, "I will remove from your body the heart of stone and give you a heart of flesh. I will put my spirit within you" (Ezek 36:26-27; 11:19) (see sidebar above: "Written on the Heart"). In light of these prophecies Paul is not at all disqualifying God's covenant with Israel but is seeing it being fulfilled in what is happening in Corinth.

Third, after the opening contrasts drawn from these prophecies, Paul integrates into his argument the account of Moses at Sinai from Exodus 32–34. (Rereading these chapters may be the sine qua non of understanding Paul here.) Death happens at Moses' first descent from Sinai when he sees the golden calf, throws down the tablets of the law, and three thousand Israelites die (Exod 32). The shift Paul makes to this Sinai story may have been triggered by his earlier reference to "the script that kills" (3:6). But his focus falls on the scene that follows about Moses' second descent from Sinai.

---

10. Because of the preconception that Paul is defending his individual apostleship, most interpreters take Paul's first-person plural defense here to apply to himself alone, at least until the "we all" of 3:18 requires that they include other believers in Christ. Paul's uses of the first-person plural are multiple and complex: M. Carrez, "Le 'Nous' en 2 Corinthiens," NTS 26 (1980): 474–86; Markus Müller, "Der sogenannte 'schriftstellerische Plural'—neu betrachtet. Zur Frage der Mitarbeiter als Mitverfasser der Paulusbriefe," BZ 42 (1998): 181–201; Christine Gerber, Paulus und seine "Kinder": Studien zur Beziehungsmetaphorik der paulinischen Briefe (Berlin: de Gruyter, 2005), 78–80; Margaret E. Thrall, A Critical and Exegetical Commentary on the Second Epistle to the Corinthians, ICC (Edinburgh: T & T Clark, 1994), 105–7, 195–96.

The Glory of God in Moses' Face

Moses came down from Mount Sinai. As he came down from the mountain with the two tablets of the covenant in his hand, Moses did not know that the skin of his face shone because he had been talking with God. When Aaron and all the Israelites saw Moses, the skin of his face was shining, and they were afraid to come near him. But Moses called to them; and Aaron and all the leaders of the congregation returned to him, and Moses spoke with them. Afterward all the Israelites came near, and he gave them in commandment all that the LORD had spoken with him on Mount Sinai. When Moses had finished speaking with them, he put a veil on his face; but whenever Moses went in before the LORD to speak with him, he would take the veil off, until he came out; and when he came out, and told the Israelites what he had been commanded, the Israelites would see the face of Moses, that the skin of his face was shining; and Moses would put the veil on his face again, until he went in to speak with him. (Exod 34:29-35)

Many recent interpreters follow Scott Hafemann, who takes the entire Sinai account in Exodus as relevant—not only Israel's "fall" in this way, but Moses' consequent step-by-step effort (Exod 33–34) to get God to set aside punishment, to allow Israel to continue to the promised land, to agree to appear to Moses in a tent outside the camp, and finally to meet Moses a second time on Sinai and renew the covenant.[11] This suggests that a new covenant comes for the people only if they face the fact of being covenant breakers and yet persist in desiring God's presence. Frances Watson thinks Paul is working here with the internal tension in the Exodus Scripture between the unconditional promise of God and the conditional law, and though Paul correlates the Gospel with the promise, he sees the law still bearing fruit where the risk of the promise is not taken.[12] Dierk Starnitzke argues that Paul chooses Exodus 32–34 because it is a story of two covenants, one carved on stone tablets that are broken before they are read and one realized by God's immediate presence with Moses on the mountain and in the tent of meeting. How Paul sees the latter happening "in Christ" (3:14), Starnitzke suggests, could come from his taking Christ himself as being the tent where God

11. Hafemann, *Paul, Moses*, 189–254.
12. Watson, *Hermeneutics of Faith*, 273–81.

is present, comparable to the way Paul calls Christ the rock that Moses struck in the desert in 1 Corinthians 10:4. Yet Starnitzke concedes that Christ the tent is not explicit and proposes an alternative that the community or person in Christ is the place where Moses' act of removing the veil and turning to God is being realized.[13]

Fourth, Paul interprets Moses' second and effective delivery of God's law to Israel positively by focusing on the glory of God reflected on Moses' face. It is hard to overestimate the importance of God's glory for Paul. In the Roman culture oriented on the honor of Rome, its emperor, and its legions, Paul continually celebrates God's glory, "for from him and through him and to him are all things; to him be the glory forever" (Rom 11:36). In 2 Corinthians everything is to be done for God's glory—preaching the Gospel, bearing affliction, supporting the needy, thanking God—and life's ultimate aim is to know the glory of God.[14] Exegetes who understand Paul to be primarily contrasting himself with Moses have said that Paul's opponents must have introduced Moses' story into the debate over leadership because Paul himself was anything but glorious by comparison.[15] But in 2 Corinthians Paul does claim to mediate God's glory, and, regardless of how the topic arose, he uses the account of God's glory on Moses' face to assert the particular kind of διακονία that he and his coworkers practice. Paul implies that because the glory on Moses' face made the people of Israel fear a return of condemnation and death, a διακονία offering vindication and life is bound to be more glorious. Three times in 3:7-11 Paul makes this argument a fortiori, from the lesser likelihood to the greater, each time developing a new aspect of the Exodus text to do this. Without doubt Paul uses the Scripture here as a positive demonstration that the new covenant is glorious by saying it eclipses even the glory of God's law-giving through Moses (3:10).

Fifth, the veiling of Moses' face also appears to have a positive role in Paul's argument. The Exodus account and its exegetical tradition in early

13. Starnitzke, "Der Dienst des Paulus," 203–5.

14. 2 Cor 1:20; 4:4, 6, 17; 8:19.

15. Dieter Georgi, *The Opponents of Paul in Second Corinthians* (Philadelphia: Fortress, 1986 [German 1964]), 270–71, 315–19. Linda Belleville notes that interacting with opponents by modifying their documents is not a hermeneutical practice in Paul's time: *Reflections of Glory: Paul's Polemical Use of the Moses-Doxa Tradition in 2 Corinthians 3:1-18* (Sheffield: Sheffield Academic, 1991), 79, n. 1; Belleville, " 'Tradition or Creation'? Paul's Use of the Exodus 34 Tradition in 2 Corinthians 3:7-18," in *Paul and the Scriptures of Israel*, ed. Craig A. Evans and James A. Sanders (Sheffield: Sheffield Academic, 1993), 186, n. 49.

Judaism see God's glory veiled by Moses largely as a concession to the people's fear, and this only after God's message has been delivered to Israel (Exod 34:30-33), while the glory on Moses' face is assumed to be permanent, though it may not appear in stories of his later life or death.[16] Paul seems to read the veiling as a disguise of the fading or passing of the glory, a disguise that he contrasts with his own frankness of speech in preaching God's glory in Christ (3:12-13). Yet when he says that Moses veiled himself in order that the people of Israel not gaze at τὸ τέλος τοῦ καταργουμένου (3:13), does he mean that they not have to face "the end of what is passing away" or does he mean that they not be blinded by "the fulfillment of what has given way"? The noun τὸ τέλος can mean "end" or it can mean "aim," "outcome," "fulfillment."[17]

Much also depends on how Paul's difficult verb καταργεῖν in 3:7, 11, 13-14 is read. The root meaning is "to deactivate," "to decommission" (NRSV, "to set aside"; REB, "to fade [or take] away"). Hafemann interprets the verb "to render inoperative," hence here "the outcome of that which was being rendered inoperative" (3:13).[18] He construes this distinctively, reading that Moses veils himself to prevent Israel's repulsion and God's punishment of its hardened heart, thus protecting the people in God's mercy. Ekkehard Stegemann stresses Paul's contrast of what is passing and what is permanent in 3:11, so that Moses shields Israel from seeing "der Ausgang des Zeitlichen," meaning roughly "the exit of the temporal" into the eternal.[19] Under influence of 3:10-11, I translate "the fullness of being eclipsed," using visual terms appropriate for glory to express how one light can make another light not separately visible without diminishing it.[20]

Finally, Paul does not leave it to a hearer's imagination to apply this Exodus narrative to his present time. Drawing on Exodus 34:30 and 33, Paul identifies Moses' veiling of his face with a hardening of the Israelites' hearts when they hear Moses (i.e., the Torah) read in Paul's own

16. The story of Moses reflecting God's glory is not developed in the Hebrew Scriptures but in Jewish writings of the Hellenistic and Roman periods. See Belleville, *Reflections of Glory*, 24–79; " 'Tradition or Creation,' " 165–86.

17. Thrall, *Second Epistle*, 258–61; Hays, *Echoes of Scripture*, 136–38.

18. Hafemann, *Paul, Moses*, 427, 347–62.

19. Ekkehard Stegemann, "Der Neue Bund im Alten: Zum Schriftverständnis des Paulus in II Kor 3," *TZ* 42 (1986): 112–13.

20. Hays, *Echoes of Scripture*, 134.

time, "it not being made known that it is eclipsed in Christ" (3:14-15).[21] This reading of the Torah need not be visualized in a distant synagogue but may be in the synagogue, workshop, or home where Paul is addressing people who come to hear Scripture or later to hear his letters read.[22]

It is with these hard-of-hearing hearers in mind that Paul says of Moses, "Whenever he turns back to the Lord, the veil is taken off" (3:16). He is quoting Exodus 34:34 (LXX): "Whenever Moses went in before the Lord to speak with him, he took off the veil until he came out." In citing Scripture Paul has made small changes that allow the reference to Moses to include the hearers of the book of Moses and that shift the verb from "went in" to "turn back"—a term that can mean "repent." Paul follows here his usual pattern of arguing by means of Scripture rather than citing before interpreting. Exegetes refer to Sternberg's Proteus Principle that every quotation is a recontextualization of meaning in the new situation,[23] and Paul is a master at this.[24] Moses becomes the vanguard among those who take off the veil and turn to the Lord.

One question remains: whom is Paul calling "the Lord" in saying "Whenever he turns back to the Lord"? Paul usually means Christ when speaking of "the Lord," but when Paul cites Scripture, "Lord" normally means God.[25] Throughout Exodus, and the Torah as a whole, "the Lord" substitutes for God's unspoken name, and there is no question that in 34:34 Moses is turning to God. But could Paul in his application to his present hearers simply be reversing his earlier line about the veil over the reading of the old covenant, "it not being made known that it is eclipsed in Christ" (3:14c)? Fortunately Paul anticipates the ambiguity of "Lord"[26] and answers immediately after quoting, "Now 'the Lord' here is the Spirit. And where the Spirit of the Lord is, there is freedom" (3:17).

21. The adverb "only" of the NRSV "only in Christ is it set aside" is not in the Greek text.

22. See 1 Cor 14:6, 23; 2 Cor 1:13; Gal 4:21; Col 4:16; 1 Thess 5:27.

23. Meir Sternberg, "Proteus in Quotation-Land: Mimesis and the Forms of Reported Discourse," *Poetics Today* 3 (1982):107–10, 144–54.

24. The fact that the Nestle-Aland twenty-eighth edition of the Greek text (cf. twenty-sixth ed.) no longer puts this line in italics to indicate a quotation shows that the editors in their effort to avoid subjective judgments now italicize only lines that have multiple identical words in sequence or explicit quotation formulas, omitting identification of many citations that the exegetical contexts make unmistakable.

25. See, for example, 1 Cor 14:21; 2 Cor 6:18; Rom 9:29; 11:34; 15:11.

26. The article before "Lord" in "The Lord is the Spirit" (3:17) indicates that "Lord" is an anaphora, a repeating to signify "the one just mentioned."

Some interpreters think Paul is speaking of the Spirit received at baptism, so the "Spirit of the Lord" that brings freedom would mean the Spirit of Christ that frees from the stipulations of the law (Rom 8:2-4; Gal 2:20-21; 4:6-7). But in the context of identifying with Moses' turning uncovered to God, most recent interpreters understand Paul to mean the Spirit of God, a common phrase throughout the Scriptures for the active power of God.[27] The freedom mentioned is then not only freedom from fear of God's judgment but also freedom for access to God's glory.[28]

But for our question of whether Paul is primarily contrasting his διακονία with that of Moses or defending it in terms of Moses, the final celebration of being transformed from glory to glory points unmistakably to the latter. This is true even for the majority of interpreters who understand the "we" who are being transformed as the communities who are in Christ in contrast to those who "until the present day" read Moses with veils over their hearts. But Paul's positive reliance on the Moses account is stronger yet if, with Marlene Crüsemann, the transformation is seen to incorporate all who turn with Moses to the Spirit of God, Jew and Gentile. And Paul's final recapitulating line, "this from the Lord, the Spirit," makes it impossible to end the reading of Paul's argument thinking of "Christ rather than Moses," or "us rather than them," since Moses, who has been made the model of a people that turn back to God, cannot be a symbol against his own people.[29]

Focusing on Paul's Interchange with the Corinthians

When Paul compares the task given him with that given Moses, he may be responding to a charge from the Corinthians or from his rivals that his message is veiled, since he says soon after: "But even if our gospel is veiled, it is veiled to those who are being lost" (4:3). The issue between them does not seem to be a theological conflict or even a difference in

---

27. Hafemann, *Paul, Moses*, 396–99; Thrall, *Second Epistle*, 272–74; Starnitzke, "Der Dienst des Paulus," 205; Martin McNamara, *Targum and Testament Revisited: Aramaic Paraphrases of the Hebrew Bible; A Light on the New Testament*, 2nd ed. (Grand Rapids, MI: Eerdmans, 2010), 172.

28. On freedom here, see Victor Paul Furnish, *II Corinthians*, AB 32A (Garden City, NY: Doubleday, 1984), 236–42.

29. Crüsemann, "Der Gottesname," *Gott ist Beziehung*, 126. This passage functions in the Corinthian correspondence parallel to Romans 9–11 in that letter. There Paul's identification with his own people brings him to affirm God's faithfulness to Israel in a way prior to, if not completely independent of, God's saving in Christ.

religious or ethical practices so much as Paul's perceived lack of clarity, impact, or effective presence. We learn later that he has some "thorn in the flesh" that hampers his work and may contribute to his difficulty in communication (12:7-10), possibly a disabling speech impediment (10:10), eye condition (Gal 4:15), and/or bodily deformity (1 Cor 15:8). He even quotes his detractors' complaints about him, "The letters are profound and strong, but his physical presence is feeble and his speaking is worthless" (2 Cor 10:10). Our earliest description of Paul from *The Acts of Paul and Thecla* in the second century retains a possible memory of his peculiarity.

Paul's Appearance

He saw Paul coming, a man small of stature, with a bald head and crooked legs, in a good state of body, with eyebrows meeting and nose somewhat hooked, full of friendliness; for now he appeared like a man, and now he had the face of an angel.[30]

Paul meets the charges against him by claiming to be confident and speak with boldness (3:4, 12). Yet his repeated assertions of confidence ring somewhat hollow and we sense he protests too much (4:1, 16). Is he provoking that reaction to prepare for his next point that his confidence is not in himself but in God? He claims that it is God who qualifies him and his colleagues to be agents (διάκονοι) of a new covenant, which is not a script that is death-dealing but a spirit that is life-giving (3:6). A better translation for διάκονος is "agent" or "mediator" rather than "minister," which now names an occupation. A διάκονος functions as a representative of another person, in this case God, in dealing with a third party, here the Corinthians.[31] That Paul uses this term rather than "apostle," and defends the διάκονοι with the plural "we" rather than the singular "I," may be a response to competing itinerants who exalt

---

30. *Acts of Paul and Thecla* 1, trans. R. McL. Wilson, in *New Testament Apocrypha*, ed. Edgar Hennecke and Wilhelm Schneemelcher, vol. 2 (Philadelphia: Westminster, 1964), 355.

31. Collins, *DIAKONIA*.

themselves as apostles.[32] It seems to be part of Paul's change in strategy since 1 Corinthians to defend himself in concert with colleagues (Titus was apparently well regarded in Corinth)[33] in preference to competing with opposing "pseudo apostles."

The "covenant" term has deep historical roots in God's covenant with Abraham to give him land and progeny, and his stubborn faithfulness in response, but it is also applied to God's earlier covenant with a renewed humanity through Noah and to God's bond with Israel through the exodus and law. Multiple covenant renewals, such as after the exile and at Qumran, confirm that one covenant does not wipe out a previous one but intensifies and reshapes it for another generation. Paul presents himself and his coworkers as mediators of a new relation or covenant with God, not a recorded one that catches people in offenses and results in death, but one that invigorates or animates, one that results in conduct appropriate to a family.[34] From 2 Corinthians it appears that Paul is now framing his role in terms of what they desire, mediating a new way of relating to God that is not external and conditional but one that God's Spirit inscribes in "hearts of flesh."[35]

Paul's assertion that he serves a new God-given relationship made not in script that kills but in spirit that animates (3:1-6) becomes the basis for his repeated argument a fortiori: if a covenant served by Moses that killed those who broke it was so glorious that Moses had to cover his face after speaking with God, how much greater will be the glory from a covenant that gives life. Though Paul dissociates the new covenant in Christ from specific commands and their consequences given in the old, he still wants to retain the basic understanding of covenant as God-given relation that allows participation in God's glory. Paul argues that the honor and glory the Corinthians claim (1 Cor 4:10) comes from the Spirit that gives life and outshines even the glory that shone in Moses' face when mediating the old covenant.

---

32. 2 Cor 11:5, 13; 12:11.
33. 2 Cor 7:15; 8:6, 16, 23; 12:18.
34. Gerber, *Paulus und seine "Kinder,"* 205–14.
35. Richard Horsley suggests that Paul in capitulating to the Corinthians' desire for glory is "compromising the Judaean apocalyptic perspective that constituted the key to his anti-imperial mission." See "1 and 2 Corinthians" in *A Postcolonial Commentary on the New Testament Writings*, ed. Fernando Segovia and R. S. Sugirtharajah (London: Bloomsbury, 2007), 237–44.

Two problems remain for Paul's argument. First, how is the glory of God on Moses' face not canceled out by the glory in Christ but credited in its own right so that the argument based on it not collapse? Apparently Paul counts on the Corinthians not only knowing but admiring the story of Moses' glory when he deduces from it the greater glory of Christ, and that admiration cannot be undermined. Second, because glory is something visible while Paul himself is not glorious, where can the yet greater glory of the new relation to God be seen as the glory of the old was seen on Moses' face?

Traditionally Christians have ignored the first problem, as though Paul were willing, or even able, to scuttle the covenant with Israel as having served its purpose. So the verb καταργεῖν at the end of 3:7 and 13 is translated as "abolished," "cancelled," or "nullified." More recently, under influence of Paul's contrasting it with what "persists" or "endures" in 3:11, it is translated "fading away," "passing away," or "set aside." Because the verb comes from a root meaning "to be idle," "not activated," Giorgio Agamben suggests "suspended," in the way that work is suspended on the Sabbath.[36] Because of the dominant visual imagery in this context and the unusual comparison of what is glorified with what has overriding glory (3:10, 13), I have translated δόξαν . . . καταργουμένην as "glory being eclipsed," in the sense of it "obscuring relative to a designated observer , . . . [causing] any temporary or permanent dimming or cutting off of light."[37] This can perhaps allow Paul's image of one glory outshining another without challenging the glory of the first that becomes in this context not visible.

Narratively, Paul meets the first problem of Israel's viability by shifting the veil on Moses' face from Moses to the faces of those who hear Moses read in Paul's time. Their minds are dulled because it is not uncovered that in Christ the glory in Moses' face has been eclipsed. Then, significantly, it is not Christ but Moses who provides Paul the model for removing the veil. Paul quotes Exodus 34:34, "Whenever Moses went in to the Lord to speak with him, he would take off the veil until he came out," changing the main verb from "he went in to the Lord" to "he turned (or turned back) to the Lord," to suggest that the people of Israel will see clearly when they, like Moses, turn back to the Lord. Most notably, in

36. Giorgio Agamben, *The Time That Remains: A Commentary on the Letter to the Romans* (Stanford, CA: Stanford University Press, 2005), 95–99.

37. *American Heritage Dictionary of the English Language*, ed. William Morris (Boston: Houghton Mifflin, 1969), 413.

the next sentence the word "Lord" to whom Moses turns is explained to be the Spirit of God (not Christ) so that "where the Spirit of the Lord is, there is freedom" (3:17). Though Paul more often uses "Lord" to signify Christ, when he is citing Scripture it usually refers to God.[38] Here the explicit identification of the Lord as Spirit indicates that Paul recognizes the broad reference to God's Spirit as more appropriate in Moses' story.

And at this point Paul takes a further step with the first-person plural pronoun, which he has been using for himself and his coworkers, by extending it to all who turn to the Lord. The particle δὲ that links the final sentence here to the previous one can be translated either as "but" or "and," yet in this case of one positive statement following another the second must begin, "And we all" (3:18). This links what the Spirit does in Moses and Israel positively with what the Spirit does in Paul and the Corinthians, incorporating Moses and the Israel that turns to God's Spirit with Paul and the Corinthians as "we all" who are beholding the same image of God and being transformed from glory to glory. Granted that Paul goes on in the next argument to identify the image of God with Christ (4:4, 6), but this comes after Moses has been claimed as the model for those who turn to the Lord.

Paul's final problem in defending his agency to the Corinthians by comparing it to Moses' agency is that his own face does not glow, not literally to the eye or even metaphorically in charisma, in spite of the second-century description of "the face of an angel" in *Acts of Paul and Thecla* above. This has made some commentators argue that the story of Moses' glory must have been brought into the discussion by Paul's opponents in Corinth in order to denigrate Paul by comparison.[39] At least some in Corinth are complaining that his Gospel is veiled (4:3), and Paul claims in response that a glory beyond even that on Moses' face is accessible in his Gospel. Yet he does this while conceding that he and his colleagues are themselves not qualified for this task. Only the Spirit of the life-generating God qualifies them to be διακόνους καινῆς διαθήκης (3:6), mediators of a new covenant with God, agents of a new relationship.

The glory that the Corinthians seek and do not find visible in Paul he finds in the work that God does through him and his coworkers, namely, in the Corinthian believers themselves. They are his letter of recommendation, or rather Christ's letter delivered by these mediators (3:2-3). As

---

38. On "the Lord" as God, see above and 1 Cor 14:21; 2 Cor 6:18; Rom 9:29; 11:34; 14:11; 15:11.

39. Georgi, *Opponents*, 254–71; Belleville, *Reflections of Glory*, 245.

he says at the conclusion of the following argument: "So death is at work in us, but life in you" (4:12). Whereas in 1 Corinthians Paul insisted that the Corinthian believers imitate him and his cruciform life,[40] now he is willing, even eager, to accept them as evidence of Christ's resurrection glory that vindicates his death-prone work. And he no longer reserves this resurrection life until Christ's triumph over death but can see it happening in the present in processes of transformation "from glory to glory" through the workings of God's Spirit.[41]

This can be seen by the Corinthians only as a vindication of those who speak in the Spirit, whether in expressing the prayers of the people to God or the prophecies of God's will to the people. That women were prominent in these roles in Corinth's community is evident both when Paul tells them to cover their heads when praying and prophesying and when he further restricts their speaking to the family circle.[42] In spite of Paul they have apparently continued to function in Corinth's community as "the image and glory of God," not as "the glory of the man" according to Paul's previous instructions (1 Cor 11:7).

What might it have meant for these women to represent God's glory? It was not at all unthinkable in that context for God's Spirit to be linked to female embodiment.[43] Not only was the Pythian priestess the most renowned prophet at the Delphic shrine directly across the gulf to the north of Corinth, but Corinth was known worldwide for Aphrodite, the goddess of beauty (called Venus in Rome), whose temple was at Corinth's acropolis to the south. And the sacred precinct at its foot being rebuilt in Paul's time by the Romans was dedicated to the goddesses Demeter and Kore.

In Paul's lifetime Philo describes a Jewish community in Egypt where women and men have withdrawn from the world for Scripture study and meditation.

40. 1 Cor 1:26–2:5; 4:8-16; 10:31–11:1.
41. 1 Cor 15:22, 49, 54; 2 Cor 3:18.
42. 1 Cor 11:2-16; 14:34-35; for a defense of the latter as the original text, see Antoinette Clark Wire, *The Corinthian Women Prophets: A Reconstruction through Paul's Rhetoric* (Minneapolis: Fortress, 1990; repr., Eugene, OR: Wipf and Stock, 2003), 135–58, and Curt Niccum, "The Voice of the Manuscripts on the Silence of Women: The External Evidence for 1 Cor 14:34-35," *NTS* 43 (1997): 342–55.
43. Wire, "Women Who Speak for the Divine—Selected Texts from the Early Empire," in *Corinthian Women Prophets*, 237–69.

A First-Century Jewish Community in Egypt

The vocation of these philosophers is at once made clear from their title of Therapeutai [healing men] and Therapeutrides [healing women], a name derived from θεραπεύω, either in the sense of "cure" . . . or else in the sense of "worship." . . . Twice every day they pray, at dawn and at eventide. . . . The interval between early morning and evening is spent [alone] entirely in spiritual exercise. They read the Holy Scriptures and seek wisdom from their ancestral philosophy . . . but also compose hymns and psalms to God in all sorts of metres and melodies which they write down. . . .

[The] common sanctuary in which they meet every seventh day is a double enclosure, one portion set apart for the use of the men, the other for the women. For women too regularly make part of the audience with the same ardour and the same sense of their calling. . . . The feast [every seven times seven days] is shared by women also, most of them aged virgins, who have kept their chastity not under compulsion, like some of the Greek priestesses, but of their own free will in their ardent yearning for wisdom. Eager to have her for their life mate they have spurned the pleasures of the body and desire no mortal offspring . . . .

After the supper they hold the sacred vigil . . . first in two choirs, one of men and one of women. . . . Then they sing hymns to God . . . hands and feet keeping time. . . . They mix and both together become a single choir, a copy of the choir set up of old beside the Red Sea . . . the treble of the women blending with the bass of the men. . . . Thus they continue till dawn, drunk with this drunkenness in which there is no shame . . . and when they see the sun rising they stretch their hands up to heaven and pray for bright days and knowledge of the truth.[44]

The attention Paul gives to wisdom thought in 1 Corinthians also suggests that Israel's wisdom texts and practices may have been present in the Corinthian community. The Wisdom of Solomon a good century earlier spoke of the glory of God's Wisdom in female form (see sidebar above, p. 45: "Who Is Wisdom?" from Wis 7:24-27).

44. Philo, *The Contemplative Life*, 2.27-32, 68, 83-89, in *Philo*, vol. 9, trans. F. H. Colson, LCL (Cambridge, MA: Harvard University Press, 1941), 113–69.

Also when the Hebrew Bible story of the glory on Moses' face was read in a synagogue in the Roman east and interpreted in Aramaic for the people to understand, it told of the presence of the Shekinah, another feminine image of God.

The Glory of the Shekinah

And Moses did not know that the splendor of the features of his face shone because of the splendor of the glory of the Shekinah of the Lord at the time the Lord spoke with him.[45]

In addition, Paul's use of Moses as a model for those who turn to the Lord parallels closely the presentation of Aseneth, the Egyptian wife of Joseph, in a Hellenistic Jewish novel. She is not only remembered as a beautiful and humble convert to God who receives a shining vision but is also held up as a model for other converts.

The Egyptian Convert Aseneth Receives a Divine Messenger

And the man [from heaven] said to her, "Courage, Aseneth, chaste virgin. Behold, I have heard all the words of your confession and your prayer. . . . And your name shall no longer be called Aseneth, but your name shall be City of Refuge, because in you many nations will take refuge with the Lord God, the Most High, and under your wings many peoples trusting in the Lord God will be sheltered, and behind your walls will be guarded those who attach themselves to the Most High God in the name of Repentance. For Repentance is in the heavens, an exceedingly beautiful and good daughter of the Most High. And she herself entreats the Most High God for you at all times and for all who repent in the name of the Most High God.[46]

---

45. *Targum Pseudo-Jonathan Exodus* 34:29; cf. 34:5, 9, in *The Aramaic Bible: Targum Pseudo-Jonathan: Exodus*, trans. Michael Maher (Collegeville, MN: Liturgical Press, 1994), 260–61.

46. *The Confession and Prayer of Aseneth* (traditionally: *Joseph and Aseneth*) 15:2, 7, trans. C. Burchard, in *The Old Testament Pseudepigrapha*, vol. 2, ed. James H. Charlesworth (Garden City, NY: Doubleday, 1985), 226–27.

Granted that Paul in 2 Corinthians does not refer explicitly to women who exhibit God's Spirit, yet in writing to a community where he knows women have been key bearers of God's Spirit (1 Cor 11:2-16; 14:26-40), he opens this section by calling the Corinthians his letter of recommendation, written not with ink but with the Spirit of the living God on hearts of flesh (3:3). In closing the argument, Paul identifies this Spirit as the one who breathes life into the human form in creation (4:6). And this is the Spirit who is the Lord that Moses turned to when he took off his veil, thus providing Paul's model for turning to God when "we all" with uncovered faces see the same image of God's glory and are transformed from glory to glory (3:16-18).[47]

47. Wire, "Reconciled to Glory in Corinth?," 263–75.

2 Corinthians 4:1-15

A Light out of Darkness,
a Treasure in Clay

Text and Its Structure (4:1-15)

Midway in defending the work he and his coworkers have done in Corinth, Paul continues to alternate between defensive statements about their much-contested work and strong affirmations of God who nevertheless reveals Christ through them. He begins with negations: we don't lose heart; we don't deceive others; we are not obscure except to blinded minds; we don't proclaim ourselves (4:1-5). Then he says they do proclaim Jesus Christ in whose face God's glory shines to give knowledge of God, the same God who first said, "Out of darkness let there be light!" (4:5-6). So Paul's defense of their challenged ministry ends in a gleaming affirmation of God's light, and this explicitly "out of darkness."

His next defensive statements allow that he and his colleagues do not meet the normal standards of excellence. They have the treasure of God's light in clay pots, not in gold vessels, and their work has been struck down and they have been afflicted and made distraught. But the clay pot, he asserts, shows in contrast that the power is God's and not theirs, and their marginal lives reveal over and over that God keeps them alive (4:7-9). Paul summarizes: they carry Jesus' death in their bodies so that Jesus' risen life can be made visible in their survival (4:10-11). And Paul's affirmation of this life-giving God culminates a second time in the brief

⁴:¹Therefore, since it is by God's mercy that we are engaged in this ministry, we do not lose heart. ²We have renounced the shameful things that one hides; we refuse to practice cunning or to falsify God's word; but by the open statement of the truth we commend ourselves to the conscience of everyone in the sight of God. ³And even if our gospel is veiled, it is veiled to those who are perishing. ⁴In their case the god of this world has blinded the minds of the unbelievers, to keep them from seeing the light of the gospel of the glory of Christ, who is the image of God. ⁵For we do not proclaim ourselves; we proclaim Jesus Christ as Lord and ourselves as your slaves for Jesus' sake. ⁶For it is the God who said, "Let light shine out of darkness," who has shone in our hearts to give the light of the knowledge of the glory of God in the face of Jesus Christ.

⁷But we have this treasure in clay jars, so that it may be made clear that this extraordinary power belongs to God and does not come from us. ⁸We are afflicted in every way, but not

but crucial "So death is working in us, but life in you" (4:12)—locating the life God makes visible, not in their ministry, but in the Corinthians who respond to it.

Finally, Paul appeals to the psalmist's three words from the Greek Old Testament (LXX):[1] ἐπίστευσα διὸ ἐλάλησα ("I trusted, therefore I spoke"). He likewise claims to speak because he trusts that God who raised Christ will also raise him and his coworkers with the Corinthians who have responded to them. And he concludes with confidence that all this is for the Corinthians' sake so that they will give more and more thanks to God's glory.

A Feminist Lens at Three Ranges on a Treasure in Clay and a Light in Darkness (4:1-15)

A Broad Focus on All Bodies in the Tension between Light and Dark, Life and Death

What does this passage tell us about Paul's vision of reality as a whole? It is not presented as a world of rural production the way Jesus saw it,

---

1. Psalm 115:1 (see NRSV 116:10). I translate πιστεύειν as "to trust" rather than "to believe" because the latter has come in English to mean believing certain concepts to be true rather than confidence in someone.

crushed; perplexed, but not driven to despair; [9]persecuted, but not forsaken; struck down, but not destroyed; [10]always carrying in the body the death of Jesus, so that the life of Jesus may also be made visible in our bodies. [11]For while we live, we are always being given up to death for Jesus' sake, so that the life of Jesus may be made visible in our mortal flesh. [12]So death is at work in us, but life in you.

[13]But just as we have the same spirit of faith that is in accordance with scripture—"I believed, and so I spoke"—we also believe, and so we speak, [14]because we know that the one who raised the Lord Jesus will raise us also with Jesus, and will bring us with you into his presence. [15]Yes, everything is for your sake, so that grace, as it extends to more and more people, may increase thanksgiving, to the glory of God.

where God makes rain fall on the just and unjust; neither is it presented as a philosopher's world the way Philo saw it, where God is the first principle and final aim of all existence. Paul's is an urban and imperial world where God is creating light out of darkness, glory out of death. It is here in the human competition for survival and meaning that Paul insists the glory of God has appeared in Jesus' dying and rising and those who see this light are being transformed into Jesus' risen life, praising and returning glory to God.

To express this view of the world, Paul cultivates a trove of images from light and darkness. The stage for this has been set by 3:4-18, where Israel's gazing at God's glory on Moses' face—first unveiled on Sinai, then veiled and again unveiled by Moses—is the basis for expressing God's overwhelming glory in Christ, so that now all who see God's glory take on God's image and are transformed from one glory to another through God's Spirit. In 4:1-15 everything is characterized either as hiding, falsifying, veiling, blinding, not seeing, darkness, and clay or as open, true, light, glory of Christ, image of God, shining, knowing, face of Christ, and (gold?) treasure. There are multiple Greek expressions for light in the first six verses alone: φανερόω, "disclose, make visible";[2] αὐγάζω, "dawn, gleam"; φωτισμός, "brightness"; δόξα, "glory, radiance"; εἰκών, "image, likeness"; φῶς, "light"; λάμπω, "shine, glow." A clearer

2. Of the thirteen uses of the verb φανερόω in Paul's seven generally recognized letters, nine are in 2 Corinthians. Dominika A. Kurek-Chomycz, "The Scent," *Theologizing in the Corinthian Conflict: Studies in the Exegesis and Theology of 2 Corinthians*, ed. Reimund Bieringer, Ma. Marilou S. Ibita, Dominika A. Kurek-Chomycz, and Thomas A. Vollmer, BTS 16 (Leuven: Peeters, 2013), 90.

translation of 4:4 might be: "The god of this age has blinded their distrusting minds so they do not see the dawning gleam of the good news of the glory of Christ who is God's image."

The light imagery that Paul uses to communicate the transforming of human life cannot be traced back to a single source. One origin may be his own initial call when he was persecuting the church. It is described by Luke some decades after Paul's death as being so bright that it blinded him until he saw the world in a new way.[3] Paul in his own letters is reticent about what happened, saying to the Galatians only that God "was pleased to reveal his son in me so I might proclaim him among the nations" (Gal 1:15-16), and to the Corinthians, "Am I not an apostle? Have I not seen the Lord?" and "Last of all, as to one born dead, he appeared also to me" (1 Cor 9:1; 15:8). Both in telling the Galatians his life-changing call and in telling the Corinthians the appearance of Jesus that made him an apostle, Paul presents his own transformation as a visual experience, a revelation, a seeing. This experience may also be shaping his appeal in 2 Corinthians 4:6 to God's first act of creation: "It is the God who said, 'Out of darkness let light shine,' who has shown in our hearts to illumine the knowing of God's glory in the face of Jesus Christ."[4] To God's words from Genesis 1:3, "Let light shine," Paul adds the phrase "out of darkness," putting it first to shape the creation story of Genesis as his own story of persecutor re-created as persecuted proclaimer of Christ.

But Paul would not have expressed his experience this way were it not for a long tradition in and around Israel of describing the divine in terms of light. The burning bush where Moses heard God's name, the fire and cloud that guided enslaved Israel out of Egypt, and the glory of God on Sinai and in the traveling tabernacle all manifest God as light. God's glory (LXX, δόξα), once conceived as a physical substance of massive weight and power, came during the Babylonian exile to be identified with light.[5] It was this glory of God that was taken to be magnified when people gave thank offerings or prayers of praise (2 Cor 1:11; 4:15).[6]

---

3. Acts 9:1-19; 22:3-21; 26:12-18.

4. Christian Dietzelbinger, *Die Berufung des Paulus als Ursprung seiner Theologie* (Neukirchen: Neukirchener Verlag, 1985); Karl Olav Sandnes, *Paul, One of the Prophets?*, WUNT 2.43 (Tübingen: J. C.B. Mohr [Paul Siebeck], 1991), 131–45.

5. George Henry Boobyer, *"Thanksgiving" and the "Glory of God" in Paul* (Leipzig: Universitätsverlag von Robert Noske, 1929), 15–34, 85–89.

6. Glory theology in Israel also produced Merkavah-type mysticism. Those seeking transformation might see Moses ascending from Sinai in a throne chariot, but specific signs of this tradition are minimal here. Yet note Robin Griffith-Jones, "Turning to the

In Hellenistic and Roman times God's presence among humans was also expressed in terms of wisdom, and some Israelite literary circles present Σοφία (Sophia/Wisdom) as a female companion or personification of God characterized by light. In praises and laments she appears active in creating the world, and yet she is rejected at every turn (Prov 1:20-33; 8:1-36; and see Wis 7:24-27, p. 45, above). Because women in Israel and the Roman east were seldom literate, Israel's texts about Wisdom probably reflect male ways to express the attractions and satisfactions they found in studying God's wisdom. But the fact that a female divine figure was available in Israel for such meditations is less likely to have come from devout men reading Egyptian or Iranian texts about such figures than from long-standing religious veneration in Israel of the female divine alongside the male YHWH. This is attested not only by Scripture's recurring prohibitions of Asherah and all worship on high places other than Jerusalem[7]—a no fishing sign means good fishing—but also by recent archaeological finds of hundreds of small female figurines[8] as well as inscriptions about "YHWH and his Asherah."[9] Women who treasured such figures may also have shaped stories, songs, or prayers that already were integrating the praise of Wisdom with Israel's YHWH worship so that no hesitancy to do this survives in scribal Wisdom meditations. Paul develops Christian wisdom theology more fully in 1 Corinthians 1–3 than in 2 Corinthians, where images of light and darkness dominate. But Paul's identifying Christ as God's image here seems to be borrowing for Jesus the epithet of Wisdom as God's image with all the brightness that implies.[10]

Lord: Vision, Transformation and Paul's Agenda in 2 Corinthians 1–8," in *Theologizing in the Corinthian Conflict*, 255–79.

7. 1 Kgs 15:13; 2 Kgs 21:7; Jer 7:18, 31; 44:2-5, 15-25.

8. Marie-Theres Wacker, "Zum Stand der feministisch-exegetischen Diskussion um die Göttinnen im Alten Israel" and "Der biblische Monotheismus—seine Entstehung und seine Folgen (1999)," in *Von Göttinnen, Göttern und dem einzigen Gott: Studien zum biblischen Monotheismus aus feministisch-theologischer Sicht* (Münster: Literatur Verlag, 2004).

9. Judith M. Hadley, "From Goddess to Literary Construct: The Transformation of Asherah into Hokmah," in *A Feminist Companion to Reading the Bible: Approaches, Methods and Strategies*, ed. Athalya Brenner and Carole Fontaine, FCB 11 (Sheffield: Sheffield Academic, 1997), 360–99.

10. Hans Lietzmann, *An die Korinther I II*, extended by W. G. Kümmel, 5th ed. (Tübingen: J. C. B. Mohr [Paul Siebeck], 1969), 201. Jacob Jervell, *IMAGO DEI: Gen 1,26f. im Spätjudentum, in der Gnosis und in den paulinischen Briefen* (Göttingen: Vandenhoeck & Ruprecht, 1960), 214–17; Margaret E. Thrall, *A Critical and Exegetical Commentary*

Paul knows another possible source of light imagery, namely, the tradition found in some early Jewish and rabbinical texts that Adam was
created as God's image with such brightness that even the angels were
not able to look at him.[11] In 1 Corinthians 11:7 Paul says, "A man need
not cover his head, being the image and glory of God, but a woman is
the glory of a man." Yet this sentence is an anomaly in Paul's letters,
since otherwise Adam—and Eve—signify for Paul the sin that alienates
humanity from God and that is overcome in Christ's dying and rising.[12]
Elsewhere Paul does not identify the image of God's glory with Adam
but consistently reserves glory to God and to those who come to reflect
God's image, above all Christ.[13]

But to what extent does Paul's Christology lock him into a light/
darkness dualism that functionally excludes much of the world and
its peoples from the light? Because Paul does span the scope of apocalyptic language in this text, moving from God's creation of light out of
darkness to a final resurrection and heavenly reunion (4:6, 14), it would
seem that all else has been consigned to blinding by the "god of this age"
(4:4). Yet an effective apocalyptic scenario is more comprehensive than
this. In spite of his reifying the god who blinds—a function more often
given by Paul to God's own hardening of hearts[14]—Paul sees darkness
here in process of being fully illuminated by light. The negative role in
Paul's dualism—hiding, shame, deceit, and cunning—can for him give
way only in the daylight when truth is exposed to the human conscience
before God (4:2; 5:11). Paul's quoting Exodus 34:34 in 3:16 just before
this passage shows Moses leading this movement by taking off the veil
when he turns to the Lord so that "we all," free and unobstructed, see the
same image of God (3:18). Yet darkness is not fully left behind and Paul
adds it to the statement that God creates light (4:6), influenced perhaps
by Genesis 1:1, Isaiah 9:2, or Psalm 112:4.

---

on the Second Epistle to the Corinthians, ICC (Edinburgh: T & T Clark, 1994), 309–10; C.
Kavin Rowe, "New Testament Iconography? Situating Paul in the Absence of Material
Evidence," in Picturing the New Testament: Studies in Ancient Visual Images, ed. Annette
Weissenrieder, Friederike Wendt, and Petra von Gemünden, WUNT 2.193 (Tübingen:
Mohr Siebeck, 2005), 293–306.

11. Jervell, IMĀGO DEI, 37–41, 96–107.

12. 1 Cor 15:21-22; 2 Cor 11:3; Rom 5:12-21.

13. 1 Cor 15:49; 2 Cor 3:16-18; 4:4; Rom 8:29; cf. Col 3:10.

14. 2 Cor 3:14; Rom 11:7, 25; cf. 2 Cor 4:4.

For Paul, darkness precedes the light of creation as death precedes life, both for Jesus and for himself.[15] Paul must carry around the dying of Jesus because it is against this dark foil that Jesus' risen life shines as the light that it is (4:10-11). The bright treasure requires the clay jar (as with us, water left for immigrants in the desert requires a plastic bottle), and Paul's bare survivals require his near extinctions (4:8-9). Darkness is not left behind but comes first and backs up the light: "death is active in us, but life in you" (4:12). Yet Paul does not take his lot bearing Jesus' death as a permanent state; rather, it is one that will give way when God who raised Jesus from the dead also raises him to be presented with the Corinthians.[16] The verb παρίστημι ("present, stand beside") is used in the Pauline tradition for a positive culmination,[17] not for standing in final judgment.[18] The point of the dualism seems to be an ultimate inclusive joy. Paul is confident that when darkness has fulfilled its task of setting off the light in contrast, it disappears in light and to God's glory.

A Mid-Range Focus on the Social, Political, and Economic Setting

Because Paul speaks here of the god of this age blinding those who do not see light in the news of Christ's glory (4:4), the question must be asked if Paul is alluding to the political power of Rome. Mid-first-century Rome did exercise pervasive propaganda in its eastern provinces through imperial temples and coins, festivals and games, both to assert its claim to universal power and to obscure the fact that the empire was created and maintained by military force for economic exploitation.[19] Some commentators take "Jesus Christ as Lord" to be Paul's counterclaim to Roman

15. Jan Lambrecht, "The *Nekrōsis* of Jesus: Ministry and Suffering in 2 Cor 4,7-15, in *Studies on 2 Corinthians*, ed. R. Bieringer and J. Lambrecht, BETL 112 (Leuven: Leuven University Press, 1994), 309–33; Robert C. Tannehill, *Dying and Rising with Christ: A Study in Pauline Theology* (Berlin: Topelmann, 1967), 84–85.

16. 2 Cor 1:14; 4:14; 13:4.

17. 2 Cor 11:2; Eph 5:27; Col 1:22.

18. Tokunboh Adeyemo, *Africa Bible Commentary* (Nairobi: World Alive Publishers, 2006), 1403. Very differently, Norbert Baumert takes Jesus' raising the believer as a repeated event in each crisis, making this presentation a present and public manifestation of Jesus' life: *Täglich sterben und auferstehen. Der Literalsinn von 2 Kor 4,12–5,10* (Munich: Kösel Verlag, 1973), 94–99.

19. See, for Rome at large, Paul Zanker's *The Power of Images in the Age of Augustus* (Ann Arbor: University of Michigan Press, 1988) and, for the Roman East, S. R. F. Price's *Rituals and Power: The Roman Imperial Cult in Asia Minor* (Cambridge: Cambridge University Press, 1984).

hegemony (4:5; cf. 1 Cor 12:3),[20] while others see Paul simply adopting the language of his time, both Jewish apocalyptic and Roman political language, to assert the preeminence of the risen Christ.[21] Yet in an imperial setting—even within an internal province of the empire such as Greece that was favored with a measure of urban-based autonomy,[22] and in Corinth with the status of a Roman colony and provincial capital—new religious movements gathering adherents could provoke opposition from Roman officials and from local groups such as synagogues whose religious practices were acknowledged by Rome.

This is made explicit when Paul describes his life and that of his co-workers: "at every turn afflicted . . . at a loss . . . pursued . . . knocked down, always carrying Jesus' dying around in our body . . . , always being delivered up alive to death for Jesus' sake" (4:8-11). Though Paul is using this description to affirm God's rescue of him at each point "so that Jesus' life is made visible," he is also describing the concrete experience of early missioners soon elaborated in the Acts of the Apostles, a life of discomfort, hardship and close calls with death, fleeing from one place to another.[23] Later, the so-called Apocryphal Acts of the Apostles, written down in the second to fourth centuries, further dramatize the political conflicts between Christian women converted by apostles and the political authorities.[24] It is significant that Paul's letters do not distinguish

---

20. Richard A. Horsley, "Rhetoric and Empire—and 1 Corinthians," in *Paul and Politics: Ekklesia, Israel, Imperium, Interpretation*, ed. Richard A. Horsley (Harrisburg, PA: Trinity Press International, 2000), 72–102; Neil Elliott, *The Arrogance of Nations: Reading Romans in the Shadow of Empire* (Minneapolis: Fortress, 2008); Neil Elliott, "Marxism and the Postcolonial Study of Paul," in *The Colonized Apostle: Paul through Postcolonial Eyes*, ed. Christopher Stanley (Minneapolis: Fortress, 2011), 34–50.

21. Jeremy Punt, "Pauline Agency in Postcolonial Perspective: Subverter of or Agent for Empire," in Stanley, *Colonized Apostle*, 53–61; Albert J. Harrill, *Paul the Apostle: His Life and Legacy in Their Roman Context* (Cambridge: Cambridge University Press, 2012). Also see the articles by Elisabeth Schüssler Fiorenza, Cynthia Briggs Kittredge, Sheila Briggs, and myself responding to the editor Richard A. Horsley in *Paul and Politics* (40–57, 103–29).

22. See the commentary above on the political context of 1:12–2:11.

23. Timothy Luckritz Marquis, *Transient Apostle: Paul, Travel and the Rhetoric of Empire* (New Haven: Yale University Press, 2013); Ulrich Mell, "Paulus: scheiternder Gescheiter: Ein historischer und literarischer Einwurf," in *Der zweite Korintherbrief: Literarische Gestalt—historische Situation—theologische Argumentation. Festschrift zum 70. Geburtstag von Dietrich-Alex Koch*, ed. Dieter Sänger (Göttingen: Vandenhoeck & Ruprecht, 2012).

24. See, for example, *The Acts of Paul and Thecla* 14–17, 20–22, 26–39, trans. R. McL. Wilson, in *New Testament Apocrypha*, vol. 2, ed. Edgar Hennecke and Wilhelm Schneemelcher (Philadelphia: Westminster, 1964), 353–64.

physical and mental distress and include being "at a loss" in this list of trials. Discouragement remains a constant threat for Paul, as can be heard in his repeated expressions of confidence[25] and in his claims that "we do not lose heart."[26]

Without doubt, this preaching of Jesus' dying and rising provokes a significant social opposition, apparently not only from local elites and Roman officials but first and foremost from fellow Jews and from fellow Christ-believers who have found less provocative ways of expressing their faith (1 Thess 2:14-16; Gal 6:12). The internal pacified provinces of the Roman east including Greece and costal Asia Minor are, in other words, a conservative culture in which religion functions traditionally to honor long-established gods under the distant but supreme patronage of the goddess Roma and her emperors. This stands in contrast to external occupied provinces and vassal states of the empire such as Judea, where Jewish prophets gathered crowds, dissenting voices were suppressed by force (see sidebar: "Theudas the Prophet"), and Israel's martyrs expected to be vindicated by receiving life from God (see sidebar: "The Mother of Seven Sons").[27]

Theudas the Prophet

During the period when Fadus was procurator of Judea, a certain impostor named Theudas persuaded the majority of the masses to take up their possessions and to follow him to the Jordan River. He stated that he was a prophet, and that at his command the river would be parted and would provide them an easy passage. With this talk he deceived many. Fadus, however, did not permit them to reap the fruit of their folly, but sent against them a squadron of cavalry. These fell upon them unexpectedly, slew many of

---

25. 2 Cor 3:4, 12; 4:13; 5:6. Stanley Norris Olson notes, "The confident tone of the assertion contrasts with the actual situation," in his "Epistolary Uses of Expressions of Self-Confidence," *JBL* 103 (1984): 596.

26. 2 Cor 4:1, 16. Michel Bouttier observes that Paul uses some form of ἔχομεν (we have) repeatedly to inventory "what remains when the ship goes down" (3:4, 12; 4:1, 7, 13; 5:1). See "La souffrance de l'Apôtre: 2 Co 4,7-18," in *The Διακονία of the Spirit (2 Co 4:7-7:4)*, ed. Lorenzo de Lorenzi (Rome: St. Paul's Abbey, 1989), 29–49, esp. 32–33. Thrall in *Second Epistle*, 298–300, translates ἐγκακοῦμεν not as "lose heart" but as "grow lax."

27. For further accounts of suppressed prophets and violated martyrs in the Hellenistic and Roman period, see my *Holy Lives, Holy Deaths: A Close Hearing of Early Jewish Storytellers* (Atlanta: Society of Biblical Literature, 2002), 200–223; 240–66; 304–73.

them and took many prisoners. Theudas himself was captured, whereupon they cut off his head and brought it to Jerusalem.[28]

Before these days Theudas rose up saying he was somebody, and about four hundred men joined up with him. He was killed, and all those won over by him were scattered and came to nothing. (Acts 5:36)

The Mother of Seven Sons

But the holy and God-fearing mother lamented none [of her sons] with any such dirge, nor urged any of them to avoid death, nor grieved over them in the moment of their death. Rather, as though she had a mind of adamant and were this time bringing her brood of sons to birth into immortal life, she encouraged them and pled with them to die for piety's sake: . . . "Remember that it is for God's sake you were given a share in the world and the benefit of life, and accordingly you owe it to

God to endure all hardship for his sake, for whom our father Abraham ventured boldly to sacrifice his son Isaac, the father of our nation; and Isaac, seeing his father's hand, with knife in it, fall down against him, did not flinch." . . . With these words the mother of the seven exhorted each one and persuaded them to die rather than transgress the commandment of God, and they knew full well themselves that those who die for the sake of God live unto God, as do Abraham and Isaac and Jacob and all the patriarchs.[29]

Paul was not a revolutionary like John of Patmos, yet even John's visions disguised Rome as Babylon (Rev 17–18). But Paul's task to proclaim God's raising and exalting a man crucified by Rome was not a safe one, particularly when this marginal religious group was recruiting women and slaves independently of their husbands and/or masters (1 Cor 7:12-

28. Josephus, *AJ* 20.97-98, in Josephus, *Ant.*, vol. 9, LCL, trans. Louis H. Feldman (Cambridge, MA: Harvard University Press, 1969), 441–43. See also Acts 5:36.

29. 4 Macc 16:12-13, 18-19, 24-25, trans. H. Anderson, *Old Testament Pseudepigrapha*, vol. 2, ed. James H. Charlesworth (Garden City, NY: Doubleday, 1985), 561–62.

24).[30] Yet Roman governors and city officials might not need to take direct action to "keep the peace" if local religious affiliates who saw their communities implicated made that unnecessary.

It remains to ask what is the social significance of the particular claims Paul and his colleagues make that Christ is the image of God's glory (4:4) and that Jesus' life is made visible in their own mortal flesh (4:4, 6, 10-11). The consistent visual metaphors suggest a new vision, a new knowledge, a new "shining in the heart" (4:6), but is new conduct implied? Compare these to the saying of Jesus that God "makes his sun rise on the evil and the good," which accompanies his ethical instruction, "Love your enemies and pray for those who persecute you so that you may be children of your Father in heaven" (Matt 5:45). Is it Paul's news of God's glory for all in the face of Christ that leads him to risk reaching out to others in spite of persecutions until all give glory to God? He is a Jew who has thrown himself into making God's glory known to all peoples or, to put it as he does, he has seen God's glory in Christ and like the psalmist cannot but trust and speak,[31] provoking rejection by bringing Jesus' risen life to light. The social implications are clear, both for him and for his coworkers, and one must assume also for the Corinthians who come through them to trust and speak (1:7; 4:13), though in this context of defending his task he is not laying the risks on them. His stubborn conviction that God's glory has been revealed in Jesus for all people—his way to say that God makes the sun rise on the evil and the good—shapes his uncompromising witness and brings on the twin effect, "So death is at work in us, but life in you" (4:12).

When Paul speaks of "Jesus' life" we cannot assume that he has in mind what we know from the gospels about Jesus' conduct in his lifetime— here interpreters agree[32]—since Paul's letters never make any reference to Jesus' healing or eating with tax collectors and prostitutes or promising recompense to the poor, hungry, and mourning. It is possible that Paul knows little of the Galilean ministry tradition if it was cultivated among women who returned to Galilee from Jerusalem after Jesus' death while the apostles and Hellenists spread news from Jerusalem of his execution

---

30. See Acts 17:4, 12, 34; 18:8; Josephus, *Antiquities of the Jews* 18.65-80; Juvenal, *Satires* 6.511-57; *Acts of Paul and Thecla*.

31. 2 Cor 4:13; Ps 115:1 LXX/Ps 116:10.

32. Maurice Carrez, "Que représente la vie de Jésus pour l'apôtre Paul?," *RHPR* 68 (1988), 155–61; Thrall, *Second Epistle*, 336, n. 1011.

and appearances.[33] It is also possible that Paul chose in the Roman and Greek cities not to tell Jesus' proclaiming God's kingdom in wondrous acts and social reversals that would be taken as revolutionary. For Paul, Jesus' death was a sufficient marker of his witness. Yet the fact that Paul—distinctively for him—refers several times here to "Jesus" without using the title "Christ/Messiah" does at least name the specific man who lived so as to die at Roman hands and was acclaimed vindicated by new life from God (4:14).[34] What matters to Paul are not the acts of Jesus' lifetime that provoked his execution but the act of God that raised this man and made God's power visible over all evil and death itself.

A Sharp Focus on the Interaction between Paul and the Corinthians

Our reading of Paul's interaction with the Corinthians in this letter is bound to be influenced by how we read the more familiar 1 Corinthians. Modern stereotypes of this community such as the "cultured snobs at Corinth" and the "muddled and recalcitrant Corinthians"[35] need to be replaced with investigations of its conflicts as important sources of early Christian thought and practice. I have studied one part of this community, its women prophets, with attention to how Paul addresses those whose social status has risen in Christ while his has fallen,[36] and I encourage others to do such specific investigations. At the same time as taking 1 Corinthians seriously, 2 Corinthians is a fresh effort by Paul to speak to these people and must be heard as the final gauge of what Paul is doing at this stage. It seems that Paul's attention has shifted from the Corinthians' problems as he sees them to his problems as the Corinthians

33. This is my argument in *Mark Composed in Performance* (Eugene, OR: Wipf and Stock, 2011), 177–86; cf. Ernst Lohmeyer, *Galiläa und Jerusalem* (Göttingen: Vandenhoeck & Ruprecht, 1936).

34. Margaret Thrall speaks of God's power taking shape in Paul's rescued life as in Jesus' resurrection, "equally visible and equally revelational" (*Second Epistle*, 334–35). Michel Bouttier compares the διάκονοι of this letter to the martyrs of our time—Bonhoeffer, Maximillian Kolbe, Oscar Romero, Martin Luther King—who are today's gospel of life out of death, spread not through letters but our media ("La souffrance," 49).

35. These phrases are from N. T. Wright's *Paul and the Faithfulness of God*, parts 3 and 4 (Minneapolis: Fortress, 2013), 725, 981. At the same time he says Paul speaks of the Corinthians as the new tabernacle where the Holy Spirit dwells (983).

36. Antoinette Clark Wire, *The Corinthian Women Prophets: A Reconstruction through Paul's Rhetoric* (Minneapolis: Fortress, 1990; repr., Eugene, OR: Wipf and Stock, 2003), 62–71.

see them. His self-defense in turn gives us new angles from which to see both Paul and the Corinthians.

Paul's present strategy to recover the Corinthians' respect and restore his relation with them is evident in this passage in three ways: in Paul's accepting their demand for visible evidence; in presenting his own role and that of his coworkers as functional, even essential, for Jesus' life and God's glory that has become visible in the Corinthians; and thereby in honoring their claim to be already experiencing life in Jesus.

First, Paul accepts their demand for visible evidence. He has already stressed what is visible in his comparison of Christ and Moses (3:3-18) and continues to do so here. But only when this is seen as a positive response to Corinthian religious experience do the images cohere and show their significance. True, he does not talk about pleasing them, which could ring false and even manipulative, but he repeatedly presents himself and his colleagues as open and above board—"commending ourselves by visible manifestation of the truth."[37] Though some Corinthians have apparently found his gospel to be veiled, he attributes any obscurity to the lack of vision of those blinded by "the god of this age" so they miss the "dawning gleam of the glorious gospel of Christ who is God's image" (4:4). This epiphanic language[38] works to draw the Corinthians in and dissociate them from the blind who disparage his Gospel as veiled, and the light imagery may be Paul's use of their way of speaking. The wisdom they value that Paul appeals to in 1 Corinthians (1 Cor 1:18–2:16) can be described in other Jewish texts of this era as the brightness or image of God (see sidebars "Who Is Wisdom?," p. 45, and "Wisdom and Mind," below). Unfortunately, the translator of Philo below capitalizes Mind as the divine archetype of the human mind but does not recognize in this way the divine personification of Wisdom, although Philo calls her the "archetypal luminary," the brilliance that guides those to the divine. Like Philo, Paul sustains throughout this part of 2 Corinthians a visual rather than an aural way of presenting the Gospel—not as good news to hear, but as the brightness of knowing God reflected in Jesus' face, as the magnifying of God's glory.[39]

---

37. 2 Cor 4:2; see also 2:17; 5:11-12.
38. I adopt the term "epiphanic" from Peter Orr's study of the presence of Christ in 2 Corinthians, *Christ Absent and Present: A Study in Pauline Christology* (Tübingen: Mohr Siebeck, 2014), 115–60.
39. 4:6, 7, 10-11, 15. Bouttier, "La souffrance," 30-32, 58-59; Marquis, *Transient Apostle*, 103–13.

Wisdom and Mind according to Philo

In former times they called the prophets "seers" . . . even the seeing of the Divine light, identical with knowledge, which opens wide the soul's eye, and leads it to apprehensions distinct and brilliant beyond those gained by the ears. For as the application of the principles of music is apprehended through the science of music, and the practice of each science through that science, even so only through wisdom [σοφία] comes discernment of what is wise. But wisdom is not only, after the manner of light, an instrument of sight, but it [Greek: "she"] is able to see its [Greek: "her"] own self besides. Wisdom [Greek: "She"] is God's archetypal luminary and the sun is a copy and image of it [Greek: "her"].[40]

By using many words for it [Greek "her"] Moses has already made it manifest that the sublime and heavenly wisdom is of many names; for he calls it [Greek "her"] "origin" and "image" and "vision of God."[41]

Neither is God in human form, nor is the human body God-like. No, it is in respect of the Mind [νοῦς], the sovereign element of the soul, that the word "image" is used; for after the pattern of a single Mind, even the Mind of the Universe as an archetype, the mind in each of those who successively came into being was molded. . . . When on soaring wing it has contemplated the atmosphere and all its phases, it is borne yet higher to the ether and the circuit of heaven, and is whirled round with the dances of planets and fixed stars, in accordance with the laws of perfect music, following that love of wisdom which guides its steps. . . . Wafted by this to the topmost arch of the things perceptible to mind, it seems to be on its way to the Great King Himself; but, amid its longing to see Him, pure and untampered rays of concentrated light stream forth like a torrent, so that by its gleams the eye of the understanding is dazzled.[42]

Second, Paul presents his own and his coworkers' hardships as essential to Jesus' life shining in the Corinthians. Their integral relation

---

40. Philo, *The Migration of Abraham* 38–40, in *Philo*, vol. 4, trans. F. H. Colson and G. H. Whitaker, LCL (Cambridge, MA: Harvard University Press, 1968), 153–55.

41. Philo, *Allegorical Interpretation* 1.43, in *Philo*, vol. 1, trans. F. H. Colson and G. H. Whitaker, LCL (Cambridge, MA: Harvard University Press, 1929), 175. Elsewhere Philo also calls the λόγος ("Word") "origin" and "image" and identifies it as the source of light: *On the Creation of the World* 29–31 and *On the Confusion of Tongues* 146.

42. Philo, *On the Creation of the World* 69–71, in *Philo*, 1:55–57.

appears whenever he broadens the first-person plural "we," which he uses largely to defend his work and that of his colleagues, to include the Corinthians as he brings each argument to a climax (3:18; 4:6; 5:5, 10). But the interdependence is most explicit when he addresses them directly with the second-person plural "you" as distinguished from the "we" of his coworkers (3:1-3; 4:5, 12, 14, 15). After naming "we" missioners as the clay jar for God's treasure, the survivors of every hardship, the embodiment of Jesus' life in his death, Paul makes a striking shift in a concluding phrase, "So death is active in us, but life in you" (4:7-12). This seems to contradict Paul's just previous lines that he and his coworkers carry around Jesus' dying so that "Jesus' life might be visible in our body" (4:10).[43] We can ask, did he mean "our body" collectively to include the Corinthians, hence, "Jesus' life in you" (4:12)? But meanwhile he has intensified his point, making this interpretation more difficult, "We were delivered up alive to death on Jesus' account so that Jesus' life might be visible in our mortal flesh" (4:11).

After this sharp claim he may anticipate their retort—"Visible in your flesh? Where?"—because he reconfigures and claims to find Jesus' life in them, "So death is active in us, but life in you" (4:12).[44] Earlier Paul moved just as quickly from calling the Corinthians "our letter" to naming them "Christ's letter delivered by us" (3:2-3). So here too, he may step back from claiming too much for himself. Jesus' life may not be visible in his body but in theirs, yet their life demonstrates how effective his risky Gospel preaching has been. The question for us is whether, with most interpreters, we slip over this[45] or whether we see that he has recognized Jesus' life in them with the hope that they will recognize the near-dying

---

43. Jan Lambrecht takes "dying" here to mean a process active in Paul ("*Nekrōsis* of Jesus," 309–33); Margaret Thrall favors the meaning "deadness," as in Romans 4:19 (*Second Epistle*, 331–34).

44. Steven J. Kraftchick observes that Jesus' death and resurrection become a metaphor for how Paul's ministry functions for the Corinthians' life, yet this is read not as a concession that serves Paul's defense but as an effort to get the Corinthians to reevaluate themselves and seek the life that dies to God's glory ("Death in Us, Life in You," in *Pauline Theology*, vol. 2: *1 and 2 Corinthians*, ed. David Mittay (Minneapolis: Fortress, 1993), 169–78; Joyce Kaithakottil recognizes the hardships Paul undergoes to bring life to others, yet she also takes this as a model for each believer (" 'Death in Us, Life in You': Ministry and Suffering; A Study of 2 Cor 4:7-15," in *BiBh* 28 [2002]: 433–60).

45. Margaret Thrall deals with 4:12 in half a page compared to six pages for the previous two verses (*Second Epistle*, 331–37).

that gave it birth, or—to mix metaphors—the mother's labor that has delivered the letter that they are. Paul's evidence of this, that the messengers must undergo dying in order for the receivers of the message to be living, is not so much explained as it is found to have happened, first in Jesus and now in Corinth, and on this Paul rests his case.

If this seems to be an odd interpretation, it is not because the text points to something else but because 2 Corinthians is normally read with prejudice against the Corinthians carried over from Paul's critique of them in 1 Corinthians, which is taken as an objective account. Interpreters have typecast the Corinthians as "enthusiasts" whom Paul must restrict and instruct. Therefore Paul is not permitted to change his strategy from insisting that they imitate his weakness in Christ to citing their strength in Christ as proof that his own work on the edge of death has been effective.[46] That he reverts in the final chapters of 2 Corinthians to criticizing them for receiving other preachers as apostles is understandable precisely because Paul has chosen not to press on the Corinthians his apostolic credentials as the last person to see the risen Christ. Possibly he has avoided this in order to allow for Corinthian experiences of Christ since that time, that is, his is not the last. But this does leave him vulnerable when others make apostolic claims. He has presented himself as one among other διάκονοι—servants, bearers, couriers, representatives, messengers—whose authority depends strictly on the message they transmit in the clay jars appropriate for a treasure as bright as gold.

This same reserve could explain the persistence with which Paul uses the plural "we" when defending the way he and his coworkers have conducted themselves, even mentioning by name Timothy and Silvanus as cofounders of Corinth's assembly in Christ (1:19) and revealing his dependence on Titus and other coworkers,[47] among whom are also women.[48] And even when Paul speaks as "I" in a citation or to defend himself

---

46. Some do see Paul's change in strategy since 1 Corinthians: Bouttier, "La souffrance," 31–34; and Marquis, *Transient Apostle*, 18. Margaret M. Mitchell traces how Paul keeps shifting his strategies as he reinterprets himself and the Corinthians' interpretations of him ("The Corinthian Correspondence and the Birth of Pauline Hermeneutics," in *Paul and the Corinthians: Studies of a Community in Conflict*, ed. Trevor J. Burke and J. Keith Elliott, NovTSup 109 [Leiden: Brill, 2003], 36–49).

47. 2 Cor 2:13; 7:6-7, 13-15; 8:6, 16-23; 9:5; 12:18. Behind this may stand a tight cooperation that has developed between Paul and some colleagues, particularly Titus, so that they think out their common strategy in the plural. It may then be we who are projecting our view of the isolated apostle upon Paul. Bouttier recognizes that apostolic claims are absent in this entire section ("La souffrance," 30–32).

48. 1 Cor 1:11, 16; 16:15, 19; Rom 16:1.

against the specific charges of vacillating travel plans, he reverts to "we" to defend the whole pattern of work pursued by these διάκονοι with whom he now identifies himself (2:12-14; 4:13-14).

Third, Paul in 2 Corinthians consistently honors the Corinthians' claim to already experience Jesus' life. This contrasts sharply with 1 Corinthians, where he mocks their exaltation: "Already you are filled! Already you are rich! Without us you rule as kings and queens! Would that you did rule so that we could rule with you!" (1 Cor 4:8).[49] In fact, some interpreters follow John Calvin's claim on the basis of these caustic sentences in 1 Corinthians that Paul is being ironic when he says in 2 Corinthians 4:12, "So death is active in us, but life in you."[50] On the contrary, Paul's openness in 2 Corinthians to their experience of Jesus' risen life is already evident when he extends his first-person plural affirmations to include his interlocutors: "We all with unveiled face see the Lord's glory" (3:18) and "The God who said: 'Out of darkness let light shine' has shown in our hearts to give light for recognizing the glory of God in the face of Jesus Christ" (4:6).[51] Paul goes on from here to show how God continues to bring light out of darkness, a treasure out of clay pots, survival out of each crisis, Jesus' life out of the διάκονοι who carry around Jesus' death, culminating with making explicit that this life is visible, not in him, but in the Corinthians: "So death is at work in us, but life in you" (4:7-12).

We want to know the nature of this life that he honors in them, but Paul does not need to tell the Corinthians about themselves and continues to defend his stand on the margin of life (4:13-14). Drawing on a psalm of affliction and thanks for rescue (Ps 116:10, in its Greek [LXX] form Ps 115:1), he takes three words, ἐπίστευσα διὸ ἐλάλησα, "I trusted so I spoke," and uses them to speak, not of his affliction, but of the wonder that he can speak at all when there is nothing to base it on but trust in God (4:13).[52]

---

49. The Greek text speaks here in generic plural verbs about ruling without any gendered nouns. Because nouns are useful for clarity in English, the NRSV supplies the masculine "kings," yet without the feminine "queens."

50. Calvin's *Commentaries*, vol. 10: *The Second Epistle of Paul the Apostle to the Corinthians and the Epistles to Timothy, Titus and Philemon*, ed. David W. and Thomas F. Torrance, trans. T. A. Small (Grand Rapids, MI: Eerdmans, 1964), 60.

51. These first-person plural statements that include his hearers keep recurring in 5:5, 10, 21, etc.

52. Stefan Alkier sees Paul in 4:7-8 interpreting his survivals through hardship as miraculous acts of God that confirm his call: Stefan Alkier, *Wunder und Wirklichkeit in den Briefen des Apostel Paulus: Ein Beitrag zu einem Wunderverständnis jenseits von Entmythologisierung und Rehistorisierung*, WUNT 134 (Tübingen: Mohr Siebeck, 2001), 231–39.

Claiming the trusting spirit of the psalmist, he and his coworkers trust God and speak in spite of being "given up to death for Jesus' sake" (4:11). The reason follows, "because we know that the one who raised the Lord Jesus will raise us too." Paul anticipates his own resurrection, and he adds a final statement that God "will present us with you" (4:14b), again addressing the Corinthians. Paul's point here is that he and his coworkers who speak out to their peril will be vindicated. But the fact that he simply assumes the Corinthians' presence on that day shows that when he affirms Jesus' life in them, he means Jesus' risen life. While the διάκονοι still struggle to embody Jesus' death and mediate his life, those who see this and trust God already know Jesus' risen life. When they ask him for evidence—"Life in your mortal flesh? Where?"—Paul has an answer, "In you." They become his boast (1:14), releasing him from charges of self-commendation and boasting. They express the new life, whether in prayer or prophesy or revelations or tongues, exhibiting the Wisdom of God and extending to others the vision of Jesus' risen life (1 Cor 1:5-7; 11:6; 14:26, 34-35).

Paul's final sentence announces that all of this happens "for your sake," not in order to make them the epitome of mortal life, but so that more and more people might praise God (4:15; cf. 1:11). But how can all things be for their sake if everything is for God's glory? The same oxymoron appears when the scribe asks Jesus, "What commandment is first of all?" and Jesus tells him to love God with all his heart, soul, mind, and strength, and, second, to love his neighbor as himself (Mark 12:28-34). With what can he love his neighbor while loving God with his entire self? When Paul says here that it's all for their sake so that all can be for God's sake, it can only be that God is altogether for them, for that neighbor.

If Paul shapes these arguments to draw in the Corinthians, what does this suggest about the spirituality and influence of that community and the women who pray and prophesy there? It makes increasing sense that the women have not reordered themselves according to Paul's earlier instructions to cover their heads in worship leadership, let alone to be silent in the assemblies (1 Cor 11:2-16; 14:34-35). Rather, they must be speaking openly for God to the people in prophecy and for the people to God in prayer. In addition, the epiphanic language Paul uses in this argument that is shaped for their ears suggests that they share a way of speaking that depicts Christ as God's image and Wisdom, that they reflect to others God's glory in Christ, and that this increases thanksgiving to God's glory.

Most surprising, when Paul says the life of Jesus is active in them (4:12) and that God will also raise him to join them (4:14), he concedes to them a present experience of Jesus' risen life. Paul says this in order to get them to concede in return that his νέκρωσις ("dying") has made it possible (4:10), but such a strategy would not work unless they claimed this experience. This claim of risen life is already implied in Paul's retort in 1 Corinthians 4:8, "Already you are filled! Already you are rich! Without us you have begun to rule!" And some interpreters read Paul's argument for God's final resurrection of the dead in 1 Corinthians 15 to have been provoked by Corinthian claims to already know resurrection in Christ and be unwilling to reserve it for the dead.[53]

To find depictions of such experience of life in Christ we do not need to go to second- and third-century Christian texts where lifetime resurrection claims are attested.[54] Closer to hand are Jewish and Christian narratives that tell visionary experiences of women[55] such as The Confession and Prayer of Aseneth (see sidebar below: "The Vision of Aseneth").[56] Paul himself, a founder of the Corinthian church, saw transforming visions (12:2-4) and writes, "I was crucified with Christ and I no longer live but Christ lives in me" (Gal 2:20; Rom 6:4). This transformation in conduct ("walking in newness of life") and this identity change ("Christ lives in me") include divine-human communication in prayer, prophecy, and speaking in tongues (1 Cor 14:1-19). That it evolves in Corinth in a way at first not congenial to Paul may come from the prominence of women as mediums of divine oracles in Greek culture, hence in Corinth, at a time when Paul was working to make a collection for Jerusalem that might get more conservative Christ followers there to recognize his mission work. But in 2 Corinthians, threatened with losing ties with the congregation in Corinth, Paul takes Christ's life in them as the treasure in his clay jar. He thinks they cannot gainsay this evidence of God's power that has happened through the death-risking διακονία of his coworkers and himself.

---

53. Wire, *Corinthian Women Prophets*, 163–76, 233–36.

54. 2 Tim 2:18; *Acts of Paul and Thecla* 14; Nag Hammadi Codex I,4, *Treatise on the Resurrection* 49.15.

55. For a collection of primary texts about women who prophesy in this era, see my "Women Who Speak for the Divine: Selected Texts from the Early Empire," in *Corinthian Women Prophets*, 237–69.

56. For an English translation of the longer version of this Greek novel, see C. Burchard, "Joseph and Aseneth," in *Old Testament Pseudepigrapha*, 2:224–27.

The Vision of Aseneth

And when Aseneth ended her confession to the Lord, behold, the morning star rose from the eastern sky. . . . And behold, close to the morning star the heaven was torn open and a light beyond description appeared. And Aseneth fell on her face on the ashes and a man came from heaven toward her. And he stood over her head and called her, "Aseneth." . . . And the man said to her,

"Courage, Aseneth, do not be afraid, but stand up and I will speak to you." And the man said to her, "Remove the veil from your head for you are a holy virgin today and your head is like the head of a young man. . . . [F]or behold, the Lord has heard the words of your confession.

"Courage, Aseneth, behold, your name has been written in the book of life and it will never be wiped out. Behold, now on you will be renewed and reformed and revived and you will eat the bread of life and drink the cup of immortality, and you will be anointed with the ointment of incorruptibility.

"Courage, Aseneth, behold, the Lord has given you to Joseph as a bride and he himself will be your bridegroom. And you will no longer be called Aseneth, but your name will be City of Refuge, because in you many nations will take refuge and under your wings many peoples will be protected and within your wall those who attach themselves to God through repentance will be defended. For Repentance is a daughter of the Most High and it is she who at all times invokes the Most High for you and for all those who repent. . . ."

And the man said to her, "Bring me a honeycomb.". . . And Aseneth went in and she found a honeycomb lying on the table, and the comb was white as snow and full of honey and its breath had the scent of life. And Aseneth took the comb and brought it to him. . . . And the man stretched out his hand and held her head and said, "Aseneth, you are blessed that the unutterable things of God have been revealed to you, and blessed are those who attach themselves to the Lord God in repentance since they will eat from this comb. For the bees of the paradise of joy have made this honey and God's angels eat from it, and whoever eats from it will never die. And the man stretched out his right hand and broke off some of the comb and ate it, and he put some with his hand into Aseneth's mouth. . . .

And bees rose up from the cells of the comb, and they were white as snow, and their wings were like purple and like the hyacinth and like threads of gold, and gold crowns were on their heads, and their stings were stakes. And the bees all entwined themselves around

| Aseneth from foot to head and other large bees like queens held Aseneth's lips. And the man said to the bees, "Go home." And they all left Aseneth and | fell to the ground and died. And the man said, "Rise up and go home." And they all rose and went off toward the courtyard near Aseneth's.[57] |

Paul's direct second-person address to "you" Corinthians that begins and ends this argument (4:5, 15) is explained by the small but crucial conjunctions that indicate his purpose. Twice he says that he embodies Jesus' death so that (ἵνα) Jesus' life might be made visible, and he concludes: "So [ὥστε] death is active in us, but life in you" (4:10-12).[58] All this leads to Paul's ultimate purpose: "so that [ἵνα] grace magnified through many people might multiply thanksgiving to God's glory" (4:15b). His aim to fuel their life through embodying Jesus' death is finally absorbed into the goal they both serve when the Corinthians embody Jesus' risen life and inspire others to glorify God.

If we read Paul's argument, not as an instruction to get the Corinthians to do this, but as his recognition of the life they are living in Christ in order to defend his own role in the process, then they have two possible responses. Either they reject him in favor of other leaders who provide more positive models or they recognize his offensive but memorable role in the life they have. The survival of the letter could suggest the latter, but the fact that it is not in circulation until well into the second century could point to the former. In either case, they remain for some years a vibrant congregation, attested at the turn of the century for recalling their elders and provoking Clement's letter from Rome.[59]

57. *The Confession and Prayer of Aseneth* 14:1-4, 11; 15:1-7; 16:1-5, 7-9, 13-17. I have translated here from the Greek text that I take to be the original shorter version of this mystical novel written in the Roman period, probably by a Jew from Egypt, as edited by Marc Philonenko, *Joseph et Aseneth* (Leiden: Brill, 1968), 109, 176–90. On the implications of this text for ancient women's experience, see Angela Standhartinger's *Das Frauenbild im Judentum der hellenistischen Zeit* (Leiden: Brill, 1995), 219–39. Ross Shepard Kraemer proposes a third-century dating in *When Aseneth Met Joseph: A Late Antique Tale of the Biblical Patriarch and His Egyptian Wife, Reconsidered* (New York: Oxford University Press, 1998), ix, 225–44. On the possibility of no single original text but various traditions see Edith M. Humphrey, *Joseph and Aseneth* (Sheffield: Sheffield Academic, 2000), 17–28.

58. Bouttier's careful analysis highlights these conjunctions ("La souffrance," 48–49, 52) as does Lambrecht ("Nekrōsis of Jesus," 325–26).

59. 1 Clement 45–47.

2 Corinthians 4:16–5:10

At Home in the Body and/or at Home with the Lord

Text and Its Structure (4:16–5:10)

Paul first claims to be confident in spite of great challenges by contrasting the life that he and his coworkers live that is external, old, afflicted, momentary, visible, and earthly with the life they are in process of realizing that is inner, new, glorified, eternal, invisible, and heavenly (4:16-17). Neither reality is softened by its presence with the other. The tension between the two is developed in three images (5:1-9). He contrasts their present tent with their heavenly dwelling, their sparse or even absent clothing now with their eventual robes of life, and their being away from the Lord now with being at home with the Lord. Finally, he states again why he remains confident (5:7-10).

Throughout, and particularly in closing, Paul reasserts his confidence (5:6, 8) because he and his coworkers live the outer life from the inner, which is "renewed day by day" as they look toward the eternal, anticipating being "swallowed up in life" (4:16-17; 5:4). And since this is not his own program Paul twice interrupts: "For we walk by trust, not by a visible presence" and "But the one who created us for this is God who has given us the pledge of the Spirit" (5:7, 5). Therefore all that matters is trusting in the Spirit's presence and pleasing God by doing good and not evil. In closing, Paul extends his first-person plural "we" to become "we all," including the Corinthians, confident that each person's work will be recognized by Christ.

97

2 Cor 4:16–5:10

4:16So we do not lose heart. Even though our outer nature is wasting away, our inner nature is being renewed day by day. 17For this slight momentary affliction is preparing us for an eternal weight of glory beyond all measure, 18because we look not at what can be seen but at what cannot be seen; for what can be seen is temporary, but what cannot be seen is eternal.

5:1For we know that if the earthly tent we live in is destroyed, we have a building from God, a house not made with hands, eternal in the heavens. 2For in this tent we groan, longing to be clothed with our heavenly dwelling—3if indeed, when we have taken it off, we will not be found naked. 4For while we are still in this tent, we groan under our burden, because we wish not to be

The point where manuscripts differ sufficiently to impact the translation (5:3) will be taken up where the clothing metaphor is discussed below.

A Feminist Lens at Three Ranges on Paul's Interpretation of Life and Death (4:16–5:10)

Broad Focus on the Ecosystem Presupposed in What Is Seen and Unseen, in Death and Life

The opening words recurring here (4:1, 16), "So we do not lose heart," remind us that this text is not Paul's schedule for what happens after death but an insistence that a difficult life can be worth living, that what seems to be a living death is rather a dying life. Nonetheless, commentaries dwell on the question of whether Paul's expectations about life after death have changed since writing 1 Thessalonians 4:13-17 and 1 Corinthians 15:51-54. Does he no longer expect to survive until the Lord appears and the sleeping dead awake at the final resurrection? Is he now thinking that immediately at death he will be with the Lord?[1] Paul's language here is richly metaphorical, and we do best to listen to all the ways he speaks for whatever is implied about life and death in his world as he faces death.

---

1. Margaret Thrall discusses at length Paul's possible change of expectations and concludes that he now realizes he may die before Christ's appearing and is convinced that he could not be other than immediately with the Lord (*A Critical and Exegetical Commentary on the Second Epistle to the Corinthians*, ICC [Edinburgh: T & T Clark, 1994], 368–70, 397–400). Fredrick Lindgård sees changes not in Paul but in the situations he is addressing. Here in 2 Corinthians it is a community not sure they can trust him, so he is open and even intimate about himself before he begins his appeal for their support (*Paul's Line of Thought in 2 Corinthians 4:10–5:10*, WUNT 2.189 [Tübingen: Mohr-Siebeck, 2005], 2, 226).

unclothed but to be further clothed, so that what is mortal may be swallowed up by life. [5]He who has prepared us for this very thing is God, who has given us the Spirit as a guarantee.

[6]So we are always confident; even though we know that while we are at home in the body we are away from the Lord—[7]for we walk by faith, not by sight. [8]Yes, we do have confidence, and we would rather be away from the body and at home with the Lord. [9]So whether we are at home or away, we make it our aim to please him. [10]For all of us must appear before the judgment seat of Christ, so that each may receive recompense for what has been done in the body, whether good or evil.*

*NRSV note: 5:3, Other ancient authorities read *put it on.*

At first Paul seems to speak of two aspects of life. There is the outer, visible self that is in process of decay, and there is the inner, not visible self that is in process of daily renewal. This reflects the body-soul dualism standard in much of Greek thought, and Hellenized Jews like Paul would have been very familiar with it (see sidebar: "Who Can Learn Wisdom?"). But Paul's point here is quite specific, not that the soul is burdened and seeks escape from the body, but that the inner self is being renewed as the outer deteriorates and that the temporary experience of affliction is minimal compared with the weight of glory produced for those who attend to what is not seen rather than to what is seen.

Who Can Learn Wisdom?

How can any human being learn what is God's plan? Who can apprehend what is the will of the Lord? The reasoning of mortals is uncertain and our plans are fallible, because a perishable body weighs down the soul, and its frame of clay burdens the mind already so full of care. With difficulty we guess even at things on earth, and laboriously find out what lies within our reach; but who has ever traced out what is in heaven? (Wis 9:13-16, REB)[2]

2. The Wisdom of Solomon is a Hellenistic Jewish praise of God's Wisdom from the second or first century BCE that appears in Roman Catholic Bibles. It was in the King James Authorized English Version until a new edition in the nineteenth century omitted all Greek texts from the Old Testament in line with Martin Luther's German translation.

In 5:1-10 Paul tries to explain how this can be with the help of three metaphors—living in a tent or house, putting on and off clothing, and being at home or away.[3] His upbeat opening, "For we know that," as well as his sustained "so we are always confident" project not a lament about bodily life but an assurance that there is no cause for alarm (5:1, 6, 8). He insists that there is a dwelling from God if the earthly tent is destroyed, though he must concede that "we cry out" longing to be so clothed. The verb in 5:3 in all the earliest manuscripts reads ἐνδυσάμενοι, "put on," not ἐκδυσάμενοι, "put off."[4] This confirms what has just been said, that the new clothing put on over the old leaves no fear of being naked and trapped in some harsh transition between embodiments depicted as clothing. Some interpreters think that Paul is saying he wants to survive until Christ appears and thereby escape death. But the culminating image of the mortal being "swallowed up by life" (5:4; see also 1 Cor 15:53-55) suggests rather that the desire "not to be unclothed but to be further clothed" is a cry for quick relief from debility and violence.

The final metaphor concerns being at home or away (5:6-10). This makes clear that Paul's cry is not only a negative reaction to the pains of his present life but a positive longing "to be at home with the Lord." The image is stronger when some translations (REB, NJB) sharpen "being away from home" into "being in exile."[5] Ostracism was a widespread way to discipline disruptive citizens in the Greco-Roman city, and since an exile could not return without an act of repeal, one can compare them to political refugees today. Paul senses a distance from Christ when "in the body" that requires living by πίστις (trust) rather than ἐίδος (a visible form or presence, not the faculty of sight). Yet he repeats, "But we have confidence, even though we would rather be exiled from the body and at home with the Lord" (5:8), so in whatever state "we aspire to please him" (5:9). In other words, the home does not shift but is a given, even at the cost of human longing.

---

3. Five of the seven Greek sentences in this section include the explanatory particle γὰρ ("for"; 5:1, 2, 4, 7, 10), and two include a consequence particle ἵνα ("in order that"; 5:4, 10).

4. Thrall, *Second Epistle*, 373–74, 377; Thrall, " 'Putting on' or 'Stripping off' in 2 Corinthians 5:3," in *New Testament Textual Criticism: Its Significance for Exegesis*, ed. Eldon Jay Epp and Gordon D. Fee (Oxford: Clarendon, 1981), 221–35.

5. See Plato, *Laws* 9, 864e; on the fate of exiles, see Demosthenes, *Oration* 2, and Philo, *Against Flaccus* 151–91.

At the end of each paragraph of his explanation about why he doesn't lose heart (5:5, 10), Paul returns to his point made in the first sentence, "We know . . . that we have a building from God [ἐκ θεοῦ]." Paul paints it as building, clothing, or a home, but he confirms, "The one who has made us for this very thing is God,[6] who has given us the Spirit as assurance" (5:5), and he concludes by insisting that everything done in the body will receive Christ's reward (5:10). Though the latter could be read as a threat, in this context it is without question another assurance that life in the body counts for something. Every act carried out in the Spirit that God has given, whatever its results in rejection or failure, is duly recognized. Because of these few but crucially placed references to God as the one who has made or created people "for a mortality to be swallowed up in life," all Paul's metaphors depict aspects of this God-created mortal life that knows its home is secure. Trusting the Spirit from God, Paul says, one need not lose heart in doing good amid attacks and longings, since the harshest affliction is feather light compared to the weight of God's glory.

Has Paul left groundwork here for centuries of Christians to cultivate a heavenly self at the expense of the earthly body and its potential? Yes. But the pointers are sharper toward a view of life and death that is neither Stoic mastering of the unruly body nor apocalyptic visions of future bliss. Granted that human beings are mortal, temporary tents subject to damage and destruction, clothing that could leave one naked, a life in exile, they are nonetheless created by God for walking in trust and doing good. Already through God's Spirit they are renewed day by day (4:16; 3:18) as they actively cry out to be swallowed up in life and welcomed home with the Lord (5:4, 8).

A Mid-Range Focus on the Political, Social, and Economic Setting

Though Paul's point here is positive—that he knows he has full security because God "has his back"—yet in saying this he betrays again how marginal his life is. He concedes he is wasting away, beset by afflictions, threatened in fact with death as he has recounted in opening the

---

6. The NRSV translates the verb κατεργάζομαι as "prepare" in 4:17 and 5:5, but this meaning is not found elsewhere and should not be invented for this text. The standard meaning is "to achieve, accomplish, bring about, produce, create." BDAG, 531. On exception it means "to overpower or conquer."

letter (1:8-9). This reality is social as well as physical because it has been caused by his persistent announcement that God raised Christ from the dead so that people of every nation are free in Christ from those who rule by threatening death. Yet is what Paul says here simply an assurance of individual vindication by having a home after death in the heavens with the Lord, as these texts are often read? Or does Paul presume here a process of social and political transformation of the world now ruled by threat of death, a process already underway in those who hear his announcement?

In spite of the fact that this text does concern a time when Paul and his coworkers faced possible death, there are several indications that Paul's response anticipates nothing less than a concrete transformation of the rule of death into the rule of life.

First, recent study of the Jewish and Christian apocalyptic tradition has come to recognize that the visions in texts such as Daniel, 1 Enoch, 2 Baruch, Mark 13, Revelation, and 4 Ezra cannot be dismissed as projections of the violent imaginations of the oppressed and depressed but need to be heard as cries of trust that God is at work in power reversal. Mary Rose D'Angelo and Luzia Sutter Rehmann have shown in different ways how apocalyptic themes functioned to maintain hope and mobilize resistance in political situations where no direct opposition was possible.[7] Feminists see the vision of Rome's downfall as a prostitute in Revelation 17–18 to be a patriarchal projection of Rome's exploitation onto women due to cities being called feminine. But they also see in the burning of a harlot who thinks she's a queen that Rome's insatiable greed is being exposed to all the merchants and ship captains whose wails show that their wealth and glory depend on it.[8] Paul himself apparently had visions,[9] and though reticent about describing them, he makes clear that his life was transformed by a vision that gave him the confidence that Christ was raised. Most apocalyptic scenarios incorporate Israel's belief

---

7. Mary Rose D'Angelo, "Remembering Jesus: Women, Prophecy and Resistance," *Hor* 19 (1992): 199–218; Luzia Sutter Rehmann, *Geh—Frage die Gebärerin: Feministisch-befreiungstheologische Untersuchungen zum Gebärmotiv in der Apokalyptik* (Gütersloh: Kaiser, Gütersloher Verlagshaus, 1995), 69–96, 115–18.

8. Elisabeth Schüssler Fiorenza, *The Book of Revelation: Justice and Judgment* (Philadelphia: Fortress, 1985), 181–203; *Revelation: Vision of a Just World* (Minneapolis: Fortress, 1991), 95–103; Tina Pippin, *Death and Desire: The Rhetoric of Gender in the Apocalypse of John* (Louisville: Westminster John Knox, 1992), 57–68.

9. 1 Cor 9:1; 15:8, 51-58; 2 Cor 12:1-4.

in God's righteous judgment as a final stage when all wrongs are righted. Paul's conclusion in 5:10 affirms this final event at which "all of us" are held accountable, so that already now, though "away from the Lord," Paul can "aim to please him" by doing good.

A second sign that Paul has social and political change in mind appears where he seems to allude in his "building from God not made with hands" to a saying widely attributed to Jesus: "I will destroy this temple made with hands and after three days I will build another not made with hands" (Mark 14:58). The development of this particular saying of Jesus is both complicated and obscure but important to try to unravel. The temple sign may have begun as Jesus' lament: "Jerusalem, Jerusalem, killing the prophets and stoning those sent to you. . . . Behold! your house is left for you desolate" (Matt 23:37-38; see also Luke 13:34-35; Jer 22:5). A prophet's lament could also be taken as a prophetic curse, a sign of coming destruction, as were Jesus' woes to the rich, to the teachers, and to Jerusalem after its destruction.[10] A lament that is unmistakably a prophetic sign of destruction is described in the story of the prophet Jesus ben Ananias (see sidebar: "The Prophecy of Jesus Son of Ananias"). Jesus of Nazareth rebukes his disciples' awe of the temple by announcing its destruction in a different saying: "Not one stone will be left on another!"[11]

It is, however, only when Jesus' word of the temple's destruction is used in gospel narratives as an accusation against him at his trial and as a taunt at his crucifixion that it appears with a claim to rebuild in three days a temple not made with hands.[12] The reference to three days could signify in apocalyptic literature an indeterminate but limited time of distress[13] but may here have come from or led to interpretations of Jesus' resurrection in three days. The Fourth Gospel attributes a related taunt to Jesus when asked for a sign of his authority to have disrupted the temple, "Destroy this temple and in three days I will raise it up!" and the narrator explains, "he was speaking of the temple of his body" (John 2:19-21). In the context of the gospels as whole narratives these sayings operate not only as taunt, accusation, lament, or curse but also and principally as vindication of Jesus at a time after the temple had been burned in the Roman War in 70 CE.

---

10. Luke 6:24-26; Matt 23:13-36; Luke 19:41-44.
11. Mark 13:1-2; Matt 24:1-2; Luke 21:6.
12. Matt 26:61; 27:40; Mark 14:58; 15:29; cf. Acts 6:14.
13. Rev 11:11; 12:14.

The Prophecy of Jesus Son of Ananias

An incident more alarming still had occurred four years before the war at a time of exceptional peace and prosperity for the City. One Jesus son of Ananias, a very ordinary yokel, came to the feast at which every Jew is expected to set up a tabernacle for God. As he stood in the Temple he suddenly began to shout: "A voice from the east, a voice from the west, a voice from the four winds, a voice against Jerusalem and the Sanctuary, a voice against bridegrooms and brides, a voice against the whole people." Day and night he uttered the cry as he went through all the streets. . . . "Woe to Jerusalem!" Those who daily cursed him he never cursed; those who gave him food he never thanked; his only response to anyone was that dismal foreboding. His voice was heard most of all at the feasts. For seven years and five months he went on ceaselessly, his voice as strong as ever and his vigour unabated, till during the siege after seeing the fulfilment of his foreboding he was silenced. He was going round on the wall uttering his piercing cry: "Woe again to the City, the people, and the Sanctuary!" and as he added a last word; "Woe to me also!" a stone shot from an engine struck him, killing him instantly.[14]

Writing before the temple's destruction, Paul does not take Jesus' sayings as prophecies of the temple's fall but hears a reference to the destruction of the body at death, as the Fourth Gospel does. Therefore if Paul is alluding to Jesus' saying with his heavenly building, dwelling, or house (οἰκία, οἰκοδομή, οἰκοτήριον [5:1-2]), it would be to a heavenly temple, which, for a Jew like Paul, would mean a single place of worship for all, a kind of communal resurrection life in Christ. Meanwhile Jerusalem itself remains central for Paul, and this letter culminates in his collecting financial support for Christ followers there (2 Cor 8–9).

Finally, the word ἀχειροποίητος, "not made with hands," has a wider significance in Jewish and early Christian texts. Whereas most Greek texts that survive from this period contrast things made with human hands (χειροποίητος) with objects of nature, an artificial hill to a natural one, the Jewish tradition had long compared things made with hands to what

---

14. Josephus, *Jewish War* 6.300–301, 306–9, in Josephus, *The Jewish War*, trans. G. A. Williamson (Harmondsworth: Penguin, 1959), 349–50.

God has made, contrasting the two different makers. The blatant offense to the Creator of creatures worshiping things they themselves make, dramatized in Romans 1:18-21 and at greater length in Wisdom 13–15, would keep clear for those who knew the Jewish Scriptures that humans were different in kind from their Creator.[15] In the Greek Bible (LXX) that Paul read, the Hebrew word אליל ("idol") in Leviticus and Isaiah is often translated simply τά χειροποιήτα (the things made with hands),[16] and this can also apply to a sanctuary where idols are worshiped (Isa 16:12). All New Testament uses of ἀχειροποιήτα refer to sanctuaries or ritual acts and highlight the same contrast between what God makes and what humans make.[17]

To conclude, when Paul asserts here, "For we know that if our earthly tent-house is destroyed we have a building from God, a home not made with hands, eternal in the heavens" (5:1), he grounds the confidence he has just claimed for the invisible but daily renewed inner self (4:16-18) not so much in the future as in the present God-created dwelling. In this way he claims for himself and his coworkers ultimate immunity from powers that attack them and threaten death. All this may be echoing Jesus' prophecy understood to mean that the body can be destroyed but God makes one that is indestructible. Out of this Paul sees himself and those he addresses freed from the limitations of social, political, and economic expediency, assured by God's Spirit to live in the body in confidence (5:5-8), so that, being renewed day by day, "all of us" might please God in doing good and not evil (3:18; 4:6; 5:9-10). The particulars of Paul's understanding of world transformation come up when he is talking about Corinth, Jerusalem, or Rome, but it all depends on his claim that "the one who has created us for this very thing is God" (5:5a).

Focusing in on the Interaction of Paul and the Corinthians

Because Paul in this section stops speaking directly to his listeners about "life in you" and "everything for you" (4:12, 15) but instead speaks in a broad first-person plural about being confident in the face of death, interpreters have compared this passage to a meditation on life and death,

---

15. Eduard Lohse, "χειροποίητος, ἀχειροποίητος," *TDNT* 9:436; Philo, *Life of Moses* 2.51, 88, 168.

16. Lev 26:1; Isa 2:18; 10:11; 19:1; 21:9; 31:7; 46:6.

17. Mark 14:58; Acts 7:48; 17:24; 2 Cor 5:1; Eph 2:11; Col 2:11; Heb 9:11, 24.

time and eternity, in the style of Augustine's *Confessions*.[18] But he begins with his usual "So we do not lose heart" (4:16) and continues "so we take courage" (5:6, 8), making this an integral piece, or even part of the final climax, in Paul's long recital of his reasons for confidence (2:14–5:21). What provoked this in writing to Corinth is the crucial question here.

It may be that some Corinthians are convinced that Paul has nothing further to offer them, seeing no evidence of leadership that they can respect after his painful earlier letter (2:1-10). Later in the present letter Paul says that the Corinthians who got his message from Titus have repented concerning something that offended Paul (7:5-11), but the fact that Paul begins with repeated remonstrances about his integrity shows that he thinks they still lack confidence in him. They may not fear a heavy hand from him at this point so much as they dismiss him as inarticulate and unimpressive (10:10; 11:6), a man with bad health, rough appearance, and a tradesman's ways of coming and going. In response it is not surprising that, to climax his assertions of confidence, he should claim to be impervious to death. Reading Paul's argument this way as a response to the people he addresses, we do not find him sinking into reverie and soliloquy but rather grasping at ways to demonstrate, even here, his sure foundation.

First, as several interpreters have noted, he concedes to dualism the sense of being at once an external self that is threatened and an inner self that is renewed, at once subject to very visible afflictions and sure of an eternal, if invisible, glory (4:17). There is no softening of the social trials and physical attacks involved: use in papyri letters suggest Paul's διαφθείρω is not "waste away" but "suffer attack," as in war or from wild animals (4:16).[19] Yet internal renewal is daily, the weight of glory makes afflictions light in contrast, and all his attention shifts from what is seen to what is eternal though unseen. Paul speaks as "we" to include his coworkers, the διάκονοι, among whom he builds his defense, but also perhaps to open up toward the Corinthians he is addressing who are explicitly included by the "all of us" in his final lines (5:10). Their interest in wisdom and the internal work of the Spirit, as suggested in 1 Corinthians 1–2 and 12–14, might well attract them to a daily renewal of life

18. Gerhard Dautzenberg, "'Glaube' oder 'Hoffnung' in 2 Kor 4,13–5,10," in *The Diakonia of the Spirit (2 Co 4:7–7:4)*, ed. L. de Lorenzi (Rome: St. Paul's Abbey, 1989), 75–104.

19. Peter Arzt-Grabner, *2. Korinther. Unter Mitarbeit von Ruth E. Kritzer*, vol. 4 of *Papyrologische Kommentare zum Neuen Testament* (Göttingen: Vandenhoeck & Ruprecht, 2014), 310–11.

out of an eternal weight of glory. Paul apparently hopes to draw them in to consider that he and his unlikely colleagues could be experiencing these transformations simultaneously with attacks and afflictions on the external self. Paul is, after all, talking not about the future but about the tensions of his present life that is grounded in the unseen and eternal.

Explication follows in terms of the three metaphors of building, clothing, and being at home or away (see the broad-range analysis above). In each case Paul falls between destruction and preservation, or, rather, claims a double possession: whenever the earthly tent collapses we know we have a building from God; we yearn to put this on like clothing over our present body so as not to be found naked; and we would rather be "at home with the Lord" and away from the body, but we move by faith through the Spirit, seeking to please him. What emerges is a life confident of the road being taken (5:6, 8). It is a chosen path (φιλοτιμούμεθα, "we make it our aim," 5:9) and yet in constant tension. This is communicated in words expressing longing (ἐπιποθοῦντες), desiring (εὐδοκοῦμεν), pleasing (εὐάρεστοι), and, most extreme, crying out and crying out in heavy labor (στενάζομεν and στενάζομεν βαρούμενοι) (5:2, 8, 9, 2, 4). Some interpreteters translate στενάζω as "sighing" and stress Paul's positive desire for what is not yet fulfilled, but since it appears a second time with "being weighed down" or "being in hard labor," it must carry negative weight as well. On the other hand, the NRSV, NEB, and NJB translations of στενάζω as "groaning" is almost entirely negative in its normal English usage, so I choose "crying out," which is open to expressing inadvertent sounds of pain or hope or both. In such extended expression of his emotions Paul makes himself vulnerable to the Corinthians and seeks to draw them toward identifying with him.

To understand this "crying out," women interpreters turn us in two fruitful directions. On the one hand, when this verb is used with "being burdened" it often signifies the pains of labor in giving birth.[20] That Paul uses this for himself is not an anomaly in his letters but part of an important metaphor he develops to communicate his role as one who gives birth to new communities of faith. Beverly Roberts Gaventa in her study *Our Mother, Saint Paul* shows that these are not simply variations on his paternal imagery. Paternity for Paul normally focuses on the single act of producing a child,[21] whereas mothering is seen as a long-term

---

20. Rom 8:22; Thrall, *Second Epistle*, 370–71.
21. Phlm 10; 1 Cor 4:15; Phil 2:22; cf. 1 Thess 2:11-12.

process of giving birth and nurture.[22] To the Galatians Paul says, "my children, with whom I am again in labor pains until Christ is formed in you" (Gal 4:19); to the Thessalonians he describes himself as "like a wet nurse nursing her own children" (1 Thess 2:7); and the Corinthians he addresses as "infants in Christ. I gave you milk, not solid food" (1 Cor 3:1-2). Although in 2 Corinthians Paul is speaking of his crying out not to leave this body but to be swallowed up in life, there is an echo of the mother's cry as she keeps going in her indispensable work. How the Corinthians take Paul's maternal stance is, of course, another question. He repeats regularly "everything is for you,"[23] but what may interest them more is his dependency on them, which he hardly conceded in 1 Corinthians but he may now be having to acknowledge.[24]

A second contribution of feminist interpreters of this text has been in developing its links with Romans 8:18-32, where Paul gives voice to creation's crying out in labor pains as it anticipates its liberation. When Paul writes to the Romans from Corinth, probably within some months after 2 Corinthians, he is on his way to Jerusalem and Rome to defend his Gospel among fellow Jews who recognize Jesus as Messiah (Rom 15:14-33). Therefore his persuasion in Romans is very differently configured. But Romans 8 interrupts with a celebration of life in God's Spirit that he could even then be experiencing in Corinth, letting him articulate in a more sustained way than when writing 2 Corinthians how God's Spirit works. Here the same verb for crying out appears with the added prefix συν- ("with, together"), συστενάζω, and this is used with a second verb explicitly referring to a woman's labor pains, with the same prefix: συνωδίνω:

> We know that all creation is crying out together and moaning together in labor pains [συστενάζει καὶ συνωδίνει] right up until now. And not only that, but we ourselves, having the first fruits of the Spirit, are also crying out inwardly, eagerly anticipating adoption, the restoration of our body. (Rom 8:22-23)[25]

22. Beverley Roberts Gaventa, *Our Mother, Saint Paul* (Louisville: Westminster John Knox, 2000); "Our Mother, Saint Paul: Toward the Recovery of a Neglected Theme," in *A Feminist Companion to Paul*, ed. Amy-Jill Levine, FCNTECW 6 (London: T & T Clark, 2004), 85–97.

23. 2 Cor 4:15; see also 1:6, 23; 4:12; 5:13; 6:11, etc. to 13:7-9.

24. 2 Cor 1:11; 3:1-2; 6:13; 7:2; 8:7, 24; 13:9; Rom 15:30-32.

25. Note that although Paul in Romans 8:1-9 has positioned the spirit (πνεῦμα) against the flesh (σάρξ) and its desires, he claims here that when people are adopted in the Spirit the body (σῶμα, singular, possibly collective) is restored, redeemed, bought back from captivity. Paul's metaphors in 2 Corinthians 5 of one house replacing another, adding rather than losing clothing, and being at home rather than in exile seem to be other ways to speak of this work of God's Spirit.

Luzia Sutter Rehmann's study of Romans 8:18-25 exposes the dominant interpretations that ignore the political context of this text and miss the meaning of the birth pains as resistance work.[26] She presents as an alternative to these Luise Schottroff's approach to apocalyptic texts as expressions of a present breakthrough in a people's structural suffering under imperial exploitation. The birth pains indicate the end of passive suffering and the beginning of the work of producing new life. Schottroff identifies this as the *Presswehen* or final pushing stage of birth when the mother is herself engaged in pushing the child out, an all-consuming and often protracted effort. Creation's crying out is this kind of active responding to and participating in a new and hope-filled expectation. The bondage from which the creation seeks freedom is not only physical decay but also violence and destruction, as Sutter Rehmann shows from the broader social meanings of φθορά in the biblical tradition.[27]

When we read Paul's Romans text from an apocalyptic hearing of birthing cries as creation's active claiming of the glory of God (Rom 8:21-23), then this human cry is poorly translated as "waiting." Ἀπεκδέχομαι normally means "eagerly anticipating," and in the context of Romans it is creation's longing for restoration after destruction and captivity (Rom 8:23). So when Paul speaks in 2 Corinthians of crying out under the burden of the tent/body (2 Cor 5:2-4), this will not mean passive sighs but active cries, straining against all obstructions toward the fulfillment of God's creation in the process of which everything subject to destruction and death is swallowed up in life.

Paul's sustained exposition in Romans of God's Spirit also can help us understand 2 Corinthians 5. Anything but passive, the Spirit is God's gift within both creation and its people (Rom 8:9, 23; 2 Cor 5:2-5) that shows they are being adopted as God's own. They know this because the Spirit empowers their common inarticulate cries of expectant labor (Rom 8:22-23) so that they can be heard and welcomed by God (Rom 8:26-27) and receive Christ's life in place of death (Rom 8:2, 11).[28] It is the Creator of whom Paul says in 2 Corinthians, "The one who has made

---

26. Rehmann, *Geh—Frage*, 69–119; Rehmann, "Turning Groaning into Labor," in Levine, *Feminist Companion to Paul*, 74–84.

27. Rom 8:21; Isa 24:3; Mic 2:10; Gal 6:8; Rehmann, *Geh—Frage*, 98–102.

28. Paul's confidence that God's restoring of creation happens in Christ's dying and rising is not restricting salvation to Christians in contrast to Jews or any other people. Paul, the Jew, sees from the revelation he has experienced of the risen Christ that God is remaking all creation and humanity, including anyone outside knowledge of God, hence his wide-open Gentile mission. It is our challenge to hear and interpret this in a pluralistic world.

us for this very thing"—death swallowed up by life—"is God who has given us the Spirit as assurance" (5:5).[29]

For the feminist, traditional Christian concepts of the Spirit have been a challenge. In the Hebrew Bible the Spirit (or "wind," or "breath") from God hovers over the waters before creation (Gen 1:2). As a feminine noun in Hebrew, רוח (spirit) may be personified here hovering over the waters, supporting a translation of the following pronoun in the feminine, that is, God breathes her into human nostrils to give life. Proverbs and Wisdom both identify this presence in creation with a feminine figure called God's Wisdom (Prov 8:22-31; Wis 7:1; 9:9). In Romans 8 "spirit" is used both in a human and a divine sense, evident in the NRSV effort to distinguish the two by capitalizing the divine.[30] This ambiguity seems to rise because Paul understands that humans have spirit in more than one sense, both as the spirit or breath of life given in creation (Gen 2:7) and as the Spirit of God given in Christ. In either case it is God's Spirit that helps them cry out to God, hear and know God, and interpret God's will to others (1 Cor 2:6-16). Yet by the church's fourth century the Spirit was becoming the third person of a triune, unmistakably masculine God who reflected a patriarchal world.

In his correspondence with Corinth Paul articulates his view of the Spirit in response to their practice of spiritual gifts. In 1 Corinthians he characterizes, caricatures, and even competes with the Corinthians' experience of the Spirit in order to instruct them and rein them in.[31] But in 2 Corinthians he reserves his sharp words until the end of the letter and

---

29. The NRSV translates the final word in v. 5 as "guarantee." It is a commercial term signifying that a major payment has already sealed the deal. The translation "down payment" or "first installment" is accurate but threatens to trivialize. Paul also uses a parallel metaphor for the Spirit taken from the temple offering practice of giving the first fruit of a crop or herd, "But we ourselves who have the first fruits of the Spirit cry out internally as we eagerly anticipate adoption" (Rom 8:23). On adoption as sons, see Kathleen E. Corley, "Women's Inheritance Rights in Antiquity and Paul's Metaphor of Adoption," in Levine, *Feminist Companion to Paul*, 98–121.

30. See the NRSV footnotes to "Spirit" in Romans 8, also "spirit" in Romans 8:15-16. Greek manuscripts before the tenth century are written entirely in capital rather than cursive letters, so they do not make this distinction. But early copyists began to abbreviate and mark with a superscribed line various names for God, including πνεῦμα (spirit), yet these marks are not Paul's, nor are they consistent. It may be instructive that this reference to God's Spirit is named from an aspect of what was taken to be human nature, which was in turn thought receptive to God's Spirit. For Paul on the Spirit, see also 1 Cor 2:6-16; 12:1-13; 14:1-5, but also 34-40.

31. 1 Cor 2:6-16; 4:8-10; 12:1–14:39.

repeatedly affirms the Spirit's work in them.[32] Having not persuaded them in 1 Corinthians by warning and instruction, in 2 Corinthians he takes the working of God's Spirit in their spirits as the fruit of his labor and claims their recognition of him on that basis. So in this passage he completes his image of the mortal tent/body's eager crying out to be wrapped up in life by insisting that "God has made us for this very thing" and "has given us the Spirit as assurance" (5:1-5).

Paul's final metaphor for his ambiguous position between life and death—being exiled rather than being at home (5:6-10)—evokes the alienation he feels both from God and from the Corinthians and leads him into recasting salvation as reconciliation (5:19-20). No pull is as strong as that of home, Paul concedes, and he wants to be with the Lord. But he knows that he is walking by faith, not by a visible presence, and he is confident he can live to please God by active anticipation of this reunion (5:7-10). Here the apocalyptic expectation of God's victory over powers of evil and a final righteous judgment appears less as a warning to do good, or even as an assurance to those who suffer evil, than as a foretaste of the longed-for homecoming in God's just creation fully restored. Yet for the Corinthians who are at home in their lively community and not under threat of death, Paul's finding the Spirit in cries of pain and longing may ring false.

32. 2 Cor 1:21-22; 3:2-3, 17-18.

2 Corinthians 5:11-21

A New Creation in Christ That Is Reconciliation

Text and Its Structure (5:11-21)

Here Paul brings his defense to a head. He begins, as before, in explicit self-defense that claims not to be self-defense (5:11-13; see also 3:1-2), attributes his confidence to Christ (5:14-17), attributes Christ to God (5:18-19), and concludes with a direct appeal to the Corinthians (5:20) and a summary statement (5:21). The conjunctions that Paul uses in this argument—γὰρ ("for," 5:13, 14), δὲ ("but," 5:18), and ὡς ὅτι ("that is," 5:19)—trace his commission back to its source in Christ's love and God's reconciliation of the world, providing the backstory of Paul's work in Corinth. Other conjunctions simultaneously point ahead to the purpose or consequences of these events—ἵνα ("so that," 5:12, 15, 21), ἄρα ("therefore," 5:14), ὥστε ("so," 5:16, 17), and οὖν ("so that," 5:20). God's purpose, as the two summary statements show (5:15, 21), is that the living no longer live for themselves but for the dying and rising one and thereby take on God's justice. Paul does not appear here as either the source or the aim of what he does. But by explaining the new creation in Christ as God's act of reconciliation for the purpose of world transformation, Paul presents himself among others as God's representative or instrument: "All this is from God who reconciled himself to us through Christ and has given us the delivery of reconciliation" (5:18).

5:11Therefore, knowing the fear of the Lord, we try to persuade others; but we ourselves are well known to God, and I hope that we are also well known to your consciences. 12We are not commending ourselves to you again, but giving you an opportunity to boast about us, so that you may be able to answer those who boast in outward appearance and not in the heart. 13For if we are beside ourselves, it is for God; if we are in our right mind, it is for you. 14For the love of Christ urges us on, because we are convinced that one has died for all; therefore all have died. 15And he died for all, so that those who live might live no longer for themselves, but for him who died and was raised for them.

16From now on, therefore, we regard no one from a human point of view; even though we once knew Christ from a human point of view, we know him no longer in that way. 17So if anyone is in

A Feminist Lens at Three Ranges on Reconciling with God as a New Creation (5:11-21)

A Broad View of All Bodies Caught between Death and Life, Old and New

If we read the first half of this key passage with the broadest questions about the structure of existence—how life can overcome in spite of death and how anything fully new is possible when the old is so well entrenched—it helps to begin with the concrete words Paul uses to describe the struggle as he faces it. He insists that he and his coworkers are well known both to God and to the Corinthians (πεφανερώμεθα, "we are revealed, wide open, transparent"). They are known not by outward appearance (προσώπῳ, "by face") but from within (ἐν καρδίᾳ, "in the heart"), and not when beside themselves (ἐξέστημεν, "we are ecstatic") but in their right minds (σωφρονοῦμεν, "we make sense"). It is Christ's love, Paul says, that constrains us (συνέχει ἡμᾶς, "holds, presses, or absorbs us"), "having determined that one died for all" (5:14). Dying for all in Paul's world could be heard as a cultic sacrifice to atone for sin, or a martyr's death to rescue a people. But these options do not fit the result that follows: "One died for all so all died." Now Paul hardly makes sense, whatever he claims, since to die for someone would surely mean to save them from dying, not that they should also die.

Fortunately, Paul restates his point, "And he died for all so that those who live might no longer live for themselves but for the one who died for them and was raised" (5:15). So Paul may be speaking metaphorically of a comprehensive change of orientation, from self-orientation to orientation on the one who died for all. Is that what he means by saying

Christ, there is a new creation: everything old has passed away; see, everything has become new! ¹⁸All this is from God, who reconciled us to himself through Christ, and has given us the ministry of reconciliation; ¹⁹that is, in Christ God was reconciling the world to himself, not counting their trespasses against them, and entrusting the message of reconciliation to us. ²⁰So we are ambassadors for Christ, since God is making his appeal through us; we entreat you on behalf of Christ, be reconciled to God. ²¹For our sake he made him to be sin who knew no sin, so that in him we might become the righteousness of God.*

* NRSV notes: 5:16, Gk *according to the flesh* twice for *from a human point of view*; 5:19, Or *God was in Christ reconciling the world to himself.*

that Christ was raised and that they are living? Though Christ's death was surely for Paul an event in past time (aorist tense), it was also more than that if it made possible for people to be transformed. A new structure of life is possible, Paul goes on to claim. "From now on we know nobody in terms of the flesh [κατὰ σάρκα, "from a human point of view" (NRSV); "by worldly standards" (NEB); "by what is external" (Moffatt)], not even Christ himself do we know this way" (5:16). And he celebrates: "So is anyone in Christ? It's a new creation! Everything old is gone! Look, everything has become new!" (5:17).

This raises two questions. First, can it be called a structural transformation if the positive life that comes out of death in Christ is presented only as a possibility for all rather than a completed fact? "He died for all so that those who live might no longer live for themselves. . . . If anyone is in Christ—a new creation!" (5:15, 17; see also Gal 6:15 and Rom 6:3-4). Earlier Paul put it in the future tense: "For just as all die in Adam, so also all will be made alive in Christ" (1 Cor 15:22). And how is the claim that life is given them by a single contemporary person demonstrated by the claim—to us even more improbable—that sin was given them by a single progenitor? Yet we can perhaps settle for Paul's point in our text that all died in one man's death, not by some external change in human nature, but by what the report of a death given for all can do to all, namely, that all die and become open to a life given for all.

This is where Paul introduces the crucial role of the reporters or news carriers, himself and his coworkers in many places (5:18-19). Paul sees the transformation already present in Jesus' death, even to the point that all die, but the new creation awaits the word of a messenger and the response to it that realizes new life. This is the reason that Paul is intent on preaching and "carrying around in his body the dying of Jesus" (4:10), since he takes Jesus' death to be the turning point that has already been accomplished, opening the way to new life for all in Christ.

The second question for us concerns the scope of this new creation that Paul is talking about. The apocalyptic tradition that Paul draws on proclaims a new creation of heaven and earth in the impending future. Comprehensive transformation is also suggested in Paul's word choice. He announces a καινὴ κτίσις (new creation)[1] and speaks not only of new people but broadly of τὰ ἀρχαῖα and καινά (5:17; "old things and new things"; "everything old, everything new" [NRSV]). Within a year Paul will go on to write to Christ followers in Rome that the whole creation cries out in the process of its new birth as it moves from bondage to decay into the freedom and glory of God's progeny (Rom 8:21-23). But to the Corinthians at this point he writes not so much of the process (as in 2 Cor 3:18) as of the present reality—the sheer surprise—of the new creation, accenting this in the clipped syntax of his three short exclamations: A new creation! Old things are gone! Look, new things are happening! (5:17).

So does this announcement of a new creation have eco-structural implications, or is he speaking strictly of the human condition? Paul's focus is on human transformation, interpreters agree.[2] The "all" for whom Christ died who themselves die are οἱ πάντες, "all people." Yet we must not be taken in by the modern bifurcation of humanity on the one side and nature on the opposite side. For Paul, surely, there is one God who creates all things (τὰ πάντα, 1 Cor 8:6), and in Romans he is explicit that even now "the whole creation [πᾶσα ἡ κτίσις] cries out in labor pains" to be released from its bondage to corruption (Rom 8:22-23). When Paul in 2 Corinthians proclaims a new creation in Christ (ἐν Χριστῷ καινὴ κτίσις) who dies for all people so that all die, he speaks of something that has implications beyond one species. The problem Paul has posed is death,

---

1. Though some have argued that κτίσις ("creation") here must mean the human creature because the sentence begins "if anyone is in Christ," Furnish counters on the basis of Romans 1:20, 25 and 8:19-22 that κτίσις means the whole creation, though he concedes it can be used to refer to a part of the creation (τις κτίσις ἑτέρα, "any other creature," Rom 8:39). See Victor Paul Furnish, *II Corinthians*, AB 32A (Garden City, NY: Doubleday, 1984), 314–15.

2. Reimund Bieringer and Jan Lambrecht, *Studies on 2 Corinthians*, BETL 112 (Leuven: Leuven University Press, 1994), 429–59; David G. Horrell, "Ecojustice in the Bible? Pauline Contributions to an Ecological Theology," in *Bible and Justice: Ancient Texts, Modern Challenges*, ed. Matthew J. M. Coomber (London: Equinox, 2011), 164–72; Jan Lambrecht, *Second Corinthians*, SP 8 (Collegeville, MN: Liturgical Press, 1999), 97.

not yet specifically sin,[3] and a death that all living things share in a way far more integrated with each other than Paul may realize. David Horrell concludes that our awakening to the ecological crisis makes it possible for us to reread Paul constructively and carry further his grasp of God's whole creation and our human responsibility within it.[4]

A Mid-Range Focus on the Social, Political, and Economic Setting of Paul's Argument

Because Paul is speaking here of what has driven him and others to spread the news of Christ, the social context in which he works is not explicitly described. But the way he presents his message draws on the two major cultures he shares and betrays his social location within them—specifically in Greek-speaking Israel and in the Roman east. And because politics is the exercise of negotiating power in social relations and economics is the system of material production that supports this, each context suggests certain political and economic implications.

Israel is the dominant tradition from which Paul draws the concept of a "new creation," particularly from its prophetic and apocalyptic voices, but also its wisdom traditions.[5] Second Isaiah (Isa 40–55), known to Paul primarily through the Greek Old Testament (LXX), challenges the exiles of Judah that God is about to do a new thing and bring them through the desert back to their own land (see sidebar: "A New Thing Now"). And when the people become disillusioned Third Isaiah repeats "do not remember the former things" and extends the promise of God's creating from a new earth to new heavens and from a restored Jerusalem to "all flesh" (Isa 65:17-18, 21-22a; 66:22-23). Some apocalyptic writers have visions of a new communal future already prepared in heaven or a new

---

3. The noun "sin" (ἁμαρτία) appears only three times in 2 Corinthians: in 5:21 twice as he incorporates the broader tradition in his summary statement, and in 11:7. Also "world" is not a negative term in this letter as 5:19 shows, and "death" must carry the negative weight. On these terms, see Edward Adams' *Constructing the World: A Study of Paul's Cosmological Language* (Edinburgh: T & T Clark, 2000), 232–37.

4. Horrell, "Ecojustice," 172–77; David G. Horrell, Cherryl Hunt, and Christopher Southgate, *Greening Paul: Reading Paul in a Time of Ecological Crisis* (Waco, TX: Baylor University Press, 2010), 117–87.

5. On the background of Paul's understanding of a new creation, see the comprehensive study of Ulrich Mell, *Neue Schöpfung: Eine traditionsgeschichtliche und exegetische Studie zu einem soteriologischen Grundsatz paulinischer Theologie* (Berlin: de Gruyter, 1989); also Margaret E. Thrall, *A Critical and Exegetical Commentary on the Second Epistle to the Corinthians*, ICC (Edinburgh: T & T Clark, 1994), 421–29.

heaven to come contrasted with the present earth.[6] Paul retains this confidence in communal new life but sees it with Second Isaiah as already beginning in God's present transformation that is good news for all.

> *A New Thing Now*
>
> Do not remember the former
> things,
> or consider the things of old.
> I am about to do a new thing;
> now it springs forth, do you not
> perceive it?
> I will make a way in the
> wilderness
> and rivers in the desert.
>
> The wild animals will honor me,
> the jackals and the ostriches;
> for I give water in the
> wilderness,
> rivers in the desert,
> to give drink to my chosen people,
> the people whom I formed for
> myself
> so that they might declare my
> praise. (Isa 43:18-21)

In Paul's first-century context, before Israel's hopes for political agency are defeated in two revolts and the rabbis shift the focus onto family Torah obedience, there is still space to speak of a new creation in communal life that shapes all people. This kind of optimism also appears in diaspora Judaism's historical novel about Aseneth, the wife of Joseph mentioned in passing in Genesis 41:45.[7] In this Hellenistic-Jewish historical novel she is an Egyptian priest's daughter who undergoes a radical conversion and, after seven days of repenting her idol worship in sackcloth and ashes, receives a heavenly visitor who announces her transformation. He renames her "City of Refuge" because many nations will take refuge in God through her. He gives her the honeycomb of life, saying, "Behold, you have eaten the bread of life and drunk a cup of immortality and been anointed with ointment of incorruptibility . . . and you shall be like a walled mother-city of all who take refuge with the

---

6. Jub. 1:29; Rev 21:1; 2 Pet 3:11-13; and see sidebar below, "A New Heaven and a New Earth," from 1 Enoch and *Biblical Antiquities*.

7. Mell, *Neue Schöpfung*, 226–57; for an extended version of the ancient text called "Joseph and Aseneth," see James H. Charlesworth, ed., *Old Testament Pseudepigrapha*, 2 vols. (Garden City, NY: Doubleday, 1983 and 1985), 2:202–47; for the shorter, probably earlier text in Greek and French, see Marc Philonenko, *Joseph et Aseneth* (Leiden: Brill, 1968); for further analysis, see Angela Standhartinger, *Das Frauenbild im Judentum der hellenistischen Zeit* (Leiden: Brill, 1995), and Ross Shepard Kraemer, *When Aseneth Met Joseph: A Late Antique Tale of the Biblical Patriarch and His Egyptian Wife, Reconsidered* (New York: Oxford University Press, 1998).

name of the Lord God" (*Confession and Prayer of Aseneth* 16.16; see sidebar on pages 94–95). This story indicates that the social world of Israel that Paul shares is broader than its prophetic and apocalyptic voices and also produces popular wisdom traditions. As in Israel's wisdom writings, Paul does not expect God's new creation to wipe out God's creation of this world but to make it over anew.

While the news that "one died for all, so all died" is indeed new in Israel, Paul makes sense of it within the experiences and expectations of his people.[8] Immediately after exclaiming about the new creation, he announces twice that it is all God's doing (5:18, 19). And to make clear that this is no new god but the same Creator and Rescuer who has challenged Israel from the start, he incorporates an early tradition, "not counting their offenses against them" (5:19), and ends with a summary that explains the power of Jesus' death to make life in terms of an exchange of sin for righteousness.[9] Paul may be the first to call life in Christ a "new creation," as several interpreters suggest,[10] but the phrase simply shows that these early Christ communities were a part—if a marginal one—of diaspora Second Temple Judaism where God's "new heaven and new earth" was anticipated (see sidebar: "A New Heaven and a New Earth").

A New Heaven and a New Earth

But when the years appointed for the world have been fulfilled, then the light will cease and the darkness will fade away. And I will bring the dead to life and raise up those who are sleeping from the earth . . . so that I may render to each according to his works. . . . And the world will cease, and death will be abolished and hell will shut its mouth. And the earth will not be without progeny or sterile for those inhabiting it; and no one who has been pardoned by me will be tainted. And there will be another earth and another heaven, an everlasting dwelling

---

8. Thrall offers six options for reading "all died" and herself thinks Paul understands it parallel to universal sin in Adam (*Second Epistle*, 409–11).

9. Ernst Käsemann proposed that with 5:19-21 Paul was quoting Christian tradition, due to such matters as the opening ὡς ὅτι that can be translated "as it is said," the plural word for sins while Paul prefers the singular, and the periphrastic verb unusual for Paul ("Some Thoughts on the 'Doctrine of Reconciliation,'" in *The Future of Our Religious Past*, ed. J. M. Robinson [New York: Harper and Row, 1971], 52–57). Others reduce the quote to 19ab (Furnish, *II Corinthians*, 334–35), and Thrall considers traditional allusions are more likely (Thrall, *Second Epistle*, 445–49).

10. Furnish, *II Corinthians*, 314–15; Thrall, *Second Epistle*, 424–29.

place[11] (*Biblical Antiquities* 3.10). There shall be the eternal judgment; and it shall be executed by the angels of the eternal heaven—the great (judgment) which emanates from all of the angels. The first heaven shall depart and pass away; a new heaven shall appear; and all the powers of heaven shall shine forever sevenfold. (1 Enoch 91.16)[12]

Distinctive to Paul in this context is his proclamation that the anticipated new world is already accomplished in Christ's death for all, so that all have died, even, it seems, those not yet knowing this. All that is lacking is that people receive the news, and this, Paul completes his argument, is the task of those who have heard, specifically himself and his coworkers. That the repenting Gentile is welcome is nothing new in Israel. The proselyte is the one called a new creation in the rabbis' writings, as with Aseneth. But now "one died for all so all died," Jews included, and Paul is ready to take the role of messenger, "carrying around Jesus' dying in the body" (4:10), and, it seems, ready to recognize the consequent appearance of Jesus' life in the Corinthians.

Politically, this means that the most important power negotiations for Paul are those within the people of Israel, and specifically among the "saints," as he calls those in Christ. But can he amass sufficient evidence that God transforms all through the death of Jesus to convince God's people Israel that Christ's life has power through those who tell and exhibit his death? This letter aims more modestly to persuade Christ believers in Corinth of this. By affirming their life in Christ, he claims recognition of Christ's death in him and thereby of God's reconciliation of the world through those who have been reconciled. Yet his accompanying economic agenda appears to threaten his success in Corinth. He is collecting funds for the poor in Jerusalem, which could reconcile Christ believers there with Paul's mission, and at the same time he is refusing in Corinth personal gifts for his own support that would make him dependent on them. Though Paul's aims are more explicit in other chapters, in this letter, where he defends his plans, Titus's mission, and the collection, his "one died for all so all died" followed by "all this is from God" identify the event of Christ's death and its universal significance as God's action to be foundational for Israel's political and economic life.

11. *Pseudo-Philo/Biblical Antiquities* 3.10, trans. Daniel J. Harrington, in Charlesworth, *Old Testament Pseudepigrapha*, 2:307.

12. 1 En. 91.16, trans. E. Isaac, in Charlesworth, *Old Testament Pseudepigrapha*, 1:73.

The imperial political context surfaces in 2 Corinthians 5:11-21 at three points at least: in Paul's universal claims of a "new creation," in his naming God's act in Christ "reconciliation," and in his calling himself "envoy" or "ambassador." In each case Paul uses arguments on behalf of Christ that are current in Roman defense of its power.[13] Although there is no alternative to speaking in the language and cultural concepts of one's time, the question arises whether Paul has been coopted by imperial thinking or whether he successfully destabilizes the imperial way of making these power claims so as to offer a distinct, or even contrary, grasp of what effective power is.

In this text it is particularly his announcement of a new creation in Christ that parallels the claim of a new age for all peoples that was made on behalf of Rome's emperors. In monumental art, inscriptions, literature, and coins, Augustus Caesar (31 BCE–14 CE) was heralded everywhere as the sign of a new world order, all the more after his death when succeeding emperors traced their authority to *Divus Augustus* (divine Augustus). In 9 BCE the cities of Asia Minor announced the "good news" of a new age that had begun from his birthday (see sidebar: "Proclamation of Augustus's Birthday"), and Virgil's Fourth Eclogue was sung to herald Augustus's arrival as the golden age.[14] Augustan propaganda often downplayed Roman military domination and highlighted the peace, prosperity, and good order of all people under his care (see figure 1, Earth Goddess bas relief at the *Ara Pacis* [Altar of Peace]).[15] The character of the "new creation" that Paul proclaims may be closer to the visions of Israel's apocalyptic seers and wisdom teachers,[16] but its present arrival provoking shouts of universal celebration is closer to the sound of Roman crowds welcoming the emperor or to the good news of his birthday decreed by provincial assemblies.

13. T. Ryan Jackson, *New Creation in Paul's Letters: A Study in the Historical and Social Setting of a Pauline Concept*, WUNT 2.272 (Tübingen: Mohr Siebeck, 2010), 60–80, 115–49; J. Albert Harrill, *Paul the Apostle: His Life and Legacy in Their Roman Context* (Cambridge: Cambridge University Press, 2012), 76–94.

14. *Documents and Images for the Study of Paul*, ed. Neil Elliott and Mark Reasoner (Minneapolis: Fortress, 2011), 110–11; *Eclogues. Aeneid*: Books 1–6, trans. H. Rushton Fairclough, rev. G. P. Gould, Virgil, vol. 1 (Cambridge, MA: Harvard University Press, 1916).

15. On the altar built by Augustus the life-size relief carving of the Goddess of Peace or Mother Earth is surrounded by infants and animals signifying fertility, peace, and prosperity. See the illustration on the next page. Yet on the opposite side of the altar there seems to be a surviving fragment of the Goddess Roma in military regalia (Paul Zanker, *The Power of Images in the Age of Augustus* [Ann Arbor: University of Michigan Press, 1988], pp. 120–23, 167–79, figs. 126, 135, 136).

16. See the thorough history of these new creation traditions in Ulrich Mell's *Neue Schöpfung*.

Figure 1. The Earth Mother Tellus or the Goddess of Peace in a garden with nursing babies and gazing animals, flanked by the *aurae*, winds blowing rain on the land (left) and transport on the sea (right). The upper left panel bas relief at the entrance of the *Ara Pacis* in Rome, constructed in 9–13 CE to honor victories of Augustus Caesar. Alinari Archive, Florence.

Proclamation of Augustus's Birthday as the Gospel of a New Era

Whereas the Providence (πρόνοια) which has guided our whole existence and which has shown such care and liberality has brought our life to the peak of perfection in giving to us [the emperor] Augustus, whom it filled with virtue (ἀρετή) for the welfare of humanity, and who, being sent to us and to our descendants as a savior (σωτήρ), has put an end to war and has set all things in order; and [whereas], having become manifest, Caesar has fulfilled all the hopes of earlier times . . . not only in surpassing all the benefactors (εὐεργέται) who preceded him but also in leaving to his successors no hope of surpassing him; and whereas, finally, that the birthday of the God [Augustus] has been for the whole world the beginning of the good news/ gospel (εὐαγγέλιον) concerning him, [therefore, let a new era begin from his birth, and let his birthday mark the beginning of the new year].[17]

Yet it is Christ's love expressed in his "death for all" that is distinctive in Paul's particular expression of a new creation (5:14). Although the cross, which was the means of Roman execution, is not stressed in 2 Corinthians as it is in Galatians and 1 Corinthians, death for others is explicit and may signify for Paul, as in Jewish martyrdom stories, a witness in face of occupying foreign rulers.[18] We cannot dismiss the political implications in Paul's claim of Christ's death for all by making a narrow cultic interpretation in terms of atonement for sin before God. In fact, Paul completes "one died for all" with "all died," not with "so others would not die." Christ's death evokes the believer's own death to self and life "for the one who died and was raised" (5:14-15), accomplishing not substitution but participation or representation.[19] And when Paul goes on to say that this new creation in Christ's death and rising

17. *Priene Inscription*, 9 BCE in *Ancient Roman Religion*, ed. and trans. F. C. Grant (New York: Liberal Arts Press, 1957), 174, followed by other examples. The Priene inscription is also cited in David R. Cartlidge and David L. Dungan, *Documents for the Study of the Gospels* (Cleveland: Collins, 1989), 13–14.

18. 2 Macc 6–7; 4 Macc 4:15–12:19; 17:17-22.

19. A. J. M. Wedderburn, "2 Cor 5:14—A Key to Paul's Soteriology," in *Paul and the Corinthians: Studies of a Community in Conflict*, ed. Trevor J. Burke and J. Keith Elliott, NovTSup 109 (Leiden: Brill, 2003), 267–83; Michael J. Gorman, *Becoming the Gospel: Paul, Participation, and Mission* (Grand Rapids, MI: Eerdmans, 2015), 247–49; Mell, *Neue Schöpfung*, 342–63.

Figure 2. The emperor, center, crowned by Senate or Goddess Roma, is holding the victory trophy over a conquered suppliant. One panel of the Sebasteion, a double stoa honoring the emperors in the Asia Minor city of Aphrodisias. New York University Excavation at Aphrodisias (G. Petrucioli).

is "from God" who is "reconciling the world to himself" (5:18-19), the claim of transformation in Christ is made universal. Though not directly contrasted with imperial claims, it cannot be made compatible with them. The emerging conflict with what becomes in Paul's century the cult of emperor worship is more sharply framed in the later letters of Colossians and Ephesians and is explicit, if in visionary language, in Revelation.[20]

In addition to a universal claim, Paul adopts in his reconciliation metaphor an image of the world at enmity with its rightful ruler. On Roman-era coins and bas reliefs we see conquered "barbarians" on their knees before the emperor, pleading for mercy and reconciliation (see figure 2, Emperor crowned by Roman Senate or the Goddess Roma with captive kneeling). In exceptional cases the emperor might favor with clemency some who had fought against Roman legions in order to display his magnanimity. When Paul uses the term καταλλάσσω (reconcile) for what God does in Christ, he could be comparing it to a family conflict that is overcome (see 1 Cor 7:11), but he more likely draws on the image of warfare that is overcome in peace, as he does later in Romans 5:10: "If when we were enemies we were reconciled to God through the death of his son, how much more will we who are reconciled be saved in his life." Some interpreters propose that Paul is influenced by Hellenistic Jewish texts that speak of God finally becoming reconciled with his people.[21] What is clear is that Paul reverses the standard expectation, also among Jews, that the offending party sends envoys to sue for peace. Paul announces that it is God, the rightful ruler, who sends envoys to seek reconciliation with an alienated creation.[22] So the highest virtue of the emperor to grant clemency to enemies who sue for peace is superseded by Paul's God who offers reconciliation to those who have never claimed it.

For Paul, all that is lacking to realize new life is news of this event, and here he draws on practices of Hellenistic and Roman diplomacy. Envoys are sent representing the ruler to inform people of the conditions for peace. Paul presents those who have been reconciled with God—himself

---

20. Col 1:15-20; Eph 1:20-23; Rev 13:1-18; 18:1–19:10.

21. 2 Macc 7:33; 8:29; Thrall, *Second Epistle*, 429–30; Cilliers Breytenbach, *Grace, Reconciliation, Concord: The Death of Christ in Graeco-Roman Metaphors* (Leiden: Brill, 2010), 177.

22. Brytenbach, *Grace, Reconciliation, Concord*, 171–205; John T. Fitzgerald, "Paul and Paradigm Shifts: Reconciliation and Its Linkage Groups," in *Beyond the Judaism/ Hellenism Divide*, ed. Troels Engberg-Pedersen (Louisville: Westminster John Knox, 2001), 241–62.

and his coworkers—as ambassadors or envoys of God's unconditional reconciliation of the world (5:18-19). Because the Greek verb Paul uses for their task, πρεσβεύομαι ("I act as elder," "I represent"), appears in nominal form in some inscriptions for the Latin term *legatus*—a representative appointed by the emperor with full authority to carry out a specific, usually military, task[23]—Margaret Thrall concludes that this "image enhances the dignity of the apostolic office."[24] And Margaret Mitchell notes that Paul begins as a prisoner in God's triumph and ends in "a traveling parade of Christ's ambassador."[25] But πρεσβεύομαι is a broad term for an appointed representative or envoy, and Paul uses it as a verb and in the plural, not just for himself or in any relation to his being an apostle. In contrast to the English noun "ambassador," which implies at least in the United States a single figurehead for one nation located in another nation, this verb signifies representation for any specific task. Granted that Paul is claiming a certain authority by using this term from Greco-Roman diplomatic practice, he claims it as a responsibility of those who have been reconciled to carry the message of God's reconciliation (5:18-20).

So in at least these three ways—the universal claim, the image of military reconciliation, and the role of representative or ambassador—Paul uses language and concepts with which the Roman Empire claims power in order to defend his claims, while in each case distinguishing the power he defends from theirs. A new creation has come for all people, not through Rome's might or for an inner circle of the empire, but through Christ's death. Reconciliation with the world ruler has come, not by the pleas of captives begging for the emperor's clemency, but by God's initiative to reconcile the world to God's self in Christ's faithfulness that leads to his death. The ambassadors or, better, representatives who have been given authority to carry the news are not from the senatorial ranks but from those who themselves have been reconciled, whose witness makes their word believable. Nevertheless, because Roman power permeates first-century Corinth—refounded as a Roman colony by Julius Caesar and functioning as Rome's provincial

---

23. G. Adolf Deissmann, *Light from the Ancient East: The New Testament Illustrated by Recently Discovered Texts of the Graeco-Roman World* (New York: Hodder and Stoughton, 1910), 379, citing David Magie, *De Romanorum iuris publici* (Leipzig: Tuebner, 1905), 86–89.

24. Thrall, *Second Epistle*, 437.

25. Margaret M. Mitchell, "The Corinthian Correspondence and the Birth of Pauline Hermeneutics," in Burke and Elliott, *Paul and the Corinthians*, 29–30.

capital of Achaea with Roman city government and Roman monumental construction—Paul's power claims may be heard and his countercultural qualifications missed, all the more so because Paul's defense
requires that he assert himself.

A Close-up of Paul's Interaction with the Corinthians, Especially the Women

Aware of Paul's systemic claims and his social-political setting above,
I focus on Paul's argument as one stage in his interaction with a particular group in Corinth, which is known in other documents to contend
for wisdom and to include active women.[26] How does the way Paul
tries to persuade these people also show us something of their previous
approaches to him, their probable reactions to this argument, and his
possible responses in turn?[27] Though a narrow view of proof excludes
such proposals about a document as speculative, in the case of a letter
the specific address is a given, and the letter's meaning cannot be understood without making assumptions, articulated or not, about the human
interaction within which its writing takes place. Due to the importance
of this passage in Paul's 2 Corinthians argument, I will take up each of
its four units in turn, following my own translation.

> So knowing we are accountable to the Lord we do persuade people,
> but we are transparent to God, and I trust also transparent to your
> consciences. It is not that we are commending ourselves to you again,
> but we are giving you a starting point for taking pride in us, so that

---

26. 1 Cor 1:17-31; 7; 11:2-16; 14:26-37; 1 Clement 11–12; 21; 44–49; 54–56.

27. See here Christine Gerber's caution that the letter must be read as an argument
shaped for a single situation not our own (*Paulus, Apostolat und Autorität, oder vom
Lesen fremder Briefe* [Zürich: Theologischer Verlag Zürich, 2012], 9–18), and Melanie
Johnson DeBaufre and Laura S. Nasrallah's aim to read Paul's letters as "sites of
vision and debate" and contested space by "privileging the ancient communities to
which Paul wrote" ("Beyond the Heroic Paul: Toward a Feminist Decolonizing Approach to the Letters of Paul," in *The Colonized Apostle: Paul through Postcolonial Eyes*,
ed. Christopher Stanley [Minneapolis: Fortress, 2011], 161–74). Bieringer analyzes
at length the relation between Paul and the Corinthians as Paul sees it, but he does
not ask how the Corinthians might see it (*Studies on 2 Corinthians*, 173–79, 197–226,
246–51). Hans Frör does provide in detail the responses of various Corinthians to
Paul, though sometimes taking Paul's critiques of them as objective characterizations
(*You Wretched Corinthians! The Correspondence between the Church in Corinth and Paul*
[London: SCM, 1995]).

you can deal with those who take pride in appearances and not in the heart. As for us, if we were out of our minds, it was for God, but if we are in our right minds, it is for you. (5:11-13)

As after each time Paul affirms in this letter what God is doing, he returns here again to defending himself. Since he and his coworkers are accountable to Christ's judgment for whatever they do (5:10), they know they are transparent to God and, Paul trusts, also to the Corinthians.[28] On this basis they have been bold to persuade people, though some might consider this presumptuous (Gal 1:10). And if it sounds like they make too much of themselves, Paul claims he does this only to show the Corinthians how to defend him and his colleagues against people who boast in the way they look and not in who they are. If this is a defense against Corinthian charges, they do find him presumptuous rather than inspiring, but he insists on reserving his ecstasies for times with God (5:13; 1 Cor 14:18-19) and on claiming authority from the news he carries rather than from his transforming experiences—though not denying he has them (2 Cor 12:1-10). Paul does not identify which factions in Corinth hold these views or whether women are leaders among those who do. But the fact that Paul's effort in 1 Corinthians to restrict women occurs at the beginning and at the climax of his reining in expressive conduct in worship (1 Cor 11:2-16; 14:34-35) suggests that he could be responding here to their continuing activity of this kind. In any case he is no longer laying down restrictions on them but has recognized his own vulnerability and defends himself as being down-to-earth and in his right mind among them.

> For Christ's love constrains us, since we have judged that one died for all so all died. And he died for all so that those who live might no longer live for themselves but for the one who died for them and was raised. So from now on we ourselves know nobody according to the flesh. Even if we knew Christ according to the flesh, we know him this

28. Ἐλπίζω (I hope) signifies for Paul not an anxious longing, as we often use the term, but a steady confidence, hence my translation "trust." (See Scott J. Hafemann, *Paul, Moses, and the History of Israel: The Letter/Spirit Contrast and the Argument from Scripture in 2 Corinthians 3* [Tübingen: J. C. B. Mohr (Paul Siebeck), 1995], 337.) Paul understands the συνείδησις (conscience) as a positive moral compass in human nature that functions for Gentiles parallel to the law for those in Israel (Rom 2:15; 13:5) (Margaret E. Thrall, "The Pauline Use of ΣΥΝΕΙΔΗΣΙΣ," *NTS* 14 [1967]: 118–25; *Second Epistle*, 131–33).

way no longer. So if anyone is in Christ—a new creation! What's old is
gone—look, what's new has come! (5:14-17)

Paul here shifts out of the direct address of "we" speaking to "you"
and begins to speak as "we" concerning "all" and finally "anyone." This
paragraph gives us an explanation (γὰρ, for; 5:14) of why Paul persists in
persuading people (5:11), namely, because he is constrained to do so by
the love of Christ. Interpreters agree that Paul means Christ's love for all
rather than Paul's love for Christ. Yet if Paul is constrained by Christ's
love, it also motivates him.[29] Would some in Corinth prefer him to let up
and leave space for other persons or interpretations? His own judgment
about what happened is radical—that "one died for all so all died," a
categorical impact on humanity later explained by Paul as God's way of
overcoming sin (Rom 5:5–6:11). But here Paul speaks in terms that may
be of greater concern to Corinth: death or life, shame or glory. The failure
or death that one person experienced for all others was a failure or death
of all people. None escape. This is presented as an accomplished fact,
whether Paul conceives the death of all as a natural death[30] due to being
implicated in violence since Adam or a metaphorical death of the self-
oriented and destructive personal or communal identity. It follows that
all people, including Christ, no longer are to be known "in terms of the
flesh" (5:16), which may mean according to earthly descent, or judging
by externals, or living for oneself and being vulnerable to failure (5:16).
Those who no longer live for themselves are "in Christ," since the death
that comes by all participating in Christ's death has allowed a new life
in God's raising Christ from the dead.

It has been proposed that Paul may have been the first to identify life
in Christ as the new creation that was anticipated in the prophets and in
apocalyptic Judaism.[31] His exclamation here does sound like a discovery: "If anyone is in Christ—a new creation! What's old has gone. Look,

29. The verb συνέχω is normally restrictive: "hold together," "constrain." Yet Bouttier argues following Deissmann that Paul's "love of Christ" means not only Christ's
love of all but also a responding human love of Christ and others (a simultaneous
subjective and objective genitive), so that life "in Christ" can be characterized as
"Christusliebe" (Christ-love) and functions to motivate as well as constrain (Michel
Bouttier, *En Christ, Étude d'exégèse et de théologie pauliniennes* [Paris: Presses Universitaires de France, 1962], 69–73; Adolf Diessmann, *Paul: A Study in Social and Religious
History*, from the German 2nd ed. 1925 [New York: Harper Brothers, 1957], 161–64).

30. See James D. G. Dunn, *The Theology of Paul the Apostle* (Grand Rapids, MI:
Eerdmans, 1998), 210–11.

31. Isa 42:5-16; 43:18-21; Ezek 36:26-30.

what's new has come!" (5:17). Yet what is unique to Paul may rather be its universal prerequisite that was accomplished in Christ's death—"and all died." It is possible that claims of a new creation in Christ were already present in the Corinthian community. They knew through Paul the tradition of a new covenant in Christ's blood (1 Cor 11:25), and they were the ones Paul once mocked, "Already you have eaten your fill! Already you are rich! Without us you have become kings!" (1 Cor 4:8). But Christ's death was not prominent in their claims, either as the prime evidence of Christ's love or as the turning point of human transformation. In contrast Paul wrote of his work in Corinth, "I decided to know nothing among you but Jesus Christ and him crucified" (1 Cor 2:2).

If the Corinthians already claimed transformation, even possibly "a new creation," in Christ's living presence, then Paul is here conceding the transformation they claim, celebrating it even, yet in a way bound firmly to and rising out of the death that Christ "died for all, so all died" (2 Cor 5:14). In order to defend his own and his coworkers' mission of "carrying around in the body the dying of Jesus" (2 Cor 4:10), he affirms that the life of Christ is becoming visible in this mission, particularly in the Corinthians, its flower: "So death is a work in us, but life in you" (4:12); "You are our letter [of recommendation]" (3:2). I suggest that this might have opened up a channel of communication between Paul and the Corinthians, if they could make sense of his conviction that they participate through him in Christ's death where "all died" and if he could sustain his openness to their creative expressions of the resulting "new creation."

> And all this is from God who has reconciled us to God's self through Christ and has given us the task of delivering reconciliation. That is, God was in Christ reconciling the world to God's self, not counting their offenses against them, and placing in us the news of reconciliation. (5:18-19)

Here Paul's argument comes to a head in two ways that reveal the interchange between him and the Corinthians. First, he coins the term "reconciliation" as a way to speak of God's work in Christ, and he does this out of his own experience of alienation from the Corinthians. Second, he exposes the breadth of his first-person plural speech to include them as both reconciled and reconcilers. How do these either respond to the Corinthians or provoke their response to him?

First, these two verses, which are one sentence in Greek, apparently describe for the first time the saving act of God in Christ as a reconciling of the alienated. Most verbs Paul uses to describe what God does in Christ appear in earlier and broader traditions about Christ—to save, redeem, justify, sanctify. But for God to take the initiative to reconcile God's self with people appears in the New Testament only here and soon after in Paul's Romans 5:10-11 and 11:15. Yet a number of interpreters contend that God's reconciling the world cannot be Paul's new coinage because he immediately refers to God's not counting offenses in a way unusual for him that suggests he is quoting Christian preaching.[32] Yet he may be quoting only a few words. In fact, Paul's constant melding of tradition and innovation points to him adopting here a phrase about sins not being counted to tie his image of reconciling in with other more cultic interpretations of Christ. Most interesting, the appearance of reconciliation language at just this point in Paul's letters suggests that it is Paul's extended alienation from the Corinthians and his deep desire for reconciliation with them that has made him sensitive to the reconciling aspect of what God does in Christ.[33] Breytenbach says that Paul's own appeals for reconciliation with the Corinthians in 6:11-12 and 7:2-4 constitute "the real point of the apostle's earlier exhortation to be reconciled to God."

Second, Christ's dying and rising are identified as "from God who has reconciled us" so as to make "us" participants not only in Christ's death and life but also in the act of reconciliation that God is doing. This sentence exposes the broadest extent of Paul's first-person plural speech. Its first half must include the Corinthians in Paul's "to us"; indeed all people are potentially included according to his just previous "one died for all so all died" (5:14). It follows that the second half of the same sentence about God's having given "us" the task of reconciliation describes not only Paul and his colleagues but all who are reconciled being given the delivery of reconciliation. Interpreters agree that Paul's "us" for the reconciled includes the Corinthians, but they differ about whether Paul takes them to be reconcilers. Robin Griffith-Jones says that the Corinthians would never understand this to include themselves. Margaret Thrall says the

32. See note 9 above.
33. Fitzgerald, "Paul and Paradigm Shifts," 257; also Furnish, *II Corinthians*, 334–37; Lambrecht, *Second Corinthians*, 104–6; J.-F. Collange, *Énigmes de la Deuxième épitre de Paul aux Corinthiens: Étude exégétique de 2 Cor. 2:14–7:4* (Cambridge: Cambridge University Press, 1972), 269, 273–75, 280; Gerber, *Apostolat und Autorität*, 74–75; Thrall, *Second Epistle*, 438; Riita Särkiö, "Die Versöhnung mit Gott—und mit Paulus: Zur Bedeutung der Gemeindesituation in Korinth für 2 Kor 5,14-21," *ST* 52 (1998): 33–34; Breytenbach, *Grace, Reconciliation, Concord*, 174–75.

Corinthians and all believers are included in the reconciled but not in the reconcilers. J.-F. Collange says the plural reference in both clauses must be kept open—Paul and the Corinthians are taken both as reconciled and reconcilers, but the Corinthians are emphasized in Paul's first point and he in the second. And Victor Furnish and Walter Rebell insist that Paul's plural pronoun be read consistently so that all reconciled become reconcilers.[34] I take Paul's point here to be that the new creation in Christ is God's doing, both "our" reconciliation and "our" having the task of reconciling. Spoken by Paul to the Corinthians, this challenges them to see each other both receiving and transmitting what God is doing.

It is Paul's next sentence that begins to distinguish roles as he broadens the scope of God's reconciling in Christ to "the world" and focuses on messengers such as Timothy, Silas, and himself in whom God has placed the λόγος (word, news) of reconciliation. Here I sense Paul is shifting back to defending the work he and his colleagues have been doing. Unlike in 1 Corinthians where Paul tried to shape the Corinthians' understanding of how to participate in Christ, here in 2 Corinthians he does not develop further their place as reconcilers but returns to persuading them of his necessary place in their new creation in Christ. It is not that he ignores them but that he recognizes what they want from him is not instruction but recognition, and within that he wants to show them how he fits in to their positive experience of Christ.

The question not broached by interpreters is what God's reconciling the world might have meant to the Corinthians, whether their alienation from Paul also disturbed them or whether they took his appeal for reconciliation as Paul's effort to regain authority over them. In what might be seen as a parallel move to Paul's, the United Presbyterian Church of the United States of America, in writing the Confession of 1967, chose to express its faith in terms of God's reconciliation in Christ because its leaders were struggling with the alienation between races and regions in the United States. Fifteen years later this confession was criticized because it assumed that the alienated wanted reconciliation in Christ

34. Robin Griffith-Jones, "Turning to the Lord: Vision, Transformation and Paul's Agenda in 2 Corinthians 1–8," in *Theologizing in the Corinthians Conflict: Studies in the Exegesis and Theology of 2 Corinthians*, ed. Reimund Bieringer, Ma. Marilou S. Ibita, Dominika A. Kurek-Chomycz, and Thomas A. Vollmer, BTS 16 (Leuven: Peeters, 2013) 276–79; Thrall, *Second Epistle*, 430–31; Collange, *Énigmes*, 268–69 and 269 n.1; Furnish, *II Corinthians*, 317; Walter Rebell, *Gehorsam und Unabhängigkeit. Eine sozialpsychologische Studie zu Paulus* (Münich: Christian Kaiser, 1986), 64–66.

when it was liberation they wanted.[35] The very fact that Paul feels himself alienated from the Corinthians and seeks their positive response suggests that they do not share his sentiment. Yet because Paul seeks reconciliation and depicts God seeking reconciliation, he must offer in exchange something that the Corinthians do want, namely, the recognition that they are not simply receivers of the good that God gives but, like Paul and his colleagues, are also channels of God's gifts and transmitters of the news of reconciliation in an alienated world.

> Therefore we are representatives on Christ's behalf as God makes the appeal through us. We plead on Christ's behalf, "Be reconciled to God!" The one who did not know sin God made sin for our sakes, so that we might embody God's justice in him. (5:20-21)

It may be in response to Corinthian doubts about reconciliation with him that Paul returns to focus on his role among them. He expresses it in a first-person plural verb, πρεσβεύομεν, literally, "we act as elders or representatives,"[36] sent by God to speak for Christ. And here Paul simultaneously explains what he does and does what he explains by challenging them, "Be reconciled to God." Reimund Bieringer argues that the verb here should be read as a deponent with a reflexive meaning, "Reconcile yourselves to God," calling for human participation in this act.[37] Margaret Thrall is doubtful that Paul means a mutual reconciliation of humans and God. Yet all agree that Paul is not only telling what he would say to unbelievers but appealing directly to the Corinthians themselves, and the imperative does call for their response. Paul's aim, Jan Lambrecht says, is their renewed reconciliation with God. This is the first imperative verb in a letter with few imperatives, and in this context it is better called an appeal than a command. It shows that there is still alienation and that Paul is approaching the Corinthians cautiously by making the first direct appeal after five chapters.

The final sentence (5:21) reads as an appendage or perhaps a summary, but it also works to include the Corinthians again in Paul's first-person

---

35. "Reconciliation and Liberation—The Confession of 1967," special issue of the *Journal of Presbyterian History* 61 (1983).

36. See the previous section on the political and social context of this text for discussion of the translation "we are ambassadors."

37. Reimund Bieringer, " 'Reconcile Yourselves to God': An Unusual Interpretation of 2 Corinthians 5:20 in Its Context," in *Jesus, Paul, and Early Christianity: Studies in Honor of Henk Jan de Jonge*, ed. R. Buitenwerf, H. W. Hollander, and J. Tromp (Leiden: Brill, 2008), 28–38; Thrall, *Second Epistle*, 436–39; Lambrecht, *Second Corinthian*s, 100.

plural of God's people. Christ's death, though not named here, is made the turning point of the exchange between Christ being made sin and "we" being made God's justice. The image is not of Christ as sin offering to God[38] but of Christ bearing for all the death that is the fate of sinners[39] or, I suggest, Christ bearing the consequences of the sin deeply imbedded in people, groups, and social structures. In return God's righteousness or justice is made possible for these very people and structures, as realized and hence realizable in Christ's life. Here sin and justice are taken as powers of evil and good respectively, not simply as evaluations of people. In our context, and it seems also in the Corinthians' context where the concern about sin was not high, this might be translated, "The one who did not know failure God made the epitome of failure so that we might become God's success in Christ," or, "The one who had no fear of death God allowed to die so that we might not fear death but take on his life." Yet Paul does introduce in this summary the ethical language of sin and its opposite, justice, recognizing that God's justice is not compromised but fulfilled in their common life in Christ. And he does this not as a rebuke or a warning to the Corinthians but in a positive claim, even a closing celebration, that "we" who are inextricably implicated in the structures of the world's sin can have, by dying in Christ's consequent death, a life that embodies God's justice.[40] Here the indicative swallows up the imperative.

And what may have been the Corinthian response to this? Tiresome as they must find it to hear Paul again commending himself by claiming not to be doing so, beginning with and returning to what he has done for their benefit (5:11-13, 18-19), he is nonetheless recognizing God's new creation in them. Yet because so much depends for Paul on Christ's death that demonstrates his love for all and draws all into dying to themselves and living for Christ in his risen life, the question must be whether they can make room for this. Without the experience that the privileged Paul has had in losing all respect when he began to represent this Jesus, can

---

38. Breytenbach, *Grace, Reconciliation, Concord*, 174–75, 180–82. Lambrecht argues that expiation of sin is not excluded in this passage but appears as Christ's representation of sinners in the reconciliation language and in the repeated preposition ὑπὲρ ("on behalf of, for," 5:14, 15, 21; see also Rom 5:10) (*Second Corinthians*, 105).

39. Thrall, *Second Epistle*, 441–42; Breytenbach, *Grace, Reconciliation, Concord*, 181–82.

40. The translation of γενώμεθα as "we might embody" I borrow from Marlene Crüsemann, "2 Korintherbrief," in *Bibel in gerechter Sprache*, ed. Ulrike Bail et al. (Gütersloh: Gütersloher Verlagshaus, 2006), 2138.

they for whom Christ has meant an expanding life see Jesus' death, his execution, as the good news of their transformation? Can they see the justice they have found in God to be grounded in Jesus undergoing injustice on their behalf? Can they see themselves as one-time enemies or aliens whom God has reconciled through Christ's death and life? It may depend on whether they have known injustice and alienation themselves, either in their families or cities, or in relation to Paul after an early bond as the women clearly have, so that they are open to see their new life in Christ as reconciling them to God—and through that possibly even to Paul.[41]

41. See the excursus "The Social Status of the Corinthian Women and Paul" in my *The Corinthian Women Prophets: A Reconstruction through Paul's Rhetoric* (Minneapolis: Fortress, 1990; repr., Eugene, OR: Wipf and Stock, 2003), 62–71.

2 Corinthians 6:1–7:4

Paul's All-Out Appeal: Open Wide Your Hearts

Text and Its Structure (6:1–7:4)

Here Paul reaches the climax in his appeal for reconciliation with the Corinthians. At once delicately balanced and almost falling into pieces, this appeal begins, revives midway, and ends in his most personal pleas for their positive response (6:1-2; 6:11-13; 7:2-4). But the two arguments that come between these pleas seem crafted both to offend and to conflict with each other, the first listing his peculiar credits (6:3-10; see "The More Specific Focus on Paul's Social, Political, and Economic Setting" below), and the second demanding their separation from unbelievers (6:14–7:1; see "The Ecosystem Paul Presupposes of Trust and Distrust, Being Wide and Narrow" below). One modern solution has been to declare this second argument to be an interpolation adapted by an editor from a lost letter of Paul (as in 1 Cor 5:9),[1] from

---

1. J. Weiss, *Der erste Korintherbrief* (Göttingen: Vandenhoeck & Ruprecht, 1910; repr., 1977), xl–xliii; Rudolph Bultmann, *The Second Letter to the Corinthians* (Minneapolis: Augsburg, 1985; German, 1976), 180.

⁶·¹As we work together with him, we urge you also not to accept the grace of God in vain. ²For he says,

"At an acceptable time I have listened to you,
and on a day of salvation I have helped you."

See, now is the acceptable time; see, now is the day of salvation! ³We are putting no obstacle in anyone's way, so that no fault may be found with our ministry, ⁴but as servants of God we have commended ourselves in every way: through great endurance, in afflictions, hardships, calamities, ⁵beatings, imprisonments, riots, labors, sleepless nights, hunger; ⁶by purity, knowledge, patience, kindness, holiness of spirit, genuine love, ⁷truthful speech, and the power of God; with the weapons of righteousness for the right hand and for the left; ⁸in honor and dishonor, in ill repute and good repute. We are treated as impostors, and yet are true; ⁹as unknown, and yet are well known; as dying, and see—we are alive; as punished, and yet not killed; ¹⁰as sorrowful, yet always rejoicing; as poor, yet making many rich; as having nothing, and yet possessing everything.

¹¹We have spoken frankly to you Corinthians; our heart is wide open to you. ¹²There is no restriction in our affections, but only in yours. ¹³In return— I speak as to children—open wide your hearts also.

¹⁴Do not be mismatched with unbelievers. For what partnership is there between righteousness and lawlessness? Or what fellowship is there

a Qumran-related text,² or from Paul's own opponents.³ Yet the same aroused tone is sustained throughout this passage, and recent interpreters are looking for ways to understand how the whole appeal can have made sense within Paul's own argument.

Three major approaches are being taken to explain the outburst against associating with unbelievers (6:14–7:1) in Paul's closing appeal. The simplest settles for technical solutions: Paul paused in dictation and began again with a strict warning;⁴ or Paul spoke this paragraph in another context, such as just before his final diatribe in 2 Corinthians 10–13, and the pages were later shuffled.⁵ But there is no positive evidence in

2. Joseph A. Fitzmyer, "Qumran and the Interpolated Paragraph in 2 Cor 6:14–7:1," *CBQ* 23 (1961): 271–80.

3. Hans-Dieter Betz, "2 Cor 6:14–7:1: An Anti-Pauline Fragment?," *JBL* 92 (1973): 88–108.

4. Hans Lietzmann, *An die Korinther I. II*, enl. by W. G. Kümmel, 5th ed. (Tübingen: J. C. B. Mohr [Paul Siebeck], 1969), 129.

5. Thomas Schmeller, "Der ursprüngliche Kontext von 2 Kor 6,14–7,1. Zur Frage der Einheitlichkeit des 2 Korintherbriefes," *NTS* 52 (2006): 219–31.

2 Corinthians 6:1–7:4   139

between light and darkness? ¹⁵What agreement does Christ have with Beliar? Or what does a believer share with an unbeliever? ¹⁶What agreement has the temple of God with idols? For we are the temple of the living God; as God said,

> "I will live in them and walk among them,
> and I will be their God,
> and they shall be my people.
> ¹⁷Therefore come out from them,
> and be separate from them,
> says the Lord,
> and touch nothing unclean;
> then I will welcome you,
> ¹⁸and I will be your father,
> and you shall be my sons and daughters,
> says the Lord Almighty."

⁷:¹Since we have these promises, beloved, let us cleanse ourselves from every defilement of body and of spirit, making holiness perfect in the fear of God.

²Make room in your hearts for us; we have wronged no one, we have corrupted no one, we have taken advantage of no one. ³I do not say this to condemn you, for I said before that you are in our hearts, to die together and to live together. ⁴I often boast about you; I have great pride in you; I am filled with consolation; I am overjoyed in all our affliction.*

* NRSV notes: 6:1, Gk *As we work together*; 6:16, Other ancient authorities read *you* for *we*; 7:2, Gk lacks *in your hearts*.

surviving manuscripts for these proposals. A second approach takes this passage as Paul's opening salvo against the rival apostles he later castigates in the final chapters of 2 Corinthians, insinuating that any who are not reconciling with him serve other gods and must be shunned.[6] Yet Paul's opponents in chapters 10–13 are Israelites proclaiming Christ (11:22-23), while here Paul is excluding association with unbelievers (ἀπίστοις, 6:14), a term he uses otherwise for the wider population met in temples, courts, and mixed marriages.[7]

6. Anacleto de Oliveira, *Die Diakonie der Gerechtigkeit und der Versöhnung in der Apologie des 2. Korintherbriefes: Analyse und Auslegung von 2 Cor 2,14–4,6; 5:11–6:10* (Münster: Aschendorf, 1990), 335–38; Franz Zeilinger, "Die Echtheit von 2 Cor 6:14–7:1," *JBL* 112 (1993): 71–80; Volker Rabens, "Paul's Rhetoric of Demarcation: Separation from 'Unbelievers' (2 Cor 6:14–7:1) in the Corinthian Conflict," in *Theologizing in the Corinthian Conflict: Studies in the Exegesis and Theology of 2 Corinthians*, ed. Reimund Bieringer, Ma. Marilou S. Ibita, Dominika A. Kurek-Chomycz, and Thomas Vollmer, BTS 16 (Leuven: Peeters, 2013), 229–53.

7. 1 Cor 6:6; 7:12-15; 10:27; 14:22-24; 2 Cor 4:4. William J. Webb, "Who Are the Unbelievers (ἀπίστοι) in 2 Corinthians 7:14?," *BSac* 149 (1992): 27–44.

The third approach looks for reasons why Paul's relative tolerance for such outsiders has suddenly been replaced by prohibiting contact. Some interpreters suggest that a warning against associating with unbelievers might be expected at this point. In a good defense speech first comes an intense arousing of pity for the defendant (the *conquestio*, as in Paul's lists of trials and his plea, 6:3-13) followed by a blast against the accusers (the *indignatio*, excoriating those who have not believed Paul, 6:14–7:1).[8] Or if Paul is depicting himself as a herald leading a religious procession, he would announce on arrival at the sanctuary that everyone unclean is forbidden entry.[9] And similarly, Moses' final song to Israel in Deuteronomy 32 that Paul draws on repeatedly (2 Cor 6:18 on Deut 32:19?) is above all a warning against apostasy.[10] Also, Paul's arguments elsewhere can end with sharp instructions and warnings.[11] So there are precedents for Paul's call to separate from unbelievers at the climax of his appeal in 2 Corinthians 6.

Other interpreters explain Paul's sharp words from a substantive effect he wants to have on the Corinthians. He could be warning a certain group of them who have not repented their immorality and still consort with unbelievers (12:21).[12] He could be evoking the Corinthians' prebaptismal instruction about being set apart from a world of unbelief.[13] Or Paul may simply take their closing the doors to worldly options as the other side of opening their hearts to the life in Christ that he presents.[14]

---

8. De Oliveira, *Diakonie*, 331–40; Zeilinger, "Die Echtheit," 71–80.

9. Paul Brooks Duff, "The Mind of the Redactor: 2 Cor 6:14–7:1 in Its Secondary Context," *NovT* 35 (1993): 60–80.

10. John W. Olley, "A Precursor of the NRSV? 'Sons and Daughters' in 2 Cor 6:18," *NTS* 44 (1998): 206–12; on Deut 11:13-16, see Jerome Murphy-O'Connor, "Relating 2 Corinthians 6:14–7:1 to Its Context," *NTS* 33 (1987): 272–75.

11. Rom 16:17-20; 1 Cor 16:22a; 1 Thess 5:12-15; Zeilinger, "Die Echtheit," 75.

12. Reimund Bieringer, "2 Korinther 6,14–7,1 im Kontext der 2. Korintherbriefes. Forschungsüberblick und Versuch eines eigenen Zugangs," in *Studies on 2 Corinthians*, ed. R. Bieringer and J. Lambrecht, BETL 112 (Leuven: Leuven University Press, 1994), 567–70; Michael Goulder, "2 Cor 6:14–7:1, an Integral Part of 2 Corinthians," *NovT* 36 (1994): 50–54.

13. Margaret E. Thrall, *A Critical and Exegetical Second Epistle to the Corinthians*, ICC (Edingurgh: T & T Clark, 1994), 25–36; Victor Paul Furnish, *II Corinthians*, AB 32A (Garden City, NY: Doubleday, 1984), 383.

14. Marlene Crüsemann, "Das weite Herz und die Gemeinschaft der Heiligen: 2 Kor 6,11–7,4 im sozialgeschichtlichen Kontext," in *Dem Tod nicht glauben: Sozialgeschichte der Bibel. Festschrift für Luise Schottroff zum 70. Geburtstag*, ed. Frank Crüsemann, Marlene Crüsemann, Claudia Janssen, Rainer Kessler, and Beate Wehn (Gütersloh: Gütersloher Verlagshaus, 2004), 362, repr. in *Gott ist Beziehung: Beiträge zur biblischen Rede von Gott*, ed. Claudia Janssen and Luise Schottroff (Gütersloh: Gütersloher Verlagshaus, 2014), 218.

Marlene Crüsemann, Margaret Thrall, and James M. Scott trace how this warning against unbelief leads into the Scripture collage where God speaks in the first person, promising Israel's restoration.[15] God's people, once called out of slavery in Egypt and then out of captivity in Babylon, are now being called out of bondage to false gods into God's own family, as if in a third exodus.[16] God's covenant promise and God's adoption in Christ require, but also motivate, total consecration, as Paul says to summarize his point (7:1), and this leads him back to plead for their reconciliation with him (7:2-4). It is these substantive readings of Paul's zeal for God in face of the surrounding world's unbelief that best reveal his moves here. It seems that in his appeal for reconciliation with God (6:1-2) he first cites his own credentials as messenger (6:3-10) and makes a personal plea (6:11-13), then raises the threat of apostasy in order to assert in contrast God's words of restoration (6:14–7:1), and ends with a final personal plea that they reconcile with him (7:2-4).

The NRSV translation is at one point deceptive. In the first sentence the words "with him" are absent in the Greek and added to connect this with what the previous chapter says about God. But for Paul it is God's people who work together.[17] Here he begins: "As we work together we also entreat you not to make God's grace come to nothing."

A Feminist Lens at Three Ranges on Paul's All-Out Appeal to the Corinthians (6:1–7:4)

The Ecosystem Paul Presupposes of Trust and Distrust, Wide and Narrow

When we read this climax of Paul's appeal for reconciliation and ask what it assumes about the world, we are first struck by the sharp dualism in Paul's warning. Five rhetorical questions dramatize that the

---

15. Crüsemann, "Weite Herz," in *Dem Tod nicht glauben*, 362–72, in *Gott ist Beziehung*, 218–27; Thrall, *Second Epistle*, 27; James M. Scott, "The Use of Scripture in 2 Corinthians 6.16c-18 and Paul's Restoration Theology," *JSNT* 56 (1994): 73–99; William J. Webb, *Returning Home: New Covenant and Second Exodus as the Context for 2 Corinthians 6.14–7.1*, JSOTSup 85 (Sheffield: JSOT, 1993), 184–99.

16. Crüsemann, "Weite Herz," in *Dem Tod nicht glauben*, 368; in *Gott ist Beziehung*, 224.

17. Rom 16:3; 1 Cor 1:24; 8:23; 16:16; Phil 2:25; 4:2; 1 Thess 3:2; Phlm 1, 24. Only 1 Cor 3:9 could suggest coworking with God but in the context indicates coworking with others for God. See Marlene Crüsemann, "Eine neue Perspektive auf Paulus," in *Gott ist Beziehung*, 137–38.

Corinthians cannot "team up" (NEB) with unbelievers, since justice makes no alliances with lawlessness, nor light with darkness, Christ with Beliar (prince of demons),[18] believers with nonbelievers, or God's temple with idols (6:14-16). Because they are God's temple, they must separate from unbelievers and cleanse themselves of all that defiles body and spirit in order to realize holiness with fear of God (6:16–7:1). Is Paul calling them to leave Corinth for the desert and an ascetic life? Paul has just defended his service for God as without offense because he has been beaten, imprisoned, caught in riots, abused, and shamed, anything but withdrawn to a life of purity. Apparently the dualism Paul asserts here is not physical separation from certain peoples or polluted things but total commitment to this righteous God's reconciling the world through Christ's death and risen life (5:14-21).

Paul assumes a world that, though created by God, seems to be ruled by lawless powers so that people live in darkness, serve idols, and compromise with evil because they see no option. Paul challenges the Corinthians not to become wrongly yoked to such a life since they are God's temple, God's people, God's sons and daughters.

The dualism that Paul projects in his rhetorical questions (6:13) is not a cosmologically given nature of reality but its aberration brought about by people who do not trust God, act lawlessly, serve gods of their own making, or in their ignorance affiliate with those who do. Paul sees his own task to inform all nations that God is reconciled with them, both the deceivers and the deceived, and to challenge them to "come out" from among those who do not trust God and be restored to God's people. Therefore Beliar appears here, not as a competing cosmic power, but as the god of this age (4:4) who has blinded the minds of those who are not trusting (ἄπιστοι; NRSV, "unbelievers")[19] so they are not illumined by the brightness of the glory of Christ, God's image (4:4; 2:14-16). Yet in his effort to explain distrust or disbelief (ἀπίστις) Paul insists that God's reconciliation is offered equally to those who receive it and those who do not. What this dualism means is that there is no middle option. Either people trust or do not, choose light or darkness, and everything

---

18. Jub. 15.33; T. Reu. 4.7; also as "Belial" in the Qumran *Damascus Document* 4.13, 15.

19. Paul's πίστις, πιστεύω can be translated "belief" and "I believe," or "faith" and "I have faith," but a more dynamic translation is "trust" and "I trust." The negative for persons (ἄπιστοι) would be "the unbelieving," "the faithless," "the distrusting."

follows from that. This is the altar call at the end of Paul's self-defense, and it is not ambiguous.

How Paul uses the categories of space and time in this passage bears attention from the feminist reader. Space that is narrow or restricted to the point of being absent is disparaged, and space that is open, wide, or full is valued.[20] Among Paul's trials he lists ἐν στενοχωρίαις (6:4; in narrow straits or tight places, being under stress or in calamity). His first plea is that the Corinthians not receive God's grace in vain, εἰς κενὸν (6:1; into emptiness, coming to nothing, to no effect; see also 1 Cor 15:10). Because God's grace is extensive, all-sufficient, and generous,[21] it must not come to nothing.

The language of space is most fully exploited in his direct pleas to the Corinthians (6:11-13; 7:2-4). I italicize his spatial terms. After listing his trials he says, "Our mouth is *opened* toward you, Corinthians, our heart is *extended*. You are not *constricted* [στενοχωρεῖσθε] from our side but you are *constricted* in your own feelings [σπλάγχνοις; 'guts, internal organs']" (6:11-12). If the Corinthians had not complained of being constricted by Paul, would he have denied it? Yet now he wants to be open with them, receptive rather than condemning, and he asks their openness in return. He challenges them, " 'Turnabout is fair play'—I speak as among children—*extend* yourselves too!" (6:13). After his sharp warning that they not be yoked with unfaithful or distrusting people because they are God's temple where God *walks around* (6:14–7:1),[22] Paul resumes his spacious plea, "*Make room* for us. . . . You are in our hearts to die together and live together! How *openly* I have spoken to you! How much I boast over you! I am *filled* with encouragement. I *overflow* with joy in all our *constraints*" (7:2-4).

Time indicators are also illuminating.[23] Parallel to the shift in space since 1 Corinthians from constricting to extending, Paul shifts from past memories and future hopes to present assurance. His initial call on the Corinthians not to receive God's grace for nothing (6:1) is supported immediately by Scripture attributed to God, "In the nick of time I heard you, and on the day for rescue I helped you" (6:2a; Isa 49:8). Although

20. See a different analysis in Jorunn Økland's *Women in Their Place: Paul and the Corinthian Discourse of Gender and Sanctuary Space* (London: T & T Clark, 2004), 157–59.
21. 2 Cor 4:15; 9:8, 14; 12:9.
22. In the pre-industrial city, the courts of the temple could be the only open space for walking.
23. On time in Paul's letters, see Giorgio Agamben, *The Time That Remains: A Commentary on the Letter to the Romans* (Stanford, CA: Stanford University Press, 2005), 59–78.

these past tenses could point backward, Paul interprets them as present, even as immediate, "Look, now is the nick of time! Look, now is the day for rescue!" (6:2a). This makes God's acts in the past confirm God's move toward them in the present. The following list of Paul's ongoing trials (6:3-10) can be heard as further proof that God's presence is carrying him through, keeping him and his colleagues effective as God's agents.

Paul then makes explicit his plea that the Corinthians reciprocate his outreach to them, speaking in the perfect tense to signify a continuing state: "Our mouth has opened to you, Corinthians; our heart has become wide" (6:11). And again in his final plea for their response, his past and perfect tenses intensify his present confession: "You are in our hearts to die together and live together. . . . I have been filled with courage. In all our constraints I overflow with joy" (7:2-4).

But between these pleas Paul warns against idolatry using future tenses (6:16-18), quoting Scripture as God's first-person speech: "I will live with them and circulate among them, and I will be their God and they will be my people." And again, "I will be your father, and you will be my sons and daughters."[24] Does this put off God's adoption of them to some future time? Paul's summary might suggest this in the way it is commonly translated, "Since we have these promises, beloved, let us cleanse ourselves . . . , making holiness perfect in the fear of God" (7:1, NRSV). But ἐπαγγελίας here is better translated "assurances" than "promises": "Having these assurances, let us cleanse ourselves . . . realizing holiness in fear of God." The present-tense meaning is confirmed by the way Paul introduces the Scriptures in which God speaks. His rhetorical questions build up to a present-tense assertion, "What contact has God's temple with idols? For we are the temple of the living God, as God said, 'I will live in them and circulate among them'" (6:16).

Though in 1 Corinthians Paul reserves until after death the realization of God's full presence in resurrection life[25] and restricts the women prophets,[26] here he not only concedes life now to the Corinthians but also promotes the present restoration of God's people and the Corinthians' role in realizing holiness in body and spirit before God.[27] Now, he says, is the right time, and Corinth, their place, is the spacious place for God's full reconciliation with and among people.

---

24. 2 Cor 6:16, 18; Lev 26:11-12; Ezek 37:27; 2 Sam 7:14.
25. 1 Cor 15:22, 49, 51-52, 54-55.
26. 1 Cor 11:2-16; 14:34-36.
27. 2 Cor 6:2, 16, 18; 7:1.

The Temple of the Living God: We or You?

In 2 Corinthians 6:16b the NRSV reads: "For we are the temple of the living God." The footnote says: "Other ancient authorities read *you*" (plural).

The best early manuscripts show the first-person personal pronoun "we." This is the choice of most translations like the RSV, NRSV, NASB, NABRE, NIV, and ESV, and this commentary affirms the "we" reading (Wire, p. 144). The "we" includes Paul with the Corinthians in being the temple of the living God. Consequently, this self-inclusion is carried over when he writes 2 Corinthians 6:18, where the phrase "sons and daughters" is found. The purported source in 2 Samuel 7:14 reads: "and he shall be a son to me." Paul changes the singular "son" to the plural and adds "and daughters." The use of "we" implies that Paul, together with the Corinthians, is one of the "sons and daughters." He is a fellow sibling of the Corinthians, and they have God as common Father (see Wire, p. lx: "only by shifting from the stance of [a] knowing father to [a] vulnerable brother could he attempt a lasting reconciliation with them"). Paul's employment of "we" tones down his use of the explicit, unequal relationship of father and children (6:13). Together, these narrative clues characterize how Paul explicitly unites himself on an equal footing with the Corinthian men and women with whom he needs to be reconciled. Paul's self-identification with the Corinthians in employing "we" reaffirms that his careful use of the plural male noun ἀδελφοί is an inclusive, egalitarian sibling language (1:8; 8:1; 13:11) that also includes the Corinthian women. This move helps advance his aim to be reconciled with all of them.[28]

Conversely, the narrative effect of the use of the plural "you" in other manuscripts favored by a few translations like KJV, World English Bible, and Wycliffe Bible is that Paul makes a more qualified and careful assertion that the Corinthians are God's children. Even if the Corinthians are distinguished from the unbelievers (6:14-15) and they are recognized as God's sons and daughters, Paul's relationship with them on an equal level is not explicit or communicated. The earlier distinction between "we" and "you" (6:1-13) spills over here and his regarding them as children (6:13) echoes, making him implicitly their father and identifying himself with God as Father to the Corinthians (6:18).

---

28. See Reidar Aasgaard, *My Beloved Brothers and Sisters! Christian Siblingship in Paul* (London: T & T Clark, 2004); also Ma. Marilou S. Ibita, "Mending a Broken Relationship," in Bieringer et al., *Theologizing the Corinthian Conflict*, 43–68.

His self-identification with the Corinthians as fellow siblings who have God as a common Father is missing. This move maintains the gap between Paul and the Corinthians and is not fully helpful in his attempt to be reconciled with them.

Thus, the decision whether Paul wrote "we" or "you" has important implications for his self-identification with the Corinthians and for his potential success in fully reconciling with them.

Ma. Marilou S. Ibita

The More Specific Focus on Paul's Social, Political, and Economic Setting

The extent of Paul's social world comes through in this final plea for the Corinthians' reconciliation with God. On the one hand, he appeals to God's own voice through Israel's Scriptures, saying, "I heard you," "I helped you," and "I will be your God and you will be my sons and daughters"—people no longer bound to an unbelieving and idolatrous world (6:1-2, 14-18). On the other hand, Paul brings to a climax his self-defense in a Greek high rhetorical style, reciting at length all he has endured in God's service on their behalf (6:3-10). He draws both together with his most personal pleas for the Corinthian believers to be reconciled with him (6:11-13; 7:2-4). In this way he demonstrates how integrally he belongs to his hybrid culture and how effectively he functions as a zealous Messianic Jew in the pagan Greco-Roman world.

I take up, first, Paul's catalogue of the trials he has endured and the virtues so exhibited (6:3-10). Note how this "commending ourselves as God's servants/agents" conflicts with his earlier claim that he and his coworkers are not "commending themselves."[29] This cannot be finessed as a simple issue of word order in which self-commending is wrong and commending oneself is right.[30] This is the double bind that characterizes Paul's plight in this letter, to be a devout Jew (Messianic or not) whose only boast is God and at the same time to operate in Greek agonistic debate.[31] Paul ties himself securely to both sides of the double bind, as-

29. 2 Cor 6:4; 3:1; 5:12.

30. John T. Fitzgerald, *Cracks in an Earthen Vessel: An Examination of the Catalogues of Hardships in the Corinthian Correspondence* (Atlanta: Scholars Press, 1988), 187.

31. For six characteristics of agonistic rhetoric and its use by Paul, see Margaret M. Mitchell, *Paul, the Corinthians and the Birth of Christian Hermeneutics* (Cambridge: Cambridge University Press, 2010), 24–27, 45–46, 63, 106–8.

serting God's prerogative to alone be praised against all idolatry and yet finding ways to commend those who proclaim God where oral competition is the order of the day.[32]

There is some order to be found in Paul's cacophonous catalogue of his trials (6:4-10), whether by counting the opening phrase, "in great endurance," among nine virtues that follow nine trials, all grouped in threes,[33] or simply by hearing his endurance proven by triads of trials followed by quadrads of strengths. In the Greek text each of these is introduced with the preposition ἐν ("in"). They are followed by three conditions introduced with διὰ ("through") and seven antitheses presented as ὡς . . . δὲ/καὶ ("as . . . and yet"). In straining to communicate the content of the catalogue, translators often lose the rhythm of Paul's recitation that carries its weight in the social ἀγών (struggle, competition) where it seeks to be heard and trusted. The specific social setting is not named, and some interpreters see that the "false apostles" Paul attacks in the letter's final chapters (10–13) are surfacing here as competitors whose praise in letters that recommend them (3:3) or in their own speaking requires a rebuttal. But Paul's focus here is less on comparing himself to others than on gaining the respect of the Corinthians themselves. He uses a device called a catalogue of dangers to cite his hardships as evidence of his devotion to God and as proof of God's power that keeps him going on their behalf.[34]

Paul's catalogues bear some resemblance to the inscriptions ordered by Hellenistic kings and Roman emperors to make known their honors and accomplishments.[35] Most famous of these is the *res gestae* of Augustus Caesar, inscribed on stone pillars in provincial cities a half century before Paul, very likely also in Corinth, in which Augustus lists in the first-person singular the honors he has received and the conquests he has made on behalf of the Roman people. The emperor, like Paul, claims the full adherence of his audience in return for his unstinting service.

32. On Paul's self-commendation, see Fitzgerald, *Cracks*, 187, yet 150–52, and Thrall, *Second Epistle*, 456.

33. Thrall, *Second Epistle*, 453–54.

34. Fitzgerald, *Cracks*, 145–48, 166–76, 184–201; Robert Hodges, "Paul the Apostle and the First Century Tribulation Lists," *ZNW* 74 (1983): 59–80.

35. Anton Fridrichsen, "Peristasenkatalog und Res Gestae. Nachtrag zu 2 Cor. 11:23ff," *Symbolae Osloenses* 8 (1929): 78–82.

Inscription of Augustus Caesar's Accomplishments

I conquered the pirates and gave peace to the seas. In that war I handed over to their masters for punishment nearly 30,000 slaves who had run away from their owners, and taken up arms against the republic. The whole of Italy of its own free will took the oath of fidelity to me. . . . I extended the frontiers of all the provinces of the Roman people, which had as neighbours races not obedient to our empire. I restored peace to all the provinces of Gaul and Spain and to Germany. . . . Egypt I added to the empire of the Roman people. . . . After I had extinguished the civil wars, having been put in supreme possession of the whole empire by the universal consent of all, I transferred the republic from my own power into the free control of the Senate and Roman people.[36]

Paul's first-person catalogues have been contrasted with Augustus Caesar's because Paul boasted his hardships rather than his achievements. But Caesar also listed his refusal of many honors and his returning to the Roman Senate the powers once given him over the empire's internal provinces, including Greece and Western Asia Minor. He does not mention that he retained for the legions in his command the resource-rich external provinces and vassal states, including Syria, Palestine, and Egypt. This political distinction between pacified provinces ruled by the Senate and occupied territories ruled by the emperor as military imperator may be worth considering in study of Paul's shaping a Gospel grounded in an occupied world for people living in pacified cities.[37] The *res gestae* of Augustus at least alert us to the fact that political influence had to be won, even by emperors, and surely by a man like Paul whose dignity was so compromised by his obsessive mission.

Closer parallels to Paul's than the *res gestae* are found where Stoics, Cynics, and historians generally extol the wise man inured to hardship (see sidebar: "Hardships Tolerated for a Higher Goal").

36. *Res Gestae Divi Augusti* 24–27, 34, trans. E. G. Hardy, *Momentum Ancyranum* (Oxford: Clarendon, 1923), 68–79; C. K. Barrett, ed., *The New Testament Background: Selected Documents* (New York: Harper & Row, 1956), 2–4.

37. See my "Women in Early Christian Stories: Serving and Served, Rural and Urban, in Occupied and Pacified Provinces," in *Bridges in New Testament Interpretation: Interdisciplinary Advances*, ed. Neil Elliott and Werner Kelber (Lanham, MD: Lexington Books/Fortress, 2018), 23–25.

Hardships Tolerated
for a Higher Goal

The noble man holds his hardships to be his greatest antagonists, . . . grappling with hunger and cold, withstanding thirst, and disclosing no weakness even though he must endure the lash or give his body to be cut or burned. Hunger, exile, loss of reputation, and the like have no terrors for him; nay, he holds them as mere trifles.[38]

[Alexander the Great to his mutinous troops:] Let any who carries wounds strip himself and show them; I too will show mine. I have no part of my body, in front at least, that is left without scars; there is no weapon, used at close quarters, or hurled from afar, of which I do not carry the mark. Nay, I have been wounded by the sword, hand to hand; I have been shot with arrows; I have been struck from a catapult, smitten many a time with stones and clubs, for you, for your glory, for your wealth.[39]

What Paul does in his catalogue is not to distinguish himself from others of his time but to exercise well the rhetorical culture he shares so that he can claim the Corinthians' respect.[40] Yet the claim would fall flat if it did not recall for people what they had seen of his conduct and that of his coworkers, and thereby it can tell us something of their social and political standing in Corinth. Paul's introduction to the catalogue—"But in every way we recommend ourselves as God's servants by great endurance"—when taken with the first triad, "in disruptions, in hardships, in tight places," gives the broad picture of this steadfast witness under opposition. The second triad, "in beatings, in imprisonments, in revolts," tells specifics that are further detailed and numbered later in the letter (11:23-25).[41] Suffering such public abuse and punishment identifies

38. Dio Chrysostom, *Eighth Discourse, On Virtue* 15–16, in *Discourses*, vol. 1: *1–11*, ed. and trans. J. W. Cohoon, LCL (Cambridge, MA: Harvard University Press, 1961), 385.

39. Arrian, *Anabasis of Alexander* 7.10.1-2, in Arrian, *Anabasis of Alexander*, vol. 2: *Books 5–7, Indica*, ed. and trans. E. Iliff Robson, LCL (Cambridge, MA: Harvard University Press, 1966), 233.

40. Note that Greco-Roman catalogues also regularly claim the favor of gods and attribute rescues to their aid: Fitzgerald, *Cracks*, 171, citing Seneca, *Epistle* 41.4-5 and Aelius Aristides, *Oration* 24.

41. On the harsh conditions of imprisonment in this period, see Angela Standhartinger's "Letter from Prison as Hidden Transcript: What It Tells Us about the People at Philippi," in *The People Beside Paul: The Philippian Assembly and History from Below*, ed. Joseph A. Marchal (Atlanta: SBL Press, 2015), 114–24.

Paul and his colleagues with the servile class (6:6-7) or with those who are so sure of the divine spirit and power in them that they take abuse lightly, not in any case with the elite who vaunt their power or with the great majority who defer to them. The third triad, "in manual labor, in nights at watch,[42] in fasting," has been interpreted to name voluntary self-disciplines, though in the longer catalogue of 11:22-29 the latter two appear alongside "in famine and thirst" and "in cold and nakedness," suggesting forced lack of sleep and food. We do know that Paul chose the manual labor of the tent-making trade rather than becoming dependent on the Corinthians for his living,[43] even though in that culture educated men did not work with their hands. So he did choose a life where sleep and food would be tenuous and recognized that this required a defense.

Paul next lists the resources that fund his and his colleagues' endurance (6:6-7), combining character traits such as holiness, knowledge, kindness, and love with their divine sources in spirit and power. It may be in response to slurs from the Corinthians that he stresses his steadfastness in the three conditions that follow: "with weapons of justice on the right and on the left,[44] with honor and dishonor, with praise and blame." And finally his juxtaposing shameful situations with antithetical outcomes makes every apparent debasement another proof of vindication. Paul claims that he and his coworkers may be thought deceptive, unknown, disciplined by God, hurting, impoverished, and dying, but it turns out they are truth-telling, recognized, and rejoicing survivors.

The explicit economic data at the end of this catalogue show both that the destitute (πτωχοί) are considered of no account and that the missioners are often destitute. Yet Paul says they enrich many when they have nothing and thereby possess everything. Has the meaning of wealth simply become metaphorical midway in this claim? I see a sharper reversal being spoken, an enriching and possessing being claimed that is broad enough to encompass material necessities in all that nourishes life. In other words, Paul is not just exchanging material for spiritual wealth, shame now for reward later, but he begins in this letter to recognize in

---

42. Literally the word ἀγρυπνία means "field sleep," regularly associated with keeping watch, so possibly keeping watch in fields of ripe crops, or on military guard; where it appears with νηστεία in 2 Samuel LXX 12:21 it seems to mean "lying all night on the ground" in repentance (see 2 Sam 12:16). Paul's itinerancy would have meant often sleeping on the ground.

43. 1 Cor 9:4-18; 2 Cor 11:7-10.

44. The sword for offense is held in the right hand; the shield for defense in the left.

these early communities an alternate structure of mutual care that is superior to the imperial and civic structures because it is sustained by enriching others. Paul's vision for this kind of subsistence polity and reciprocating economy probably derived from the common life of some Jews in Hellenistic cities that Paul saw extended to all people through Jesus' death and rising.[45] Finally, the antitheses of 6:8-10 show that Paul is not seeking pity or even respect for himself and his coworkers so much as he is claiming to have all that one could want—survival through times of discipline and pain, recognition, joy, and the chance to be made rich by enriching others. Without social status or political clout, he claims to have all that matters.

On this basis he launches immediately into his plea that the Corinthians receive him, and he recapitulates the plea at the end of this passage (6:11-13; 7:2-4). But between these he adds a sharp warning, apparently fearing that they will revert to their previous associations (6:14–7:1). Here the rhetoric of Israel's anti-idolatry polemic shows that Paul knows the seductions of the social world in which they live with its rituals, festivals, and temples. He depicts a stark contrast between God's justice and this chaos, light and darkness, Christ and Beliar, those who trust God and those who do not. By means of a text from Isaiah 52:11—in the heart of the prophet's Servant Song—Paul demands that they "come out from among them," no longer meaning from Babylon for the return to Jerusalem but from the culture that wants to satisfy them with Greek gods dressed in Roman power.

Against this allure he asserts in God's voice, "And I myself will gather you in" (6:17).[46] He imbeds this Scripture in two others with the strongest possible assurances that they are God's temple and God's people: "God has said, 'I will live in them and circulate among them and I will be their God and they will be my people'" (6:16).[47] "And I will become a father to you and you will become sons and daughters to me" (6:18).[48] Paul concludes, "Since we have assurances like these, beloved ones, let

---

45. Crüsemann, "Weite Herz," in *Dem Tod nicht glauben*, 362–72, in *Gott ist Beziehung*, 218–27.

46. Ezek 20:34, 41 LXX points toward translating εἰσδέχομαι not simply as "accept" or "receive" but as "gather into" or "gather up."

47. 2 Cor 6:16; Lev 26:11; Ezek 37:27.

48. 2 Cor 6:18; 2 Sam 7:14. On the present-tense meaning of this prophetic future, see above near the end of the section on the broad focus. On Paul's adding "daughters" to the Scripture, see below on his interaction with the Corinthians.

us wash from ourselves every pollution of body and spirit as we realize holiness in the fear of God" (7:1). Is Paul here instilling in them fears of pollution and anxiety before God? Or is this an assurance that since they are God's temple, God's people, God's children, they must not miss the chance to realize this life? At least Paul could not be clearer that in an imperial world, though they are already in Christ, they must continually make this choice.

The Focus Sharpened onto This Interaction between Paul and the Corinthians

Because at the beginning, middle, and end of this text Paul makes a direct and personal plea to the Corinthians (6:1-2, 11-13; 7:2-4), these three pleas are our best key to understanding their interaction. Each one harks back to the letter's first imperative verb at the climax of the previous chapter: "We beg on Christ's behalf, be reconciled with God" (5:20). In each of these pleas Paul's "we" challenges "you" in an appeal, a denial, and an offer. Our question as we look at these pleas is what Paul wants from them and what he implies they want from him.

The first plea is brief (6:1-2) and the appeal could not be more explicit: "we urge you." The denial comes immediately as part of the appeal, "not to receive God's grace in vain." Paul wants them to agree that the grace God has given them comes to nothing if it is not fruitful. The threat that all might come to nothing is a repeated theme in Paul's letters, especially those to Corinth.[49] The Corinthians apparently remain confident that they receive and express God's grace, whereas Paul quotes God's voice through Isaiah, "On the day for rescue I helped you" (Isa 49:8 LXX), and he updates this rescue to each present crisis, "Now is the day of rescue." This offer of repeated rescue completes Paul's plea, and he goes on to catalogue how his service for God (διακονία) and that of his coworkers depends on incessant divine rescue (6:3-10). Yet the catalogue of hardships is apparently not introduced as a blueprint for the Corinthians but as a defense of his own service. He wants them to respect itinerants like himself whose marginal survival has made them rich, indicating a different role for the Corinthians than for himself (see 4:12; 13:9).

The second plea (6:11-13) moves in reverse order, from offer to appeal through a denial. Paul offers himself and those who work with him and addresses the Corinthians explicitly, "Our mouth is opened toward you,

---

49. 1 Cor 1:17; 15:10, 58; 2 Cor 9:3; Phil 2:6; 1 Thess 3:5.

O Corinthians, our heart is extended." He then denies what must have been charged against him or he would not have put it this way: "You are not constricted from our side, but you are constricted from within yourselves," literally, in your guts, wombs, internal organs.[50] This charge of his having constricted them, literally narrowed their space, could have come from the women Paul tried to restrict in clothing and speech (1 Cor 11:2-16; 14:34-35), perhaps acting in concert with others who also rejected his food, sex, or worship regulations in 1 Corinthians. Paul claims, in contrast, that they are narrow toward him, not he toward them. He ends with the appeal: " 'Turnabout is fair play'—I speak as among children— extend yourselves too!" Marlene Crüsemann notes that Paul speaks here as the vulnerable party, asking for reciprocity as children do.[51]

Before the final and fullest plea, Paul warns the Corinthians against a mixed yoking with nonbelievers (ἄπιστοί; 6:14–7:1). Five rhetorical questions pit good against evil, followed by the words "for we ourselves are the temple of the living God" (6:16). Paul thus grounds his call that the Corinthians not be yoked with unbelievers in the fact of their identity as God's temple, confirmed by God's voice from Scripture, "I will live in them and circulate among them, and I will be their God and they will be my people" (Lev 26:11-12; Ezek 37:27). Thus he places the Corinthians on the side of all that is good, not so much making a demand on them as recognizing their present status.[52] Even the imperatives that follow in the Scripture collage—"Therefore come out from them and be separate from them, says the Lord . . . and I myself will gather you in" (6:17)—are less an instruction to them than an echo of God's gathering of Israel out of the nations (Ezek 20:34, 41), which for Paul is the gathering of the nations into Israel, what Marlene Crüsemann has called the third exodus,[53] their "coming out" not from Egypt or from Babylon but from unbelieving or distrusting nations into a people who trust God.

This positive meaning of God's act in Corinth is confirmed by the final line of Scripture taken from God's assurance to David concerning his son (2 Sam 7:14): "I will be father to him and he will be son to me." Paul

---

50. τὰ σπλάγχνα is used by Paul for deep-felt positive emotions (2 Cor 7:15; Phil 1:8; 2:1; Phlm 7, 12).

51. Crüsemann, "Weite Herz," in *Dem Tod nicht glauben*, 353–54, n. 11, in *Gott ist Beziehung*, 209, n. 11.

52. See the broad range view above on Paul's use of these present, past, and future verbs.

53. Crüsemann, "Weite Herz," in *Dem Tod nicht glauben*, 368, in *Gott ist Beziehung*, 224.

directs his quotation to the Corinthians and adds the word "daughters" to the word "sons": "I will become your father, and you will become my sons and daughters" (6:18). Scholars suggest that Paul is influenced here by the prophets who speak of sons and daughters to signify the fruitfulness and prosperity of God's people in Israel's postexile restoration.[54] But Paul does not take large families or wealth as signs of his Gentile mission. More likely, Paul is making explicit the women in his audience who claim parity as God's daughters.

A second allusion to them may be found in Paul's summary that concludes this quotation: "Having these assurances, beloved ones, let us cleanse ourselves from all pollution of body and spirit" (7:1). This echoes his 1 Corinthians statement that the "unmarried women and the virgins" are free to "concern themselves with the Lord's matters in order to be holy both in body and in spirit" (1 Cor 7:34). It may be that Paul's entire warning not to be yoked with unbelievers that ends with this summary (2 Cor 6:14–7:1) intends to appeal to the more strict or ascetic Corinthian believers to assure them of his support.[55] The women prophets, for example, will not be impressed by Paul's catalogue of trials and virtues if he does not also affirm their identity as God's holy people. Their recognition of him will not be won without his recognition of them. Interpreters who dismiss this passage as an interpolation (see the introduction, "One Letter or Many?," and the introduction to this chapter) have excluded the possibility that Paul might change his own stance in order to achieve reconciliation with the Corinthians. Whether or not the women in Paul's audience are primarily in mind, they are the ones Paul explicitly adds to the citation, including them as daughters among God's children. Both unmarried women who had refused remarriage in favor of prophetic roles in order to be holy "in body and spirit" and married women who had separated from unbelieving husbands, not to mention virgins who decided not to marry,[56] might now be more prone to "make room" for Paul when he follows this with his third and last plea (7:2).

Paul's final plea reverts to the order of the first: an appeal, a denial, and an offer (7:2-4). The appeal is short: "Make room for us." The denial

---

54. Isa 43:6; 49:22; Jer 31:13.

55. See Antoinette Clark Wire, *The Corinthian Women Prophets: A Reconstruction through Paul's Rhetoric* (Minneapolis: Fortress, 1990; repr., Eugene, OR: Wipf and Stock, 2003), 73–97, for evidence in 1 Corinthians 7 that women's initiative was crucial in the movement away from sexuality in the Corinthian congregations.

56. 1 Cor 7:34, 13-16, 25-38.

is more elaborate: "We have wronged no one, we have corrupted no one, we have cheated no one. Nor is my point condemnation" (7:2-3). These denials would be strange for Paul to introduce if he had not been accused of such offenses, unless he were dissociating himself from others who had done them. Paul does taunt the Corinthians in the letter's closing diatribe (10:1–13:10) with having tolerated such abuse from other leaders (11:20-21). Yet in the present context Paul is not competing with others so much as dramatizing that he and his colleagues are innocent of all serious offenses, thus minimizing the charge that must have provoked his final denial: "Nor is my point condemnation." The Corinthians clearly took Paul's 1 Corinthians letter and his intervening conduct to be condemning them, as is reflected in their reputation down through Christian history. At this point, however, Paul claims not to condemn them, yet they (and we) remain unpersuaded. Our question can be: Is Paul willing in this letter to reconcile with them as they are? Or is Paul still working to remake them in his image?

Paul's offer that follows the appeal and denial could not be more conciliatory or more personal (7:3-4). He cuts back his normal practice in this letter of speaking for all his coworkers and shifts into the first-person singular: "Nor is my point condemnation, for I told you before that you are in our hearts to die together and live together. Let me be very frank with you. I am very proud of you. I am filled with encouragement. I overflow with joy in all our trials" (7:3-4). It is an ancient commonplace that friends pledge to live and die together. But Paul speaks of death first, then life, mirroring the sequence of Jesus' death and resurrection life but also the sequence of his "carrying around the dying of Jesus" (4:10-11) and the Corinthian's experience of Jesus' risen life. He has summarized, "Death is at work in us, but life in you" (4:12), but now he sees dying and rising enacted in them both and bringing them together. Whereas he began the letter defending himself and calling on them to give thanks for him and be proud of him, now he says frankly that they are his pride and joy.

This is difficult to read as manipulation, except perhaps in the broadest sense of a change of strategy in his relation to them. He speaks in this letter not as apostolic advisor and authoritative teacher but as one of the διάκονοι, the servers or deliverers of the good news, who model Jesus' dying and receive Jesus' life as it is revealed in those who believe them— the treasure in their clay pot (4:7). Yet even so, we must ask if this is for him strictly a strategy, a means to some larger end, such as Corinthian support for his collection and a resulting Jerusalem recognition of his work in Asia and Greece. Or is he truly frank when he says he is proud of them, calling them his letter of recommendation (3:2-3) because he recognizes their community life as the rich fruit that proves his service to God? Is his joy in fact overflowing?

Feminist readers will differ in our answers to these questions, but we will ask them and not pass over Paul's arguments quickly, since we have not, like so many readers, already deified or dismissed Paul. In this passage Paul does link reconciliation with God to reconciliation with himself, in that God's first-person assurances from Scripture ground his first-person appeals that they open up to him (6:1-2, 16-18; 7:1-4). But in the process he concedes unconditionally the Corinthians' claim to be God's sons and daughters and recognizes that it is their present life in Christ that makes his present death in Christ not a dead end but a dying and living together.

What is it then that Paul wants of the Corinthians, and what do they want from him? If Paul concedes that the Corinthians are God's temple in which the living God dwells and walks around (6:16) according to God's promise in Leviticus 26:11-12 and Ezekiel 37:27, then what Paul wants when he pleads for them to be reconciled with God is in fact that they be reconciled with him. They must be quite alienated from him, apparently convinced that he stands in judgment against them (7:3), probably because they have not followed his earlier instructions. It is not clear if they are also distressed by their alienation from him or if they have dismissed him as a figure in their past—Paul's extended self-defense suggests the latter—but he clearly cannot tolerate being estranged from them.

Yet why does he claim reconciliation with them in terms of reconciliation with God? Apparently, he so identifies his work with God's outreach toward them that the reconciliation with them that he desires as he writes this letter becomes a new way to speak of God's desire, and "reconciliation" becomes for the first time that is attested a metaphor for God's act in Christ parallel to "salvation," "redemption," and "justification." This is the contradiction Paul finds himself in, calling those already in Christ to be reconciled to God, that has led some interpreters to say that Paul is using prebaptismal instructions in this passage: "be reconciled to God," "now is the right time," "come out . . . be separated." Yet Paul's letters are full of imperatives that follow indicatives in this way. And the metaphor "reconciliation," as with "repent" and "return," is particularly open to repeated use in a world where "coming out" is a process, not a single step, and restoration has a long history.

As for the Corinthians, it seems increasingly clear that they want to be recognized as God's people, as witnesses to Jesus' risen life. The unmarried women and virgins among them and the women who pray and prophesy have added reason to seek recognition after Paul's restrictions of them in his earlier letter. If we ask why Paul does not cancel these restrictions explicitly, or apologize, the answer is not hard to come by. He could think that this would highlight his previous position that did not succeed, whereas he wants to diffuse the conflict. He does this not by using apostolic credentials (Paul has not claimed to be an "apostle" since the opening sentence of the letter) but by identifying himself with his coworkers as διάκονοι, servers of the Gospel who enact Christ's death in itinerant trials, and by identifying the Corinthians he has offended with the congregation as a whole who enact Christ's risen life as God's temple, God's people, and God's sons and daughters. Other less generous interpretations of Paul's conduct are also possible, but it is not accurate to ignore the changes in Paul's perspectives and arguments or to assume that the women leaders have melted away. He has taken the vulnerable position of the defendant, has conceded considerable space, and should be evaluated accordingly.

2 Corinthians 7:5-16

Titus's Report and Paul's Joy

Text and Its Structure (7:5-16)

The structure of this section is not ambiguous. Paul gives a running account of arriving in Macedonia, meeting Titus, and hearing his report from Corinth. He then responds to the report, both apologizing for his earlier letter and defending it, and concludes with Titus's reactions. Yet, far from a dry travelogue, this passage continues to focus on Paul's feelings, the Corinthians' feelings, and Titus's feelings.[1] Paul seems to be seeking a restoration of good relations with the Corinthians by elaborating on their positive response to him via Titus and by expressing full confidence in them. Ivan Vegge calls this psychagogy, "leading the soul," in this case by praising them and amplifying the partial reconciliation so as to carry them toward a full reconciliation.[2]

What is difficult is reconstructing the cause and nature of their estrangement from the allusions Paul makes to it here and in 2:1-13. A previous letter from Paul is involved, also a man who has done wrong

---

1. Victor Paul Furnish, *II Corinthians*, AB 32A (Garden City, NY: Doubleday, 1984), 393–98; L.L. Welborn, "Paul's Appeal to the Emotions in 2 Corinthians 1.1–2.13; 7.5-16," *JSNT* 82 (2001): 31–60.

2. Ivan Vegge, *2 Corinthians: A Letter about Reconciliation; A Psychagogical, Epistologographical and Rhetorical Analysis*, WUNT 2.239 (Tübingen: Mohr Siebeck, 2008), 37–52, 71–106.

⁷·⁵For even when we came into Macedonia, our bodies had no rest, but we were afflicted in every way—disputes without and fears within. ⁶But God, who consoles the downcast, consoled us by the arrival of Titus, ⁷and not only by his coming, but also by the consolation with which he was consoled about you, as he told us of your longing, your mourning, your zeal for me, so that I rejoiced still more. ⁸For even if I made you sorry with my letter, I do not regret it (though I did regret it, for I see that I grieved you with that letter, though only briefly). ⁹Now I rejoice, not because you were grieved, but because your grief led to repentance; for you felt a godly grief, so that you were not harmed in any way by us. ¹⁰For godly grief produces a repentance that leads to salvation and brings no regret, but worldly grief produces death. ¹¹For see what earnestness this godly grief has produced in you, what eagerness to clear

to another person, perhaps to Paul, and to some extent to the whole community (7:8-12; 2:5). He has now been disciplined by the community and Paul wants them to forgive him (2:6-11). To explain this, interpreters have developed a thesis that Paul has just sent Titus to Corinth with a letter admonishing the Corinthians to discipline a person who insulted or otherwise offended Paul at his recent brief visit and that Paul's joy reflects them having done so.[3] I follow the earlier assumption now being revived that Paul is referring to the letter we call 1 Corinthians and probably to the man living with his father's wife whom Paul had instructed them to punish. This thesis will be developed below in discussing Paul's interaction with the Corinthians. But it is clear in any case that the purpose of this passage is not to solve the man's case, which was settled in 2:6-11, but to restore the Corinthians' confidence in Paul and pave the way for Corinth's resuming the collection for Jerusalem (7:12-13a; 8:1–9:15).

At one point only do manuscripts differ so as to put the NRSV translation in question. In 7:12 some scribes have shifted the pronouns because the Greek words for "your" and "our" had come to be pronounced alike.

3. For proposals on the nature of the man's offense, see C. K. Barrett's "Ο ΑΔΙΚΗΣΑΣ (2 Cor. 7.12)," in his *Essays on Paul* (Philadelphia: Westminster Press, 1982), 108–17; Margaret M. Thrall's "The Offender and the Offence: A Problem of Detection in 2 Corinthians," in *Scripture: Meaning and Method*, ed. B. P. Thompson (Hull: Hull University Press, 1989), 65–78; and Victor Furnish's *II Corinthians*, 163–68.

yourselves, what indignation, what alarm, what longing, what zeal, what punishment! At every point you have proved yourselves guiltless in the matter. [12]So although I wrote to you, it was not on account of the one who did the wrong, nor on account of the one who was wronged, but in order that your zeal for us might be made known to you before God. [13]In this we find comfort.

In addition to our own consolation, we rejoiced still more at the joy of Titus, because his mind has been set at rest by all of you. [14]For if I have been somewhat boastful about you to him, I was not disgraced; but just as everything we said to you was true, so our boasting to Titus has proved true as well. [15]And his heart goes out all the more to you, as he remembers the obedience of all of you, and how you welcomed him with fear and trembling. [16]I rejoice, because I have complete confidence in you.

The original could have been "our zeal on your behalf," as Chrysostom read it in the fourth century,[4] rather than "your zeal on our behalf."

A Feminist Lens at Three Ranges on Paul's Joy at Titus's Report (7:5-16)

With a Broad Focus on All Reality in the Tension between Grief and Joy

In this passage Paul finally ends the suspense set up in 2:12-13 by telling what happens when he meets Titus in Macedonia and how he reacts to Titus's news about them. He defends his earlier letter in spite of their initial negative reaction and rejoices in their positive response to Titus. But at key points where he speaks of God there are also glimpses of his underlying assumptions about pain and comfort, death and life, misunderstanding and knowing. These are set off in contrast to each other in a way that points from the negative to the positive pole.

That pain gives way to comfort appears immediately in his description of having found no relief in Macedonia until God comforted him with Titus's arrival and with good news from Corinth (7:5-7). Though it is the Corinthians' intense response that relieves Paul, he attributes it to the God who gives courage to the downcast (7:6; 1:3-4, 9-11; Isa 49:13), presuming a constant and sure support not dependent on human vicissitudes.

---

4. John Chrysostom, *Homilies on Second Corinthians* 15.3.

The final time he refers to his previous letter (7:12), he claims to have written it not because of the person who did wrong or the one who was wronged but so that something the Corinthians didn't know might be revealed to them before God. Though manuscripts of 2 Corinthians differ on whether it is Paul's zeal for them or their zeal for Paul that he says they have now discovered, it is clear that their knowledge of this relationship before God makes all the difference to Paul. Moreover, he assumes that their bond before God is secure, even in spite of ongoing conflict, and needs only to become better known.

Between these two indications of a firm foundation in God's giving courage to the downcast and revealing their mutual relationship, Paul refers again to God in his primary point of defending his previous letter (7:8-11). He contrasts λύπη (pain, grief) that is τοῦ κόσμου (of the world) and λύπη (pain, grief) that is κατὰ θεόν (according to God). Here the translation can be deceptive. The NRSV speaks of "worldly grief" and "godly grief," vitiating the contrast. Frances Young and David F. Ford translate "the world's hurt" and "hurt under God," suggesting to me that the person is God's victim.[5] The Revised English Bible is better, where "pain borne in the world's way" is contrasted with "pain borne in God's way." In any case, Paul's point is that the former produces death, while the latter, through μετάνοια (a change of heart, repentance), produces salvation or life (σωτηρία, from σώζω, "save, live"). The dualism here is best seen as a contrast of two ways to deal with pain, and Paul claims that, at least in the case of "the man who did wrong" (7:12), their hearts were changed to recognize and discipline him so that now forgiveness is possible (2:5-11; 1 Cor 5:1-13). Paul is saying that life is available rather than death when pain caused by human conflict is faced in God's way, that is, in open acts of justice aiming toward restoration. Whether Paul is presenting this to the Corinthians with full disclosure of the conflict between himself and them—whether there are other matters rankling than this man's case, whether he is open to change on his side—remains unclear.

With Focus on the Social, Political, and Economic Context

Although this passage seems to be dealing with personal issues between Paul and this community and with Titus as the mediator, certain social, political, and economic factors are in play as Paul seeks the reso-

---

5. Frances Young and David F. Ford, *Meaning and Truth in 2 Corinthians* (London: SPCK, 1987), 268–69.

lution he hopes for. He is writing 2 Corinthians from Macedonia, a larger
Roman province north of Achaia where Corinth is a central city (1:1). In
Macedonia, Paul has just met Titus, who brought him news about how
the Corinthians had received his earlier letter (7:5-13). Macedonia's two
major cities, the Roman colony of Philippi, founded by Augustus as a site
to settle his Roman veterans after the long civil wars, and the provincial
capital of Thessalonica, each had assemblies of Christ believers generated by Paul and his colleagues. It becomes apparent in 2 Corinthians
that Corinth's believers competed with these groups for Paul's attention; witness the way Paul defends his plans to travel to Macedonia as
having been arranged for the benefit of the Corinthians (1:15-23). Now
he writes from Macedonia, delaying again his coming to Corinth and
explaining again that this is for their benefit, not only because he had to
wait there for Titus to arrive with news from Corinth, but also because
he wants to spare them his judgment that will fall if he comes before
they are reconciled.[6]

Rivalry in the Greek-speaking world between Achaia and Macedonia
had deep roots in early competitions among city-states. Achaean cities
such as Athens, Sparta, and Corinth dominated until Philip I of Macedon
and his son Alexander the Great built an empire in the late fourth century
BCE. Rome's destruction of Corinth in the second century for organizing
a league of cities against Roman expansion was another humiliation for
Corinth that was in no way compensated for a century later by Rome's
building and populating a colony there called *Colonia Laus Julia Corinthiensis*. Greek-speaking people who returned or who arrived in Corinth
to make a living in the trades and service areas where Paul circulated
had no citizenship or social standing. Meanwhile Roman investments
in Macedonia were increasing as legions and their supplies were sent to
put down rebellions and fortify Thrace and areas along the Danube, so
that for a time Achaia was even absorbed with Macedonia into Moesia
as an imperial province under the Roman Legate Poppeaus Sabinus.[7]

This competition can only have exacerbated the Corinthians' sense
of frustration with Paul, who managed to get to Macedonia but not to
Corinth. So in this section of 2 Corinthians, where he picks up again his
account of having gone to Macedonia, he stresses that he did so even at
the risk of his work in Asia in order to meet Titus and get word about

---

6. 2 Cor 2:1-2; 12:20-21; 13:2, 10.

7. For a fuller description of this, see the "Social, Political, and Economic Setting"
of 1:12–2:11 above.

Corinth (2:12-13). He reports his arrival in Macedonia: "our flesh had no relief . . . strife without, fears within," until Titus arrives with good news about them (7:5-7). And in concluding this section (7:14-16) Paul points out that his earlier boast to Titus about them had been vindicated and now he could rejoice with Titus. So Paul plays on Corinthian competition with Macedonia to encourage their sense of his special relation with Corinth. This will become explicit in the following two chapters.[8]

Titus's role is significant on several levels. He appears as Paul's agent in visiting Corinth after a negative reaction to Paul's letter, and he brings back positive news, at least about one case. This suggests, along with Paul's boasting about the Corinthians to Titus before sending him there, that Titus not only carried word back and forth but was briefed ahead and expected to be instrumental in working toward a solution to the problem. A similar role is described for Timothy in 1 Thessalonians 3:1-6, where he is said to have been sent "to strengthen and encourage" them.

This kind of representing another person was essential to political administration in the Roman Empire,[9] where even provincial governors in internal provinces such as Italy, Greece, and Western Asia Minor traditionally returned to Rome at the year's end to report to the Roman Senate, though by this time reporting no longer occurred annually. The emperor himself ruled the external provinces of the empire through his personal authority delegated to military tribunes, governors, vassal kings, special legates, procurators, tax officials, and administrative slaves who represented him at every level. By the time the Roman Republic had been replaced by the Roman Empire in the second half of the first century BCE, rule by those representing the larger body of people had given way to rule by the personal authority of an individual will. Personal authority also shaped Paul's self-understanding in that he had been sent by God's will as apostle to the Gentiles (Rom 11:13). Did Titus understand himself as a representative of Paul's personal authority? Or does Paul's first-person-plural defense of God's διάκονοι (representatives, ministers; 3:1–7:4) show that they would both take themselves to be delegates of God's authority? In either case, Roman patterns of personal and representational authority are not far off.

---

8. Hans Dieter Betz, *2 Corinthians 8 and 9: A Commentary on Two Administrative Letters of the Apostle Paul* (Philadelphia: Fortress, 1985), 48–53.

9. Margaret M. Mitchell, "New Testament Envoys in the Context of Greco-Roman Diplomatic and Epistolary Conventions: The Example of Timothy and Titus," *JBL* 3 (1992): 641–62.

Titus appears in Paul's recognized letters only in 2 Corinthians and in Galatians 2:1-3, where Titus is noted as being Greek and yet not required to be circumcised when taken along some years before to the Jerusalem council that recognized Paul's outreach to Gentiles. That Titus was an uncircumcised Greek was not a problem in largely Gentile Corinth. He seems to be favored there over Paul, so that Paul sends him to investigate Corinthian opposition to his earlier letter. Later Paul pleads his own innocence by comparing himself to Titus (12:16-18). Was it Titus's relative youth, good looks, and speaking ability that contrasted with Paul's, considering Paul's apparent sight or speech disability?[10] Or was it Paul's authority as a founder of the community[11] and his demanding temperament that put off the Corinthians, while Titus might conciliate Corinthian leaders, including its women prophets, having a Greek person's assumptions about meal, dress, and prophecy practices? Titus's skill in bringing the Corinthians to a measure of agreement with Paul here, and Paul to accepting them, turns out to be crucial in the next chapters, where Paul designates Titus to return to Corinth to organize the collection for Jerusalem (8:16-24).

With Focus Narrowed to This Interaction of Paul and the Corinthians

Here we see how little our broad focus above on the structure of reality or the more specific focus on the social and political setting can reveal about what is going on where the composer touches the issue most sensitive to the recipients. We can tell there has been a serious falling-out between Paul and the Corinthians, one related to a letter he wrote about a certain person who wronged someone else (7:8-13), perhaps Paul himself. We are not told what the man did because everyone to whom Paul is writing knows. In fact, Paul himself wants to get beyond the incident now that they have disciplined the man and Paul has urged them to forgive him (2:5-11). Why, then, does Paul return here to the issue of this letter? Clearly, more is at stake than one man. Paul seems to be using their willingness to follow his lead in this case that Titus has reported—their μετάνοια (REB: "change of heart"; NRSV: "repentance")—for another purpose.[12] Yet he does not apply it as a model to create change about other

---

10. 2 Cor 10:10; 11:6; Gal 4:13-15.

11. 2 Cor 1:19; 10:13-14.

12. This is the thesis of Reimund Bieringer, *Studies on 2 Corinthians*, BETL 112 (Leuven: Leuven University Press, 1994), 156–69. An alternate thesis proposes that

specific matters where they differ from him. What he wants is a change in their relationship, from contention to acceptance of each other (7:12).

Apparently the letter that provoked the conflict involved other matters, matters that are still rousing resentment in Corinth, which Paul wants neither to press nor to concede explicitly. Instead, he is ready to settle for a reconciliation of different roles: he delivers Christ's letter, which they are (3:3); he provides the clay pot for God's treasure in them (4:7); he enacts Jesus' dying and they Christ's life (4:10-12). This is possible for Paul because he has shifted his strategy from expecting them to imitate him (1 Cor 4:16; 11:1) to recognizing a complementarity between himself and them, allowing him to accept conduct in them he does not practice in order to be accepted as integral, even essential, to their experience of Christ. But to achieve this Paul must not ignore their reaction to his letter. The letter cannot have been one written after a single, recent, and otherwise unknown incident about a certain man, as most interpreters propose from Paul's not discussing other issues. Rather, it is the letter he has poured himself into, shaping multiple instructions for different groups, a number of which have not been accepted in Corinth, hence the conflict. First Corinthians was this letter, according to ancient interpreters.[13] A full argument for this was developed by F. C. Baur in the mid-nineteenth century,[14] and it has been defended against other modern theories by Niels Hyldahl.[15] It points to the man who "has his father's wife" (1 Cor 5:1) as the likely "one who did wrong" (2 Cor 7:12), a thesis often rejected because Paul's call for ostracism in 1 Corinthians seems irreversible, whereas here Paul forgives (2 Cor 2:5-11).[16] Or does the difficulty arise from the modern classification of the offense as incest? Paul may have come to see it differently, if he had heard, for example, that the father had married his son's friend before himself dying.

I focus on four questions in exploring what 2 Corinthians 7:5-16 reveals about Paul's interaction with the Corinthians. First, since Paul has already shared the anguish in which he wrote 1 Corinthians (2 Cor 2:1-4)

---

the offender was not an individual but a group whose repentance and forgiveness is still pending: Christopher Land, *The Integrity of 2 Corinthians and Paul's Aggravating Absence* (Sheffield: Sheffield Phoenix, 2015).

13. John Chrysostom, *Homilies on Second Corinthians* 15.3.

14. Ferdinand Christian Baur, "Die beiden Briefe an die Korinthier," in *Paulus, Der Apostel Jesu Christi*, vol. 1, 2nd ed. (Leipzig, 1866–67; repr. Osnabrück, 1968), 337–43.

15. Niels Hyldahl, "Die Frage nach der literarischen Einheit des Zweiten Korintherbriefes," *ZNW* 64 (1973): 289–306, summary: 305–6.

16. Furnish, *II Corinthians*, 165–66.

and told how he headed to Macedonia to get word from Titus about the Corinthians, why, then, does he delay five chapters before reporting here that he reached Macedonia and got positive news about Corinth? Second, when Paul goes on to provide multiple excuses for having written as he did, why does he not take up any further objections they made to the letter but dwells strictly on their feelings about him? Third, why does Paul highlight the messenger Titus both before and after defending his letter to the Corinthians? And fourth, is Paul really joyful and confident in the Corinthians here, or is he simply preparing the ground to seek donations for Jerusalem in chapters 8–9 or to undermine their support for rival apostles in chapter 10–13?

Paul's delay in reporting Titus's news needs an explanation once we read Paul's letters in the way we read letters that we ourselves receive, that is, not as objective descriptions of a static world, but as attempts to move and persuade the receivers. Were the delay in telling the story not deliberate we would hardly expect Paul to introduce his urgency to meet Titus in Macedonia, as he did so vividly (2:12-13), and then not tell what Titus said or how he himself reacted until five chapters later. Paul does burst out in thanks to God just after the mention of going to Macedonia (2:12-16), so the Corinthians might think he remembers how Titus had spoken well of them. But Paul leaves them unclear if he is thanking God that Titus has made it back safely or that Titus brought good news about them. The suspense would be greater because the Corinthians would know, as the letter as a whole shows us,[17] that Titus found ambiguous attitudes toward Paul in Corinth. They might be wondering if Titus had told Paul the worst. Would Paul lash out against those who had not followed his directives, such as, perhaps, virgins who still refused marriage, speakers in tongues, or women prophets? Would he now stir up his earlier converts, Crispus and Stephanus, to discipline others?[18] Could Christ really be speaking through a man so strong in his letters but inarticulate and ineffective in person (13:3; 10:10)?

Paul apparently had reason to defend himself for several chapters against charges of self-praise, deceit, and incompetence and to reshape his message while keeping them alert as they waited for the other shoe to drop about what he heard from Titus.[19] Paul's defense ends with a

17. 2 Cor 6:1-2; 7:1; 10:10-11; 12:20-21; 13:2-5.
18. 1 Cor 1:14-16; 16:15-18; Acts 18:1-3, 18.
19. Thomas Schmeller, *Der zweite Brief an die Korinther, Teilband 1: 2 Kor. 1:1–7:4* (Neukirchen-Vluyn: Neukirchener Varlag, 2010), 146–47.

plea to be reconciled with God, which turns out to be inextricable from reconciliation with Paul.[20] Only then do they learn that Paul takes their warm, even vehement, response to Titus as their zeal on his own behalf and their longing to see him (7:7, 11, 15).

Second, why does Paul provide multiple excuses for his letter that offended them—it hurt him too, it led to their regret, it didn't harm them, it showed they cared for him, it comforted him—but yet not take up any other specific points where they do not comply than the single offender they punished? It is this that has caused most interpreters to say that Paul is not referring to 1 Corinthians but must have written another letter with tears concerning a man who did wrong. Paul does commend them ἐλυπήθετε γὰρ κατὰ θεόν ("you were pained in God's way" or in the NRSV "you felt a godly grief," 7:9). That led to repenting how they had once treated the man because they discovered in disciplining this man and vindicating Paul how much they care for Paul. But if this issue is so well solved, why does Paul still defend his letter so vehemently and preface this with chapters defending his work among them and calling for reconciliation? It is both simpler and more adequate to the evidence to conclude that Titus went to Corinth, as Timothy had earlier gone to Thessalonica (1 Thess 3:6-10), on a fact-finding and peacemaking trip for Paul after word came of their not implementing his instructions in 1 Corinthians.

Now that Titus has returned with at least one piece of good news—apparently that they repented their support of the man who lived with his father's wife (1 Cor 5:1-5)—Paul chooses to take their discipline of this man as a sufficient sign of their concern for him. He interprets their intense response—"your longing [ἐπιπόθησιν], your mourning [ὀδυρμόν], your zeal [ζῆλον] for me" (7:7)—as a sign of their change of heart concerning himself. "Grief according to God's will," he says, filled them with "such self-defense [ἀπολογίαν], such indignation [ἀγανάκτησιν], such fear [φόβον], such longing [ἐπιπόθησιν], such zeal [ζῆλον], such vindication [ἐκδίκησιν]!" (7:11).[21] Would that we could know all that stood behind

---

20. 2 Cor 5:20; 6:1-2, 11-13; 7:2-4.

21. My translation. See the NRSV above. The Revised English Bible tries to make sense of the words in light of the situation: "You bore your pain in God's way, and just look at the results: it made you take the matter seriously and vindicate yourselves; it made you indignant and apprehensive; it aroused your longing for me, your devotion, and your eagerness to see justice done" (7:11). See also the German feminist *Bibel in gerechter Sprache* 2006 translation: "Seht doch, welch grosses Bemühen gerade

their fervent reaction that Titus reported and Paul interprets![22] Paul chooses to take it both as evidence that they are innocent in the matter of the wrongdoer and as proof that they now know how deeply they care for him (7:9, 12). Yet the letter he is writing shows that this support is the very thing Paul is still struggling to bring off. When he concludes, "In this we are encouraged" (διὰ τοῦτο παρακεκλήμεθα; 7:13) and "I rejoice that in all matters I am confident in you" (χαίρω ὅτι ἐν παντὶ θαρρῶ ἐν ὑμῖν; 7:16), we sense, as in his many statements of self-confidence, that he is working to persuade both himself and them.[23]

Third, why does Paul give such prominence to the conduct and feelings of Titus, the messenger, when the issue is his own reconciliation with the Corinthians? He dramatizes his eagerness to hear from Corinth by telling how he leaves for Macedonia from Troas because Titus had not arrived there (2:12-13). When he resumes the story after five chapters with his arrival in Macedonia, he speaks first of waiting there for Titus, next of his joy at Titus's arrival, and only then of Titus's report about them. And this is told in terms of Titus being encouraged by their concern for Paul, as if it were Titus who had been through the tension of waiting (7:5-7). After Paul defends his letter as good for them, if painful, because of their change of heart about the man and about Paul himself (7:8-13), Paul returns to Titus and claims to have been even more encouraged by Titus's joy over them and by the vindication of his own earlier boast about them to Titus. And finally, Paul reports that Titus's feelings for them (σπλάγχνα, "bowels, guts"; NRSV: "heart") are only intensified as Titus remembers how warmly they received him (7:13-15), leaving unsaid that receiving the one sent is tantamount to receiving the sender.

This praise of the messenger reveals two key aspects of Paul's interaction with the Corinthians. First, Titus had been able to touch the hearts of the Corinthians in a way that Paul had not. This was not likely due only to Paul's disadvantage in speech, sight, or appearance but due to his authority, with Timothy and Sylvanus, as a church founder (1:19).

---

diese gottgewollte Traurigkeit bei euch hervorgebracht hat, dazu Entschuldigung, Entrüstung, Angst, Sehnsucht, Engagement und Rechtsprechung!" (p. 2139).

22. Benjamin Lapprenga takes ζῆλος and σπουδή (zeal and eagerness) as synonyms and yet argues that ζῆλος can indicate emulation, that the Corinthians are patterning themselves after the less-than-noble Paul: *Paul's Language of ζῆλος: Monosemy and the Rhetoric of Identity and Practice*, BibInt 137 (Leiden: Brill, 2015), 179–83. I hear Paul's ζῆλος here signifying the intense concern for another person or project (7:7, 11).

23. Stanley Norris Olson, "Confidence Expressions in Paul: Epistolary Conventions and the Purpose of 2 Corinthians" (PhD diss., Yale University, 1976), 57–83.

The letter being defended by Paul was his own 1 Corinthians. Titus did not arrive with another letter from Paul making demands but was free to inquire and to persuade until they punished the offender, or at least to interpret their act to Paul as a change of heart bringing on Paul's forgiveness in this present letter. Paul was apparently ready to let other matters go, but one sign of change of heart on both sides was needed to mend the relationship, and this was mediated by Titus. Paul's other instructions in 1 Corinthians about food, marriage, and worship, including women's sexual choices and leadership, have not been raised. Paul's joy about an opening toward reconciliation with Corinth reveals his debt to Titus.

The other equally important reason Paul highlights Titus is evident in the following chapters. We hear in 8:16-24 that Paul is sending (or has sent) Titus back to Corinth to renew the collection for Jerusalem, which Paul wants them to complete before he comes himself. The success of this collection is arguably the primary aim of 2 Corinthians, and Paul introduces it only after he has dealt with the Corinthians' doubts about him, defended his service for God, and made a start in resolving their differences with the help of Titus. Then he pleads for a generous collection for Jerusalem (chaps. 8–9). Finally, Paul makes an attack on those who denigrate his work (chaps. 10–13), and here again he appeals to their good experience with Titus to prove that he and his colleagues would never exploit them as others have done (12:17-18).

My fourth question asks whether Paul can be genuinely joyful and confident in the Corinthians at this point and yet in chapters 10–13 go on to sharp critique and threats of judgment. This can only be properly considered after a complete review of the letter. Yet one cannot on principle deny him times of joy and confidence simply because they come and go. A related, and perhaps more difficult, question concerns whether Paul's interest is in the Corinthians or in the collection he is raising for Jerusalem and whether the collection is for the poor in Jerusalem or for gaining in Jerusalem recognition for his work among people like the Corinthians. This may be less a question to be solved than a conundrum to be left open in our search for how the Corinthians will have reacted to the present letter.

As feminist interpreters we may also question the methods Paul uses to get the support of the Corinthians for his collection. Is the man with what Paul considers a sexual offense made a kind of scapegoat in Paul's recovering good relations with this community? No wonder Paul is constrained to release him from the exclusion or other discipline that was applied (2:5-11). And was it ethical to use Titus as a front man to face the hostility that the Corinthians felt at Paul's 1 Corinthians letter? Is Paul's effusive praise of Titus a compensation for having asked so much of him? Nonetheless, I find it impressive that Paul and Titus do not walk away from work that in its inter-cultural complexity is close to impossible to bring off. Convinced that they have a calling from God, they keep at relating and communicating,[24] shifting strategies to bring off what must therefore have been an evolving vision, one that had to incorporate aspects that the Corinthians were not willing to give up.

24. Ulrich Mell, "Paulus: scheiternder Gescheiter: Ein historischer und literarischer Einwurf," in *Der zweite Korintherbrief: Literarische Gestalt—historische Situation—theologische Argumentation. Festschrift zum 70. Geburtstag von Dietrich-Alex Koch*, ed. Dieter Sänger (Göttingen: Vandenhoeck & Ruprecht, 2012), 215–17.

2 Corinthians 8:1–9:15

A Culminating Appeal
for the Jerusalem Poor

Text and Its Structure (8:1–9:15)

In these two chapters Paul promotes the collection for the poor in Jerusalem. Hans Dieter Betz argues that each chapter is a separate administrative letter written by Paul at nearly the same time: the first letter asking Corinth's congregations to complete their collection and recommending his envoys; the second mobilizing others in the wider province of Achaia to help Corinth do so.[1] But most other interpreters today read chapter 8 or both chapters as a continuation of the preceding letter, not only because themes of joy (χαρά), eagerness (σπουδή), and abundance (περίσσευμα) are already present in earlier chapters,[2] but because this intense and extended appeal for their Jerusalem offering is a fitting culmination of Paul's previous equally intense appeal for their reconciliation with himself and with God (5:20–7:16). And before that Paul has built his self-defense with sufficient care (2:14–5:21) that he now feels able to ask Corinth to make their contribution, prodding them with

---

1. Hans Dieter Betz, *2 Corinthians 8 and 9: A Commentary on Two Administrative Letters of the Apostle Paul* (Philadelphia: Fortress, 1985), 39–41, 87–95, 129–40.
2. Nils Alstrup Dahl, *Studies in Paul* (Minneapolis: Augsburg, 1977), 38–39.

2 Cor 8:1–9:15

8:1We want you to know, brothers and sisters, about the grace of God that has been granted to the churches of Macedonia; 2for during a severe ordeal of affliction, their abundant joy and their extreme poverty have overflowed in a wealth of generosity on their part. 3For, as I can testify, they voluntarily gave according to their means, and even beyond their means, 4begging us earnestly for the privilege of sharing in this ministry to the saints—5and this, not merely as we expected; they gave themselves first to the Lord and, by the will of God, to us, 6so that we might urge Titus that, as he had already made a beginning, so he should also complete this generous undertaking among you. 7Now as you excel in everything—in faith, in speech, in knowledge, in utmost eagerness, and in our love for you—so we want you to excel also in this generous undertaking.

8I do not say this as a command, but I am testing the genuineness of your love against the earnestness of others. 9For you know the generous act of our Lord Jesus Christ, that though he was rich, yet for your sakes he became poor, so that by his poverty you might become rich. 10And in this matter I am giving my advice: it is appropriate for you who began last year not only to do something but even to desire to do something—11now finish doing it, so that your eagerness may be matched by completing it according to your means. 12For if the eagerness is there, the gift is acceptable according to what one has—not according to what one does not have. 13I do not mean that there should be relief for others and

news of the Macedonians' generosity and luring them with recognition that they were among the first who wanted to give.

When read as part of a continuing letter, the collection appeal proceeds in four major parts. The first is a report of the Macedonians' generosity as a challenge to Corinth's own, with assurance that he wants them only to complete what they started, to give what they have to give, and to foster greater equality for the benefit of all (8:1-15). In the second part he recommends to them Titus and two exemplary brothers who will ensure the security of the collection (8:16-24). Third, he claims he wouldn't need to write them about the collection except that he told the Macedonians that Achaia was prepared to give since last year, and now he needs them to back him up (9:1-5). Fourth, and most substantively, he argues for theirs to be a generous gift, saying less about the needs of the Jerusalem poor than about their own needs as nature and Scripture teach—that those who sow richly reap richly, that God is able to give them all they need for living and great giving, and that their gift will cause those who receive it to praise God and to pray to God for them (9:6-15).

pressure on you, but it is a question of a fair balance between [14]your present abundance and their need, so that their abundance may be for your need, in order that there may be a fair balance. [15]As it is written,

"The one who had much did not have too much,

and the one who had little did not have too little."

[16]But thanks be to God who put in the heart of Titus the same eagerness for you that I myself have. [17]For he not only accepted our appeal, but since he is more eager than ever, he is going to you of his own accord. [18]With him we are sending the brother who is famous among all the churches for his proclaiming the good news; [19]and not only that, but he has also been appointed by the churches to travel with us while we are administering this generous undertaking for the glory of the Lord himself and to show our goodwill. [20]We intend that no one should blame us about this generous gift that we are administering, [21]for we intend to do what is right not only in the Lord's sight but also in the sight of others. [22]And with them we are sending our brother whom we have often tested and found eager in many matters, but who is now more eager than ever because of his great confidence in you. [23]As for Titus, he is my partner and co-worker in your service; as for our brothers, they are messengers of the churches, the glory of Christ. [24]Therefore openly before the churches, show them the proof of your love and of our reason for boasting about you.

[9:1]Now it is not necessary for me to write you about the ministry to the

Only at one point is the wording of these chapters seriously contested in the different manuscripts. When Paul cites the Corinthians' talents (8:7) he lists their faith, speech, knowledge, and energy, ending with either "and the love you have for us" or "and the love we have for you." The latter is found in more early manuscripts ($\mathfrak{P}^{46}$ and the Vaticanus codex [B]). Also it is the more difficult reading in this context, hence probably the original that some scribes have "corrected." So Paul brings in his own love for them as the final evidence that they can afford to be generous.[3] At another point the translation is contested: Paul's ὑποστάσις in 9:4 could refer back to his "project" or "undertaking" of the collection

3. Margaret E. Thrall, *A Critical and Exegetical Commentary on the Second Epistle to the Corinthians*, ICC (Edinburgh: T & T Clark, 1994), 529–30; Victor Paul Furnish, *II Corinthians*, AB 32A (Garden City, NY: Doubleday, 1984), 403.

saints, [2]for I know your eagerness, which is the subject of my boasting about you to the people of Macedonia, saying that Achaia has been ready since last year; and your zeal has stirred up most of them. [3]But I am sending the brothers in order that our boasting about you may not prove to have been empty in this case, so that you may be ready, as I said you would be; [4]otherwise, if some Macedonians come with me and find that you are not ready, we would be humiliated—to say nothing of you—in this undertaking. [5]So I thought it necessary to urge the brothers to go on ahead to you, and arrange in advance for this bountiful gift that you have promised, so that it may be ready as a voluntary gift and not as an extortion.

[6]The point is this: the one who sows sparingly will also reap sparingly, and the one who sows bountifully will also reap bountifully. [7]Each of you must give as you have made up your mind, not reluctantly or under compulsion, for God loves a cheerful giver. [8]And God is able to provide you with every blessing in abundance, so that by always having enough of everything, you may share abundantly in every good work. [9]As it is written,

"He scatters abroad, he gives to
     the poor;
   his righteousness endures
     forever."

in general (NRSV)[4] or perhaps more pointedly to his "confidence" or "steadfastness" in boasting about them.[5]

A Feminist Lens at Three Ranges on Paul's Appeal for the Jerusalem Collection (8:1–9:15)

The Ecosystem Assumed in Paul's Collection Appeal

Though Paul is most explicit about the whole cosmos in his Romans letter, where he speaks of the created universe groaning in its birth pains (Rom 8:18-25), here he promotes the Jerusalem collection by drawing on what Betz calls a widespread ancient agricultural theology: "The one who sows sparsely will reap sparsely, and the one who sows richly will reap richly" (9:6; close to Prov 11:24). Paul then sees this confirmed by several other words from Scripture, "God loves a happy giver" (9:7; Prov 22:8a LXX);[6] "He has scattered; he gave to the poor; his justice remains forever"

---

4. Thrall, *Second Epistle*, 568–70; Furnish, *II Corinthians*, 427–28.

5. Georg Heinrici, *Der zweite Brief an die Korinther*, rev. ed. (Göttingen: Vandenhoeck & Ruprecht, 1900; German, 1887), 298–99. But see BDAG, 1041.

6. This addition to Prov 22:8 in Greek is absent in the Hebrew text that the NRSV translates.

¹⁰He who supplies seed to the sower and bread for food will supply and multiply your seed for sowing and increase the harvest of your righteousness. ¹¹You will be enriched in every way for your great generosity, which will produce thanksgiving to God through us; ¹²for the rendering of this ministry not only supplies the needs of the saints but also overflows with many thanksgivings to God. ¹³Through the testing of this ministry you glorify God by your obedience to the confession of the gospel of Christ and by the generosity of your sharing with them and with all others, ¹⁴while they long for you and pray for you because of the surpassing grace of God that he has given you. ¹⁵Thanks be to God for his indescribable gift!*

* NRSV notes: 8:1, Gk *brothers* for *brothers and sisters*; 8:4, Gk *grace* for *privilege*; 8:6, Gk *this grace* for *this generous undertaking*; 8:7, Other ancient authorities read *your love for us* not *our love for you*; Gk *this grace* for *this generous undertaking*; 8:9, Gk *the grace* for *the generous act*; 8:18, Or *the gospel* for *the good news*; 8:19, Gk *this grace* for *this generous undertaking*; 8:23, Gk *apostles* for *messengers*; 9:4, Other ancient authorities add to the sentence *of boasting*; 9:9, Or *benevolence* for *righteousness*; 9:10, Or *benevolence* for *righteousness*.

(9:9; Ps 111:9 LXX; 112:9 NRSV);[7] and "The one providing seed for the sower and bread for the eater" will provide seed for you and make the fruit of your justice grow (9:10; Isa 55:10). In other words, Paul appeals here not to Christ or to God's covenant with Israel but to what we call nature as Jesus also appealed, "Love your enemies. . . and be children of your father in heaven, for he shines the sun on the bad and the good and rains the rain on the just and unjust" (Matt 5:45). Paul's argument for generous giving challenges the Corinthians to join in the natural process of sowing and reaping richly. He contrasts it to giving that is sparse (9:6; 8:7), commanded (9:7; 8:8), imposed from without (8:10-11; 9:5), beyond the giver's means (8:11-12), or to the giver's disadvantage (8:13-15). This may be why Paul interrupts his argument for the collection to recommend Titus and the brothers (8:16-24), because he wants to stress that not only the Macedonians (8:3-4, 8) are eager (σπουδή) and ready (προθυμία) to voluntarily (αὐθαίρετος) join in this effort but Titus (8:16-17) and the second brother (8:22) have the same enthusiasm for the task. It is as though the soil has already been sown by the eagerness

7. The Septuagint Greek Psalm 111/112 is speaking of the righteous or just person, whereas Paul speaks in this context of God, but he immediately shows its consequence for persons in 9:11. See Betz, *2 Corinthians 8 and 9*, 98–100, 114–15.

of so many people, including themselves in their initial desire to give (8:10), that they can be confident the harvest will be rich and will want to join in and complete their gift (8:11).

We may have difficulty with this argument in a time when sparse sowing and sparse reaping of the earth's resources seem more appropriate after years of overconsumption. David Horrell reminds us that we cannot expect Paul's letters to be addressing our ecological crisis.[8] What we can do is see the way that Paul in his Corinthian crisis of mutual suspicion and losing heart takes the ecosystem of plant life into account as a model and challenges those who have enough to use what they have toward the needs of others, thereby sowing richly and harvesting richly. In this way they can extend their connections and build what will come back, as Paul says, only to their benefit (8:13-14). While we who have plenty want to live more sparingly and preserve the resources and nutrients of the earth, we know that others today still have little and need to sow and reap richly. Solutions to climate change such as cap and trade and quotas based on level of development begin to recognize this difference. Paul rounds off his argument with the experience of Israel in the wilderness when God gives food according to family size, "the one with much got not too much and the one with little not too little" (8:15; Exod 16:18). The ecojustice of God is taken as the standard. God's sufficient supply of grain for food and for the next year's seed is what increases "the produce of your justice" (9:10). And here Betz documents that this concept, that God provides resources for a generosity that in turn realizes God's righteousness, is not distinctive to Paul or to Judaism but is widely present in Greek moral and religious discourse.[9]

Although Paul prefers to ground his argument here in Scripture's proverbs rather than in descriptions of God and Christ,[10] he does integrate this exhortation into a comprehensive theology through his wide use of

---

8. David G. Horrell, "Ecojustice in the Bible? Pauline Contributions to an Ecological Theology," in *Bible and Justice: Ancient Texts, Modern Challenges*, ed. Matthew J. M. Coomber (London: Equinox, 2011), 158-77, esp. 161-62, 172-73; David G. Horrell, Cherryl Hunt, and Christopher Southgate, *Greening Paul: Reading Paul in a Time of Ecological Crisis* (Waco, TX: Baylor University Press, 2010), 160-80, 190-200; Ernst Conradie, "Towards an Ecological Biblical Hermeneutics: A Review Essay on the Earth Bible Project," *Scriptura* 85 (2004): 123-35; Conradie, "The Road towards an Ecological Biblical and Theological Hermeneutics," *Scriptura* 93 (2006): 305-14.

9. Betz, *2 Corinthians 8 and 9*, 98-100, 103, 105, 107-8, 115-17.

10. 2 Cor 8:15; 9:6, 7, 9, 10; Linda L. Belleville, "Scripture and Other Voices in Paul's Theology," in *Paul and Scripture: Extending the Conversation*, ed. Christopher D. Stanley (Atlanta: Society of Biblical Literature, 2012), 233-41.

the single term χάρις (grace).[11] Unfortunately this is made invisible in the NRSV of 2 Corinthians 8 and 9, where χάρις is translated in six different English terms: "grace" (8:1; 9:14), "privilege" (8:4), "generous undertaking" (8:6, 7, 19), "generous act" (8:9), "blessing" (9:8), and "thanks" (8:16; 9:15), with the latter three references not even identified as grace (χάρις) in the footnotes. Paul's breadth of usage rises from the concrete meaning of χάρις as favor or goodwill that also indicates an attitude of graciousness or generosity, including its effects of blessing or privilege and the response to it of thanks.[12] Paul makes it one name for the collection itself, translated in the NRSV as "generous undertaking" (8:6, 7, 19), and it is also the favor or privilege of taking part by contributing (8:4). But first and foremost it is God's grace that is given to those who give (8:1; 9:14), the blessings of God that make the gift possible (9:8), and, crucially for Paul, the generous act of Jesus Christ who "became poor so that by his poverty you might become rich" (8:9). Finally χάρις is even the thanks that comes back to God from recipients of the grace that makes all this happen (8:16; 9:15).[13] To get the impact of this, see my more literal translation of these two chapters in indented paragraphs under "The Interaction of Paul and the Corinthians as Seen in His Collection Appeal" below.

This entire circuit of grace—from God's giving life and the food that sustains life, to the richness of life in Christ and the privilege of participating in this giving, and finally to the thanks and praise to God's glory—can be called the most comprehensive theme of this letter.[14] It comes to a head in these central chapters about the collection but has already been expressed in one sentence about Paul's recent rescue in 1:10-11 and reaches an earlier climax at 4:15: "For everything is on your account, so that grace as it extends to more and more people, may increase thanksgiving to God's glory." It recurs in Paul's final vision, "My grace is enough for you" (2 Cor 12:9).[15] This suggests that the collection appeal

---

11. Marlene Crüsemann, "Eine Christologie der Beziehung: Trost, *charis* und Kraft der Schwachen nach dem 2 Brief an die Gemeinde in Korinth," in *Gott ist Beziehung: Beitäge zur biblischen rede von Gott*, ed. Claudia Janssen and Luise Schottroff (Gütersloh: Gütersloher Verlagshaus, 2014), 191–97.

12. Henry George Liddell and Robert Scott, *Greek-English Lexicon* (Oxford: Clarendon, 1968), 1715–16.

13. Thrall is right to correct the NRSV of 9:13: it is the recipients of the gift and not the Corinthians who are glorifying God with their thanks (*Second Epistle*, 588–92).

14. Dieter Georgi, *Remembering the Poor: The History of Paul's Collection for Jerusalem* (Nashville: Abingdon, 1992; German 1965, rev. 1994), 106–7; John M. G. Barclay, *Paul and the Gift* (Grand Rapids, MI: Eerdmans, 2015), 562–74.

15. See more on this circle of grace on pages 255–57 below.

is the climax of Paul's argument. Not only humans but the plants sown and harvested in the earth with the animals so kept alive are integral to this giving or grace that begins and ends in God.

Χάρις *(Grace) for Jerusalem*

What fascinates me most about the way Paul pursues his primary concern in 2 Corinthians—organizing the donation project—is the weight he gives to his key word, χάρις. Unheard of to Lutheran ears, χάρις is God's grace and love that not only flows from above to humanity below, making God the sole giver of grace, as the traditional reading of Romans 3:21-26 has it, but is the divine element that works horizontally as people give it and share it with each other (2 Cor 8:4, 7, 8, 19; 9:8). Grace is at once a material and a spiritual giving that all who participate practice. Even God is said to experience grace from people—in their thanks (8:16; 9:15).

This opens up a great network of relations of reciprocal activity in which all who take part, the divine included, turn out to be at once needy and rich, receiving and giving. Both giving and taking are classified as χάρις—a loving, acted-out affection and solidarity across all gaps. It is God who enables and sustains this network through giving the Messiah Jesus and through an endless overflow of giving (περισσεύειν, 9:8). But yet God too receives grace! God needs the action and interaction of people.

This is what Paul states in so many words as his theological and practical vision, quite apart from whether or not he was able to complete his project. And we can get even more from his letter, namely, what Paul thinks the Corinthian congregation is like from how he works to persuade them in formulating his perspectives. This lets us see a certain distance into the life of this community. As Anne Wire suggests, they are gifted, eager, and open yet also cautious and suspicious of his moves.

Much less can be said about those for whom the money is being gathered, the "saints" (8:4). These saints live in Jerusalem, we are told, not by 2 Corinthians, but by 1 Corinthians 16:1 and 3. Paul says more precisely in Romans 15:26 that they are "the poor among the saints who are in Jerusalem." But does "saints" refer here to the Jewish Christ congregation in Jerusalem, or does the word stand for what the Old Testament calls Israel (Lev 19–20), that is, the people of God in general? This is Luise Schottroff's view, that Paul had the collection made for the poor of Israel as a whole and that he himself joined in taking it to the priesthood in the temple, as Acts 24:17 has Paul say: "I came to deliver donations and offerings for my people" (εἰς τὸ ἔθνος μου).[16] And even if Paul intended it for the Messianic community only, that community was for Paul not the mother of Christendom but a representation of Israel, which the nations of the world were honoring with their gifts.[17]

Marlene Crüsemann

But must a feminist hermeneutic of suspicion alienate us from such a totalizing vision? Is Paul's God in whom this grace begins and ends, "from whom are all things and we for him" (1 Cor 8:6), a magnified and yet disguised image of the male will to dominate and be glorified? Or is this God the outside limit of human will to power and hence the possibility of human transformation in Christ, "through whom are all things and we through him" (1 Cor 8:6)? The name of Christ appears in these collection chapters twice briefly—the assemblies in Christ are his glory, the confession is of his gospel (2 Cor 8:23; 9:13)—but only once centrally: "You know the grace of our Lord Jesus Christ that for you he who was rich became poor, so that you might become rich in his poverty" (8:9). John Barclay says that being rich is reinterpreted by Paul as having all it takes to be gracious: "Whatever elements there may be of imitation and obedience, the chief effect of the Christ event is the transformation of the Corinthians into grace-formed givers, as the momentum of χάρις is carried forward into the world."[18] It matters to me that Paul does not call them to poverty in imitation of Christ but to equalizing, a fair balance (8:12-15).[19] Paul's point is not to press the Corinthians to be transformed into his own model or even Christ's model but to argue that, since they have been transformed and become rich in Christ, they are free to live graciously without fear of loss. I recognize that Paul's language can

16. Luise Schottroff, *Der erste Brief an die Gemeinde in Korinth* (Stuttgart: Kohlhammer, 2013), 334.

17. Klaus Wengst, *"Freut euch, ihr Völker, mit Gottes Volk!" Israel und die Völker als Thema des Paulus* (Stuttgart: Kohlhammer, 2008), 431.

18. John M. G. Barclay, " 'Because He Was Rich He Became Poor,' Translation, Exegesis and Hermeneutics in the Reading of 2 Cor 8–9," in *Theologizing in the Corinthian Conflict: Studies in the Exegesis and Theology of 2 Corinthians*, ed. Reimund Bieringer, Ma. Marilou S. Ibita, Dominika A. Kurek-Chomycz, and Thomas Vollmer, BTS 16 (Leuven: Peeters, 2013), 343.

19. On this see further below.

be used, and has been used, for human aggrandizing; nor was Paul's support for Jerusalem free from his own interest in gaining Jerusalem support for his work, so great caution is called for.

Yet visions are needed, and it is hard to suppress the power of comprehensive grace. Nestor Miguez writes from Latin America on this text, speaking for those victimized by certain models of sacrificial grace.[20] He insists that grace is God's praxis in performing justice. God is able to overwhelm the Corinthians with all grace so that they never lack the self-sufficiency needed to do good because God gives to the poor in eternal righteousness (9:8-9). This means God does not tolerate injustice but practices retribution with transformation so that new life appears through God's presence in the natural, personal, and social spheres. Miguez sees Paul's collection appropriately called grace in this sense, not as poverty and loss, but as riches and gain through a mutual giving that shapes new symmetries of power (8:13-15). Marlene Crüsemann identifies this as the power of the relationship between God and people and among people linked by God's χάρις (grace), which she translates *Zuwendung*, a turning toward, giving oneself to, expending for.[21] She sees Paul's collection working as God's grace not only to alleviate the poor in Jerusalem but to accomplish an exodus in which the nations of the world leave a world of domination and act out their adoption into Israel as people of God's grace.[22]

When we read Paul in this way we face the further challenge of understanding the fact that, though a collection did apparently get carried with Paul to Jerusalem (Rom 15:25-26), it did not result in restoration of the unity that Paul envisioned. When Paul writes to the Romans not long after this letter, he is already anxious about the outcome of the gift going to Jerusalem (Rom 15:30-32). The book of Acts, written near the end of the century, culminates its elegy of Paul with his arrest in Jerusalem and his judicial appeal to Rome, not with Jerusalem's welcoming of a collection in praise to God. Paul's letters, with the possible exception of

20. Nestor Miguez, "Grace in Paul's Theology: Political and Economic Projections," *Neot* 46 (2012): 287–98.

21. Crüsemann, "Christologie der Beziehung," 191–97; *Bibel in gerechter Sprache*, 2139–43.

22. Marlene Crüsemann, "Das weite Herz und die Gemeinschaft der Heiligen: 2 Kor 6,11–7,4 im sozialgeschichtlichen Kontext," in *Dem Tod nicht glauben: Sozialgeschichte der Bibel. Festschrift für Luise Schottroff zum 70. Geburtstag*, ed. Frank Crüsemann, Marlene Crüsemann, Claudia Janssen, Rainer Kessler, and Beate Wehn (Gütersloh: Güersloher Verlagshaus, 2004), 362–72, repr. in *Gott ist Beziehung: Beiträge zur biblischen Rede von Gott*, ed. Claudia Janssen and Luise Schottroff (Gütersloh: Gütersloher Verlagshaus, 2014), 218–27.

Philippians,[23] tell nothing of the time in Rome, and later writings speak of Paul martyred there.[24] So Paul's vision of grace seems to outstrip the reality in which the collection vanishes, Paul is killed and Jerusalem's temple is destroyed by the empire. Later Paulinists settle for a unity of peoples in a cosmic Christ, now become head of his body the church. He is no longer the body in which all are parts.[25] This feeds the process toward legitimating hierarchy in the church, relegating Jerusalem to the past, and distorting Judaism into the church's contrasting foil.

The Social, Political, and Economic Contexts of Paul's Collection for Jerusalem

Paul's argument in 2 Corinthians 8–9 that Corinth's Christ community complete their collecting for Jerusalem takes place at once in a senatorial province of the Roman Empire, in a voluntary association of a Greek city, and in a sect of diaspora Judaism. These contexts are not simply backgrounds but are the worlds in which Paul operates. I consider each in turn, conceding that separating them is artificial.

Paul's Collection in a Roman Senatorial Province. Corinth's province of Achaia with Macedonia on its north; Pontus, Bithynia, and Asia on the east; and Italy and coastal Gaul, Spain, and North Africa to the west (plus the major islands) made up the internal, pacified provinces of the Roman Empire. These the Emperor Augustus returned to the Roman Senate's civil rule in 27 BCE after decades of war between Roman generals, and he restricted all Roman legions to the border provinces and vassal states of the empire under his personal command. This meant that citizens and even temporary residents of the pacified provinces were shielded from the abuses of military occupation and benefitted from special privileges extended to certain free cities (Athens, Sparta), Roman colonies (Corinth, Philippi), and provincial capitals (Corinth and Thessalonica). The relative peace in this area fostered trade and benefitted especially the cities like Corinth located on key sea routes that brought the mineral and agricultural wealth of the surrounding occupied provinces toward Rome.[26]

---

23. Hans Dieter Betz, *Der Apostel Paulus in Rom* (Berlin: de Gruyter, 2013); *Studies in Paul's Letter to the Philippians*, WUNT 343 (Tübingen: Mohr Siebeck, 2015).

24. 1 Clement 5.

25. Col 1:15-20; 2:17-19 and Eph 1:7-12, 20-23; 4:15-16; cf. 1 Cor 12:12-27; Rom 12:4-8.

26. On Caesar Augustus's division of the provinces between himself and the Senate, see my "Women in Early Christian Stories: Serving and Served, Rural and Urban, in

Yet how tenuous this was became evident in 15 CE when Emperor Tiberius responded to petitions from Achaia and Macedonia for Rome to lower taxes by a decree absorbing these two provinces into the occupied border province of Moesia, making them vulnerable not only to high taxes but to troop movements and crop and labor confiscations as Rome attacked revolting tribes in the north along the Danube River. This inferior status continued until Emperor Claudius returned their dignity as senatorial provinces in 44 CE, a mere decade before Paul was writing to Corinth. A second and longer-term problem for people of pacified provinces was that the increasing wealth in coastal cities seems to have been spent on buying up or confiscating for debts the surrounding agricultural lands. The resulting plantations where land was profitable were tended by slaves or local people become semi-serfs while the more marginal lands were left unused, shifting dispossessed farmers toward cities where they sought work and stretching further the gap between rich and poor.[27]

It is in this context that Paul chose to work in coastal cities of the pacified senatorial provinces, favoring Roman provincial capitals (Thessalonica and Corinth) and Roman colonies (Alexander Troas, Philippi, Corinth), in sharp contrast to Jesus' itineration among rural villages of occupied and vassal lands. Was Paul's eye on rural people cut loose from their lands and seeking survival in cities?[28] Was he intent on itinerant artisans like himself?[29] Or was he thinking that major cities would include people with resources who could donate to those in need?[30]

Without doubt the Roman peace in pacified provinces eased the spread of news about Christ. Roads were continually being built or improved, especially in the north for communication with occupied areas. Sea travel was safer from pirates than before, and Paul was one among many who traveled constantly and sent others as envoys to carry messages or make arrangements (8:16-24; 9:3). The patronage structures may not have been as formal as in Rome, where clients went to the patron's home daily to show respect, but giving and receiving still built the connections between

---

Occupied and Pacified Provinces," in *Bridges in New Testament Interpretation: Interdisciplinary Advances*, ed. Neil Elliott and Werner Kelber (Lanham, MD: Lexington Books/Fortress Academic, 2018), 23–25, and the analysis of the social and political context of 1:12–2:11 above.

27. Susan E. Alcock, *Graecea Capta: The Landscapes of Roman Greece* (Cambridge: Cambridge University Press, 1992), 37–49, 74–92.

28. Alcock, *Graecea Capta*, 33–92.

29. On the wide variety of manual workers in first-century cities, see Peter Oakes, *Reading Romans in Pompeii: Paul's Letter at Ground Level* (Minneapolis: Fortress, 2009).

30. Betz, *2 Corinthians 8 and 9*, 50–53.

people in the provinces that gave life some security. Paul does foster donations to Jerusalem by saying that one day they may be helping you (8:14). Good roads, ships, and human networks also facilitated Rome's tax collecting in pacified provinces. Paul's effort to raise money for distant use by others may have appealed as little as did Roman taxes to the Corinthians who knew how to invest money for visible use at home.[31]

Poverty in Corinth

I did not enter Corinth after all, for I learned in a short time the sordidness of the rich there and the misery of the poor. For example, at midday, after most people had bathed, I saw some pleasant-spoken, clever young fellows moving about, not near the dwellings but near the Craneum, and particularly where the women who peddle bread and retail fruit are accustomed to do their business. There the young fellows would stoop to the ground, and one would pick up lupine pods, another would examine the nutshells to make sure that none of the edible part was left anywhere and had escaped notice, another would scrape with his fingernails the pomegranate rinds (which we in Attica are accustomed to call sidia) to see whether he could glean any of the seeds anywhere, while others would actually gather and greedily devour the pieces that fell from loaves of bread—pieces that had by that time been trodden under many feet. . . . Possibly the women have Aphrodite Guardian of the City as their cult goddess, whereas the men have Famine.[32]

A further impact of Roman rule was the increased competition between Roman provinces that we see in 2 Corinthians 8 and 9. Because Greek cities could no longer deliberate foreign policy or military actions, their civic assemblies often devolved into arenas for celebrating benefactors and outdoing other provinces in honoring Rome with declarations,

31. Hans Klein, "Die Begrundung für den Spendenaufruf für die Heiligen Jerusalems in 2 Kor 8 und 9," in *Der zweite Korintherbrief: Literarische Gestalt—historische Situation—theologische Argumentation. Festschrift zum 70. Geburtstag von Dietrich-Alex Koch*, ed. Dieter Sänger (Göttingen: Vandenhoeck & Ruprecht, 2012), 125–27.

32. Alciphron, *Letters of Parasites* 24 (3.60), in *The Letters of Alciphron, Aelian, and Philosotratus*, trans. Allen Rogers Benner and Francis H. Forbes, LCL (Cambridge, MA: Harvard University Press, 1962), 211–13; cited by Jerome Murphy-O'Connor, *St. Paul's Corinth: Texts and Archaeology* (Wilmington, DE: Michael Glazier, 1983), 119–20. He notes that Alciphron reflects the situation in the century after Paul and from the perspective of a resident of the competing city of Athens.

statues, or temples. Such competition was permitted, even encouraged, by Roman emperors refusing most such honors. Paul first praises the Macedonians in order to stir up the embers of Corinth's collection for Jerusalem (8:1-6, 8), then boasts about Achaia's earlier preparations for the collection to the Macedonians, saying he doesn't want to be ashamed when Macedonians come to see the Achaian gift (9:2-4).[33] By playing on this competition, Paul is able to lure the Corinthians to give without making authority claims for himself or using imperative verbs except when he asks them to finish what they themselves began (8:10-11).

Paul's Collection in a Greek City. Paul writes not only in a pacified Roman province but also in a city in Greece where some are prosperous. Greek cities are known to have assisted other Greek cities in times of draught, famine, and earthquake, and Paul may be appealing to that sense of one's obligation to others like oneself.[34] He uses administrative terms that reflect Greek commercial life and standards of financial practice.[35] Though Corinth is now a Roman colony with resettled Roman citizens and structures, Greeks who have returned with other noncitizens carry the workload. Paul appeals in these two chapters to certain long-standing values of Greek city life: the ἐκκλεσίαι, civic assemblies whose name is taken for the gatherings of believers (8:1, 18-19, 23-24); χειροτονηθείς, elected leaders chosen by the raising of hands (8:19); αὐθαίρετος, someone self-chosen or acting voluntarily (8:3; 17); and ἰσότης, equality, parity, or fair distribution among people (8:13-14). Is there in Corinth some distant memory of self-rule from the time before the rich, and then the Romans, took control? Are there remnants of democratic practices sustained in civic or voluntary associations like the one Paul is addressing? Interpreters say that by Roman times the voluntary associations focus on titles and honors, replicating the hierarchical structures of the later Greek city, and the assemblies in Christ only too soon follow.[36] Yet Anna Miller shows from the writings of Dio Chrysostom and Plutarch that Greeks in the early empire continue to value democratic participation in common life.

---

33. Betz, *2 Corinthians 8 and 9*, 90–93.

34. Verlyn D. Verbrugge, *Paul's Style of Church Leadership Illustrated by His Instructions to the Corinthians on the Collection* (San Francisco: Mellen Research University Press, 1992), 157–75, 240–43.

35. Betz, *2 Corinthians 8 and 9*, 45–46, 70–86.

36. John S. Kloppenborg and Richard S. Ascough, *Greco-Roman Associations: Texts, Translations, and Commentary*, vol. 1: *Attica, Central Greece, Macedonia, Thrace* (Berlin: de Gruyter, 2011), 8.

She argues from Paul's letters that the Corinthian ἐκκλησίαι (assemblies, churches), including the women, practice such democratic discourses in their speech and wisdom (1 Cor 1–4; 11:2-16; 14:26-40).[37]

Private Greek associations remain important in imperial times, whether as trade guilds, religious clubs, or burial societies, and the communities to whom Paul wrote very probably were seen as such voluntary groups.[38] Though fewer inscriptions have survived from Corinth and the Peloponnesus,[39] Attic, Macedonian, and coastal Asian Greek cities have produced hundreds of dedications to donors, priestesses, and treasurers of such groups. Some inscriptions list the names of male and female members, including the enslaved (see sidebar: "Banqueters Association Inscription"). Most groups survived on the dues of their members or special gifts of an office holder, and many inscribed in stone the generosity of the donors (see sidebar: "Inscription of the Dyers Guild Honoring a Priestess"). Groups dedicated to a god could require sexual propriety and other appropriate social conduct,[40] but the primary aims seem to have been conviviality in common meals, worship of the group's god, and mutual support.

The groups Paul addressed in cities of the pacified provinces were one kind of private association, and Paul appeals to their common commitment, worship of God and mutual support (9:13-15). It is understandable in this context that they are hesitant to contribute large sums to be sent outside the city to meet a commitment he has made (Gal 2:10). Hence Paul assures that he has no command for them but only good advice (2 Cor 8:8-11), that

---

37. A. C. Miller, "Not with Eloquent Wisdom: Democratic *ekklēsia* Discourse in 1 Cor 1–4," *JSNT* 35 (2013): 323–64; Anna C. Miller, *Corinthian Democracy: Democratic Discourse in 1 Corinthians* (Eugene, OR: Pickwick Publications, 2015), 40–67, 90–114, 140–53, 176–86; Mary E. Hunt, "Feminist Catholic Theology and Practice: From Kyriarchy to Discipleship of Equals," in *Toward a New Heaven and a New Earth: Essays in Honor of Elisabeth Schüssler Fiorenza*, ed. Fernando F. Segovia (Maryknoll, NY: Orbis Books, 1998), 468–71; Elisabeth Schüssler Fiorenza, *The Power of the Word: Scripture and the Rhetoric of Empire* (Minneapolis: Fortress, 2007), 71–72; G. Adolf Deissmann, *Light from the Ancient East: The New Testament Illustrated by Recently Discovered Texts of the Graeco-Roman World* (New York: Hodder and Stoughton, 1910), 112–14. Others argue that ἐκκλησία is derived from Israel's communal roots: G. K. Beale, "The Background of ἐκκλησία Revisited," *JSNT* 38 (2015): 151–68.

38. John S. Kloppenborg, "Greco-Roman *Thiasoi*, the *Ekklēsia* at Corinth and Conflict Management," in *Redescribing Paul and the Corinthians*, ed. Ron Cameron and Merrill P. Miller (Atlanta: Society of Biblical Literature, 2011), 187–218.

39. Kloppenborg and Ascough, *Greco-Roman Associations*, 1: vii; Richard S. Ascough, Philip A. Harland, and John S. Kloppenborg, eds. and trans., *Associations of the Greco-Roman World: A Sourcebook* (Waco, TX: Baylor University Press and de Gruyter, 2012), 33–35.

40. Ascough, Harland, and Kloppenborg, *Sourcebook*, 82–84, # 121.

this is a voluntary gift, not an obligation (9:5), and that their generosity will build ties and reap benefits for them (8:13-14; 9:11-14).

Banqueters Association Inscription

The banqueters (οἱ σιτήθεντες) at the time that Nikoles was council member (πατρονόμος):[41]

Eurybanassa daughter of Sidektas, priestess;

Tyndares son of Sidektas, priest; . . .

Damokrates son of Damokrates, master builder;

Mantikles son of Sosikrates, carver;

Damokrates son of Damodrates, guilder;

Philonidas Darneoneikos son of Philonidas;

Aristopolis daughter of Damocharis recognized as legitimate;

Pratonikos freedman of Perphila, spinner;

Hippomedon son of Nidandros, paean singer;

Nikokles freedman of Tyndares, maker of palm branch crowns;

Andronikos son of Nikokles, purifier;

Zilotos freedman of Panteimia, secretary;

Damippos son of Agathokles, dyer; . . .

Eunous freedman of Aristokrates, baker;

Clodia, slave of Akamantia, dealer in crowns;

Philodamos freedman of Euthykles, butcher;

Diokles slave of Kallisthenia.[42]

Inscription of the Dyers Guild Honoring a Priestess

The dyers (*bapheis*) set this up from their own resources to honor Claudia Ammion— daughter of Metrodoros Lepidus and wife of Tiberius Claudius Antyllos who was head of the gymnasium three times— priestess of the Augusti (*Sebastoi*) and high priestess of the city for life, having served as director of contests in a magnificent and extravagant manner, and having conducted her life in purity and with self-control.[43]

---

41. Identified in Liddell and Scott, *Lexicon*, 1349, as an office instituted by Cleomenes III in Sparta.

42. Banqueters Association Members List, Ascough, Harland, and Kloppenborg, *Sourcebook*, 35, #29 (Sparta, First Century BCE. IG V, 1 209 = PH 30559).

43. Honors by Dyers for a Priestess of the Augusti (Thyatira [Lydia], ca. 50 CE. TAM V. 2 972 = IGRR IV 1242). Ascough, Harland, and Kloppenborg, *Sourcebook*, 87, # 129.

Paul's Collection in a Diaspora Messianic Sect. The socio-economic setting of Paul's collection also depends heavily on Jewish practice because he is writing to communities that were marginal sects of Judaism. Most critical, they worshiped the one God of Israel, creator of all life, and saw all good coming from this one source and rightly returning in thanks to God.[44] Paul presents Christ here as the one who enacts this grace of God by becoming poor so that the Corinthians might become rich, whether this act refers to Jesus' incarnation (Phil 2:5-11) or, more likely in this letter, to Jesus' death embodied by Paul and Jesus' resurrection as God's life-giving power richly realized in the Corinthians (4:12; 13:9).

After worship of God, the second basic obligation of the Jew is to give to those in need. Though God is to be loved with all one's heart, soul, mind, and strength (Deut 6:4; Mark 12:28-30), this somehow does not exclude but rather requires loving one's neighbor as oneself (Lev 19:18; Mark 12:31-34), so Paul calls on them to complete their collection for the saints.[45] Stories told later by the rabbis dramatize the honor given to those who are generous—even to a fault—in their donations for orphans and widows (see sidebar: "Eleazar the Righteous"). Yet, in the diaspora at least, Jewish donating seems to have been local, and evidence for major charitable drives in this period is very slight.[46] Many of Paul's names for the collection do highlight what Greek-speaking Jews would consider religious experience or practices:[47] χάρις (grace, gift, benevolence; 8:1, 6, 7; 9:8), διακονία (relief ministry; 8:4; 9:1, 12), εὐλογία (blessing, bounty; 9:5, 6), ἔργον ἀγαθόν (good work, mitzvah; 9:8), λειτουργία (public offering from private means, 9:12).[48] But these terms are also used for benevolences in the Greek city context and need not signal a distinctive Jewish practice.[49]

44. See above in "The Ecosystem Assumed in Paul's Collection Argument."

45. On Paul's not mentioning here the destination of the gift or dramatizing the poverty of the people in Jerusalem, see below on "The Interaction of Paul and the Corinthians as Seen in His Collection Appeal."

46. Tessa Rajak, "Benefactors in the Greco-Jewish Diaspora," in *The Jewish Dialogue with Greece and Rome: Studies in Cultural and Social Interaction* (Leiden: Brill, 2001), 372–91, 389.

47. Furnish, *II Corinthians*, 411–13.

48. David Bolton, "Paul's Collection: Debt Theology Transformed into an Act of Love among Kin?," in Bieringer et al., *Theologizing in the Corinthian Conflict*, 347–49, 357–59; Betz, *2 Corinthians 8 and 9*, 117–18.

49. Betz, *2 Corinthians 8 and 9*, passim.

Eleazar the Righteous

When the alms-collectors would see Eleazar, a man of Birtah, they would hide from him because he would give them all he had. One day he went up to the market to outfit his daughter for marriage. The alms-collectors saw him and hid from him. He went and hurried after them. He said to them, "I adjure you, tell me what you are working on!" They said to him, "[Providing for] an orphan boy and an orphan girl." He said to them, "By the temple service, these go before my daughter." He took all that he had and gave it to them. One zuz remained to him and he bought wheat and carried [it] and poured it into the storeroom.

His wife came and said to his daughter, "What did your father bring?" She said to her, "Everything he brought he poured into the storeroom." When she went to open the storeroom door she saw the storeroom full of wheat, even bursting out the socket of the doorway, and the door would not open due to wheat.

His daughter went to the house of study and said to him, "Come and see what your Beloved has done for you!" He said to her, "By the temple service, look! it is consecrated and you will have no more part in it than any of the poor of Israel."[50]

To support his financial appeal Paul draws a number of times on Israel's Scripture, twice explicitly[51] and otherwise by allusion.[52] These references are used as proverbial sayings or general wisdom, probably drawn orally from this people's long experience. Though Betz thinks that Paul closes the argument by alluding to his legal agreement to support the Jerusalem poor as a "submission to the confession" (9:13; Gal 2:10),[53] this has not been accepted by most other interpreters.[54]

50. b. Ta'an. 24a. For comments on this story, see Antionette Clark Wire, *Holy Lives, Holy Deaths: A Close Hearing of Early Jewish Storytellers* (Atlanta: Society of Biblical Literature, 2002), 158–61.

51. In 8:15 on Exod 16:18; in 9:9 on Ps 111:9 LXX, 112:9.

52. In 9:6 to Prov 11:24; in 9:7 to Prov 22:8a LXX; in 9:10 to Isa 55:10.

53. Betz, *2 Corinthians 8 and 9*, 122–25.

54. Thrall, *Second Epistle*, 589–90; Furnish, *II Corinthians*, 451–52.

The obvious parallel to Paul's collection in Jewish socio-economic practice is the half-shekel each adult male Jew was expected to send annually to support the temple in Jerusalem.[55] The parallel is both in the destination city and in the purpose of collecting since the half-shekel supported not only the sacrifices in Jerusalem but also the priesthood and their benevolences for the city's poor and festival pilgrims. The delivery process that Paul arranges reflects the way Jewish collectors from many places gathered to carry the diaspora gifts just before the Passover pilgrimage.[56] Paul may see his delegation parallel to this joyous pilgrimage of those carrying the annual gifts from each city. Yet Paul's explicit emphasis here is not on a joyous gift but on security, on sending people who are reliable or elected by the donors, so that no one can criticize the process of collecting and carrying the funds.[57] Security will also have been an issue with the Jewish temple tax. A large gift before the invention of paper money and money orders, let alone digital transfers, would be heavy as well as highly vulnerable to highway thieves and pirates at sea. Paul implies that the Corinthians were also concerned about his own reliability.[58] In any case, Paul does not present this collection as a tax on everyone or require a designated amount but insists on the gift being voluntary (αὐθαίρετος, "self-taken") and proportional to ability, (ἰσότης, "equal, fairly balanced").[59] He cites the example of Israel in the desert, able to gather only enough manna for the size of each family (Exod 16:16-18).

Yet a parallel to the temple tax remains in that Paul shows an obligation not only to the place where people are in need but also to Jerusalem as the source or symbolic center of the community of faith, which can confirm the unity of the scattered communities "confessing the good news of the Christ/Messiah" (9:13). Some interpreters say Paul meant the collection to be a first fulfillment of the prophets' words that Gentiles

55. John M. G. Barclay, *Pauline Churches and Diaspora Jews*, WUNT 275 (Tübingen: Mohr Siebeck, 2011), 110–17.

56. S. Safrai, "Relations between the Diaspora and the Land of Israel," in *The Jewish People in the First Century: Historical Geography, Political History, Social Cultural and Religious Life and Institutions*, vol. 1, ed. S. Safrai and M. Stern (Philadelphia: Fortress, 1971), 188–93.

57. 2 Cor 8:18-21; 12:17-18.

58. 2 Cor 2:17; 4:2; 12:18.

59. 2 Cor 8:3, 8, 10-15; 9:7.

would bring their wealth and worship God in Jerusalem.[60] Marlene Crüsemann takes this a crucial step further by calling the gift-carrying a "quasi third exodus" for Israel when people from all nations turn from false gods to יהוה (YHWH) in Jerusalem, binding together Jew and Gentile in God's people.[61] At the least Paul envisions that this relief collection will overcome any distance between the Corinthians and Jerusalem when its poor begin to thank God for their partnership (9:13). And to close, Paul joins the prayer, "Grace be to God for his indescribable gift!" (9:15).

The Interaction of Paul and the Corinthians as Seen in His Collection Appeal

Here we focus down from tracing the broad ecosystem Paul assumes and the socio-economic context of his collection to asking how chapters 8 and 9 expose the interaction between Paul and the Corinthians. Because a letter writer will try to speak so as to impress the minds of those who are to hear the letter read, the words should reflect what makes the hearers hear.[62] And this in turn tells us more about the hearers than whatever description of them is offered, assuming that the persuader is motivated and effective. So the speaker and hearer of this message meet in the process of its communication, and what we learn can hardly be more about the one than the other.

It is important not to approach a letter with fixed assumptions about either party. Yet Paul's stance in 1 Corinthians—written many months if not a few years, before 2 Corinthians—regularly colors our reading. Margaret Thrall cautions that Paul in 2 Corinthians 8 and 9 is no longer giving commands but is testing their energy for the collection, even announcing that he has no command for them but only a word of advice (8:8, 10; cf. 1 Cor 16:1-4).[63] Verlyn Verbrugge notes that Paul in 2 Corinthians has shifted from the imperative verb forms to more indirect

---

60. Isa 2:2-4; 60:5-7; Mic 4:1-4; Georgi, *Remembering the Poor*, 100; Johannes Munck, *Paul and the Salvation of Mankind* (Richmond, VA: John Knox, 1959), 285–308; Bolton, "Paul's Collection," 357.

61. Crüsemann, "Weite Herz," in *Dem Tod nicht glauben*, 368, in *Gott ist Beziehung*, 224.

62. Christopher D. Stanley, "The Rhetoric of Quotations: An Essay on Method," in *Early Christian Interpretations of the Scriptures of Israel: Investigations and Proposals* (Sheffield: Sheffield Academic, 1997), 18–27.

63. Thrall, *Second Epistle*, 530–32.

requests, often in the subjunctive, participle, or jussive form.[64] Margaret Mitchell speaks of meanings Paul negotiates with the addressees, Hans Dieter Betz of redundancies Paul uses to deal with their impatience, Victor Paul Furnish of theology Paul shapes in the delicate task of asking for money.[65] I will take up each section of Paul's collection appeal in turn following my own translation of that part of the letter and ask how Paul's approach reflects an interaction with those he wants to persuade.

> And we want you to know, brothers and sisters, of God's grace given in our assemblies[66] of Macedonia, that in a severe testing by affliction their extreme joy and their deep poverty excelled in a wealth of single-heartedness so that, offering what they could—and I swear, even more than they could—they begged us in many appeals for the grace to share in this service for the saints. And not only as we hoped, they gave themselves first to the Lord and by God's will also to us so that we encouraged Titus, since he had begun it before, that he complete this grace also among you.
>
> And as you excel in everything—in faith and speech and knowledge and all diligence, and in our love for you—we trust that you also excel in this grace. I do not speak to command you but I am testing the genuineness of your love by the earnestness of others. For you know the grace of our Lord Jesus Christ who, though he was rich, became poor on your account, so that you in his poverty might become rich. And I do give my opinion on this, that it is better for you, who last year already began not only to do it but to want to do it, that you now complete what you are doing, matching your desire to do it by completing it from what you have. For if the willingness is present it is welcome according to what you have, not what you don't have, since the point is not relief for others by hardship for you, but an equalizing. At the present time your excess can serve their lack in order that their excess might serve your lack, so there may be equality. As it is written, "The one with much did not have more than enough, and the one with little did not have less." (8:1-15)

64. 2 Cor 8:7, 24; 9:7, 11; Verbrugge, *Paul's Style*, 247–60.

65. Margaret M. Mitchell, "The Corinthian Correspondence and the Birth of Pauline Hermeneutics," in *Paul and the Corinthians: Studies of a Commmunity in Conflict*, ed. Trevor J. Burke and J. Keith Elliott, NovTSup 109 (Leiden: Brill, 2003), 36–53; Betz, *2 Corinthians 8 and 9*, 91; Furnish, *II Corinthians*, 446–53.

66. I translate ἐκκλησίαις as "assemblies" to recognize the broad civic use of this term, appending "our" to make clear that Paul is speaking of the assemblies in Christ.

Paul's topic to start is God's grace that made the Macedonians so devoted that, in spite of their affliction and poverty, they voluntarily gave far beyond their means (1:1-6). Yet this six-verse sentence in Greek begins and ends with the Corinthians: "We want you to know" about their devotion (8:1) "so that we encouraged Titus . . . to complete this grace among you" (8:6). Paul clearly expects the Macedonians' exceptional interest in giving to arouse the Corinthians to take part, in line with the competition between the two Roman provinces. Yet the reference to Macedonian poverty would have no effect if the Corinthians did not know that Macedonia was largely rural and poor except for a few coastal cities.[67] But since that could be said of Greece in this period as well, Paul may be exaggerating Macedonian poverty to dramatize its generosity,[68] or increased poverty could be among the afflictions of new believers there.[69]

And how did Paul want this to play in Corinth? Is the believing community in Corinth hard pressed (1 Cor 1:26) and is Paul foreclosing excuses from them about having nothing to spare? More likely, he is encouraging a larger gift from Corinth, a city known for its wealth. This does show that a good collection there is still in question, and he needs to approach the "ask" indirectly, knowing that the Corinthians had not sustained their initial collecting (8:6). And by speaking of the Macedonians' devotion to God and their begging to participate in this joyful relief work, Paul makes this a competition not only in coin but in attitude. Paul wants not only the Corinthians' money but their hearts.[70] To get Corinth on board he addresses them as "brothers and sisters" (8:1)[71] and maintains the upbeat tone of his earlier pleas for reconciliation and intimacy,[72] expecting this to attract them where his complaints and instructions had not.

67. Thrall, *Second Epistle*, 521–22.

68. Gesila Nneka Uzukwu, "The Poverty and Wealth of the Macedonians: A Grammatical and Rhetorical Analysis of 2 Corinthinas 8:1-5," in Bieringer et al., *Theologizing in the Corinthian Conflict*, 319–30.

69. 2 Cor 8:2; 1 Thess 1:6-7; 3:2-4; Phil 1:27-30.

70. Furnish, *II Corinthians*, 451–52.

71. This form of address appears otherwise in 2 Corinthians only in Paul's letter opening and closing (1:8; 13:11). See my comment on this NRSV translation on p. 12, n. 20.

72. 2 Cor 5:20–6:2; 6:11-13; 7:2-15.

*Shifting Relationships
in 2 Corinthians*

The Corinthian Christians, as
a new social group, developed
structural and anti-structural
roles in the community.[73] The
structural roles in the community
are hierarchical and segmentarily
differentiated. Paul is superior
as founding apostle with various
ministries, and the Corinthians,
the "church of God," have
an inferior role as founded
community (1:1). The break in
their social relationship happened
mostly in the structural roles.[74]

FIGURE 1: SOCIAL RELATIONSHIPS IN 2 CORINTHIANS 1-13 (explicit roles: **bold**; *implicit: italics*)				
STRUCTURAL ROLES	ANTI-STRUCTURAL ROLES			
	Superior -Inferior	Unclear	Equal	Inferior
Superior: Apostle **(1:1; 12:11-12;** *3:6, 8, 9; 5:18-20; 11:1)*				
	Superior: parent *(6:13;* **12:14)**	*lover (parent)?* *(7:1; 12:14-15, 19)*		
			siblings (brothers and sisters, **1:8; 8:1; 13:11)** *beloved and lover (see 1:8; 2:4;* **7:1)**	Paul: Corinthians' slave for Jesus' sake **(4:5)**
	Inferior: children *(6:13;* **12:14)**	Beloved (children) *(7:1;* **12:14-15, 19)**		
Inferior: church of God in Corinth (1:1)				

73. See Norman Petersen, *Rediscovering Paul: Philemon and the Sociology of Paul's Narrative World* (Philadelphia: Fortress, 1985), 89–199, esp. 152.

74. See Ma. Marilou S. Ibita, "Mending a Broken Relationship: The Social Relations and the Symbolic Universe of 2 Corinthians 1–7," in Beiringer et al., *Theologizing the Corinthian Conflict*, 43–68.

In response, Paul appeals explicitly and implicitly to the antistructural roles to complete the dynamic process of reconciliation and close the relationship gap in various and shifting places. The antistructural roles expressed in metaphorical kinship language provide communal intimacy and subvert the structural relationship in manifold ways. Antistructurally, Paul as parent is still superior while the Corinthians as children are inferior. Yet the hierarchical gap in their relation is tempered with love. Their relationship as lover-beloved is unequal if it means the parent-children relation. Equality may be implicit in 2:3-4, however, if it continues the siblingship in **1:8** that is repeated in **8:1** and **13:11**. "Beloved" also seems to express mutuality (**7:1; 12:19**). The words "beloved" (7:1) and "complete confidence" (7:16) buttress the siblingship expression (8:1) that opens the highly rhetorical collection appeal. Reidar Aasgaard holds that "beloved" is used with the sibling metaphor and at times replaces it.[75] In addition to these varying social relationships, Paul also claims an inferior role as the Corinthians' slave for Jesus' sake (**4:5**).

The **siblingship** seems to have an edge among the other relationships, employed as it is in the letter's beginning (**1:8**), middle (**8:1**), and end (**13:11**). Yet the extent of equality regarding Paul's and the male Corinthians' sibling relationship with the Corinthian women during the writing of 2 Corinthians and beyond is difficult to ascertain. Paul's use of the masculine plural ἀδελφοί could be consciously inclusive of the sisters or not at all. While Paul's sibling metaphors do seem to affirm the common identity of Christians, instill a family "feel," and fortify bonds of solidarity, the sibling address does not necessarily imply "equality in power."[76] Even today, considering the world before the text of this letter, equality between the metaphorical siblings in the church remains incomplete and inadequate worldwide.

Ma. Marilou S. Ibita

When Paul calls on the Corinthians to excel in this grace—this collection—just as they "excel in faith and speaking and knowledge and in all eagerness and in our love for you"[77] (8:7), my question is whether he is

75. Reidar Aasgaard, *My Beloved Brothers and Sisters! Christian Siblingship in Paul* (London: T & T Clark, 2004), 4.

76. Ibid., 284.

77. On the textual variant, "your love of us," see p. 175 above.

praising them strictly to manipulate them in his cause. In fact, Paul has been speaking about "excelling" throughout the letter, with cognates of this περισσεύειν term appearing more times in 2 Corinthians than in all of Paul's other surviving letters combined, and with more than half of these coming in 2 Corinthians 8 and 9 and the lines just preceding (7:13-16). These περισσεύειν terms are translated in the NRSV so differently that his emphasis does not come through. The NRSV translates περισσεύειν cognates as "still more" (7:13); "all the more" (7:15); "abundant" (8:2); "overflowed" (8:2); "excel" (twice in 8:7); "abundance" (twice in 8:14); "not necessary" (i.e., excessive; 9:1); "abundance" (9:8); "abundantly" (9:8); "overflows" (9:12).

Paul's exuberance here is far more than a quick bait to catch the Corinthians' eye. Unless we reduce him to a shyster, this represents a change in the way he presents what God is doing among them. He does not challenge them to sacrifice through self-discipline, nor does he disparage their gifts of faith, speech, knowledge, and eagerness, but he offers them the "privilege of sharing"—literally "the grace of participation"—in the collection for Jerusalem as another way in which to excel (8:4, 7). This praise of their talents ends, not with an imperative verb, "so excel," or even with the NRSV, "so we want you to excel," but with a subjunctive: "so that you might excel" or "so that you could excel."[78] Verbrugge contrasts this positive and receptive approach by Paul in 2 Corinthians with the imperative tone of much of 1 Corinthians, noting that a request like this using ἵνα with the subjunctive is often spoken from "a subordinate or uncertain position," as though making a proposal.[79]

Any doubt about Paul's stance should be put to rest by his next words, "I do not say this as a command" (8:8). Yet he is aware that it could be heard as pressure from him and claims he is only testing that their love is genuine, measured up to the eagerness of the Macedonians (8:8). The Paul of 1 Corinthians would have pressed further, using as their model Christ crucified who shows God's foolishness in choosing the weak in the world like themselves to shame the strong (1 Cor 1:18-25; 4:8). Here in 2 Corinthians Paul says that "Christ, though rich, became poor on your account, so that in his poverty you yourselves might become rich" (2 Cor 8:9). Whether Christ's poverty means, as most interpreters take

78. Yet this is taken as an imperative by Furnish (*II Corinthians*, 403) and Martin (*2 Corinthians*, WBC 40 [Waco, TX: Word Books, 1983], 262), while Thrall (*Second Epistle*, 529) calls it a weak command.
79. See Gal 2:9-10; Matt 20:33; Mark 5:23; Verbrugge, *Paul's Style*, xvi, 2, 7, also 247–51 and 259–60.

it, his incarnation in human form (Phil 2:5-11)[80] or, more likely in this letter, his harsh suffering and death that Paul claims to embody (2 Cor 4:10-12), the Corinthians are not challenged to embody his poverty in order to acquire his wealth. On the contrary, Paul concedes that they have already become rich by the "grace" and "through the poverty of our Lord Jesus Christ" (8:9).

It is on this basis that Paul encourages them to give. Since they not only started the collection some time ago but themselves wanted to do so,[81] it is only to their advantage to complete it from whatever they have available, not waiting until they can give more or burdening themselves to relieve others. All he wants is equalizing (ἰσότης, softened in the NRSV to "fair balance"). And he states again the advantage for themselves using the περισσεύειν (to exceed) term, "Let your present excess be for their lack so that their excess might be for your lack, thus becoming equal" (8:14), confirming this with the Scripture about God providing just enough manna for each family in the desert (8:15; Exod 16:18).

This argument from the Corinthians' wealth and excess, while allowing they may not have much to give, seems fashioned to persuade people who have something to give but cannot be pressured or manipulated to do so. The Corinthians know they became rich in Christ (8:9), are gifted in many ways (8:7), and were in on the earliest plans for this collection (8:10). Yet they will enrich others only when they are recognized for whom they are and what they have, and it seems that Paul by this point has learned to give them recognition. He not only asks for money but offers relationships that will come back to bless them—relationships with himself and now with God's people in Jerusalem (8:14; 9:14). Interpreters consider it unrealistic that Paul expects Jerusalem to send support to Corinth,[82] yet Paul appeals to the Corinthians' good sense that nothing pays like wide connections. I translate again:

> Grace be to God, who put this same eagerness about you into Titus's heart, for he not only got my encouragement but, being all the more eager, went off on his own accord to you. And we sent with him the brother whose reputation in the gospel is known in all our assemblies.

80. Thrall, *Second Epistle*, 532–34; Furnish, *II Corinthians*, 417. Heinrici takes "poverty" here to refer to Jesus' life, to which his death was the climax (*Der zweite Brief*, 276).

81. Paul reverses the expected "they not only wanted to do it but did it" by saying "they not only did something but wanted to do it," stressing their desire yet also exposing that what they wanted is not yet done (8:10-11).

82. Furnish, *II Corinthians*, 419–20. Thrall cautions that Paul couldn't know the revolt was coming and the temple would be burned in 70 CE (*Second Epistle*, 542).

Not only that, but he has also been elected by the assemblies to be our fellow traveler in this grace that is being carried out by us to show the Lord's glory and our goodwill. We want to avoid just this, that anyone could blame us in the way we carry out this abundant gift, since we have in mind to be acceptable not only in the Lord's eyes but also in people's eyes. And we have sent along with them our brother whom we have tested in many times and places and found eager, but now even more eager and with much confidence in you. If you ask about Titus—he is my partner and fellow worker among you, or about our brothers—they are apostles [ἀπόστολοι] of our assemblies, the glory of Christ. So you can demonstrate before all our assemblies the evidence of your love for us and the proof of our pride in you. (8:16-24)

Before Paul reverses the Macedonians' role in his argument from being model donors in the Corinthians' eyes (8:1-7) to being the eyes observing the Corinthians' donations (9:1-5), Paul introduces the people sent to supervise the collection and carry it with Paul to Jerusalem (8:16-24). He says that Titus was given by God such eagerness for them that he not only welcomed Paul's request but went voluntarily. This is the same Titus who has just been to Corinth and returned to Paul with good news, at least about their disciplining an offender on Paul's behalf (7:5-13), suggesting that Titus has been more successful with the Corinthians than Paul himself (see 12:18). Paul stresses not his technical qualifications as an organizer but his eagerness to work with the Corinthians, showing that Paul expects the Corinthians to take such zeal as the highest possible qualification.[83]

Paul next recommends the representative who is a well-known proclaimer of the Gospel, presented not as someone eager but as one elected by the assemblies to travel with Paul and Titus (8:18-19). The verb "elected" (χειροτονηθείς) comes from the root of showing hands. Though no assembly of all congregations is conceivable at that time to have carried out what we would call an election, popular support is indicated by that term, which

---

83. Paul uses completed past-tense verbs (aorist) in urging Titus to go to Corinth and in sending the two brothers. This leaves unclear whether they have already gone or whether he is writing so as to be read aloud on arrival: "I urged . . . I sent along . . . ," using what is called the epistolary aorist. A later mention that Titus and one brother have already (perfect tense) demonstrated their reliability in Corinth (12:18) could refer to Titus' earlier visit, or the accompanying brother could indicate that Titus and the elected brother have gone ahead (aorist past tense). When Paul includes a commendation of a second brother, "our brother," he may be sent along now to carry this letter (epistolary aorist). This would explain the brothers' very separate introductions as well as the mention of only one brother in 12:18.

may have been appealing in Corinth, and it does get lost in the NRSV translation of "appointed." Next Paul says he wants the collection to be above board in every way (8:20-21), suggesting that this person is known, not as one of Paul's associates, but as one who brings an independent eye. Clearly Paul thinks some Corinthians are suspicious that the collection is serving Paul's interests, if not filling his pockets.

Paul then goes on to add a second "brother" with whom he has worked extensively, one who is eager not only about the collection for Jerusalem but even more about the Corinthians' participation in it (8:22). By adding this person Paul makes the wide and eager eyes in this delegation outweigh the squinting or suspicious eyes, assuring that this special collection is not taken up as an official tax for headquarters but as an eager gift for those most in need. Adapting his approach to Corinthian sensibilities, he stresses positive relationships and experiences without ignoring the security factor.

Several other aspects of this recommendation give clues about Paul's interaction with the Corinthians. In Paul's closing list of the three being recommended, he calls Titus "my coworker" and the two brothers "apostles of the assemblies/churches" (8:23). The noun "apostle" simply means "sent out" or "commissioned," hence representing these communities. Though Paul calls himself "apostle of Christ Jesus" at the start of this letter and defends himself against others called apostles near its end—"I am not a bit inferior to these super-apostles, even though I am nothing. The signs of an apostle were done among you" (1:1; 12:11-12)— these instances cannot make the letter Paul's defense of the title "apostle" for himself as it is regularly presented.[84] Yet interpreters import from 1 Corinthians both Paul's self-defense as apostle[85] and the Corinthians' recalcitrance at his discipline,[86] allowing no shifts in his presentation of himself or of them. In fact, in 2 Corinthians Paul calls himself, alongside his coworkers, διάκονος χριστοῦ (servant, representative, agent of Christ; 3:1–5:21), shifting the focus from his personal status to his function among those who brought them the good news of Christ (1:19). His emphasis here is on his own transparency before God (8:20-21) and on shaping a broad enough delegation to allay any suspicions.

84. Stanley Norris Olson, "Confidence Expressions in Paul: Epistolary Conventions and the Purpose of 2 Corinthians" (PhD diss., Yale University, 1976), 236.

85. 1 Cor 9:1-5; 15:7-11.

86. 1 Cor 4:18-21; 11:16, 22; 14:37-38.

In concluding his recommendation Paul speaks of the assemblies, calling the two brothers ἀπόστολοι ἐκκλησιῶν, δόξα χριστοῦ ("apostles of the assemblies, Christ's glory") and challenging the Corinthians "to demonstrate before the assemblies" what he has been boasting about them (8:23-24). Paul could not speak more highly of "the assemblies" than to call them God's glory, and among them he understands the Corinthians about whom he has boasted. Nonetheless, his sending of this delegation is the concrete pressure he is putting on them to contribute to the collection. And he has taken "the assemblies" as his means to this end—through their choosing one brother, through their delegating the two brothers as their apostles, and through their watching to witness if Paul's boast about the Corinthians holds water (8:19, 23, 21, 24). It remains significant that Paul does not use imperative verbs in challenging the Corinthians to give but uses instead a participle, making the last sentence of this chapter best translated "you can be people showing proof" (8:24). In all, Paul is banking not on commands based on his authority as their apostle and spiritual father[87] but on the Corinthians wanting to measure up to their peers and be recognized with the other assemblies as "the glory of Christ" (8:1-6, 23-24).[88]

> About this service for the saints, it would be excessive for me to write you since I know your eagerness which I have praised you for to the Macedonians—"Achaia was ready a year ago"—and your zealousness has aroused most of them. But I have sent the brothers so that our praising of you in this matter would not come up empty—that I said you were ready—lest if some Macedonians should come with me and find you not ready, we ourselves might be shamed, not to speak of you, in this condition. So I thought it necessary to urge the brothers to precede me toward you and to prepare ahead the blessing you have promised. In that way it can be ready as a blessing and not as an appropriation under pressure. (9:1-5)

Hans Dieter Betz takes the ninth chapter as a second administrative letter because Paul seems to begin again introducing the collection at

---

87. Cf. 1 Cor 4:14-20, 9:1-2.

88. Many Christian interpreters since Luther have been satisfied with the Corinth Paul projected in 1 Corinthians and they decry this theology of glory that Paul learns to respect. Is Paul's new stance to be dismissed as the rhetorical statement of a man desperate to pull his collection project out of defeat? Or has he delineated in 2 Corinthians that life on the other side of Christ's cross can also be embodied and so is challenging the Corinthians to demonstrate that glory among the assemblies in Christ (3:17-18; 4:12; 8:23; 13:4)?

9:1, now calling on believers in the province of Achaia as a whole to become active in Corinth's completing its collection.[89] But Achaia could be mentioned here to highlight its early readiness that Paul has boasted in contrast to Macedonia's recent response. Eve-Marie Becker reads these chapters through text-linguistics as part of a two-sided correspondence between Paul and the Corinthians.[90] She sees the distinctive element in this part of 2 Corinthians to be not that we have a single letter or an edited sequence of letters but that this church received and preserved written appeals for the collection rather than visits from Paul, allowing us to track an evolving relationship through changes over years. (Would that he had preserved their side of the correspondence! [1 Cor 7:1]) Furnish thinks Paul resumes his collection appeal here within the same letter, explaining why he is sending people ahead to prepare it before he comes himself.[91] Paul claims both his reputation and theirs is at stake if he arrives with some Macedonians to find that nothing has been done and make their gift look like a forced response (9:4-5).

When we read the opening of chapter 9 as a resumption of Paul's appeal, most surprising is the change of the Macedonians' function in Paul's argument. They are no longer the model of giving but have become the witnesses to Corinth's giving in light of Paul's high expectations. Paul's purported praise of the Corinthians here could be nothing but a strategy to produce a gift and protect his own reputation. But if so, why is he so open in speaking of the cost to himself in humiliation if they don't give or in the appearance of extortion if they give under pressure? There may be truth on both sides—that Paul is zealous for a good collection to show what he has done in the Greek-speaking cities, but also he is "anxious for the assemblies" (11:28) and specifically for Corinth. He could be shifting his praise from the Macedonians to the Achaians and to Corinth itself in hopes that their gift could be a turning point, not only for him and the receivers, but also for the Corinthians.

89. Betz, *2 Corinthians 8 and 9*, 90–97, 139–40.

90. Eve-Marie Becker, "Stellung und Funktion von 2. Korinther 8–9 im literarischen Endtext: Anmerkungen zum Stand der literarischen Diskussion," in Bieringer et al., *Theologizing in the Corinthian Conflict*, 301–4.

91. Furnish, *II Corinthians*, 425–26, 429–33. As evidence that chapter 9 continues the previous argument, Furnish notes the explanatory participle γὰρ in its opening, whereas δὲ would be expected in the περὶ δὲ form were Paul opening a new discussion (1 Cor 7:1, 25; 8:1; 12:1; 16:1). He sees the μὲν of 2 Corinthians 9:1 linking it to the δὲ of 9:3, while the neuter pronoun in τὸ γράφειν suggests "the aforementioned writing" (9:1). See also Heinrici, *Der zweite Brief*, 293–96.

As this says, "He who sows stingily will reap stingily and he who sows with blessing will reap a blessing," let each one give as she determines in her heart, not due to pain or pressure, "for God loves a happy giver." And God is able to make all grace overflow toward you so that, having all sufficiency in all things at all times, you might overflow in all good works! As it is written, "He scattered abroad. He gave to the poor. His righteousness continues forever!" And the one who "provides seed for the sower and bread for eating" will provide and multiply your seed and make the produce of your righteousness grow. You are enriched in every way in all singleness of heart, which produces thanksgiving to God through us, since carrying out this public offering is not only supplying what the saints lack but also overflows through many people in thanksgivings to God. From the evidence of this service they will glorify God for your faithfulness to the confession of the good news of Christ and for your singlehearted sharing with them and with all. And in their prayers for you they will long for you on account of the overwhelming grace of God at work in you. Let grace resound back to God for God's inexpressible gift! (9:6-15)

The final words on the collection are Paul's substantive argument for why it is good to give. They will have been shaped for maximum impact on the Corinthians and so offer maximum chance to see where they stand.[92] He begins very broadly with a proverb known throughout the ancient world about sowing richly to harvest richly (9:6; Prov 11:24),[93] followed by assurance about giving whatever seems right to you because, in another proverb, God loves those who give gladly (9:7; Prov 22:8 LXX).[94] Paul explains the reason you will not run out of resources to give in a sentence using the word "all" five times: "And God is able to make all grace overflow toward you so that, having all sufficiency in all things at all times, you might overflow with all good works!" (9:8). This boundless confidence is supported by two further Scripture texts: God scatters freely and gives to the poor so God's justice lasts forever (9:9; Ps 111:9 LXX, 112:9 NRSV),[95] and God provides seed for the sower and bread for the eater, making the fruit of your justice grow (9:10; Isa 55:10). Though Psalm 112 is speaking about the justice of the human giver, Paul

92. On this section, see also above "The Ecosystem Assumed in Paul's Collection Argument."

93. Betz, *2 Corinthians 8 and 9*, 102–5.

94. Here the Greek text that Paul remembers differs from the Hebrew original that the NRSV translates in Proverbs 22:8.

95. Though the psalm recounts the believer's justice and good works (Ps 111:8 LXX), the third-person pronouns in Paul's series of Scriptures all apply to God, with the second person bringing in the believer (9:8, 10).

applies it to God as the eternal source of justice who provides those who give not only food for today but seed for next year's crop—expenses and savings—extending justice indefinitely.

This entire argument for giving gladly mentions sparse sowing only to dismiss it with multiple affirmations of rich sowing, glad giving, abundant good works, and fruits of justice (8:6-10). Without doubt Paul is appealing to people who are positive and confident. He uses ancient proverbs and wise sayings that he expects the Corinthians to grasp and apply to themselves. This does not necessarily indicate that the Corinthian community is highly educated but that it lives in a culture where traditional wisdom is valued and well-known sayings are favored in oral speech to make a point. Such wisdom may even be most respected where people are not literate or where written sources are not accessible to most people.[96]

Respect for Wisdom in China

In 2002 I visited a church gathering outside Nanjing, China, in a tiny four-room home along a passageway that let in a little noon sun between long rows of self-made one-story buildings. Every inch of space was full of people seated on chairs, benches, and low stools, with others sitting outside the door. They found me a seat and a Chinese Bible. The local leaders were women, one old and blind, one young from the choir of a downtown church who had invited me.

After many songs and prayers a man visiting from that downtown church stood between rooms and began to read aloud very slowly the third chapter of Proverbs. After each verse the people repeated the saying, following with their fingers in their own Bibles. I was counting ahead how much longer the thirty-five verses would take when he finally finished. Then it appalled me that everyone begged him to read it again and he reluctantly agreed. No one else seemed impatient for another half-hour, all following each word, then repeating each saying. I realized at last that people were not only memorizing the sayings but most of them were learning for the first time the characters that held them, not having had schooling. They could use the sayings with their children and with coworkers on vegetable market streets and bicycle repair corners, and such reading of the Bible and song book would eventually let them read street signs and then newspapers.

96. Lee A. Johnson, "Paul's Letters as Artifacts: The Value of the Written Text among Non-Literate People," *BTB* 46 (2016): 25–34.

Paul's affirmative rather than demanding approach continues as he moves into the climax of his argument for their giving (9:11-15). The opening participle in "you are enriched in every way in all singleness of heart"[97] is sometimes translated as an imperative, "be enriched," or with the NRSV as a future tense following the previous sentence, "you will be enriched," suggesting future reward. But the present-tense participle is Paul's recognition that "they are made rich" and that, since the time he and Timothy and Silvanus brought them word of Christ (1:19), this "produces thanksgiving to God through us" (9:11). Thanksgiving to God from the gift's recipients brings the gift of God's grace full circle (see χάρις [grace] as the ecosystem Paul assumes on pages 178–81 above). Made possible by God's grace, the collection that Paul also calls grace or "the work of this public service" (ἡ διακονία τῆς λειτουργίας ταύτης) "not only fills up what the saints [in Jerusalem] are lacking but overflows through many thanksgivings to God" (9:12). This then serves as a test or proof of Paul's ministry and of theirs as well, that God is glorified by the poor who see evidence of the Corinthians' loyalty in confessing the good news of Christ (9:13). He even expects such a partnership to be created that the recipients will be praying for them and longing to know them because of God's grace overflowing in them (9:14). By this point Paul exhausts his powers of description and can only praise God for this indescribable gift (9:15).

And what can the way Paul has pressed for Corinth's participation in the Jerusalem gift tell us about the Corinthians? In the first place, unless we dismiss as manipulation all Paul's talk about their gifts and his boasting about them (8:7; 9:2-4), we begin with Paul having a changed attitude toward them. He seems to have not only a new strategy with them but a new respect for what they experience and practice in Christ, having shifted his role from instruction to defending his Gospel. Yet in these two chapters he arrives at what he does want from them, namely, an eager participation in this gift, and the way he argues shows us what he thinks can make them want to give. I list some of the ways that he characterizes them, summarizing each in a word.

1. Gifted: They see themselves, unlike the Macedonians who give out of their poverty, as people gifted with great faith, speech, knowledge, and energy, from whom much can be expected (8:1-7).

---

97. ἁπλότης is a noun indicating simplicity, frankness, sincerity. The adjective ἁπλοῦς (simple, straightforward) is the opposite of διπλοῦς (doubled, twofold), itself close to δίψυχος (doubleminded, duplicitous) (Jas 1:8; 4:8).

2. Rich: For Paul and his colleagues, "Christ is Lord" means he is their model of the rich becoming poor, but for the Corinthians "Christ is Lord" means that he has drawn them out of poverty to become rich in him (8:9; 9:11).

3. First: They won't be interested in a project started in Macedonia, so Paul argues that they themselves once wanted to give and now need to complete what they began (8:10-11; 9:5).

4. Eager: The eagerness to give that Paul sees in the Macedonians and Titus was once also present in Corinth (8:10-11), and they are challenged to remember this and outstrip the others by finishing as they began.

5. Independent: They will not give under pressure but will make up their own minds in light of reasons to give that they consider valid, not going beyond what they have to give or making themselves suffer while others are relieved (8:12-13).

6. Just: They are expected by Paul to see the justice of having more equality among believers, even if dubious that gifts at such a distance could be reciprocated (8:13b-15).

7. Careful: They will want a careful eye on any money they send with Paul, hence his description of each carrier (8:16-23). They may insist on sending along their own representative as Paul had once offered them (1 Cor 16:3).

8. Respected: They recognize that it is the assemblies that are Christ's glory, and it matters to them that their reputation remains high among the assemblies (8:23–9:4).

9. Suspicious, But Open: Some Corinthians see Paul putting pressure on them to give. So Paul justifies his sending Titus and the assembly leaders ahead from his wanting them to give voluntarily, not give under pressure when he arrives (9:5).

10. Wise: Paul's many proverbs and sayings from Scripture appeal to Corinthian wisdom about the natural world and God's justice in provision (8:15; 9:6-10).

11. Empirical: Though Paul concedes their freedom to decide what to give so that they give gladly, he insists that God provides more than enough for distant giving (9:7-10) while they may understand God's justice in terms of local, visible, and reciprocal giving.

12. Expressive: Knowing that the Corinthians celebrate being rich in Christ and glorify God in the Spirit (1 Cor 2:6-16; 4:8, 10; 14:26-40), Paul presents the collection as the work of God's grace that allows them to give grace to others and return grace to God (2 Cor 9:11-15).

The Corinthians are visible not only in these assumptions about them, as Paul writes, but also in their response to Paul's argument, but this is much harder to ferret out. One can argue that the Corinthians reconcile with Paul and contribute liberally (7:6-9, 16; Rom 15:26). Yet the observation that no Corinthians are included in the Acts 20:4 list of delegates said to accompany Paul to Jerusalem could suggest that their gift was minimal. The fact that most interpreters now take 2 Corinthians 10–13 either as a part of this letter or one written soon after would point to continuing conflicts with Paul's leadership. I will return to this after reviewing those chapters.

Yet the issue could be considered moot because we have no evidence that the collection was ever received by the Christ followers in Jerusalem. Acts may not have told what happened to the collection because it was publicly rejected in Jerusalem under pressure of rising sentiment against Gentile influence only a decade before the Jews revolt against Rome. Or did the money more likely disappear into hands that could use it to meet dire needs in the harsh times ahead? At least Acts makes clear that Paul did not receive from Jerusalem the public support he wanted for his wider mission; nor did the Corinthians get something back. Yet people may have been fed, God praised, donors blessed, and grace happen. Even a giving without a receiving could be grace.

The question remains whether Paul's harsh words in the letter's final four chapters so overshadow the whole that his interaction with Corinth in the first nine chapters is eclipsed. This issue can be discussed only after all chapters are reviewed. But to this point it is clear that he has laid his cards on the table, defended his conduct,[98] and asserted his confidence that the good news in Christ has made them rich and wise and effective in speaking.[99] He has opened his mouth to them and poured out his heart,[100] seeking reconciliation and cooperation, particularly in this act of public service to Jerusalem.[101]

98. 2 Cor 1:12–2:4; 2:14–3:6; 4:1-15.
99. 2 Cor 3:18; 4:12; 5:17; 7:13-16; 8:7.
100. 2 Cor 6:11-13; 7:2-4.
101. 2 Cor 5:20; 6:2; 8:7, 10-11; 9:3, 8, 11-13.

Though we do not know their response to this appeal, it is significant that Paul shows himself no longer hesitant or anxious but confident, even buoyant, expecting that they will be welcoming his delegation, gathering a good gift, and preparing to receive him when he arrives.[102] Since their relation was quite strained in the past, "fights without, fears within,"[103] his confidence must come from some change in the relationship, on the one hand, the change that Titus reported when he returned from Corinth—that they took his side in a conflict with an offender[104]— but also that he takes their side now in affirming their distinctive and expressive life in Christ.[105] He is ready to be a clay pot to their role as God's treasure, a courier to their letter from Christ, a bearer of Christ's death to their bearing of Christ's life.[106] His confidence that this will make sense to them indicates that it likely does.

But how they negotiate with him the practice of this relationship so that it maintains their expressive leadership in community prayer and prophecy and in words of wisdom we do not know, because we are reading the final letter that survives in this correspondence. Possibly clues to this will yet be found somewhere between the lines of his or other early Christian writings. At the end of the century a Roman bishop does write to Corinth berating them for recalling elders who hold office for life, so there is no end to the process.[107]

---

102. 2 Cor 8:16-24; 9:1-5, 11-15. Furnish, *II Corinthians*, 452.
103. 2 Cor 2:1-4; 7:8; 9:3-5.
104. 2 Cor 2:12-13; 7:5-16.
105. 2 Cor 3:18; 4:12; 5:17; 7:13, 16; 8:7.
106. 2 Cor 4:7; 3:3; 4:12.
107. 1 Clement 44–47.

2 Corinthians 10:1–11:21a

Paul's Rebuttal of His Rivals' Charges

Text and Its Structure (10:1–11:21a)

Having worked to reconcile with the Corinthians (2 Cor 1–7) and get them to participate in the gift for Jerusalem (2 Cor 8–9), Paul ends his letter with a harsh rebuttal against the accusations of some opponents (2 Cor 10–13). The change in tone is so abrupt that many interpreters take these last four chapters to be a separate letter[1] (see the introduction: "One Letter or Many?"). But it is more likely that as Paul prepares to end 2 Corinthians his attention shifts to his forthcoming arrival in Corinth where he has been discounted, even vilified, by other missionaries who also speak for Christ.[2] This provokes Paul to give

---

1. Margaret E. Thrall, *A Critical and Exegetical Commentary on the Second Epistle to the Corinthians*, ICC (Edinburgh: T & T Clark, 1994), 595–96; Victor Paul Furnish, *II Corinthians*, AB 32A (Garden City, NY: Doubleday, 1984), 36–41. Others propose that this four-chapter letter was written first, expressing Paul's pain after a brief interim visit: Jerome Murphy-O'Connor, "The Date of Second Corinthians 10–13," in *Keys to Second Corinthians: Revisiting Major Issues* (Oxford: Oxford University Press, 2010), 149–69; Margaret M. Mitchell, "The Corinthian Correspondence and the Birth of Pauline Hermeneutics," in *Paul and the Corinthians: Studies of a Community in Conflict*, ed. Trevor J. Burke and J. Keith Elliott, NovTSup 109 (Leiden: Brill, 2003), 21, 30–34.

2. Defenders of the letter's unity explain the break variously. Some propose that further news from Corinth arrives as Paul composes (Wolff; Schnelle), others that Paul's

210   *2 Corinthians*

2 Cor 10:1–11:21a

10:1I myself, Paul, appeal to you by the meekness and gentleness of Christ—I who am humble when face to face with you, but bold toward you when I am away!—2I ask that when I am present I need not show boldness by daring to oppose those who think we are acting according to human standards. 3Indeed, we live as human beings, but we do not wage war according to human standards; 4for the weapons of our warfare are not merely human, but they have divine power to destroy strongholds. We destroy arguments 5and every proud obstacle raised up against the knowledge of God, and we take every thought captive to obey Christ. 6We are ready to punish every disobedience when your obedience is complete.

7Look at what is before your eyes. If you are confident that you belong to Christ, remind yourself of this, that just as you belong to Christ, so also do we. 8Now, even if I boast a little too much of our authority, which the Lord gave for building you up and not for tearing you down, I will not be ashamed of it. 9I do not want to seem as though I am trying to frighten you with my letters. 10For they say, "His letters are weighty and strong, but his bodily presence is weak, and his speech contemptible." 11Let such people understand that what we say by letter when absent, we will also do when present.

12We do not dare to classify or compare ourselves with some of those who commend themselves. But when they

the full weight of his rebuttal so that when he arrives the Corinthians will be ready to welcome him (10:2; 13:10). Only then can he carry out his God-given task to build them up, not tear them down (10:8; 12:19;

---

earlier statements of confidence in the Corinthians were an idealization (Vegge), or that the letter closes with a "sharp postscript" to prepare for his arrival (Schmeller), or that his argument is coherent for hearers in the context if not cohesive for readers today (Becker); more complex arguments for unity are provided by Young and Ford and by Bieringer. See Christian Wolff, *Der zweite Brief des Paulus an die Korinther* (Berlin: Evangelische Verlagsanstalt, 1989), 1–3, 190–93; Udo Schnelle, "Der 2. Korintherbrief und die Mission gegen Paulus," in *Der zweite Korintherbrief: Literarische Gestalt—historische Situation—theologische Argumentation. Festschrift zum 70. Geburtstag von Dietrich-Alex Koch*, ed. Dieter Sänger (Göttingen: Vandenhoeck & Ruprecht, 2012), 318–20; Ivan Vegge, *2 Corinthians: A Letter about Reconciliation; A Psychagogical, Epistologographical and Rhetorical Analysis*, WUNT 2.239 (Tübingen: Mohr Siebeck, 2008), 95–118, 370–91; Thomas Schmeller, "No Bridge over Troubled Water? The Gap between 2 Corinthians 1–9 and 10–13 Revisited," *JSNT* 36 (2013): 73–84; Eve-Marie Becker, *Letter Hermeneutics in 2 Corinthians: Studies in Literarkritik and Communication Theory*, trans. Helen S. Heron (London: T & T Clark, 2004), 1–38; Frances Young and David F. Ford, *Meaning and Truth in 2 Corinthians* (London: SPCK, 1987), 28–40; R. Bieringer and J. Lambrecht, *Studies on 2 Corinthians*, BETL 112 (Leuven: Leuven University Press, 1994), 156–73, 560–70.

measure themselves by one another, and compare themselves with one another, they do not show good sense. [13]We, however, will not boast beyond limits, but will keep within the field that God has assigned to us, to reach out even as far as you. [14]For we were not overstepping our limits when we reached you; we were the first to come all the way to you with the good news of Christ. [15]We do not boast beyond limits, that is, in the labors of others; but our hope is that, as your faith increases, our sphere of action among you may be greatly enlarged, [16]so that we may proclaim the good news in lands beyond you, without boasting of work already done in someone else's sphere of action. [17]"Let the one who boasts, boast in the Lord." [18]For it is not those who commend themselves that are approved, but those whom the Lord commends.

[11:1]I wish you would bear with me in a little foolishness. Do bear with me! [2]I feel a divine jealousy for you, for I promised you in marriage to one husband, to present you as a chaste virgin to Christ. [3]But I am afraid that as the serpent deceived Eve by its cunning, your thoughts will be led astray from a sincere and pure devotion to Christ. [4]For if someone comes and proclaims another Jesus than the one we proclaimed, or if you receive a different spirit from the one you received, or a different gospel from the one you accepted, you submit to it readily enough.

13:10). This explains why Paul's attack on his detractors is not addressed to the accusers themselves but to the Corinthians who have tolerated their ways (11:4, 19-20). It seems that Paul's sharp words in these final chapters corroborate the rivals' accusation that his letters are bold—this because he expects to be, perhaps can only be, weak and pliable when he is present with them (10:9-10). In this he identifies himself with the meekness of Christ, conceding in his own words, "I am humble when present with you and bold toward you when away" (10:1), bold to press the Corinthians to make a choice before he comes, but his aim remains reconciliation with them.

The argument of the last four chapters is highly wrought rather than carefully organized. It may be best described as intercalated in that a second point always begins before a first is completed. So while Paul is responding to their charges in this section he begins to speak of his own boasting as a fool already in 10:8, asks their forbearance for this in 11:1, and finally both denies he is a fool and asks to be accepted as one in 11:16-18 and 21b, all before he begins the fool's boast with a list of his credentials in 11:22-29. Even here he interrupts his boast three times to comment on a fool's boasting (11:30; 12:1, 5-6), and he closes with a reflection on having

⁵I think that I am not in the least inferior to these super-apostles. ⁶I may be untrained in speech, but not in knowledge; certainly in every way and in all things we have made this evident to you.

⁷Did I commit a sin by humbling myself so that you might be exalted, because I proclaimed God's good news to you free of charge? ⁸I robbed other churches by accepting support from them in order to serve you. ⁹And when I was with you and was in need, I did not burden anyone, for my needs were supplied by the friends who came from Macedonia. So I refrained and will continue to refrain from burdening you in any way. ¹⁰As the truth of Christ is in me, this boast of mine will not be silenced in the regions of Achaia. ¹¹And why? Because I do not love you? God knows I do!

¹²And what I do I will also continue to do, in order to deny an opportunity to those who want an opportunity to be recognized as our equals in what they boast about. ¹³For such boasters are false apostles, deceitful workers, disguising themselves as apostles of Christ. ¹⁴And no wonder! Even Satan

boasted as a fool (12:11-13). All this metacommunication about his way of speaking will be considered in my next chapter about his fool's boast (11:21b–12:10). The letter ends with Paul's challenge to the Corinthians to prepare for his arrival in Corinth (12:14–13:13). But now I focus on his opening rebuttal of the charges he faces (10:1–11:21a).

Paul meets the charges made against him, not one by one, but in the process of self-defense. He can quote his opposition verbatim, yet more often he insinuates their moves in his countermoves. I first ask what is the ecosystem or worldview underlying Paul's argument and what are the primary contrasts he draws that expose it to us. Second, I try to reconstruct the charges made against Paul, explicit and implied, and the wider social, political, and economic context within which these make sense. Finally, I take up Paul's interaction with the Corinthians, how what he says to them suggests their stance toward him, both in what they have said and done to which he is responding and how he expects them to react now.

A Feminist Lens at Three Ranges on Paul's Rebuttal to His Rivals' Charges (10:1–11:21a)

The Broad Ecosystem or Worldview Underlying Paul's Rebuttal of Rivals

Because Paul in this section is doing all he can to expose and undermine rival teachers who have come to Corinth, he stresses values that

disguises himself as an angel of light.
[15]So it is not strange if his ministers also disguise themselves as ministers of righteousness. Their end will match their deeds.

[16]I repeat, let no one think that I am a fool; but if you do, then accept me as a fool, so that I too may boast a little. [17]What I am saying in regard to this boastful confidence, I am saying not with the Lord's authority, but as a fool; [18]since many boast according to human standards, I will also boast. [19]For you gladly put up with fools, being wise yourselves! [20]For you put up with it when someone makes slaves of you, or preys upon you, or takes advantage of you, or puts on airs, or gives you a slap in the face. [21]To my shame, I must say, we were too weak for that!*

* NRSV notes: 10:2, 3; 11:18, Gk *according to the flesh* for *according to human standards*; 10:3, Gk *in the flesh* for *as human beings*; 10:4, Gk *fleshly* for *merely human*; 10:14, 16; 11:7, Or *gospel* for *good news*; 11:3, Other ancient authorities lack *pure*; 11:9, Gk *brothers* for *friends*.

oppose each other: the true versus the false, the measured versus the excessive, the known versus what is thought up, doing versus speaking, loving versus abusing, lifting up versus tearing down—all told, the ways of God versus the ways of the flesh, which turn out to be Satan in disguise. These contrasting values to which Paul appeals are not distinctive to him but are basic to ancient cultures both in Israel and in the Hellenic and Roman worlds. As feminist interpreters we reject this sharp polarization and insist on space for diversity. At the same time we see that Paul is under direct attack from others who are working to replace him, and he argues from widely accepted polarities to show that he measures up and they do not.

Paul's accusers have charged that he writes powerful letters but cannot speak with any impact when he is present (10:10). They indicate that it is time for him to move on and not disturb this community with his letters, making demands he cannot bring off. They apparently expect itinerant preachers like Paul and themselves to operate seriatim, some apostles opening up new territory and others arriving to raise the spiritual level of the communities when they are ready for more. This has led to competition between preachers, but the Corinthians have found it stimulating. Though Paul once said, "I planted and Apollo watered, but God gave the growth" (1 Cor 3:6), here he rejects any notion of a sequence of leaders in time and asserts a distribution in space: "We do not boast beyond measure but according to the measure of the boundary that the measuring God has measured out for us to reach even to you" (10:13). And he contrasts himself to those who overstep their boundaries and work in other people's fields (10:14-16). This indicates a geographical division of labor, one measured not by whatever gifts a speaker cultivates and whatever needs evolve over time but by the place and culture in which one is set and the flourishing of the people there.

Yet Paul is far from a true conservative who aims to maintain a completed creation without change. In fact, he immediately challenges the Corinthians to grow in faith so that "among you our boundaries may be greatly expanded for the good news to be proclaimed in regions beyond you—yet not boasting in what is already opened up by others" (10:15-16). The reference to their growing faith suggests that he anticipates their carrying the news beyond themselves within an expanded region that he opens up (10:15).[3] Note in this connection that the letter has been addressed not only to the Corinthians but "to all the saints in Achaia" (1:1), the Roman province that includes not only Corinth but the Peloponnesus, Attica, and all of what is southern Greece today, making Corinth a channel toward multiple towns and villages.

If so, there may be not only a struggle here between itinerants who call themselves apostles over whether they should be distributed in time or in space but also a struggle to shape and protect an indigenous mission. Paul shifts at this point from speaking as "I" to speaking as "we" (10:3-6, 11-16), which has been interpreted to include the wider mission group of Timothy, Sylvanus, and Titus,[4] or is he thinking of the Corinthians themselves: Chloe, Gaius, Crispus, Stephanus, and the local prophets and teachers (1 Cor 1:11, 16; 11:4-5; 12:29; 14:29-31)? Paul may sense as he moves on to new areas in the west (Rom 15:17-24) that the Christ assemblies of the east must grow out from within, that local

---

3. The verb for preaching the gospel is an infinitive, not a first-person plural, but the sentence is regularly translated so that it is Paul's further preaching that is anticipated. But then why is it delayed until their faith has grown (10:15-16)?

4. Loïc P. M. Berge's detailed study shows that Paul's first-person plural in 2 Corinthians refers largely to "un travail d'équipe" (the work of a team), "la collégialité apostolique de groupe paulinien" (the apostolic collegiality of the Pauline group); see *Faiblesse et force, présidence et collégialité chez Paul de Tarse: Recherche littéraire et théologique sur 2 Co 10–13 dans le contexte du genre épistolaire antique* (Leiden: Brill, 2015), 212–16, 221–24. Marquis interprets Paul's task geographically but takes this as the measure of Paul's personal authority "to the extent that an arrival of an apostle in a region constituted the arrival of God's spirit." God "thus established the apostle as authority over the community, as its 'father'" (Timothy Luckritz Marquis, *Transient Apostle: Paul, Travel, and the Rhetoric of Empire* [New Haven: Yale University Press, 2013], 42).

cultures are best addressed by their own people. Or is this belied by his plan to head for Spain, where he speaks neither the local languages nor the international Latin? Possibly he knows of enclaves of Greek-speaking Jews in Spain where he can ignite something that others can spread. At least he sees himself propelled by a God who measures out assignments geographically, expects heavy local cultivation over time, and blocks rank violations from outsiders.

Yet Paul seems blind to his own position as outsider. Now that postcolonial biblical interpreters are raising our awareness that local residents have authority over their own wellbeing and that of other living things and the land itself,[5] we see local mission as a local responsibility, world ecosystems and climates as both local and worldwide responsibility.[6] There is an analogy here to Paul's effort to mobilize a local community to take responsibility under threat from confident and powerful outsiders.

The Social, Political, and Economic Context of Paul's Rebuttal

So who are these opponents appearing suddenly near the end of Paul's letter? They are not dignified with names, nor are their specific theology or practices opposed with any consistency, as is the case in Paul's letter to the Galatians. We can patch together only a general description: that certain preachers of Christ (10:7, 14; 11:23), who, like Paul, are part of Israel's tradition (11:22), have come to Corinth from elsewhere with letters of recommendation and new interpretations that are threatening Paul's influence in an assembly that he and his colleagues founded (1:19; 3:1; 10:20; 11:4, 23). Our best bet for understanding this conflict is to work backward from Paul's defense against these people, reconstructing their charges against him and drawing in whatever aspects of the social, political, or economic setting that can illuminate the conflict.

Paul's opening salvo, "I myself, Paul, appeal to you with Christ's meekness and kindness," can only be meant sincerely, but the next line, "I who am humble when face to face with you but bold when away" (10:1),

---

5. Musa W. Dube, *Postcolonial Feminist Interpretation of the Bible* (St. Louis: Chalice, 2000); R. S. Sugirharajah, *The Bible and the Third World* (Cambridge: Cambridge University Press, 2001); Musa W. Dube Shomanah, Andrew Mütüa Mbuvi, and Dora R. Mbuwayesango, eds., *Postcolonial Perspectives in African Biblical Interpretation* (Atlanta: Society of Biblical Literature, 2012).

6. David G. Horrell calls for "an ecologically reconfigured Pauline theology" in "Ecojustice in the Bible? Pauline Contributions in Ecological Theology," in *Bible and Justice: Ancient Texts, Modern Challenges*, ed. Mathew J. M. Coomber (London: Equinox, 2011), 158–77.

reflects ironically the charge of his rivals, which he quotes soon after, "For, they say, the letters are hefty and strong, but his physical presence is weak and his speaking despicable" (10:10). They are charging him with being ineffective on the ground and therefore deceptive in his bold writing. He concedes his weak presence—is it a disability of stance or of sight or of speech?—but he denies that he is deceptive: "Let these people consider that the way we speak in letters when absent we will act when present" (10:11). Paul shifts the focus from inconsistency in writing and speaking where his skills are apparently very different, to consistency in word and deed, to his moral integrity.[7] Whatever his inadequacies, he says, he will follow through and carry out what he threatens to do.

Meanwhile Paul explains why he writes so forcefully, namely, to avoid a worse conflict when he arrives in Corinth (10:2; 13:10). It has come to this, he complains, because certain persons are saying that they are "agents of Christ" (10:7; 11:23) and that we are "walking according to the flesh" (10:2; NRSV, "acting according to human standards"). This charge against Paul could reflect suspicions about how he handles money. On the one hand, he does manual labor and refuses their financial support, a subject to which he returns (11:7-11), and, on the other, he expects them to donate for Jerusalem, where he has obligations (8:1–9:15; Gal 2:10). Or they may consider him more generally "on the make." Paul concedes that he acts "in the flesh," though not "according to the flesh," yet he claims to wield weapons that have divine power to tear down fortresses raised up against knowledge of God and take every thought captive to Christ until all disobedience is punished (10:2-6).

Against what he calls their exalted way of thinking Paul uses here the image of a city besieged until it falls and its people are enslaved and ring-leaders executed, Rome's way of dealing with rebellious cities. At this point Jeremy Punt sees Paul as the colonial appropriating the colonizer's rhetoric, mimicking not only his opponents but the empire as a whole.[8] J. Albert Harrill argues that Paul shares the rhetoric and ideologies of Roman culture and develops alternatives within it over against other

---

7. Paul appeals here to the requirement that word and deed match: Seneca, *Moralia* 52.8; 108.38; 4 Macc 5.38. See Bärbel Bosenius, *Die Abwesenheit des Apostels als theologische Program: Der zweite Korintherbrief als Beispiel für Brieflichkeit der paulinische Theologie* (Tübingen: Franke, 1994), 128–31.

8. Jeremy Punt, "Paul and Postcolonial Hermeneutics: Marginality and/in Early Biblical Interpretation," in *As It Is Written: Studying Paul's Use of Scripture*, ed. Stanley E. Porter and Christopher D. Stanley, SymS 50 (Leiden: Brill, 2008), 276–79. On the military imagery see also Thrall, *Second Epistle*, 610–11.

Christ-oriented alternatives, not over against Roman power.[9] It may be most telling that Paul is speaking here to people in Corinth, a Roman colony built a century earlier (44 BCE) on the near-abandoned site of the great Greek city of Corinth. That city had suffered exactly this fate at Roman hands yet a century before that (164 BCE) when its citizens had organized a league of Greek cities to stop Rome's advance. (See the sidebar from the geographer Strabo, "Corinth Destroyed for Resisting Rome in 164 BCE," who minimizes both the Corinthians' offense and the Roman atrocity.) Paul's threat is bound to have some resonance in a Greek-speaking community of this Latin-ruled Roman provincial capital still named Corinth. Though it is the "arguments" and "thought" of outsiders that Paul intends to destroy, not the people of Corinth, one can see why they have called his letters bold. In response, he insists that he does not want to frighten them but only to make clear that he belongs to Christ every bit as much as these rivals do (10:9, 7).

Corinth Destroyed for Resisting Rome in 164 BCE

The Corinthians, when they were subject to Philip [of Macedon], not only sided with him in his quarrel with the Romans, but individually behaved so contemptuously towards the Romans that certain persons ventured to pour down filth upon the Roman ambassadors when passing by their house. For this and other offences, however, they soon paid the penalty, for a considerable army was sent thither, and the city itself was rased to the ground by Leucius Mummius; and the other countries as far as Macedonia became subject to the Romans, different commanders being sent into different countries; but the Sicyonians [from the next town to the west] obtained most of the Corinthian country. Polibius . . . says that he was present and saw paintings that had been flung to the ground and saw soldiers playing dice on these. . . .

Now after Corinth had remained deserted for a long time, it was restored again, because of its favourable position, by the deified Caesar, who colonised it with people that belonged for the most part to the freedmen class.[10]

---

9. J. Albert Harrill, *Paul the Apostle: His Life and Legacy in Their Roman Context* (Cambridge: Cambridge University Press, 2012), 76–94.

10. Strabo, *Geography* 8.6.23, in Strabo, *Geography*, vol. 4: *Books 8–9*, trans. Horace Leonard Jones, LCL (Cambridge, MA: Harvard University Press, 1927, repr. 1968), 199–203. Strabo's description is annotated by Jerome Murphy-O'Connor in *St. Paul's Corinth: Texts and Archaeology* (Wilmington, DE: Michael Glazier, 1983), 63–69.

Next Paul attacks his rivals' boasting (10:12-18).[11] In seven verses he uses seven negative particles (οὐ, οὐκ), laying out all the ways he is not like them. After speaking as "I" he has resumed the plural "we" (10:11), blunting the edge of what could be heard as a boast in his own powers. He contrasts himself and his colleagues with those "who measure themselves by themselves," repeating the word "themselves" five times in one sentence and ending, "This is nonsense" (10:12). The challenge for Paul is to expose the foolishness of his rivals' competitive self-assertions without becoming just another player in the competition. He contrasts their boasts with "our not boasting in unmeasured ways but only according to the limited measure which God measured out for us to reach even as far as yourselves" (10:13). Here repeated cognates of the word "measure" stress the fact that he and his colleagues arrived in Corinth first with news of Christ while others have moved in on their work, boasting in what was already accomplished.[12] Against such boasts he appeals to Scripture, " 'Let the one who boasts boast in the Lord' [Jer 9:24], since it is not the one that commends himself that is tested and approved but the one whom the Lord commends" (10:17-18). Here Paul also gets traction from ancient Greek traditions such as Plato's "God is the measure of all things" and the Delphic maxim μηδὲν ἄγαν (nothing in excess).[13] It is clear that Paul's rivals came to Corinth after he did and competed for the Corinthians' attention by comparing themselves with Paul and each other, confident that his personal weaknesses and speaking difficulties would eliminate him in the contest. (We recall the line that women cannot preach because our voices are lighter.)

In response to his accusers Paul highlights again his priority in Corinth by presenting himself as the Corinthian believers' progenitor (11:2-3). He takes on the persona of the father of a virgin engaged to Christ and now beguiled away as Eve was by the snake. Like a father in a Jewish or Greek family of the time, he is held responsible to protect the daughter until she is safely married, all the more so after the betrothal. The possibility that this image was chosen particularly to address women in Corinth will be considered in the next discussion on the interchange between Paul and the Corinthians. For understanding Paul's opponents,

11. See Furnish, *II Corinthians*, 480, on competitive practices of teachers in the Roman provinces.

12. See comments on the ecosystem implied in this text above.

13. Hans Dieter Betz, *Der Apostel Paulus und die sokratische Tradition: Eine exegetische Untersuchung zu seiner "Apologie" 2 Korinther 10–13*, BHT 45 (Tübingen: J. C. B. Mohr [Paul Siebeck], 1972), 130–31; henceforth *Apostel Paulus*; Thrall, *Second Epistle*, 644.

Jews like himself (11:22), the significant factor is that Jews took betrothal as the key point of public commitment. Paul's image depicts his rivals seducing the Corinthians away from their single commitment to Christ, just as the serpent deceived Eve. They become not merely latecomers in his work area but deceivers opposed to God, like Satan himself, who by this time in Jewish exegesis can be associated with the snake.[14]

Paul then identifies their deception. They proclaim another Jesus, a different Spirit, and a different gospel than Paul has taught them (11:4). But what this difference is remains unspoken, either because he assumes the Corinthians know it, because he doesn't want to give it a hearing, or because his point is really not their Christology but that they do not thoroughly understand and genuinely stand behind what they boast.[15] He insists that he may be unskilled in speech but not in knowledge, and the Corinthians know this well enough because he has been open toward them in everything (11:5-6). His rivals have charged that he "lives according to the flesh" (10:3), and he claims that they deceive and seduce people (11:2-3). It all comes down to who one can trust. The backdrop here is the relative freedom of travel in the internal Roman provinces that attracts charlatans of every stripe who ply their snake oil or sophistries and leave town when they are exposed.[16]

A Swindler Satirized

Alexander was just getting his beard when the death of the Tyanean [who taught him "his whole bag of tricks"] put him in a bad way, since it coincided with the passing of his beauty, by which he might have supported himself. So he abandoned petty projects for ever. He formed a partnership with a Byzantine writer of choral songs . . . and they went about the country practicing quackery and sorcery, and "trimming the fatheads"—for so they style the public in the traditional patter of magicians. Well, among these they hit upon a rich Macedonian woman, past her prime but still eager to be charming, and not only lined their purses fairly well at her expense, but went with her from Bithynia to

14. Wis 2:23-24; 2 Enoch 31.4-6; 2 Cor 2:11; 4:4; 11:14; Thrall, *Second Epistle*, 662.

15. For an effort to reconstruct the opponents' theology, see Thrall, *Second Epistle*, 667–71.

16. These were apparently depicted sharply in the lost satires of Menippus and taken up by Lucian of Samosata: Betz, *Apostel Paulus*, 19–42, 53–54, 64–66, 85–86; Joel C. Relihan, *Ancient Menippean Satire* (Baltimore: Johns Hopkins University Press, 1993).

Macedon. She came from Pella, a place once flourishing in the time of the kings of Macedon but now insignificant, with very few inhabitants. There they saw great serpents, quite tame and gentle, so that they were kept by women, slept with children, let themselves be stepped upon, were not angry when they were stroked, and took milk from the breast just like babies. So they bought one of the reptiles, the finest, for a few coppers; and, in the words of Thucydides: "Here beginneth the war!". . .

For some days he remained at home [in Abonoteichus], expecting what actually happened—that as the news spread, crowds of Paphlagonias would come running in. When the city had become over-full of people, all of them already bereft of their brains and sense . . . he seated himself on a couch in a certain chamber, clothed in apparel well suited to a god, and took into his bosom his Asclepius from Pella, who, as I have said, was of uncommon size and beauty. . . . When they went in, the thing, of course, seemed to them a miracle, that the formerly tiny snake within a few days had turned into so great a serpent, with a human face, moreover and tame. They were immediately crowded towards the exit, and before they could look closely were forced out by those who kept coming in. . . .

When it was time to carry out the purpose for which the whole scheme had been concocted— that is to say, to make predictions and give oracles to those who sought them—taking his cue from Amphilochus in Cilicia, who, as you know, after the death and disappearance of his father Amphiaraus at Thebes, was exiled from his own country, went to Cilicia, and got on very well by foretelling the future, like his father, for the Cilicians and getting two obols for each prediction—taking, as I say, his cue from him, Alexander announced to all comers that the god would make prophecies, and named a date for it in advance. He directed everyone to write down whatever he wanted and what he especially wished to learn.[17]

Paul's defense that follows the charges against him is financial (11:7-11), showing where the attack hit home. He may be accused of fleecing the community, peddling bad goods (4:2). Or some interpreters argue that he offends the Corinthians by operating independently from them,

17. Lucian, *Alexander the False Prophet*, 6–8, 15–16, 19, trans. A. M. Harmon, vol. 4, LCL (Cambridge, MA: Harvard University Press, 1961), 183–85, 195–97, 201.

supporting himself by manual labor or gifts from others (11:7-9) and refusing to accept them as his patrons.[18] Well-trained teachers in the Greco-
Roman city might be supported as "friends" of a rich family or club and
be responsible to them, whereas Paul insists on earning his own living
and being responsible only to his God. They see him as aloof, which he
denies, yet he will not budge (10:10-11). He claims that he has humiliated himself (by manual labor?) and "plundered" the Macedonians so
as not to burden them with his support (11:7-8). Some Corinthians may
also find it suspicious that Paul raises money for Jerusalem, a practice
that non-Jews might well take as a cover for something else (8:18-21).

He meets the rumors of deception against him by charging his rivals
with deception. Their boasts prove they are false apostles, Satan in disguise, and their actions will expose them to God's judgment (11:13-15).
This shows us that they do claim to be apostles—Paul would not deny
it otherwise. Rather than claiming to be an apostle himself where the
term has been debased (12:11), Paul banks on his priority and integrity
in Corinth and concludes this argument with a bitter slur against his
rivals' personal and financial abuses (11:20).

In return we can ask if there is any formal difference between Paul and
his rivals. Neither was part of the group of apostles who told of Jesus
appearing to them upon his rising from the dead. Paul did claim to have
seen the Lord when he was persecuting believers and to have become
an apostle to the nations,[19] but his opponents also claimed to belong to
Christ, to speak for Christ, and to be apostles, likely with visions and
revelations to back this up.[20] Paul, then, could be our best example of
these maverick apostles and prophets because his letters survive. The
question then becomes how he, out of them all, finally won for himself
a place among recognized apostles. Was it because of grace from God
not given to others? Was it because he worked the hardest?[21] Was it his
effective persuasion? Was it Luke's Acts of the Apostles that made him
the hero of the Gentile mission, even though Luke did not count him as
one of Christ's apostles? Was it, as he says, the faith of the Corinthians
that proved his effectiveness?[22] Or, we can ask, was it his apparently

---

18. Peter Marshall, *Enmity in Corinth: Social Conventions in Paul's Relations with
the Corinthians*, WUNT 2.23 (Tübingen: J. C. B. Mohr [Paul Siebeck], 1987), 218–58.

19. Gal 1:1, 15-17; 1 Cor 1:1; 9:1; 15:8-10; 2 Cor 1:1; 12:11-12.

20. 2 Cor 10:7; 11:5, 13, 23; 12:1, 11; 13:3.

21. 1 Cor 15:10; 2 Cor 11:23-29.

22. 1 Cor 9:1-2; 2 Cor 3:1-2; 13:3-6.

atrocious speaking ability (10:10; 11:6) that forced him to put in writing for repeated congregational reading his self-defense and his tailor-made articulations of the gospel before he dared to appear in person in Corinth and in Rome?[23] For some or all of the above reasons he is known to us and can represent for us the many later apostles and prophets active among early Christ followers in cities of the Roman east, including his rivals and the women prophets of Corinth.

This Specific Interaction between Paul and the Corinthians

Paul's argument concerning his rivals is consistently addressed, not to them, but to the Corinthians. He speaks to the Corinthians as "you" in the second-person plural,[24] and he speaks about his rivals as "someone" or "them."[25] This point has been made by many interpreters,[26] yet it is often ignored. At one point the NRSV even applies his description of the rivals to the Corinthians (10:7bc). The earlier RSV had translated, "If anyone is confident that he is Christ's, let him remind himself that as he is Christ's, so are we." The NRSV applies this to "you"—"If you are confident you belong to Christ, remind yourself"—probably to avoid restricting the reference to the male gender but thereby missing the fact that Paul is comparing himself to his rivals, not to the Corinthians.[27] Better to translate in the plural: "If they are confident they belong to Christ, let them remind themselves that as they are Christ's, so are we." In other words, the Corinthians are being charged not with boasting but with letting themselves be deceived that Paul's rivals are more Christ's than he is.

But if the rivals were having no impact on the Corinthians there would be no reason for Paul to be alarmed by the charges against him, so clearly some Corinthians are listening to the new voices. In fact, they recognize that Paul, though articulate in his letters, has been singularly unimpressive on the ground in comparison to these others, especially in his speaking, nor has he bothered to come back and follow through with them.[28]

---

23. 2 Cor 10:2, 10; 11:6; 13:10; Rom 1:9-16; 15:24, 30-32.
24. 2 Cor 10:1, 6, 7, 8, 9, 12, 13, 14, 15, 16; 11:1, 2, 3, 4, 6, 7, 8, 9, 11, 16, 19, 20, 21.
25. 2 Cor 10:2, 7, 10, 11, 12, 18; 11:4, 5, 12, 13, 15.
26. Betz, *Apostel Paulus*, 19, 43; Bieringer, *Studies on 2 Corinthians*, 173–79, 246–51.
27. Thrall concurs that Paul is referring to his rivals (*Second Epistle*, 619).
28. Some interpreters project that between composing 1 and 2 Corinthians Paul made an interim visit to Corinth that ended badly or even shamefully for Paul, followed by his tearful letter before sending Titus to set things straight (2 Cor 1:12–2:11). But it is simpler to see that 1 Corinthians was written and received with more anguish

Twice Paul works to bring the Corinthians around. First, sharpening the distinction between "them" and "you Corinthians," he says he will be bold with God's weapons against every thought of theirs that exalts itself over knowing God, but this only "when your obedience is complete" (10:5-6), because "our authority [is] to build you up, not tear you down" (10:8). In other words, he will not come and attack his rivals until the Corinthians dissociate themselves from them. He insists he will not destroy what God gave him to construct, namely, themselves as a community of faith.

Second, when defending against intruders in Corinth, he says he will not overextend himself beyond his God-given field to move in on others as has been done to him (10:12-14). But "when your faith grows" he has hopes of the Gospel being extended far beyond Corinth (10:15-16). Essentially he is waiting for the Corinthians to move in his direction, as he makes explicit in closing the letter (13:5-10). The ball is now in their court. All his irony and invective against the rivals are nothing but strokes in this single game with the Corinthians. And he projects his work with this community as the turning point toward a future when many peoples whose faith is growing extend the good news beyond themselves.[29]

I find that Paul's response to Corinth about his rivals' charges includes arguments that are shaped particularly to persuade women there, suggesting their central role in the deliberations of the community. In 1 Corinthians Paul restricted women for what he called the good order of the community. He first advised that they be married or stay married, although women who prophesy were expected to be independent;[30] then he told them to cover their heads when praying and prophesying

---

than previously recognized, and the offense of Paul's not coming when he said he would had led to still greater alienation (1:23–2:4). Bosenius argues that Paul planned to visit Corinth only when the conflicts had been resolved in his favor, writing letters to settle disputes and reserving visits for strengthening solidarity (Bosenius, *Abwesenheit des Apostels*, 1–6, 10–13).

29. Most translations of 10:15-16, including the NRSV, leave the impression that the growing faith of the Corinthians will permit Paul to extend his preaching further. But the Greek text leaves open who will be doing this proclaiming. And since this "great enlarging of our field among you," which Paul hopes for, depends on "their faith growing," all indications are that he sees the Corinthians active in the goal "that the good news be proclaimed in regions beyond you."

30. 1 Cor 7:2-5, 9-10, 13, 20, 36; Antoinette Clark Wire, *The Corinthian Women Prophets: A Reconstruction through Paul's Rhetoric* (Minneapolis: Fortress, 1990; repr., Eugene, OR: Wipf and Stock, 2003), 72–97.

in worship, although this symbolized their subordination;[31] and finally he instructed that they not speak at all in the assemblies.[32] When Paul writes 2 Corinthians, perhaps a year later, the tensions between him and the community are far greater, suggesting that his instructions have not been followed and the women prophets have continued their independent lives and uncovered worship leadership. That Paul in 2 Corinthians does not repeat or even allude to his earlier instructions indicates that he has changed his approach to them. Now he defends himself according to their values, affirming Christ's risen life and glory being revealed in them and challenging them to recognize that he embodies Christ's death, which has brought Christ's life to them.[33]

A first hint in this passage that Paul could be aiming particularly to persuade women appears after he contrasts himself with those who work in a territory already developed and boast in the labors of others. He then says, " 'Let the one who boasts, boast in the Lord,' since it is not the one who commends himself that is tested and approved but the one whom the Lord commends" (10:17-18). The Scripture that Paul quotes here is usually traced back to Jeremiah 9:24: "Thus says the Lord: 'Let the one who boasts boast in this, that he understands and knows me, that I am the Lord doing mercy and judgment and righteousness on the earth.' "[34] But the Greek Bible, which Paul uses, offers a possible alternative source in an extension of the Hebrew text midway in 1 Samuel 2:10: "Let the one who boasts boast in this, to understand and know the Lord and to do judgment and righteousness in the earth." The latter is slightly closer to Paul's rendition in its third-person reference to the Lord. Though Paul is quite capable of changing syntax when he quotes, it seems unlikely he would drop the authority of God's voice—"I am the Lord"—if he were recalling Jeremiah. Another sign that he draws from 1 Samuel is his quoting the same sentence in 1 Corinthians 1:31, where he develops the theme that God reverses human fortunes and eliminates all grounds for boasting, a key feature of the 1 Samuel passage (1 Cor 1:26-29; 1 Sam 2:5-8), not of Jeremiah 9.

31. 1 Cor 11:2-16; Wire, *Corinthian Women Prophets*, 116–34.

32. 1 Cor 14:32-36; Wire, *Corinthian Women Prophets*, 135–58.

33. 2 Cor 3:16-18; 4:7-12; 13:3-4, 9-10. See further analysis of this on the pages where these particular texts are discussed in my comments on the interaction of Paul and the Corinthians.

34. Furnish, *II Corinthians*, 474; Thrall, *Second Epistle*, 652.

Finally, 1 Samuel 2:1-10 is the song of Hannah at the dedication of her infant son Samuel to the temple, one of the fourteen Scripture songs so well known that they were later collected as a separate book of odes placed after the Psalms in the Greek Bible (LXX). The Greek song of Hannah ends with a paean of praise to God in which these words about boasting in the Lord were inserted well before Paul's time, probably from Jeremiah. The Hebrew song of Hannah shows signs of being from Israel's monarchic period, and Kyle McCarter has proposed from its short symmetric lines and its closing praise of the king "his anointed" that it was composed for an "occasion of royal thanksgiving, quite possibly the birth of an heir to the throne," and that it later found its way into the Samuel narrative.[35] A third, yet longer, recording of the song is found in the Qumran 1 Samuel scroll (4QSam2). McCarter takes it to be "the only surviving witness of the primitive text,"[36] and at the least it confirms long-standing and widespread use of Hannah's song.[37] Other parts of the song are adapted in Mary's Magnificat, showing that it was not only well known in Paul's era but continued to be associated with women's praise to God at giving birth (Luke 1:46-55). Paul will have known Hannah's song in its Greek form, likely both from the text and from hearing it sung, and he could be quoting from it in Corinth to appeal to women who return praise to God for blessing them.

A possible second indication that Paul has particular interest in persuading women in Corinth appears when he compares himself to a father who has betrothed the Corinthian community as his virgin daughter to Christ and now fears that they are being seduced to another Jesus, another spirit, and another gospel (11:2-4). This image not only turns the rivalry between proclaimers of the Gospel into an open conflict between a protecting father and deceptive suitors, but by comparing his rivals with the serpent deceiving Eve, Paul suggests a Satanic force with an irreversible impact.[38] Yet even these two independent feminine images that Paul draws on—the vulnerable daughter and the gullible Eve—might not themselves signal his interest in persuading the Corinthian women were it not for his positive characterization of the virgin as "chaste," "pure," or

---

35. P. Kyle McCarter Jr., *1 Samuel*, AB 8 (Garden City, NY: Doubleday, 1980), 73–76.

36. Ibid., 67–70.

37. See also 1 Clement 3.1, cited by Christian Wolff, who supports Paul's dependence on 1 Samuel 2:10 (*Der zweite Brief*, 206–8; cf. Furnish, *II Corinthians*, 474).

38. Elsewhere Paul uses the figure of Adam to signify the entry of sin into the world (1 Cor 15:21-22; Rom 5:12-19; cf. 1 Tim 2:14).

"holy" (παρθένον ἁγνήν, 11:2). Paul makes clear in his advice about marriage in 1 Corinthians 7 that unmarried women devoted to "pleasing the Lord" took particular interest in being ἁγία καὶ τῷ σώματι καὶ τῷ πνεύματι ("holy in body and spirit," 7:34). This might have been especially necessary for women who prophesied, whose speech could otherwise be suspect of influence from their husbands. Therefore Paul's reference here to the "chaste virgin with simple and pure devotion to Christ" as his image for the Corinthians might have been intended for special effect on women in Corinth who have chosen to remain virgins, leave marriages, or stay widows in order to lead in the community.[39] The rivals of Paul with their different Christ are thus classified as threats to the commitment these women have made.

Yet what do we twenty-first-century feminists make of Paul's alternately threatening and caustic rebuttal of his rival's charge that "his letters are heavy and strong, but his physical presence is weak and his speaking is worthless" (10:10)? Writing to persuade a small community of Corinthians and perhaps particularly its women leaders who had not accepted his restrictions, he culminates his rebuttal in bitter irony: "You bear it well enough when someone enslaves you, or devours you, or takes you in, or humiliates you, or strikes you in the face. To my shame, I say, we were too weak for that" (11:20-21). This picks up the rivals' accusation that he is weak and reverses its value. Gentleness is not only Christ's way, as Paul said to start (10:1), but also his own way of dealing with them in contrast to the newcomers' manipulations and abuses. In other words, he doesn't deny he is weak when with them in Corinth, but he shows it is good for them that he is.

The charge against him that he is bold only at a distance (10:10) is confirmed by this bold counter-attack at the letter's end against his accusers. Because it is his chosen strategy to come back only when he is welcomed (10:6; 13:10), he cannot sign off on this letter seeking reconciliation with the Corinthians before he sees his accusers' attack boomerang back to hit them, if only by making the charges against him work in his favor where he cannot deny them. As it is said, "The powerful command, the powerless argue."[40]

---

39. 2 Cor 11:2-3; 1 Cor 7: 4-5, 8, 10-11, 13, 36, 39; Wire, *Corinthian Women Prophets*, 72–97.

40. Sundermann quotes Wolf Schneider's applying to Paul this statement from the philosophers of rhetoric Chaim Perelman and L. Olbrechts-Tyteca, *The New Rhetoric: A Treatise on Argumentation* (Notre Dame, IN: University of Notre Dame Press, 1969;

The final and sharpest charge against Paul, that his speech is despicable (10:10), he also concedes—he is not trained in speech-making, he says, but has knowledge of God for them (10:4-5; 11:6)—and he leaves no doubt which of the two is more important. His own counter-attack that follows, accusing his rivals of cutting in and claiming credit for his work in Corinth, is proven by his having been in Corinth first, and his never taking their money is contrasted to his rivals' abuses of them. Everything from his opening military threats to his caustic climax here tells the Corinthians that he means business against whoever thinks they can come between him and them, between, as he puts it, a father and his virgin daughter betrothed to Christ (11:2-3).

Feminist interpretation of 2 Corinthians has been consistently critical of Paul's metaphor of himself as father of a community betrothed to Christ and tempted to desert him as Eve was tempted by the snake. Caroline Vander Stichele notes that Paul here identifies passive vulnerability through Eve with woman's sexuality[41] ("snake" being masculine in Hebrew and Greek), though he elsewhere associates humanity's sin with Adam. Paul is not saying here with 1 Timothy 2:14, "Adam was not deceived but the woman was deceived," yet he makes way for that, and the wider cultural meaning of the Eve myth pointed that way. Vander Stichele does reject any reading of Paul's defensive rhetoric as normative.[42] Annette Merz describes how Paul prepares the ground here for Ephesians 5:22-33, which calls the church the pure bride of Christ in an effort to make the wedded wife normative and delegitimate ascetic women.[43] Reimund Bieringer sees Paul's betrothal image claiming an

---

French, 1958), 19–20; Hans-Georg Sundermann, *Der schwache Apostel und die Kraft der Rede: Eine historische Analyse von 2 Kor 10–13* (Frankfurt am Main: Peter Lang, 1996), 265. Paul's marginal social position is confirmed in Ryan Schellenberg's "Paul, Samson Occom, and the Constraints of Boasting: A Comparative Reading of 2 Corinthians 10–13," *HTR* 109 (2016): 512–35.

41. Caroline Vander Stichele, "2 Corinthians," in *Feminist Biblical Interpretation: A Compendium of Critical Commentary on the Books of the Bible and Related Literature*, ed. Luise Schottroff and Marie-Theres Wacker, trans. Everett Kalin, Nancy Lukens, Linda M. Maloney, Barbara Rumscheidt, Martin Rumscheidt, and Tina Steiner (Grand Rapids, MI: Eerdmans, 2012), 593–602.

42. Ibid.

43. Annette Merz, "Why Did the Pure Bride of Christ (2 Cor. 11.2) Become a Wedded Wife (Eph. 5.22-33)? Theses about the Intertextual Transformation of an Ecclesiological Metaphor," *JSNT* 79 (2000): 130–47; trans. Brian McNeil from *Paulus: Umstrittene Traditionen—lebendigen Theologie*, ed. Claudia Janssen, Luise Schottroff, and Beate Wehn (Gütersloh: Christian Kaiser/Gütersloher Verlagshaus, 2001), 148–65.

exclusive relation with the Corinthian community,[44] and Christine Gerber, who concedes this, stresses that Paul does not take for granted this authority as a father to demand obedience but is struggling with multiple metaphors to shape a relation to them that is much contested.[45]

Paul's argument is a tour de force. It is bold, an exercise in pressure if not physical force, demanding they make peace with him. How do the Corinthian women prophets hear this? How will they have responded, we should ask, because they will have had to respond. Second Corinthians itself, I have proposed, is best read as evidence of their earlier response to 1 Corinthians. Paul's sharp defensiveness in 2 Corinthians suggests that Corinth rejected many of his initial instructions, the women prophets continuing to maintain independent lives and to prophesy and pray uncovered in the assemblies. Provoked to change his approach to them, Paul is no longer instructing them by his sights but defending himself by their sights. But he will not let them go. He wagers that they can tolerate frank speech and bold argument. And since he cannot debate well in person, he will do so in writing and trust that the person who reads his words to them—will it be Titus? Stephanus? Prisca?—can bring them around.

The Corinthians' response to this attack on his accusers will have depended on several factors. Would Paul's sharp language be considered acceptable or not? Had Paul's rivals been experienced as abusive or not? Most important, did Paul leave space for the Corinthians' way of life and worship leadership or not? Paul's language, which includes bitter irony and personal invective (11:13-15, 19-21), was more common in arguments of that time between people in contention and would probably in itself not have offended to the point of becoming ineffective.[46] Whether Paul's rivals were abusive is a more difficult question. We have no way to determine this except to note that Paul banks his entire argument on the Corinthians' recognizing his opponents in what he insinuates and

44. Bieringer, *Studies on 2 Corinthians*, 249–51.

45. Christine Gerber, *Paulus, Apostolat und Autorität, oder vom Lesen fremder Briefe* (Zürich: Theologischer Verlag Zürich, 2012), 16–17.

46. Margaret Mitchell characterizes Paul's speech in 2 Corinthians as the "agonistic rhetoric" taught in Greco-Roman education and expected in the law courts (*Paul, the Corinthians and the Birth of Christian Hermeneutics* [Cambridge: Cambridge University Press, 2010], 23–27, 81–87). Severin Koster distinguishes reproof from invective in that the latter intends not only to censure but to eliminate the shamed person from the situation (*Die Invektive in der griechischen und römischen Literatur* [Meisenheim am Glan: Anton Hain, 1980], 32–34, 353–54).

exposes about their actions, choosing not to develop any critique of the content that they teach except to reject it as different from what he teaches (11:4). Paul's rivals must at least be assertive, competitive, and demanding, but so is Paul.

The question that remains is whether Paul was ready to respect the Corinthians' practices and leadership. This might be concluded from the fact that he no longer was telling the women whether to marry or how to worship as he once did.[47] Yet since he was setting aside all instructing, they could wonder if it would return later. He does distinguish them sharply from the rivals that he excoriates. And he is waiting for their response on two fronts: he will punish the rivals only "when your obedience is complete," that is, when they support him in this, and he expects the work in Achaia to be expanded only when "your faith grows," thereby spreading the good news further (10:6, 15-16). Paul keeps repeating at the start, midway, and finish of his closing peroration that the authority God has given him is for building them up, not for tearing them down (10:8; 12:19; 13:10). If they trust him in this, they may choose to work with him.

---

47. 1 Cor 7:9, 11, 13, 16, 25-26, 39-40; 11:5-6, 10, 13-16; 14:33b-36.

2 Corinthians 11:21b–12:13

Paul's Defense of Himself as a Fool

Text and Its Structure (11:21b–12:13)

In the previous argument (10:1–11:21a) Paul has accused others who have come to Corinth to preach Christ. He claims that they commend themselves and boast their superiority while only those commended by the Lord are validated (10:12-18). Yet he is under pressure in Corinth to prove he is not inferior to them and so alternates between two distinct ways of speaking, boasting his own credentials, on the one hand, and discounting all human boasts as foolish, on the other. In fact, he combines the two in this passage by making a positive boast explicitly as a fool. This begins with a blow-by-blow comparison of himself to the new arrivals (11:21b-23a), continues with a list of all he has endured (11:23b-33), and ends with an account of his visions and revelations (12:1-10). Having already discounted his boasts as "a bit of foolishness" (10:8; 11:1), asking the Corinthians to tolerate him as a fool since they tolerate fools so well (11:16-21), he begins to boast as a fool, even as a madman (11:21b, 23a). At the same time he keeps interrupting himself to disparage his boasting. Midway through, he decides he will boast only in his weakness (11:30; 12:5), though he has received revelations such that he could do otherwise (12:6-7). Finally, on the basis of Christ's words to him, "Power is realized in weakness," he claims his weakness as the place of his strength (12:7-10).

[11:21]But whatever anyone dares to boast of—I am speaking as a fool—I also dare to boast of that. [22]Are they Hebrews? So am I. Are they Israelites? So am I. Are they descendants of Abraham? So am I. [23]Are they ministers of Christ? I am talking like a madman—I am a better one: with far greater labors, far more imprisonments, with countless floggings, and often near death. [24]Five times I have received from the Jews the forty lashes minus one. [25]Three times I was beaten with rods. Once I received a stoning. Three times I was shipwrecked; for a night and a day I was adrift at sea; [26]on frequent journeys, in danger from rivers, danger from bandits, danger from my own people, danger from Gentiles, danger in the city, danger in the wilderness, danger at sea, danger from false brothers and sisters; [27]in toil and hardship, through many a sleepless night, hungry and thirsty, often without food, cold and naked. [28]And, besides other things, I am under daily pressure because of my anxiety for all the

Looking back on his boast, he blames the Corinthians for having made him a fool because they did not defend him (12:11-13).

Alongside the repeated defensive comments about his foolishness, Paul delivers the positive credentials that he thinks can demonstrate his superiority and divine insight (11:21b–12:10). These credentials, both in endurance and in revelations, are often taken as the climax of the letter. Or is it the accompanying nervous comments about boasting that are most telling? There he reveals in spite of himself his deepest conviction that whoever boasts can only boast in the Lord (10:17), that what he has accomplished, however little or much, remains God's miracle in spite of his weakness, not his achievement at all. That he proves himself a fool by boasting what he has done, however, also demonstrates his boasting rivals to be fools and brings down his competition, "For I lack nothing that these super-apostles have, even though I am nothing" (12:11).

Among the Greek manuscripts from which this text is derived there are differences significant for translation at only two points. The scribe of an early papyrus (copied by some others) apparently thought the first phrase of 12:7 belonged with the next words and so dropped after it the conjunction διό (therefore), while scribes of several early codices recognized that the phrase was part of the previous sentence and avoided this "correction."[1] At 12:9 the best early manuscripts read the words at-

---

1. Thrall retains διό but still takes the previous clause as part of verse 7; see *A Critical and Exegetical Commentary on the Second Epistle to the Corinthians*, ICC (Edinburgh: T & T Clark, 1994), 803–5.

churches. [29]Who is weak, and I am not weak? Who is made to stumble, and I am not indignant?

[30]If I must boast, I will boast of the things that show my weakness. [31]The God and Father of the Lord Jesus (blessed be he forever!) knows that I do not lie. [32]In Damascus, the governor under King Aretas guarded the city of Damascus in order to seize me, [33]but I was let down in a basket through a window in the wall, and escaped from his hands.

[12:1]It is necessary to boast; nothing is to be gained by it, but I will go on to visions and revelations of the Lord. [2]I know a person in Christ who fourteen years ago was caught up to the third heaven—whether in the body or out of the body I do not know; God knows. [3]And I know that such a person—whether in the body or out of the body I do not know; God knows—[4]was caught up into Paradise and heard things that are not to be told, that no mortal is permitted to repeat. [5]On behalf of such a

tributed to the Lord simply "for power is realized in weakness," though some scribes added a pronoun for clarification, making it "my power," thus specifying, but also perhaps narrowing, the meaning.

A Feminist Lens at Three Ranges on Paul's Speech as a Fool (11:21b–12:13)

To deal with Paul's complex argument I take up his speech in three parts. First, his daring boast of superiority to his rivals and the catalogue of dangers he has faced expose some key aspects of his political and economic context (11:16-33). Therefore I take this up first in contrast to my sequence in other chapters. Second, his claim to have visions and his account of someone's journey to paradise expose something of the worldview or ecosystem that he draws on (12:1-6). And third, Paul's story of asking for relief from a thorn in his flesh and his reaction after speaking as a fool expose best the interaction of Paul and the Corinthians (12:7-13). I open each of these with my own translation of that part of Paul's speech.

The Political, Economic and Social Setting of Paul's Speaking as a Fool (11:21b-33)

[11:21b]Whatever anyone dares to say—I'm talking nonsense—I dare to say too. [22]Are they Hebrews? Me too. Are they Israelites? Me too. Are they seed of Abraham? Me too. [23]Are they agents of Christ? I'm out of my head—me all the more, with more hard labor, more jailings, more

one I will boast, but on my own behalf I will not boast, except of my weaknesses. [6]But if I wish to boast, I will not be a fool, for I will be speaking the truth. But I refrain from it, so that no one may think better of me than what is seen in me or heard from me, [7]even considering the exceptional character of the revelations. Therefore, to keep me from being too elated, a thorn was given me in the flesh, a messenger of Satan to torment me, to keep me from being too elated. [8]Three times I appealed to the Lord about this, that it would leave me, [9]but he said to me, "My grace is sufficient for you, for power is made perfect in weakness." So, I will boast all the more gladly of my weaknesses, so that the power of Christ may dwell in me. [10]Therefore I am content with weaknesses, insults, hardships, persecutions, and calami-

beatings, often at death's door! [24]Five times I got the forty-minus-one lashes from Jews, [25]three times I was beaten with rods, once stoned, three times shipwrecked, one night and day left afloat; [26]always on the road, in danger of rivers, in danger of thieves, in danger of kinfolk, in danger of strangers; threatened in the city, threatened in the wilderness, threatened on sea, threatened by false friends; [27]in trials and tribulations, in nights on the ground, in hunger and thirst, without food, cold, and naked. [28]And beyond all these is my daily task of caring for all our assemblies! [29]Who is weak and I am not weak? Who is brought down and I am not incensed?

[30]If I must boast I will boast my weaknesses. [31]The God and Father of the Lord Jesus who is blest forever knows I am not lying. [32]In Damascus the ethnarch of King Aretas searched the Damascans' city to seize me [33]and I was dropped through the wall in a rope basket and fled from his hands!

In 11:16-18 Paul has already challenged the Corinthians to tolerate a little senseless boasting from him (10:8; 11:1) since they tolerate this and much worse from others. He now dares to boast whatever others are boasting, beginning with his heritage: Are they Hebrews? Israelites? Seed of Abraham? And, finally, are they agents of Christ (διάκονοι Χριστοῦ)? Each time he claims to be yet more so. This launches him into the longest list he makes in any letter of his credentials (11:23-29).[2] The result is that, since he must boast, he ends up conceding that he boasts his weaknesses (11:30). And, swearing he speaks the truth, he adds the final

2. Compare 1 Cor 4:9-13; 2 Cor 4:8-12; 6:4-10.

ties for the sake of Christ; for whenever I am weak, then I am strong.

[11]I have been a fool! You forced me to it. Indeed you should have been the ones commending me, for I am not at all inferior to these super-apostles, even though I am nothing. [12]The signs of a true apostle were performed among you with utmost patience, signs and wonders and mighty works. [13]How have you been worse off than the other churches,

except that I myself did not burden you? Forgive me this wrong!*

* NRSV notes: 11:26, Gk *brothers*; 11:32, Gk *ethnarch* for *governor*; Other ancient authorities read *and wanted to* for *in order to* Gk *through the wall*; 12:7, Other ancient authorities lack *to keep me from being too elated*; 12:9, Other ancient authorities read *my power*.

illustration of his flight from Damascus (11:31-33). I point to some signs in this argument of the political, economic, and broader social context in which Paul is operating.

The political setting is not explicit, but this can be expected in an imperial world where provincials compete with each other for influence in the narrow range of local religious and social life not taken over by the empire. In this sense, Paul's competition with rival Christian missionaries is a miniature of the competitions at that time among elite provincial men for largely honorary offices[3] and among eastern cities for permission to build imperial temples.[4] The distinctive element on Paul's part is the way he lists the hardships he has experienced rather than his achievements as his primary credentials. He claims to be a superior agent of Christ because he has endured more jailings, more beatings, and come closer to death (11:23), punishments that in Roman colonies like Corinth and Philippi would occur under Roman law, otherwise under Greek municipal law. He counts out having undergone three beatings by rods, a Roman discipline, as well as one stoning by a mob[5] and five

3. Steven Friesen, "The Cult of the Roman Emperors in Ephesos: Temple Wardens, City Titles, and the Interpretation of the Gospel of John," in *Ephesos: Metropolis of Asia; An Interdisciplinary Approach to Its Archaeology, Religion, and Culture*, ed. Helmut Koester (Valley Forge, PA: Trinity Press International, 1995), 229–50.

4. S. R. F. Price, *Rituals and Power: The Roman Imperial Cult in Asia Minor* (Cambridge: Cambridge University Press, 1984), 53–77, 98–100, 126–32.

5. See Acts 14:19; 16:22; Thrall, *Second Epistle*, 738–42; Victor Paul Furnish, *II Corinthians*, AB 32A (Garden City, NY: Doubleday, 1984), 516.

times having suffered a synagogue's discipline of forty lashes minus one,[6] not to mention betrayals by false friends among Christ followers (11:25-26). Finally, Paul tells of his Damascus escape in a rope basket from the Roman vassal Aretas's henchman. This indicates that various political systems, from imperial to municipal to ethnic to sectarian, have been consistently restricting Paul, if not stopping him. That he chooses to boast these events shows both that he gauges his survival an effective witness to Christ's power in him and that he thinks they can persuade the Corinthians of his devotion to God on their behalf. That the scenes are not pretty, let alone proof of Paul's power, he concedes by stating at the end and for the first time, "If I must boast, I will boast in the things that show my weakness."[7] Clearly he has not amassed political power. Yet his proclaiming a universal message of divine blessing threatens the very foundations of imperial power that sanctions only traditional religions for specific groups of people, not any offers of universal blessing other than its own.

Economic issues play a major role in this letter. Paul claims in self-defense that he has not burdened the Corinthians with supplying his needs as his rivals have done (11:7-11, 20). At the same time the heart of his letter is an extended request for the Corinthians to join the χάρις ("grace"; NRSV: "gracious act"), a collection for poor believers in Jerusalem (2 Cor 8–9). This exposes a sharp conflict over where the Corinthians' resources should be going. Also when Paul lists his hardships he shows the economic conditions in which he operates as an itinerant preacher. Walking the roads to carry the news, he is always in danger from crossing deserts, rivers, bandit-hiding mountains, and—in ships— rough seas (11:25-26). He cites specifically his lack of adequate sleep, food, drink, housing, and clothing (11:27). These conditions would be much ameliorated had he an armed escort, a pack animal, or rich patrons to host him rather than having to find shelter and work in each place. The second-century story in the *Acts of Paul and Thecla* gives the picture (see sidebar: "Paul on the Road, a Second-Century Account"). Paul is not writing in order to secure better economic conditions, but he has lived well enough in the past to be sensitive to the disadvantages he operates under. And he intensifies this in his balanced phrasing, steady rhythm, and rising amplifications, making the hardship catalogue a formidable display of economic straits.

---

6. See Deut 25:2-3; Thrall, *Second Epistle*, 736–38; Furnish, *II Corinthians*, 515–16.
7. 2 Cor 11:30; 12:5, 9, 10; 13:4, 9.

Paul on the Road, a Second-Century Account

And Paul was fasting with Onesiphorus and his wife and the children in an open tomb on the way by which they go from Iconium to Daphne. And when many days were past, as they were fasting[8] the boys said to Paul: "We are hungry." And they had nothing with which to buy bread, for Onesiphorus had left the things of the world and followed Paul with all his house. But Paul took off his outer garment and said: "Go, my child, [sell this and] buy several loaves and bring them here." But while the boy was buying he saw his neighbor Thecla. . . . And the boy said, "Come, I will take thee to him, for he has been mourning for thee and praying and fasting six days already." But when she came to the tomb Paul had bent his knees and was praying and saying: "Father of Christ, let not the fire touch Thecla, but be merciful to her, for she is thine!" But she standing behind him cried out: "Father, who didst make heaven and earth, the Father of thy beloved Son [Jesus Christ], I praise thee that thou didst save me from the fire, that I might see Paul!" . . . And within in the tomb there was much love, Paul rejoicing, and Onesiphorus and all of them. But they had five loaves, and vegetables, and water, and they were joyful over the holy works of Christ.[9]

On the social front Paul lists dangers he has experienced in cities and in open country, from his own people and from other peoples, and from those he calls "false brethren" (11:26). Is he mentioning Gentile opposition just to balance his reference to Jewish opponents who discipline their members with forty lashes minus one? More likely, he thinks of Gentile magistrates who react with floggings and jailing to the strife Paul stirs up in the Jewish communities. Final stress in this list of opponents falls on "false brothers and sisters," as the NRSV translates ψευδαδέλφοις because its editors recognize that the masculine plural is generic (11:26), indicating possible women in Corinth who are Paul's immediate competitors,

---

8. The verb νηστεύω, here translated "fasting," appears in its noun form, νηστεία, in 2 Cor 6:5 and 11:27 to indicate going hungry for lack of food. The story of Paul and Thecla suggests as much here. See "νηστεία," in *Greek-English Lexicon*, ed. Henry George Liddell and Robert Scott (Oxford: Clarendon, 1968), 671.

9. *The Acts of Paul and Thecla* 23–25, trans. R. McL. Wilson, in *New Testament Apocrypha*, vol. 2, ed. Edgar Hennecke and Wilhelm Schneemelcher (Philadelphia: Westminster, 1964), 359–60.

also called apostles (11:5, 13; 12:11). That there are women among Paul's rivals is supported by the fact that itinerant preachers of Christ at the time regularly traveled in mixed company.[10] Paul ends the catalogue speaking of the assemblies he writes to: "Besides all this there is my daily condition of worry about all our assemblies. Who is weak and I am not weak? Who is tripped up, and I am not fuming?" (11:28-29).

How can Paul take this opposition he stirs up in every place and the turmoil he experiences and make it work as credentials that he can boast? His own answer comes immediately after the catalogue when he decides to boast in what proves him weak (11:30). But the sheer quantity of instances seems to point as much to his persistence and endurance through all such trials, showing the strength that is more explicit in his earlier lists (4:8-12; 6:4-10). True, he is not strong in the mode of Hercules but perhaps in the way of God's servant according to Isaiah who shows what God's agent can suffer (Isa 52:13–53:12). And Paul presents all of this as the boast of a fool, a braggart, and a bungler, because he can't escape the absurdity of people competing with others to exhibit God's power.

The social context in which Paul argues here is not unlike ours today, where we are required to boast our superiority in CVs, job interviews, and candidate speeches until we almost believe them ourselves. In the classical world even the emperor was not exempt from having to list his accomplishments. Or, better put, the emperor in his display of power on Rome's coins and inscriptions and in monumental art made himself the epitome of power as display.[11] The prime example of royal catalogues is Augustus Caesar's *res gestae* (things done, benefit performed), a compendium of his accomplishments inscribed on stone and set up in provincial capitals across the empire shortly before his death in 13 CE (see sidebar on p. 148 above: "Inscription of Augustus Caesar's Accomplishments").

Anton Fridrichsen has identified in the *res gestae* certain signs of the form that Paul is using: first-person claims in the completed past tense, numbering of instances, attention less on offices and honors for himself than on gains made for all.[12] Augustus claims to melt down statues of himself to

10. Mark 15:41; Luke 8:1-3; 1 Cor 9:5.
11. Paul Zanker, *The Power of Images in the Age of Augustus* (Ann Arbor: University of Michigan Press, 1988).
12. Anton Fridrichsen develops this analysis in "Zum Stil der paulinischen Peristasenkatalogs 2 Cor. 11:23ff," *Symbolae Osloenses* 7 (1928): 25–29; and "Peristasenkatalog un Res Gestae. Nachtrag zu 2 Cor. 11:23ff.," *Symbolae Osloenses* 8 (1929): 79–82. Fitzgerald rejects Fridrichsen's thesis that Paul's catalogues and the *res gestae* have a common genre (*Cracks in an Earthen Vessel: An Examination of the Catalogues of Hardships in the Corinthian Correspondence* [Atlanta: Scholars Press, 1988], 17–22).

make gifts to the gods, and he cites lands he has conquered for the empire while returning to the Senate the administration of the pacified provinces. Paul refuses financial support for himself while asking it for the poor in Jerusalem, claiming from the Corinthians not titles but allegiance. It is not the lives of Augustus and Paul that are comparable but the rhetoric with which they defend themselves as worthy of leadership. True, Augustus presents himself, alongside the goddess Roma, as the embodiment of Rome's power while Paul presents himself as a boasting fool. But because of the competitive social world, Paul does boast what he has done, or rather what has been done to him, and ends with a paradoxical boast in his weakness as an instrument or location of divine power on the Corinthians' behalf.

When Paul has claimed the list of hardships as a catalogue of his weaknesses and sealed it by swearing that God knows he tells the truth (11:30-31), he adds a final incident about what happened in Damascus (11:32-33). Because this story dangles loosely on the end of a tightly constructed catalogue of hardships and tells one scene in detail, some interpreters dismiss it as a later gloss, possibly written in the margin from the account in Acts about Paul's escape from Damascus (Acts 9:23-25), colored by Rahab's feat in Joshua 2:15, and inserted here by a later copyist.[13] Yet no manuscript lacks it, and it is better taken as Paul's twist to end the catalogue.[14] Is he painting the ultimate humiliation of flight by dangling in a rope basket like a caught fish, the opposite of what might have been expected when Paul was asked to tell his Damascus experience (see Acts 9:1-19)? Others have thought this story might be a parody of the Roman *corona muralis* ("crown of the wall," a wreath given to the soldier who first scaled the wall of a besieged city).[15] At least it is clear

---

Punt takes the social context in Corinth to be one of "consensual Roman domination" and sees Paul choosing to assert his marginality and weakness in order to subvert conventional values, making this a counter-appropriation by the colonized of the colonizers rhetoric ("Paul and Postcolonial Hermeneutics: Marginality and/in Early Biblical Interpretation," in *As It Is Written: Studying Paul's Use of Scripture*, ed. Stanley E. Porter and Christopher Stanley, SymS 50 [Leiden: Brill, 2008], 273–87).

13. Hans Windisch, *Der Zweite Korintherbrief* (Göttingen: Vandenhoeck & Ruprecht, 1924, repr. 1970), 363–66; Hans Dieter Betz, *Der Apostel Paulus und die sokratische Tradition: Eine exegetische Untersuchung zu seiner "Apologie" 2 Korinther 10–13*, BHT 45 (Tübingen: J. C. B. Mohr [Paul Siebeck], 1972), 73, n. 201, henceforth *Apostel Paulus*.

14. See Thrall's analysis in *Second Epistle*, 763–71.

15. E. A. Judge, "The Conflict of Educational Aims in New Testament Thought," *Journal of Christian Education* 9 (1966): 32–45, esp. 44–45; Bärbel Bosenius, *Die Abwesenheit des Apostels als theologische Program: Der zweite Korintherbrief als Beispiel für die Brieflichkeit der paulinische Theologie* (Tübingen: Franke, 1994), 175; Thrall, *Second Epistle*, 765–66; Furnish, *II Corinthians*, 542.

that Paul does not shape his catalogue of hardships and its final epitome simply to claim virtue in endurance as might a Stoic or cynic sage.[16] He is flouting his widespread trials and massive dangers as evidence of his singular—we might say obsessive—devotion to a new order, not the imperial order of expanding military power or his rivals' impressive speaking, but God's power in the weakness of Christ's agents.

The Broad Ecosystem or Cosmology That Paul Assumes in Speaking as a Fool (12:1-6)

> [12:1]It is necessary to boast. It serves no purpose, but I will go on to visions and revelations of the Lord: [2]I know a person in Christ who fourteen years go—if in the body I don't know, or out of the body I don't know, God knows—who was snatched up to the third heaven. [3]And this person I know—if in the body or out of the body I don't know, God knows—[4]was snatched up into paradise and heard unspeakable speech that no one is allowed to speak. [5]About this one I'll boast, but about myself I won't boast—except in my weaknesses. [6]Now if I should want to boast I will not be a fool since I will speak the truth. But I hold back so no one thinks more of me than they see of me or hear from me—even due to the excess of revelations. (my translation)

Here Paul seems to make cosmological claims. After agreeing under pressure of his competitors' accounts of visions to tell his visions and divine revelations, Paul begins to describe a "person in Christ" who fourteen years before was "snatched up to the third heaven" into paradise where he heard words that are forbidden to be spoken (12:1-4). Does Paul assume a three-level heaven above earth that a person could visit to receive messages from God? Here interpreters split into two opposing camps. Though they agree that Paul perforce uses metaphorical language and that he refuses to be known for esoteric wisdom or heavenly powers, boasting only in his weakness, some take the heavenly journey purely as a rhetorical argument, a parody of the claims Paul's rivals make, while others take it as Paul's effort to speak without boasting of his own transcendent experience.

In 1972 Hans Dieter Betz proposed that Paul was using irony here to release his hearers from the grip of charlatans, as Socrates uses questions

---

16. Fitzgerald takes the Stoics and Cynics as Paul's primary models for the catalogues in 4:8-9 and 6:4-10 but doesn't test this thesis on 11:23-29: *Cracks*, 47–201.

to deal with the Sophists.[17] This would mean that Paul is mimicking the esoteric claims of false apostles in order to rouse the Corinthians from their enchantment.[18] Betz compares Paul's account with stories of heavenly and underworld journeys from the comedies of Aristophanes and the satires of Lucian of Samosota that expose how comic such false claims are.[19] Betz sees Paul constructing the story of a "person in Christ" who loses full consciousness and claims to have reached paradise, all in order to attract the Corinthians' interest, yet the journey produces nothing seen or heard that can be told. Hans-Georg Sundermann, following Betz, says that interpreters who read this as a disguised account of Paul's own heavenly experience have themselves been taken in and come out with nothing.[20]

Most interpreters nonetheless take the alternate view that Paul, pressed to compete with newly arriving preachers, tells visions and revelations from his own life.[21] He seems to claim transcendent experiences in several

17. Hans Dieter Betz, "Eine Christus-Aretalogie bei Paulus (2. Kor. 12,7-10)," *ZTK* 66 (1969): 288–305; *Apostel Paulus*, 89–92.

18. This view has recently been defended by Jeremy W. Barrier in "Two Visions of the Lord: A Comparison of Paul's Revelation to His Opponents Revelation in 2 Corinthians 12:1-10," in *Finding a Woman's Place: Essays in Honor of Carolyn Osiek, R.S.C.J.*, ed. David L. Balch and Jason T. Lamoreaux (Eugene, OR: Wipf and Stock, 2011), 272–90.

19. See Aristophanes's *The Frogs* and *The Clouds* and Lucian of Samosata's *The Downward Journey or the Tyrant, Icaromenippus or the Sky-man, Menippus or the Descent into Hades*, and *The Dialogues of the Dead*, variously written under the influence of the now lost *Necyia* of Menippus.

20. Hans-Georg Sundermann, *Der schwache Apostel un die Kraft der Rede: Eine historische Analyse von 2 Kor 10–13* (Frankfurt am Main: Peter Lang, 1996), 159–62.

21. John Chrysostom, *Homilies on Second Corinthians* 26.1; Christopher Rowland, *The Open Heaven: A Study of Apocalyptic in Judaism and Early Christianity* (New York: Crossroad, 1982), 374–86; James D. Tabor, *Things Unutterable: Paul's Ascent to Paradise in Its Greco-Roman, Judaic, and Early Christian Contexts* (Lanham, MD: University Press of America, 1986), 113–27; Alan F. Segal, *Paul the Convert: The Apostolate and Apostasy of Saul the Pharisee* (New Haven: Yale University Press, 1990), xi, 35–38, 58–62, 156–58; C. R. A. Morray-Jones, "Paradise Revisited (2 Cor 12:1-12). The Jewish Mystical Backgrounds of Paul's Apostolate," *HTR* 86 (1993): 177–217, 265–92; Margaret E. Thrall, "Paul's Journey to Paradise: Some Exegetical Issues in 2 Cor 12:2-4," in *The Corinthian Correspondence*, ed. R. Bieringer (Leuven: Leuven University Press, 1996), 347–63; Bernhard Heisinger, "Paulus und Philo als Mystiker? Himmelreisen im Vergleich (2 Kor 12,2-4; Spec. Leg. III 1-6)," in *Philo und das Neue Testament*, ed. R. Deiser and K.-W. Niebuhr, WUNT 172 (Tübingen: Mohr Siebeck, 2004), 203–4; Marlene Crüsemann, "Die Gegenwart des Verlorenen: Zur Rede vom 'Paradies' im Neuen Testament," in *Gott ist Beziehung: Beiträge zur biblischen Rede von Gott*, ed. Claudia Janssen and Luise Schottroff (Gütersloh: Gütersloher Verlagshaus, 2014), 228–30, 236–43.

letters where he tells a "mystery" or "word of the Lord" about what will happen in the future resurrection.[22] His very identity in Christ he attributes, not to knowing the man Jesus or being instructed by those who did, but to a specific personal experience that happened when he was persecuting Christ followers. Yet he offers no account of it, as does Luke concerning the Damascus Road,[23] only saying in his defense, "Have I not seen Jesus our Lord?" and, "Last of all, as to a miscarried fetus, he appeared also to me," and with slightly more detail, "The one who set me apart from my mother's womb and called me through his grace was glad to reveal his son in me so that I would proclaim him among the nations."[24]

The journey to paradise described by Paul is distinct enough in timing, location, and message that these interpreters do not take it as a further description of Paul's initial vision of Christ. But each aspect of this text is probed for possible clues to Paul's transcendent experiences. Pressed to tell "visions and revelations of the Lord," most interpreters think Paul means visions given by Christ, but he could as well mean visions in which Christ appears or speaks to him. C. R. A. Morray-Jones takes Paul's journey as confirmation that the medieval hekhalot's first-person account of Rabbi Akiba being received in paradise for his goodness (see sidebar: "An Account of Rabbi Akiba in Paradise") reflects an earlier form of Akiba's story than the Talmudic versions in which Akiba's ordained status qualified him for paradise. Morray-Jones concludes that paradise (*pardes*) was already a technical term among the early rabbis for mystical ascents to God's glory in higher heaven.[25]

An Account of Rabbi Akiba in Paradise

Akiba said: We were four who went into *pardes* [paradise]. One looked and died, one looked and was stricken, one looked and cut the shoots, and I went in in peace and came out in peace.

Why did I go in in peace and come out in peace? [sentence omitted in some mss.]

Not because I am greater than my fellows but my deeds [or they] have caused me to fulfill the teaching that the sages taught in the Mishnah: "Your deeds will bring you near and your deeds will keep you afar."
. . .

At that time, when I went up to the heavenly height, I made more signs in the entrances of the *raqia*

22. 1 Thess 4:15-17; 1 Cor 15:51-52.
23. Acts 9:1-9: 22:6-11; 26:12-18.
24. 1 Cor 9:1; 15:8; Gal 1:15-16; cf. 2 Cor 3:18; 4:4, 6.
25. Morray-Jones, "Paradise Revisited," 198–208, 265–68.

[dome] than in the entrances of my house, and when I arrived at the curtain, angels of destruction came forth to do me violence. The

Holy One, blessed be He, said to them: "Leave this elder alone, for he is worthy to behold my glory [or to behold me]."[26]

Paul tells about "a certain person in Christ" who was "snatched up into paradise," a place referred to in the Greek Bible as primeval Eden and in some Jewish apocalyptic texts as the fruit-bearing orchards prepared as a resting place for the righteous in God's presence (see sidebar: "Enoch in Paradise").[27] Margaret Thrall reads Paul's ascent in light of such biblical and Jewish apocalyptic texts as 2 Enoch and takes Paul's references to the third heaven and to paradise as a single ascent told in an intensifying parallelism.[28] Because the biblical Enoch and Elijah are described as taken up to heaven bodily,[29] whereas in 1 En. 71.1, 5 his body remains behind when his spirit is taken up, she interprets that Paul has doubled this common narrative element to stress his lack of comprehension (2 Cor 12:2-3).[30] If not a sign of modesty in his telling, Thrall says, Paul's purported ignorance could indicate the sense of displacement during visions, but in either case it suggests that the person that Paul means is really himself.[31] This at least becomes clear when he says that the thorn in his flesh was given to keep him from pride in his revelations (12:6-7).

Enoch in Paradise

And the [two great] figures took me from there. They brought me up to the third heaven. And they placed me in the midst of Paradise. And that place has an appearance of pleasantness that has never been seen. Every tree was in full flower. Every fruit was ripe, every food was in yield profusely; every fragrance was pleasant. And the four rivers were flowing past with gentle

26. Hekhalot Zutarti and Merkabah Rabbah; see Morray-Jones, "Paradise Revisited," 196–98. Translations of *pardes* and *raqia* are my own.

27. *Apocalypse of Moses* 37.5; 2 En. 8.1–9.1; *Life of Adam and Eve* 25.1-3; 29.1-3; cf. Rev 22:1-5; Thrall, *Second Epistle*, 792–93.

28. Thrall, "Paul's Journey," 356–58; Thrall, *Second Epistle*, 778–98.

29. Gen 5:24; 2 Kings 2:11.

30. Thrall, "Paul's Journey," 356.

31. Ibid.

movement, with every kind of garden producing every kind of good food. And the tree of life is in that place, under which the Lord takes a rest when the Lord takes a walk in Paradise. And that tree is indescribable for pleasantness of fragrance. And another tree is near it, an olive, flowing with oil continually. . . .

And I said, "How very pleasant is this place!" The figures answered me: "This place has been prepared, Enoch, for the righteous, who suffer every kind of tribulation in this life . . . and who carry out righteous judgment, to give bread to the hungry, and to cover the naked with clothing, and to lift up the fallen.[32]

James Tabor's full monograph on Paul's story proposes an initial ascent to the third heaven followed by a further ascent to paradise itself, where Paul hears secrets too holy to divulge.[33] Tabor finds heavenly ascent stories not only in apocalyptic and rabbinic Judaism but also in the Hellenistic and Roman worlds more broadly—in Apuleius's tall tale of *The Golden Ass*, in the esoteric conversations attributed to Poimandres, and in Mithras liturgies.[34] Tabor interprets the visions of Paul in terms of a Hellenistic "new cosmology" described by Martin Nilsson.[35] In contrast to the ancient cosmology in which people understood themselves to be at home in their native places on earth while the gods were at home in heaven, widespread social disruption brought on a new cosmology in which people felt at a loss or even imprisoned in the physical world and sought release into heaven or recovery of their heavenly identities. Tabor reads Paul's proclamation of glory through identification with the risen Christ as one gospel among many within this new cosmology,

32. 2 En. 8.1–9.1, manuscript A, trans. F. I. Andersen, in *Old Testament Pseudepigrapha*, ed. James H. Charlesworth, vol. 1 (Garden City, NY: Doubleday, 1983), Text A, 115–17. In light of Andersen's detailed notes on page 106 that "'man' might mean simply 'person'" and "we are to suppose angels in human form," I replace his "men" with "figures."

33. Tabor, *Things Unutterable*, 115.

34. Ibid., 66, 89–95.

35. Ibid., 58–69, 98; Martin Nilsson, *Greek Piety* (New York: Norton, 1969), 92–185; Nilsson, "The New Conception of the Universe in Greek Paganism," *Eranos* 44 (1946): 20–27.

with Paul's account of ascent to paradise being the evidence Paul gives when he is pressed to do so.[36]

It is tempting to explain the conflict between the two major interpretations of Paul's ascent story—as ironic parody or as mystical experience—by recognizing that German Lutherans cannot tolerate any theology of glory or mystical ascent whereas the British and Americans take psychological experience as an intriguing source of knowledge. But the issue is how Paul interprets his own story, and the two sentences that follow may answer that (12:5-6). Sundermann, in defense of a parody, reads Paul's opening words in the first sentence together with the closing of the second sentence, "I will boast in that person . . . but I refrain lest anyone think of me more than he sees or hears from me with such excess of revelations" (12:5a, 6b, 7a).[37] The intervening vow to be speaking the truth is thus dissociated from the tall tale about the person. But read in its written order, Paul's words concede a boast for this person at one remove from himself but not a boast for himself because he wants to be known only from what people see him do and hear him say—though if he boasted he'd be speaking the truth. I take this to mean that a boast for the person as himself would be true if he wanted to make it because it is himself. Granted, there is heavy irony in Paul's manner of telling his story, using the third person, dwelling on his not knowing how it happened, and telling nothing that he hears except that it cannot be told. Yet, if by proxy and irony, he has made the claim that he thinks the Corinthians require and without boasting in himself. This shows that the story he tells need not be a fictional parody in order to mock the way others tell their stories.

As to the ecosystem or cosmology being assumed, to use Nilsson's distinction adapted by Tabor above, Paul is committed to a traditional cosmology in which mortals belong on earth as seen and heard with all their trials, and God alone belongs in heaven: "Let whoever boasts boast in the Lord" (10:17). Yet the new cosmology has gained ground across the Hellenistic world, including Judaism. By Paul's time people seek ascent or recovery of divine light, and Corinth has taught him that he cannot ignore this. To compete for their ears it is insufficient to offer past acts of God's power or future resurrection in Christ as compensation for present suffering. But how can a person's transformation in Christ's dying and

---

36. Tabor, *Things Unutterable*, 33–34, 44–45, 122–25.
37. Sundermann, *Schwache Apostel*, 165–66.

rising be experienced and affirmed without false boasting since God alone is the source of all goodness and the aim of all praise? Paul's ascent to paradise told by a fool with every effort not to boast is a product of just this conflict of cosmologies. Though hardly attractive to our time because modes of expressing transcendence have changed so much, it shows that Paul, like the Corinthians, attributes his present and positive experience of Christ to God alone, yet by telling it he, like other competitors, shows himself up to be a boasting fool. It is only sad that, the less to boast and constrained by standard metaphors, Paul gives us no wider glimpse of the life-sustaining orchards of paradise as he, and doubtless others in Corinth, saw them lit with the dawning glory of Christ.

Focusing in on the Interchange of the Corinthians and Paul Speaking as a Fool (12:7-13)

> [12:7]So that I not be exalted a thorn was given me in the flesh, an angel of Satan—so that I not be exalted. [8]About this I begged the Lord three times to take it away from me. [9]And he said to me, "My grace is enough for you, since power is realized in weakness."
>
> I am more than glad to boast in my weaknesses so that Christ's power might rest on me. [10]So I delight in weaknesses, in abuses, in oppression, in persecutions, in confinements—for Christ's sake—for when I'm weak, then I'm strong!
>
> [11]I've been a fool—it was you that forced me to it. For I ought to have been commended by you, since I am inferior in nothing to those hyper-apostles, even though I am nothing. [12]For the signs of an apostle were worked among you in all patience—signs and wonders and mighty works. [13]For what is there that you lack which the other assemblies have except that I myself have not burdened you? Forgive me this injustice!

In the last four chapters of 2 Corinthians Paul has changed his tone from conciliation to something close to threat. After quoting someone saying, "His presence in the flesh is weak and his speech worthless" (10:10), he has challenged that these new arrivals are boasting their own powers, claiming credit for the work he has done, seducing the Corinthians to follow another Jesus, and abusing them in every way. Some interpreters say Paul has written to frighten away these rival preachers,[38]

---

38. Josef Zmijewski, *Der Stil der paulinischen "Narrenrede": Analyse der Sprachgestaltung in 2 Kor 11,1–12,10 als Beitrag zur Methodik von Stiluntersuchungen neutestamentlicher Texte* (Köln-Bonn: Hanstein, 1978), 413–14.

yet everything he says and the way he says it points in another direction. He is speaking to the Corinthians in Christ themselves in order to turn them against his competitors and to reconcile them with himself,[39] addressing them as "you" throughout[40] and speaking of the new arrivals as "them" or "someone."[41] He challenges the Corinthians, "Bear with me in a little foolishness. Do bear with me" (11:1, 16). The bitter irony in this apparently meek request comes to light when he uses the same verb (ἀνέχεσθε) to caricature their patience with his rivals, "You bear it well enough if someone enslaves you, devours you, takes you in, insults you, spits in your face! To my shame I say, we were too weak for that" (11:20-21a, cf. 11:4).

At that point Paul sets aside the familiar "you" address and steps on stage before his Corinthian audience to play the fool (11:21b–12:10). The fool (ἄφρων) that Paul enacts is not the king's jester or wise fool as in Shakespeare's *King Lear* but the bungling and bombastic fool of ancient comedy, the target of every slapstick joke (see sidebar: "Strepsiades the Fool in Aristophanes's *The Clouds*"). The role of fool allows Paul to boast his credentials to the Corinthians and yet undermine his boast in three ways. First, he boasts his work as agent or servant of Christ (διάκονος Χριστοῦ) by telling all the troubles he's had that show his weaknesses (11:23b-33). Second, he boasts his revelation in paradise that produces only unspeakable speech (12:1-6). Finally, he boasts that Christ speaks to him and answers his request, but in the negative (12:7-10). After all this, Paul steps off the stage and, speaking directly to the Corinthians, blames them for not having defended him and spared him the indignity of playing the fool (12:11). He claims to have proven that "I am inferior in nothing to those hyper-apostles, even though I am nothing," thereby exposing them as nothing. And he throws in at the end as of little weight[42] the acts of power in Corinth that came through his presence, insisting that Corinth has received as much from him as any other community (12:12-13).

39. Betz, *Apostel Paulus*, 18–19, 43; Bieringer, *Studies on 2 Corinthians*, 195–99.

40. 2 Cor 10:1, 6, 7, 8, 9, 13, 14, 15, 16; 11:1, 2, 3, 4, 6, 7, 8, 9, 11, 16, 19, 20; 12:11, 12, 13.

41. 2 Cor 10:2, 7, 8, 9, 13, 14, 15, 16, 18, 20, 21, 22, 23.

42. Ulrich Heckel, *Kraft in Schwachheit: Untersuchungen zu 2 Kor 10–13*, WUNT 2.56 (Tübingen: J. C. B. Mohr [Paul Siebeck], 1993), 40.

Strepsiades the Fool in Aristophanes's *The Clouds*

Strepsiades: Oh, here, dear Socrates!
Socrates   Well, my old friend.
St.   I've found a notion how to shrink my debts.
So.   Well then, propound it.
St.   What do you think of this?
                  Suppose I hire some grand Thessalian witch
                  To conjure down the Moon, and then I take it
                  And slap it into some round helmet-box,
                  And keep it fast there, like a looking glass,—
So.   But what's the use of that?
St.   The use, quotha:
                  Why if the Moon should never rise again,
                  I'd never pay one farthing.
So.   No! Why not?
St.   Why, don't we pay our interest by the month? . . . .
So.   How to prevent an adversary's suit
                  Supposing you were sure to lose it; tell me.
St.   O, nothing easier.
So.   How, pray?
St.   Why this,
                  While there was yet one trial intervening,
                  Ere mine was cited, I'd go hang myself.
So.   Absurd!
St.   No, by the Gods, it isn't though:
                  They could not prosecute me were I dead.[43]

And what does all Paul's foolishness suggest about the Corinthians' own side of the interchange? Paul assumes that they remember or, if they are new, at least have heard about the year or more that he and Timothy and Sylvanus first preached Christ in Corinth (1:19). But Paul did not return as expected,[44] and others who were more articulate came with letters of recommendation that Paul lacked, telling further revelations of Christ and experiences of God's Spirit (3:1; 11:4; 12:1). Though they competed with each other and with what Paul had done (10:12), this was apparently

43. Aristophanes, *The Clouds* 774–82, in Aristophanes, vol. 1, trans. Benjamin Bickley Rogers, LCL (Cambridge, MA: Harvard University Press, 1924, repr. 1967), 335–39.
44. 2 Cor 1:15–2:4. Some interpreters propose that he returned once for a brief and ineffective visit. See more discussion of his shifting travel plans in the next chapter.

less a problem in Corinth than a stimulus to further expressions and wider participation. Paul had written letters to Corinth advising multiple kinds of self-discipline[45] in response to their bold conduct and slogans (6:12; 7:1; 10:23), yet this only intensified the alienation, forcing Paul in 2 Corinthians to shift his stance from adviser to defendant. He knew what they knew, that he was not a strong debater in person and would need to bring this dispute to some resolution in writing before he came.[46]

Paul's account of the thorn in his flesh at the end of his fool's speech culminates his defense as a fool. Interpreters think that the thorn refers to a long-standing disability that Paul has, whether of sight[47] or speech,[48] or—Thrall proposes—some illness such as epilepsy, migraine, or malarial fever that beats on the body.[49] Paul's explanation that this "angel of Satan" was given him (likely a divine passive form) to keep him from being elated by so many revelations is not a clue to what the condition was or when it began, as some have suggested, but rises from his present challenge of persuading the Corinthians. He is claiming that the very condition everyone sees and many reproach him for—"his presence in the flesh is weak" (10:10)—was itself ordained by God to offset his divine insight and keep him from self-congratulation (12:7; 11:6).

Paul tells how he once prayed fervently for relief, multiple times, as in the stories of Elijah praying for healing and for rain and of Jesus pleading for his life in Gethsemane.[50] Because triple prayer is also attested in Hellenistic miracle stories, Hans Dieter Betz takes Paul's plea that ends in refusal to be a parody of the miracle story form, a tale made up to mock the miracle claims of the other preachers to the Corinthians. Yet what Paul achieves is not only an exposé but a positive claim. The Lord answered and spoke to him, the perfect tense of that speaking indicating a past event that makes a present and permanent state:[51] "My grace is enough for you, since power is realized in weakness" (12:9a). Paul then interprets the Lord's words: "I am more than glad to boast in my weaknesses, so that Christ's power might rest on me" (12:9b). Finally,

---

45. 1 Cor 5:9; 1:10, 26-29; 3:3, 18, 21; 4:16; 5:7, 11, etc.

46. Bosenius, *Abwesenheit des Apostels*, 1–6, 86, 91–95; François Vouga, "Der Brief als Form der apostolischen Autorität," in *Studien und Texte zur Formgeschichte*, ed. Klaus Berger et al. (Tübingen: Francke Verlag, 1992), 36.

47. Gal 4:15; 6:11; 1 Cor 16:21; Phlm 19; Acts 7:58; 9:8-9, 18.

48. 2 Cor 10:10; 11:6; 13:3.

49. Thrall, *Second Epistle*, 807–18; Windisch, *Zweite Korintherbrief*, 386–88.

50. 1 Kgs 17:21; 18:41-46; Mark 14:32-42.

51. Thrall, *Second Epistle*, 821.

he concludes the entire fool's speech: "So I delight in weaknesses—in insults, in pressures, in persecutions, and in restrictions—for Christ's sake—for when I'm weak, then I'm strong" (12:10). Each of these three statements repeats the point that he has found power in weakness. I will ask how they function in his interaction with the Corinthians to show their different understandings both of weakness and of power.

It is after listing his hardships, after dissociating himself from "someone" who goes to paradise, and after failing to get his disability taken away that Paul in each case affirms his weakness (11:30; 12:5; 12:9-10). This makes clear that he means by his weaknesses the concrete and harsh reality of his life as a disabled person who extends himself in a dangerous environment. Integral to this is the shame of being considered weak by others, yet Paul insists on being judged strictly from what people see of him and hear from him (12:6). In other words, in admitting his weakness Paul concedes what "someone" of his detractors said about him, that his letters may be strong but his presence on the ground is weak and his speech is of no account (10:10). Yet Paul presents his weakness not as a virtue but as a fact in his case. Apparently he has no choice but to defend himself as weak, or at the very least he chooses to cite this charge against him and concede the point.

This is important for feminist interpretation. We cannot let others champion Paul's affirmation of weakness as though it were a virtue for us to imitate, nor can we use it to excuse our own timidity. But when Paul tells of the Lord saying to him, "Power is realized in weakness," and then concludes, "When I am weak, then I am strong" (12:9-10), some interpreters universalize this and think Paul is modeling for the Corinthians a life of weakness as the location of God's power.[52] This reads Paul's self-defense as an instruction without any basis in the text. Due to a negative stereotype of the Corinthians drawn from Paul's 1 Corinthians restrictions, interpreters look for more restrictions in this letter. But Paul does not ask them to imitate him in this letter.[53] Now he wants them to accept him as different from themselves. He recognizes their claim to represent the life of Christ and asks them to recognize that this came about by his embodying

---

52. Zmijewski, *Der Stil*, 383–84; Bosenius, *Abwesenheit des Apostels*, 191. Others stress that Paul is speaking about his own weakness, not about human powerlessness in general: Thrall, *Second Epistle*, 825; Furnish, *II Corinthians*, 550–52.

53. Cf. 1 Cor 4:16; 11:1. Marlene Crüsemann, "Eine Christologie der Beziehung: Trost, *charis* und Kraft der Schwachen nach dem 2. Brief an die Gemeinde in Korinth," in *Gott is Beziehung*, 187.

Christ's death, "so death is active in us, but life in you" (4:7-12). He sees himself as a clay pot that holds God's treasure in them, and he confirms this when he returns to theological language in closing (13:3-4, 9). But here he defends himself with an account of being refused healing and hearing that God's grace makes him strong while yet weak.

Risky Generalizations?

The tendency to generalize Paul's celebration of weakness and suffering carries significant risks for women, so long seen as "weaker vessels" (1 Pet 3:7) and associated with self-sacrifice, even as it also potentially dignifies their social position. This paradox is provocatively explored throughout the history of women's literary writing.

On the one hand, for instance, in 1611 Aemilia Lanyer published "Eve's Apology in Defense of Women," arguing that Eve cannot be blamed for the Fall because as a woman she was weak, whereas Adam should have known better and thus deserves the blame: "What Weaknesse offered, Strength might have refusde."[54] In embracing the association of women with weakness, Lanyer finds a way to refute the tradition of blaming women for sin's entrance into the world.

In a similarly redemptive mode, two hundred years earlier, Julian of Norwich elevated women's status as childbearers by associating the experience with Christ: "Our own true Mother Jesus . . . [s]ustains us within himself in love and labor until the full time when he gladly suffered the sharpest throes and most grievous pains that ever were or ever shall be."[55] Again, Julian accepts that womanhood means suffering, but she implicitly shows the divine power in that suffering by using it as a metaphor for the salvation of humanity.

On the other hand, many writers reject a redemptive vision of female weakness or suffering. Toni Morrison makes this point devastatingly clear in her 1987 novel *Beloved*, in which the protagonist Sethe's sufferings—her dehumanizing experiences of chattel slavery, her loss of loved one after loved one, the impossible ethical situation she faces when the master arrives to return her children to captivity—absolutely refuse to be idealized. One cannot "delight in" (NIV), "take pleasure in" (KJV), or indeed be "content with" (NRSV) these

---

54. Emilia Lanier, "Eve's Apology in Defense of Women" in *Salve Deus Rex Judaeorum*, introduced by A. L. Rowse (New York: Clarkson N. Potter, 1979), 103.

55. Julian of Norwich, *Revelation of Love*, ed. and trans. John Skinner (New York: Image Books, 1996), 134.

"weaknesses, insults, hardships, persecutions, and calamities" (2 Cor 12:10). To do so would be obscene.

Likewise, Katherena Vermette's 2016 novel *The Break*, which traces the aftermath of a sexual assault in Winnipeg's North End, exposes how its Indigenous women characters are subjected to police officers' racism and misogyny, generational trauma, and the devastating effects of rape. The novel refuses to celebrate any of these sufferings or to find any redemptive quality in them.

Yet these narratives don't instead champion traditional masculinist visions of strength or power as autonomy and control. Vermette's characters manifest a nuanced blend of brokenness and resilience. The solution to their pain and permeability is not some self-contained authority but mutual dependence. Similarly, Sethe's way forward in *Beloved* is to lean into the care of her friend and lover Paul D, including his insistence, despite prevalent cultural teachings about women and mothers, that she is her own "best thing."[56]

In these insights, Morrison's *Beloved* and Vermette's *The Break* echo Adrienne Rich in *Of Woman Born: Motherhood as Experience and Institution* when she argues that the term "power" itself must be redefined.[57] Rejecting the power that is "authority and control of another,"[58] Rich writes instead of the freedom to undergo "decision, struggle, surprise, imagination, and conscious intelligence."[59] This mode of power, marked above all else by courage, involves risk taking and even "enormous pain,"[60] but such suffering, and the "weakness" of tenderness and openness to others, is a far cry from a culturally mandated feminine inferiority or self-sacrifice. In fact, it is closer to Paul's own experience of *choosing* to suffer, to emphasize his weaknesses, to play the part of the fool, as he says, for the sake of his beloved Corinthians (2 Cor 12:19). The question posed by a great cloud of women writers is this: What will it take for women to be seen as strong and whole, for their suffering or even powerlessness to result from freely chosen self-gift rather than being systemically imposed?

And the question for interpreters is: Whose experience do we overlook when we turn one man's experience into a paradigm for all?

Cynthia R. Wallace

---

56. Toni Morrison, *Beloved* (New York: Plume, 1987), 273.
57. Adrienne Rich, *Of Woman Born: Motherhood as Experience and Institution* (New York: Norton, 1976), 67.
58. Ibid.
59. Ibid., 280.
60. Ibid., 215.

To determine how Paul's professed weakness strikes the Corinthian women is difficult. Paul's newly arrived competitors do reveal to them how limited Paul is by contrast, both in specific abilities due to his disability but also in communication because his way of speaking is not exemplary or even standard: "his speech is worthless" (10:10).[61] We do know that conventions of voice and gesture and style were becoming more uniform in the imperial period while he may have betrayed his eastern upbringing or synagogue patterns in this provincial capital. Though Paul must surely have been disarming in his approach to get the initial response he did in several cities, his speech was somehow offensive. It may have been due to a speech impediment, or simply a practice of talking only to people standing around while he worked with his hands, or speaking as though to himself, or speaking interrupted by times of thought.

Was Paul considered weak because he had not promoted himself as others had done? Christine Gerber argues in a recent article that the disdain for blatant self-commendation was so firmly established in Greco-Roman rhetoric that Paul's rivals would hardly have boasted in themselves as he charges.[62] She says that Paul attributes this boasting to them in order to justify his defense—this because only people defending themselves under attack were tolerated for giving their credentials and telling their accomplishments.[63] She does concede that Paul in this argument faces actual rivals who receive support in Corinth and have provoked charges there against Paul, yet his caricature of these people as self-promoting super-apostles she traces to his own need to make the Corinthians open to his defense. Even if Gerber may exaggerate her case here, Paul surely exaggerates the self-promotion of these rivals (10:12; 11:20) and opens up the question of how the Corinthians saw them. She concludes, "Why shouldn't the community that Paul founded profit from further missionaries who enrich them with spiritual words and deeds?"[64]

According to Gerber, Paul claims an exclusive relationship to the Corinthians in Christ because he founded the church and thereby became its apostle.[65] Her point is not that he appeals to this as a recognized

---

61. 2 Cor 10:10; 11:6; 13:3.

62. Christine Gerber, "καυχᾶσθαι δεῖ, οὐ συμφέρον μέν . . . (2 Kor 12,1): Selbstlob bei Paulus vor dem Hintergrund der antiken Gepflogenheiten," in *Paul's Graeco-Roman Context*, ed. Cilliers Breytenbach (Leuven: Peeters, 2015), 213–34.

63. Ibid., 242–49.

64. Ibid., 248, my translation.

65. Christine Gerber, *Paulus, Apostolat und Autorität, oder vom Lesen fremder Briefe* (Zürich: Theologischer Verlag Zürich, 2012), 35–51, 55.

understanding of apostolic authority but that, at a time before there was a common understanding of Christ's apostles, he was working to promote this one in Corinth. The Corinthians apparently did not have the same understanding as Paul did, perhaps expecting some apostles to lay the groundwork in a community and others to build on it, a division of tasks over time rather than a division in space as they each founded and nurtured their own assemblies (10:13-15). If so, the Corinthians see themselves nurtured by various itinerants in turn rather than being devoted to one person as their apostle. There is a pattern visible in the Corinthian congregation: their openness to multiple voices and practices in 1 Corinthians,[66] their interest in other voices than Paul's in 2 Corinthians, and their impatience with long-established local leaders at the turn of the century in 1 Clement (see sidebar: "Church Elders Dismissed in Corinth at the End of the First Century").[67] If they want varied leadership and new experience, Paul's insistence on faithful attachment to those who brought the first news of Christ would seem restrictive, and Paul's defensive response to other preachers would be taken as weakness. This, combined with his physical disability and his absence from Corinth, means there is much that tells against him.

Church Elders Dismissed in Corinth at the End of the First Century

Our Apostles also knew through our Lord Jesus Christ that there would be strife for the title of bishop. For this cause, therefore, since they had received perfect foreknowledge, they appointed those who have been already mentioned, and afterwards added the codicil that if they should fall asleep, other approved men [males]

---

66. 1 Cor 5:1-2; 6:12; 8:1; 10:23; 11:2-34; 14:20-40; 15:12; Antoinette Clark Wire, *The Corinthian Women Prophets: A Reconstruction through Paul's Rhetoric* (Minneapolis: Fortress, 1990; repr., Eugene, OR: Wipf and Stock, 2003).

67. See L. L. Welborn, *The Young against the Old: Generational Conflict in First Clement* (Lanham, MD: Lexington/Fortress, 2018). In this interesting demographic study of the uprising at the end of the century against Corinthian church elders appointed for life, Welborn recognizes "the young men and women who instigated the revolt" (201) and calls it a "brief revival of the Pauline polity in which age was not a qualification for leadership" (206). Yet he relegates women to a supporting role (148, 173) and ends by projecting without specific evidence in the text that young male leaders were financed by their mothers (193–96). He does not weigh the possibility of a revival of the women's leadership that Paul faced.

should succeed to their ministry. We consider therefore that it is not a just action to remove from their ministry those who were appointed by them, or later on by other eminent men [males], with the consent of the whole Church and have ministered to the flock of Christ without blame, humbly, peaceably, and disinterestedly, and for many years have received a universally favourable testimony. For our sin is not small, if we eject from the episcopate those who have blamelessly and holily offered its sacrifices. Blessed are those Presbyters who finished their course before now, and have obtained a fruitful and perfect release in the ripeness of completed work, for they have now no fear that any shall move them from the place appointed to them. For we see that in spite of their good service you have removed some from the ministry which they fulfilled blamelessly.[68]

And what is the power that Paul claims rests on him when he is weak? Each of the three parallel statements about power in weakness that culminates Paul's fool's speech tells a key aspect of how he sees this power (12:9a, 9b, 10). First, he says the Lord spoke to him, "My grace is enough for you since power is realized in weakness" (12:9a).[69] Magdalene Frettlöh identifies "grace" as Paul's word for "originary giving," a giving that is out of fullness or excess, unlike all giving that occurs within systems of exchanging limited resources.[70] Whereas that giving favors the receiver who now has more goods, or rather the giver who gains dependents and hence social power, as Marcel Mauss showed in the anthropological classic, *The Gift*,[71] she accepts Derrida's critique of Mauss that giving is no better than receiving because it seeks a return, so that any genuine giving, any freely given gift, becomes impossible.[72] Nonetheless, Bernhard Waldenfeld has argued in studies of Mauss and Derrida that if giving

68. 1 Clement 44:1-6, trans. Kirsopp Lake, in *The Apostolic Fathers*, vol. 1, ed. G. P. Goold, LCL (Cambridge, MA: Harvard University Press, 1975), 83–85.

69. See also concerning grace pp. 178–82 above.

70. Magdalene Frettlöh, "Der Charme der gerechten Gabe," in *"Leget Anmut in das Geben": Zum Verhältnis von Ökonomie und Theologie*, ed. Jürgen Ebach, Hans-Martin Gutmann, Magdalene Frettlöh, and Michael Weinrich (Gütersloh: Chr. Kaiser/Gütersloher Verlagshaus, 2001), 123–36.

71. Marcell Mauss, *The Gift: The Form and Reason for Exchange in Archaic Societies*, trans. W. D. Halls (London: Routledge, 1990 [French 1925]).

72. Jacques Derrida, *Given Time: 1. Counterfeit Money*, trans. P. Kamuf (Chicago: University of Chicago, 1992 [French 1991]).

is indeed an answer, a response, then giving assumes a previous giving from beyond any system of exchange that our conduct erects, a giving that must be free and set no obligation of return because its origin is not in lack but in fullness.[73] Since our giving is only possible as an answer to this other giving, Frettlöh concludes quoting Waldenfeld, "The one who gives is not necessarily in the stronger position, since within this giver there is a receiving, an 'inner weakness,' that keeps the giver from being fully the giver."[74] This, she points out, parallels Paul's account of the Lord's words to him in answer to his request for relief, "My grace is enough for you since power is realized in weakness."

Grace in this reading of Paul is the strength given from outside the grip of gift exchange that empowers those who realize that they are first and foremost responders. Boundless grace alone breaks the vicious cycle of "give to take" and generates further giving among and beyond its receivers. Paul also sees it producing an overflowing response, a gracious cycle, in thanks and praise to God.[75] Hence the Jerusalem collection, itself called a χάριν (grace; NRSV: "generous undertaking"),[76] is made possible by the χάριν τοῦ θεοῦ (grace of God)[77] and gives rise to the χάρις τῷ θεῷ (grace or thanks to God).[78] But does this not simply magnify the debt common in gift exchange into a stranglehold, if all of life is a gift for which thanks is due? Or is it the case that what is given from a boundless source, from what we might visualize as an artesian spring, requires no response because nothing is being counted and for the same reason calls forth the greatest response? (See sidebar: "Memory's Mercies.") Frettlöh suggests that this gracious cycle takes two forms, giving being previous to receiving in God and receiving being previous to giving in people.[79]

---

73. Bernhard Waldenfels, *Antwortregister* (Frankfurt am Main: Suhrkamp, 1994), 586–626.

74. Frettlöh, "Gerechten Gabe," 135, quoting Bernhard Waldenfels, "Un-ding der Gabe," in *Einsätze des Denkens, Zur Philosophie von Jacques Derrida*, ed. H.-D. Gondek and B. Waldenfels (Frankfurt/Main: Suhrkamp, 1997), 385–409, at 402.

75. 2 Cor 1:11; 4:15; 9:11-15. On the gracious circle, see Dieter Georgi, *Remembering the Poor: The History of Paul's Collection for Jerusalem* (Nashville: Abingdon, 1992; German 1965, rev. 1994), 131–33; Frettlöh, "Gerechten Gabe," 157–59; Crüsemann, "Christologie der Beziehung," 197–207; John M. G. Barclay, *Paul and the Gift* (Grand Rapids, MI: Eerdmans, 2015), 575–79.

76. 2 Cor 8:6, 7, 19.

77. 2 Cor 8:1; 9:14; cf. 8:5; 9:8.

78. 2 Cor 8:16; 9:15; Crüsemann, "Christologie der Beziehung," 191–97.

79. Frettlöh, "Gerechten Gabe," 141, n. 80.

Memory's Mercies

Memory's mercies
mostly aren't

but there were
I swear
    days
veined with grace

like a lucky
rock
    ripping
electrically over

whatever water
there was—

ten skips
    twenty
in the telling:

all the day's aches
eclipsed

and a late sun
belling

even sleeping Leroy
back
    into his body
to smile
at some spirit-lit

tank-rock
skimming the real

so belongingly
no longing
    clung to it
when it plunged

bright as a firefly
into nowhere,

I swear.

Christian Wiman[80]

Whether the Lord who offers grace to Paul is understood to be the God to whom he appealed for relief, or to be Christ whose power he will say "rests on him" (12:8-9),[81] he claims that this voice not only legitimates him but identifies the place in his experience where God's power is realized/perfected/completed/fulfilled (τελεῖται; 12:9), namely, in his weakness. By telling this Paul seeks a hearing from the Corinthians who respect visionary insight and want proof that Christ speaks in him (12:1; 13:3). Because they find their own strength in God's power in Christ, likely confirmed in visions and revelations (1 Cor 14:26; 2 Cor 12:1), Paul wagers that they will recognize this power in him even though it is realized in his weakness (4:12; 13:9).

80. Christian Wiman, "Memory's Mercies," *Hammer Is the Prayer: Selected Poems* (New York: Farrar, Straus and Giroux, 2016), 165–66.

81. Crüsemann, "Christologie der Beziehung," 198–99.

Paul's second statement tells his response to the Lord's words: "I am all the more glad to boast in my weaknesses, so that Christ's power may rest on me" (12:9b). Paul puts the opening stress on being glad rather than being disappointed that his plea for relief was refused,[82] since this is how Christ's power rests on him. The verb ἐπισκηνώσῃ that appears only here in the Greek Bible (LXX) I translate as "rest on" with the RSV, NEB, and JB (NRSV: "dwell"). The verbal root is σκηνόω (to make one's tent [σκηνή], take up residence, live for a time). It appears in various forms in the Greek Old Testament (LXX) for God's mobile presence in the tent of meeting or tabernacle that followed Israel in the wilderness (Exod 29:45-46) and often in the New Testament, both for Jesus' presence ("The word became flesh and tented among us" [John 1:14]) and for God's ultimate presence ("Behold, God's tent is among people, and he will make his tent among them" [Rev 21:3; see also Ezek 37:27; Zech 2:10-11 (LXX 2:14-15)]).[83]

As if the weight of this tradition were not enough to make Paul's point, in appending the prefix ἐπί (on) in place of the more common κατά (down) to the verb σκηνόω (I make my tent, I settle), Paul could be influenced by the verb ἐπισκιάζω (to overshadow, rest on), used in Torah for the cloud of glory that covered and filled the tabernacle (Exod 40:34-35) and later for the divine presence in the New Testament annunciation and transfiguration stories.[84] There is a possible allusion in this verb to the Shekinah, a feminine form for this presence of God derived from the same consonants. This name for God appears by the second and third century CE in the Targums, which translate the Hebrew Bible into the spoken Aramaic for common understanding, suggesting that it is familiar by that time in Jewish liturgies.[85] (See the sidebar: "The Glory of the Shekinah," from Targum Neofiti, with italics indicating words not paralleled in the Hebrew text.) "Shekinah" occurs in the phrase "the glory of the Shekinah of the Lord" in the Targums Neofiti and Pseudo-Jonathan and is a divine name for God's appearance among the people

---

82. Zmijewski, *Der Stil*, 386.

83. Philip Edgcumbe Hughes, *Paul's Second Epistle to the Corinthians* (Grand Rapids, MI: Eerdmans, 1962), 452–53, n. 141.

84. Luke 1:35; 9:34; Mark 9:7; Matt 17:5. Thrall, *Second Epistle*, 827–29; Hughes, *Paul's Second Epistle*, 452–53, n. 141.

85. Martin McNamara, *Targum and Testament Revisited: Aramaic Paraphrases of the Hebrew Bible; A Light on the New Testament*, 2nd ed. (Grand Rapids, MI: Eerdmans, 2010), 146–54 on Shekinah glory, 255–83 on probable dating of these Targums.

2 Corinthians 11:21b–12:13 259

in Targum Onqelos and Targum Jonathan to the Prophets. The term apparently came to be used to avoid speaking of God as visible while yet signifying God's chosen dwelling with Israel as visible glory.

> ### The Glory of the Shekinah
>
> And the cloud covered the tent of meeting, and the Glory of *the Shekinah of* the Lord filled the tabernacle. And Moses could not enter the tent of meeting, because he had made *the Glory of the Shekinah of the Lord* rest upon it, and the Glory *of the Shekinah* of the Lord filled the tabernacle. And when the cloud was taken up the children of Israel used to journey in all their journeys. And if the cloud was not taken up, they used not to journey until the day it was taken up. Because the cloud of *the Glory of the Shekinah of* the Lord was upon the tabernacle by daytime, and a fire was in it by night to the eyes of all the house of Israel in all their journeys.[86]

The feminine form of Shekinah encouraged personification and may have allowed more intimacy in conceiving of God. When Paul says, "I boast in my weaknesses so that Christ's power may rest on me [ἐπισκηνώσῃ ἐπ' ἐμέ]," does he imply that Christ's power appears in his weaknesses as God's Shekinah glory dwelling with people? The juxtaposition of God's glory and intimacy in Shekinah is as difficult to grasp as that of Christ's power in weakness. Yet it may put in other words how Paul is defending himself in Corinth, claiming, if you will, that the Shekinah glory that the Corinthians know in Christ is not alien from but intimate with, even at home in, the harsh realities of his human life. Some later Talmudic stories speak of the Shekinah as God-at-hand, hearing the cries of the poor, appearing to visionaries, and arguing with the contentious (see sidebar: "The Poor Rabbi and the Shekinah"). It is up to the Corinthians who respond to Paul to weigh whether or not his weakness has worked or can now work to foster God's Shekinah glory in Corinth.

---

86. Exodus 40:35-38, in *Targum Neofiti 1: Exodus*, ArBib 2, ed. Martin McNamara (Collegeville, MN: Liturgical Press, 1987), 157–58.

The Poor Rabbi
and the Shekinah

Rabbi Eleazar ben Pedat was
hard pressed by poverty.
 He was bled and there was
nothing for him to taste.
 He found the skin of a piece
of a garlic, threw it in his mouth,
and felt weak.

 The Rabbis came to him. They
saw him crying and laughing
 and a ray of fire came out from
his forehead.
 When he woke up they said
to him,
 "What is the reason that the
Master was crying and laughing
 And a tuft of fire came out
from his forehead?"
 He said to them, "I saw
Shekinah and I said before her,
 "How long will I go on living
in this need?"

 She said to me, "Is it better for
you
 that I destroy the world and
create it again?
 Possibly you will fall into a
time of your sustenance."
 I said before her, "All this and
'possibly'?"

 I said before her, "What will
you give me in the world to
come?"
 She said to me, "I will give
you thirteen rivers carrying
balsam in which to enjoy
yourself."
 I said before her, "And not
more?"
 She stung me by snapping her
fingers at my forehead and said
to me,
 "Eleazar my son, Do my
arrows heap up in you?"[87]

Paul's third restatement of power in weakness brings the entire fool's speech to its climax: "So I delight in weaknesses, in abuses, in oppression, in persecutions, in confinements—for Christ's sake—for when I'm weak, then I'm strong" (12:10). The opening verb, εὐδοκῶ (I am satisfied, pleased, delighted), has a broad range of meanings, and the NRSV settles for the weakest, "I am content," to stress Paul's realism when his request for healing is denied. But after the superlative, ἥδιστα (most gladly), in Paul's previous sentence, everything points toward the strongest meaning, "I delight." With a sense of full satisfaction Paul recaps his catalogue of hardships, now specifically including the rivals' insults

---

87. b. Ta'an. 25a, in *The Treatise Ta'anit of the Babylonian Talmud [Hebrew and English]*, ed. and trans. Henry Malter (Philadelphia: Jewish Publication Society of America, 1928), 113–14. On this selection see Antoinette Clark Wire, *Holy Lives, Holy Deaths: A Close Hearing of Early Jewish Storytellers* (Atlanta: Society of Biblical Literature, 2002), 166–67.

and the persecution he meets on Christ's behalf. For the first time he claims not only that God's power works in him but that it characterizes him: "for whenever I am weak, then I am strong" (12:10). Yet even here he does not say that he possesses Christ's power (δύναμις) but that he is powerful, strong (δυνατός), that is, he is able to speak of Christ and for Christ (11:23; 13:3), and their faith in Christ is proof of this (1:14; 3:2; 10:14). Also the condition given, "when I'm weak," keeps a temporal limit on his claim. The Shekinah is not at his disposal but "rests on" him under certain conditions. Nevertheless, he claims a delight that can match the boasts of his rivals—if in weakness and as a fool—and this challenges the Corinthians to recognize him for what he has enabled among them.

Immediately after this confident "When I'm weak, then I'm strong" (12:10), Paul steps off the fool's stage and is overwhelmed with the absurdity of his bragging: "I have become a fool," and he blames them for forcing him to defend himself because they did not speak for him. He explains, or rather exclaims, "In nothing do I come short of these hyperapostles, even if I am nothing!" This brings his competitors down with him to nothing and without claiming anything for himself. Betz considers this the high point of Paul's argument and takes it to be grounded in a long-standing Greek tradition that extends from the Delphic maxim γνῶθι σεαυτόν (know yourself) to Plato's Socrates's insistence against the Sophists that he is not wise, that the immortal God is to be called εἶ (you are) in contrast to the mortal human οὐδέν εἰμι (I am nothing).[88]

Paul has stopped playing the fool and yet goes on to speak of signs, wonders, and mighty works of an apostle that he did among the Corinthians so that they lacked nothing that other congregations had except the chance to pay his expenses—for which he apologizes (12:12-13). Under a veneer of remorse his irony here reflects bitterness at the way he thinks they have treated him. The Corinthians have apparently complained that other communities are hearing these stimulating people who confirm they are apostles by doing "signs and wonders and mighty works." Interpreters agree that at the time this phrase meant miracles such as predictions, healings, or acts controlling nature, but what Paul is saying about himself is a point of contention. Some take him at face value to be claiming legitimacy on the basis of miracles he did in Corinth.[89] Others

---

88. Plato, *Theaetetus* 172D–176B; Betz, *Apostel Paulus*, 87–89, 121–24, 127–28, 143–47; Wolfgang Schadewaldt, *Der Gott von Delphi und die Humanitätsidee*, 2nd ed. (Stuttgart: Neske, 1965), 5–28.

89. Thrall, *Second Epistle*, 838–41, and Furnish, *II Corinthians*, 556, though they see that miracles are not Paul's primary evidence.

point out that Paul's letters, in contrast to Acts, never tell about himself (or Jesus) performing such a miracle and mention miraculous power only in terms of God's Spirit working in him to bring the Gentiles to Christ (Rom 15:18-19; Gal 3:1-5; 1 Thess 1:5). Therefore they see Paul's claim to have done wonders not intending to revive some memory of his healings among them but to reassert that their own transformation into a community in Christ is the wondrous act of God worked through him.[90] Betz presses this yet further, hearing not only that Paul confirms their transformation as miracle but also that he exposes his rivals' "signs of an apostle" as fraudulent, signs he has just mocked in his parody of an aborted miracle story when his triple prayer came up empty.[91]

It is here, for the first time since the opening sentence of 2 Corinthians, that Paul claims to be an apostle or, if not that, at least to have done the signs of an apostle and not to be inferior to these super-apostles (12:11-12). In chapters 2–7 the term "apostle" does not appear,[92] though commentators continue to title this section "The Apostolic Defense" or "The Ministry of the Apostle" (NRSV heading before 4:1).[93] He promotes the collection for Jerusalem in chapters 8–9 without mentioning his being an apostle. Only here in his final diatribe against rivals who claim to be apostles does Paul speak again of himself as an apostle, this in order to insist he is not inferior to others who claim the title. I suggest that the name "apostle" has become debased by its use in these power claims so that Paul has gone on to other ways of defending himself.

Christine Gerber makes three crucial points on Paul's apostleship in her recent study, *Paulus, Apostolat und Autorität*. First, Paul's letters do not assume a given meaning of an apostle's authority, but they are working to shape his authority in relation to certain groups where "apostle" has

90. Stefan Alkier, *Wunder und Wirklichkeit in den Briefen des Apostel Paulus: Ein Beitrag zu einem Wunderverständnis jenseits von Entmythologisierung und Rehistorisierung*, WUNT 134 (Tübingen: Mohr Siebeck, 2001), 223–48, 291, 302–7; Crüsemann, "Christologie der Beziehung," 199–205.

91. Betz, "Eine Christus-Aretalogie," 288–305; *Apostel Paulus*, 70–100, esp. 92–94.

92. Antoinette Clark Wire, "Reconciled to Glory in Corinth? 2 Cor 2:14–7:4," in *Antiquity and Humanity: Essays on Ancient Religion and Philosophy Presented to Hans Dieter Betz on His 70th Birthday*, ed. Adela Yarbro Collins and Margaret M. Mitchell (Tübingen: Mohr Siebeck, 2001), 263–65, 272–75; Gerber, *Apostolat und Autorität*, 42.

93. Ralph P. Martin, *2 Corinthians*, WBC 40 (Waco, TX: Word Books, 1983), 43; Jan Lambrecht, *Second Corinthians*, SP 8 (Collegeville, MN: Liturgical Press, 1999), 37; Furnish, *II Corinthians*, 173; Thrall, *Second Epistle*, 188.

no standard meaning.[94] Whereas in 1 Corinthians Paul claims a more hierarchical relation to his hearers by giving instructions about the Corinthians' conduct and asking them to imitate him,[95] in 2 Corinthians he is defending himself, and not primarily as an apostle but as one among other agents or representatives of Christ (διάκονοι Χριστοῦ).[96] That is, Paul's understanding of his role evolves. He has learned something.[97] Second, Gerber recognizes that in both letters to Corinth Paul does introduce himself as "an apostle of Jesus Christ by God's will,"[98] sent out (ἀπο-στέλλω) as witness of the risen Christ. Because he sees this calling as a special "grace" given to one not present when Jesus rose (1 Cor 15:9-10), he takes the faith of those who first heard the news of Christ through him as confirmation that he is an apostle sent to them.[99]

Third, Gerber shows that Paul does not depend primarily on theological language to tell the Corinthians how he is related to them but instead banks on metaphors that offer multiple points of comparison. Among these Gerber privileges Paul's image of father or matchmaker who has betrothed them as bride to Christ and now fears the seduction of conniving suitors.[100] She sees Paul thereby making an exclusive claim to be the one who founded their community, and she reads his other metaphors to confirm this.

Yet most metaphors in 2 Corinthians that Paul uses to explain himself appear in the plural, which I take with Loïc P. M. Berge to signify *un travail d'équipe* (the work of a team or cohort, the διάκονοι Χριστοῦ, agents of Christ):[101] "We are the fragrance of Christ to God"; "we have this treasure in clay jars"; "we are ambassadors for Christ" (2:15; 4:7; 5:20). Even in the 2 Corinthians 10–13 context of "false apostles" who have arrived in his absence, Paul shows his attachment to those he converted, not by telling

---

94. Gerber, *Apostolat und Autorität*, 16–17, 38–39. See 2 Cor 8:23 where NRSV translates ἀπόστολοι as "messengers"; also Acts 13:1-4; 14:4, 14 where Paul and Barnabas are called apostles because sent out from Antioch although Luke does not otherwise speak of them as apostles.

95. Gerber, *Apostolat und Autorität*, 79–90.

96. Ibid., 30, 42; 2 Cor 3:1–6:10; 10:12-16.

97. Ibid., 9–18.

98. 1 Cor 1:1; 2 Cor 1:1.

99. Gerber, *Apostolat und Autorität*, 38–41.

100. Ibid., 53–77.

101. Loïc P. M. Berge, *Faiblesse et force, présidence et collégialité chez Paul de Tarse: Recherche littéraire et théologique sur 2 Co 10–13 dans le context du genre épistolaire antique* (Leiden: Brill, 2015), 221–24.

stories about how he gave birth to this community (see 1 Cor 1:14-17; Gal 4:13-20), but by listing his past and present hardships. Any mother knows that giving birth is not the only challenge considering the long and hard task of raising a child from scratch in an often hostile world. This task we observe him also sharing with his colleagues Timothy and Titus and other agents or ministers of Christ (διάκονοι Χριστοῦ) as well as with local leaders he calls his coworkers (συνεργοί μου). The authority he defends in 2 Corinthians is not to be called apostle alongside the twelve but to be recognized for the work given to him alongside others—this in face of those he sees as betraying the task.

To recover the Corinthians' perspective on this power struggle and specifically on the power that Paul claims, it is chancy to project their reactions to Paul's letter. We can better see them reflected in the way Paul shapes his argument to meet and persuade them where he thinks they stand. This letter as a whole aims to recover Paul's earlier intimacy with a community (1:1–7:16), to get them to join in a collection for Jerusalem (8:1–9:15), and to disabuse them of his competitors in Corinth (10:1–13:13). This makes unmistakable that the Corinthians he addresses are still alienated or at least dissociated from Paul in spite of a partial reconciliation (7:6-11) and have followed others called apostles in some new directions (11:4-6, 13-15). Paul charges the Corinthians with tolerating newcomers who strike, rob, and enslave them (11:20), obvious exaggerations, yet they would not rankle with his hearers if high-handed conduct were not present. Gerber thinks that it is Paul's arriving first in Corinth that he considers violated by his rivals' claims of apostleship. Or has Paul refocused "apostle" from resurrection witness to church founder in order to hold ground against late-arriving "super-apostles" he considers false and abusive?

In any case, the presence of multiple apostles has apparently not posed a problem for the Corinthians. They are attracted to many aspects of the power that Paul's rivals display. When Paul in this speech as a fool (11:21b–12:10) asserts his own equal heritage in Israel plus all the hardships he has undergone (11:23-29), he offers kinds of power he thinks the Corinthians admire—the ancient tradition of Israel and total commitment to the point of personal sacrifice. Though Paul adds this up to be the boast of a fool in his weaknesses (11:30), he knows that it will impress them. Even the Damascus vignette displays not only Paul's shame in dangling over the wall but also his status of being the object of an ethnarch's city-wide search (11:32-33). The Corinthians apparently do want to interact with well-connected, forceful, and prominent leaders, and Paul does present himself as such.

When Paul considers himself forced to "go on to visions and revelations of the Lord" (12:1) it must be that these are in demand. Here he undercuts his boast by attributing his heavenly journey to someone else and by telling that his pleas for healing are rejected, but he does claim visions to the extent that he must disguise his identity in one account and settle for his disability in the second in order to keep from becoming elated by his revelations (12:2-4, 7-10). The Corinthians are clearly interested in hearing and experiencing visions and revelations (1 Cor 14:26), perhaps especially accounts of spiritual transport and inspiring words from Christ (13:3). Even the particular words of Christ that Paul transmits to them—"My grace is enough for you, since power is realized in weakness" (12:9)—need not be a downer for them if they are able to hear Paul say that divine grace through his weaknesses serves their strength. Paul had said this when first describing his weakness, "We carry around Jesus' death in the body so that Jesus' life might be made visible ἐν τῷ σώματι ἡμῶν ('in our [plural] body [singular]'. . . . Thus death is at work in us but life in you" (4:10, 12). And he concludes in his last chapter, "For we rejoice when we are weak but you are strong" (13:9; see also vv. 3-4). Here in the fool's speech his point is to show that Christ's power is realized in his weakness because God's grace is sufficient, and they are deceived to seek it in his rivals where God's grace is redundant.

Whether they respond positively to Paul's persuasion we do not know. Paul's confidence here and in the closing chapter suggests that he thinks they will. Yet the intensity of his overdetermined argument could point to doubt about his own success. Interpreters have taken the outcome of the Jerusalem collection as a gauge of the letter's success because his aim there is uncontestable (8:1–9:15). But the interpreters' conclusions span the spectrum. Albert Harrill calls the collection Paul's "crowning achievement" because Paul tells the Romans that Achaia did contribute—but little or much? and including Corinth?[102] Ulrich Mell calls the lack of any report in Acts about the money being received in Jerusalem a sign of the final blow to Paul's mission to unite in Christ all nations within Israel.[103] Most interpreters plead ignorance.[104] When Paul writes from

102. Rom 15:26; J. Albert Harrill, *Paul the Apostle: His Life and Legacy in Their Roman Context* (Cambridge: Cambridge University Press, 2012), 69.

103. Ulrich Mell, "Paulus: scheiternder Gescheiter: Ein historischer und literarischer Einwurf," in *Der zweite Korintherbrief: Literarische Gestalt—historische Situation—theologische Argumentation. Festschrift zum 70. Geburtstag von Dietrich-Alex Koch*, ed. Dieter Sänger (Göttingen: Vandenhoeck & Ruprecht, 2012), 118–19.

104. Thrall, *Second Epistle*, 515–20; Furnish, *II Corinthians*, 453.

Corinth to the Romans, "Now that there is no longer a place for me in these regions, I desire to come to you" (Rom 15:23), he could mean his work in the Aegean area is, as we might say, locked in, or that he is locked out, or perhaps some places this and some that, but he is moving on.[105]

Our next report about Corinth's congregation in the letter of Clement from Rome at the end of the century shows that they have dismissed their elders, so the independent spirit continues.[106] (See sidebar: "Church Elders Dismissed" on pp. 254–55.) It will be up to the Corinthians after hearing Paul's 2 Corinthians letter, "when you are assembled and my spirit is present with the power of the Lord Jesus" (1 Cor 5:4b), to decide how they will respond out of their far better knowledge than ours of both Paul and his contenders. The women prophets among them will have influence. I expect that the community will both welcome his coming visit and continue to receive other preachers—to Paul's confounding—confident that they can discern the Spirit.

---

105. Paul's practice to move on and leave communities he started to local leadership has been called the genius of his work: Roland Allen, *Missionary Methods: St. Paul's or Ours?* (Chicago: Moody Press, 1959).

106. *1 Clement* 44.1-6.

2 Corinthians 12:14–13:13

Paul's Plan to Come to Corinth

Text and Its Structure (12:14–13:13)

The closing part of Paul's letter is often dismissed by readers as though it were the envelope telling details about the sender and receivers that are not relevant today. But if we read the letter less to cull one universal message than to see our concrete struggles in light of some of the earliest recorded efforts to live "in Christ," then how Paul closes his letters is crucial. Here he reveals why he has argued as he has, how he hopes the Corinthians will respond, and what he is doing now to bring that off. In fact, it is the letter opening and closing with the central chapters 8 and 9 arranging the collection for Jerusalem that let us make sense of Paul's intervening self-defense, theological appeals, and harsh warnings. The envelope may be our key to the letter as a whole.

At this point Paul is making arrangements for coming to Corinth. First, he announces that he is ready to come and that he does not want to burden them with his expenses or to manipulate them, not even to defend himself, but to somehow avoid mutual disappointment and the strife and humiliation he fears might happen when he arrives (12:14-21). Second, Paul asserts that he is now indeed coming and warns any who have sinned and not repented that, though he is weak, God's power will act among them to set things right (13:1-4). Third, he instructs them, not

¹²:¹⁴Here I am, ready to come to you this third time. And I will not be a burden, because I do not want what is yours but you; for children ought not to lay up for their parents, but parents for their children. ¹⁵I will most gladly spend and be spent for you. If I love you more, am I to be loved less? ¹⁶Let it be assumed that I did not burden you. Nevertheless (you say) since I was crafty, I took you in by deceit. ¹⁷Did I take advantage of you through any of those whom I sent to you? ¹⁸I urged Titus to go, and sent the brother with him. Titus did not take advantage of you, did he? Did we not conduct ourselves with the same spirit? Did we not take the same steps?

¹⁹Have you been thinking all along that we have been defending ourselves before you? We are speaking in Christ before God. Everything we do, beloved, is for the sake of building you up. ²⁰For I fear that when I come, I may find you not as I wish, and that you may find me not as you wish; I fear that there may perhaps be quarreling, jealousy, anger, selfishness, slander, gossip, conceit, and disorder. ²¹I fear that when I come again, my God may humble me before you, and that I may

with any specific orders, but to test themselves to know whether Christ is in them, and he claims that their restoration is his highest aim. In fact, he is writing ahead, he says, so that he will only need to encourage them further when he comes (13:5-10). And fourth, he closes the letter as usual by encouraging, greeting, and blessing them (13:11-13).

Translations of this passage differ less due to differing Greek manuscripts than to differing understandings of Paul's plans as he describes them. Many modern interpreters have taken Paul's "coming this third time" (12:14; 13:1) to require a second visit after his founding period in Corinth, a visit when he was humiliated by an offender and left town in disgrace, writing a "letter of tears" that has not survived (2:1-4; 7:8, 12). Others see that letter surviving in 2 Corinthians 10–13 or take 2 Corinthians as a whole to be a series of letter fragments that Paul once wrote in an order that ended happily in the reconciliation seen in 1:1–2:13 and 7:5–8:24. On the basis of such theories Paul's closing announcement of coming a third time is understood to be repeating a warning made "when present on my second visit" (13:1-2, NRSV). Yet Paul does not speak of a second or third "visit" (12:14, NEB; 13:1), but he says, "This third time I am ready to come to you" (12:14), which may refer back to two previous times he was ready to come (1 Cor 16:5-6; 2 Cor 1:15-16). His final announcement then stresses his certainty: "This third time I am (indeed) coming to you" (13:1). When he repeats an earlier warning

have to mourn over many who previously sinned and have not repented of the impurity, sexual immorality, and licentiousness that they have practiced. [13:1]This is the third time I am coming to you. "Any charge must be sustained by the evidence of two or three witnesses." [2]I warned those who sinned previously and all the others, and I warn them now while absent, as I did when present on my second visit, that if I come again, I will not be lenient— [3]since you desire proof that Christ is speaking in me. He is not weak in dealing with you, but is powerful in you. [4]For he was crucified in weakness, but lives by the power of God. For we are weak in him, but in dealing with you we will live with him by the power of God.

[5]Examine yourselves to see whether you are living in the faith. Test yourselves. Do you not realize that Jesus Christ is in you?—unless, indeed, you fail to meet the test! [6]I hope you will find out that we have not failed. [7]But we pray to God that you may not do anything wrong—not that we may appear to have met the test, but that you may do what is right, though we may seem to have failed. [8]For we cannot do

"the second time as present and now absent," he seems to contrast that warning when present with his warning when absent now (13:2). But this warning to "spare no one if I come again" assumes Paul was absent when he threatened and points to a counter-factual translation of ὡς παρὼν, "as though present" (13:2; see also 1 Cor 5:3)—a formula that letter writers used to express feeling present while absent. This suggests that Paul is not referring to a warning on an interim visit to Corinth but is saying: "I warned [in 1 Cor 4:18-21?] the second time as though present and I warn now when yet absent,"[1] and he stresses this double warning by starting his sentence with the two verbs of warning (13:2).

The phrase that Paul repeats in 13:3-4, εἰς ὑμᾶς, is normally translated "toward you" or "for you," not "dealing with you" as in the NRSV. This means that Paul is more likely speaking of God's power that empowers

---

1. Ferdinand Christian Baur, "Die beiden Briefe an die Korinthier," in *Paulus, Der Apostel Jesu Christi*, vol. 1, 2nd ed (Leipzig, 1866–67; repr., Osnabrück, 1968), 343; Bärbel Bosenius, *Die Abwesenheit des Apostels als theologische Program: Der zweite Korintherbrief als Beispiel für die Brieflichkeit der paulinische Theologie* (Tübingen: Franke, 1994), 12–13; Niels Hyldahl, "Die Frage nach der literarischen Einheit des Zweiten Korintherbriefes," *ZNW* 64 (1973): 304–5.

anything against the truth, but only for the truth. [9]For we rejoice when we are weak and you are strong. This is what we pray for, that you may become perfect. [10]So I write these things while I am away from you, so that when I come, I may not have to be severe in using the authority that the Lord has given me for building up and not for tearing down.

[11]Finally, brothers and sisters, farewell. Put things in order, listen to my appeal, agree with one another, live in peace; and the God of love and peace will be with you. [12]Greet one another with a holy kiss. All the saints greet you.

[13]The grace of the Lord Jesus Christ, the love of God, and the communion of the Holy Spirit be with all of you.*

* NRSV notes: 13:4, Other ancient authorities read *with him* for *in him*; 13:11, Gk *brothers* for *brothers and sisters*. Or *rejoice* for *farewell*. Or *encourage one another* for *agree with one another*; 13:13, Or *and the sharing in* for *and the communion of*.

them to test themselves, not of God's power in Paul's judgment when dealing with them.[2]

These translation issues are no small matter, as is clear in Paul's summary sentence before signing off on this letter. He claims his entire strategy has been to delay enough in coming and to be sufficiently sharp in writing that they discipline themselves, and his eventual coming is a time, not of judgment, but of mutual encouragement (13:10).[3] Why? He clearly expects to be more effective in writing than in speaking (10:10; 11:6). But he is also conceding that only they can judge the life that Christ has given them: "Examine yourselves if you are in the faith. Test yourselves. Do you not know yourselves that Jesus Christ is in you? If not, you are frauds" (13:5). And Paul, in spite of his threatening tone, says more than once that the Lord has not given him authority for their destruction but for their construction (13:10; 10:8; 12:19). How do we as feminists evaluate such a strategy?

2. Marlene Crüsemann, "Eine Christologie der Beziehung: Trost, *charis* und Kraft der Schwachen nach dem 2. Brief an die Gemeinde in Korinth," in *Gott is Beziehung: Beiträge zur biblischen Rede von Gott*, ed. Claudia Janssen and Luise Schottroff (Gütersloh: Gütersloher Verlagshaus, 2014), 201–4. She translates εἰς ὑμᾶς "unter euch" ("among you,"13:3) and "bei euch" ("with you, at your place," 13:4).

3. Bosenius, *Abwesenheit des Apostels*, 10–13, 41–43.

A Feminist Lens at Three Ranges on Paul's Preparing Corinth for His Arrival (12:14–13:13)

With Broad Focus on the Ecosystem, Worldview, or Theology That Paul Assumes

Paul's claims to legitimacy in opening and closing the letter are made not in terms of apostolic credentials or even his likeness to Christ but in terms of ἐν Χριστῷ λαλοῦμεν (our speaking in Christ, 12:19) or ἐν ἐμοὶ λαλοῦντος Χριστοῦ (Christ speaking in me, 13:3). And when he shifts the focus in the last chapter from his own legitimacy to that of the Corinthians, he challenges them to recognize that Ἰησοῦς Χριστὸς ἐν ὑμῖν (Jesus Christ is in you, 13:5). It is this identity "in Christ" that is at stake in 2 Corinthians, and Paul's earlier letter to Corinth already shows that it was demonstrated there largely by different kinds of speaking. The Corinthians were known for "all speech and knowledge as the witness of Christ has been strengthened in you"; and "when you gather, each one has a psalm, a teaching, a revelation, a tongue, an interpretation" (1 Cor 1:5-6; 14:26). The women are active not only in song or speaking in tongues but in what seem to be the central worship roles of praying for the people to God and prophesying God's word to the people (1 Cor 11:5; 14:1-25). The question is what Paul now means by this "speaking in Christ" on which he bases his legitimacy at the end of 2 Corinthians (12:19; 13:3) and by which he challenges them to test themselves: "Don't you recognize that Jesus Christ is in you" (13:5)?

Paul suggests three aspects of this "speaking in Christ." In order to deny that he is speaking in self-defense at the end of this letter, he counters: "We are speaking in Christ before God, and all these things, loved ones, are for your construction" (12:19). His point is that "speaking in Christ" does not benefit the speaker but those to whom it is spoken. Similarly in opening the letter he answers charges that he has not come back to Corinth as he promised: "Jesus Christ who was proclaimed among you by me and Sylvanus and Timothy was not 'yes' and 'no' but there is nothing but 'yes' in him" (1:19). Because speaking in Christ can only be good for those who hear it, Paul is writing sharply before he comes to press the Corinthians to test themselves so that the authority he has been given works as intended for their construction, not their demolition (10:8; 13:10).

A second aspect of "speaking in Christ" also appears in 12:19 when Paul proclaims: "Before God in Christ we speak!" This is almost an oath, as if to say that speaking before God in Christ cannot be manipulating the truth. This echoes his earlier point: "For we are not like so many people, peddlers of God's word, but transparently as from God we speak before God in Christ" (2:17; see also 1:12). It is when Paul insists most fervently on his integrity and sincerity that he makes this claim to speak in Christ, as he does to the Romans when affirming his solidarity with Israel (Rom 9:1-3).

A third aspect of Paul's "speaking in Christ" beyond its benefitting others and confirming the speaker's integrity appears in the final chapter when Paul announces that this third time he is indeed coming to Corinth (2 Cor 13:1; see introduction of this text above). Here he faces the fact that they want proof that Christ is speaking in him (13:3). Perhaps because his speaking is physically or culturally inferior ("his speech is despicable," 10:10), or because prophets always make claims beyond what is evident and Corinthian prophecies have come into conflict with his, they doubt if Christ is speaking in him—all the more after hearing the visions and revelations of his rivals. Paul concedes in response that in the Corinthians Christ is not weak but is powerful (13:3b), but since Christ was crucified in weakness yet lives from God's power, so "we are weak in him, but we live with him from God's power toward you" (13:4).[4] This is often taken in context as a threat that Paul will now come to judge them by "God's power toward you" (NRSV: "in dealing with you"). Yet Marlene Crüsemann insists that Paul is drawing the Corinthians here into recognizing Christ's crucifixion as the location of God's resurrection power in them, challenging them to take stock of their mutual relation and their common future in the presence of Christ.[5] Weakness, she hears Paul say, is not alien to power but is the human condition also shared by Christ who rules in weakness and transforms what ruling is.

This may be implied in the text, but it is explicit that Paul concedes to the Corinthians: "Christ is not weak toward you, but is powerful in you" (13:3b). In contrast, Paul says that he and his coworkers embody the weakness of the crucified Christ, yet "we live with him by the power of God toward you" (13:4b). Where many interpreters hear Paul threatening to

---

4. Here I follow the earliest manuscript of this line ($\mathfrak{P}^{46}$), which gives the verb "we live" in the present tense, assuming that other copyists shifted to the future under the influence of statements in which Paul speaks of future life in Christ (2 Cor 4:14; 1 Cor 6:14; Rom 6:8; 1 Thess 4:14-17), an element dominant in early Christian piety.

5. Marlene Crüsemann, "2 Korintherbrief," in *Bibel in gerechter Sprache*, ed. Ulrike Bail et al. (Gütersloh: Gütersloher Verlagshaus, 2006), 2131–32; "Christologie der Beziehung," 204–5.

judge by God's power toward them, what it says is that the life-making power of God is present in the Corinthians through the weakness of other speakers in Christ. Here the mutuality of Paul and the Corinthians is even closer than if they both see themselves as weak, since power and weakness are in fact not evenly distributed. The Corinthians have been dependent on these weak speakers in Christ for the news of Christ (1:19), and now Paul ends up dependent on the Corinthians in whom God's power is realized.[6] This is clear when Paul proceeds, not to judge them case by case, but to challenge them to test themselves, since the authority God has given him is not to destroy but to construct.[7] So Paul is saying that "speaking in Christ" cannot be characterized either by the power or the weakness of those who speak. Through the weakness of Paul's speaking, the Corinthians came to believe, and now Paul says, "we live with him by the power of God toward you" (13:3-4). It follows that it is God's power in raising the crucified Christ, not any speaker's power, that is being realized among them in speaking the "yes" of God's promises come true (1:20).

Beyond "speaking in Christ," another ambiguous key term is the verb δοκιμάζετε (13:5; NRSV: "test"; NEB: "put to the test") with its cognates ἀδόκιμοι (13:5, 6, 7; NRSV and NEB: "failing to meet the test"), δόκιμοι (13:7; NEB: "winning approval"; NRSV: "meeting the test"), and δοκιμή (13:3; NRSV and NEB: "proof"). What kind of test has Paul in mind when he uses this term? How high a grade is necessary to "meet the test"? The Greeks used these terms for evaluating coins minted in many different metals, including brass, silver, and gold, by cities, client kingdoms, and the Roman Senate itself, each coin worth its weight in that metal yet readily counterfeited. The δοκιμάζω stem refers to testing whether a coin was genuine or adulterated by weighing it, or even by biting it to test for hardness. Because coins were either valued as stamped by the mint or were of virtually no value, made to purchase something for next to nothing, Paul's point is not that the Corinthians should evaluate how well they measure up to others or chart their own incremental development. He wants them to find out if they are true or false, genuine or counterfeit, in Christ or in disguise. We might use the image of the straight or crooked nail because once a nail is bent it can't be hammered in straight and is good for nothing. Paul not only states twice that he cares more about them than about himself being proven

---

6. 2 Cor 13:3-4; see also 3:1-2; 4:12; 13:9.
7. 2 Cor 13:5-10; 10:8; 12:19c.

genuine (13:7, 9) but also shows confidence that they are genuine by challenging them to test themselves before he comes.

What can be gained from Paul's use of "speaking in Christ" and "test yourselves" to understand the world as Paul sees it? On the one hand, he distinguishes sharply between "speaking in Christ" and all other speaking that is so disguised but in fact seeks one's own benefit, is deceptive, and relies on one's own power. This sounds highly dichotomous and might be used to exclude all other voices but his own. On the other hand, in this context Paul seems to use it to include rather than exclude. In the first place, while insisting that they test themselves rather than testing him, he is also conceding that they, not he, do the testing. He twice gives initial stress in a phrase to the word "yourselves" (ἑαυτοὺς, 13:5) and repeats it a third time: "Yourselves it is that you must test whether you are living in the faith. Yourselves it is that you must assay. Or do you not know yourselves that Jesus Christ is in you?—unless you are frauds!" Second, he provides only the broadest of guidelines for such testing, having just spoken against conflict in the community and against immorality without pointing to any specific act of contention or immorality that they have done (12:20-21) and allowing for repentance of those who have offended (2:7; 7:9-10). Compare this to his 1 Corinthians stipulations of what to do in each situation. Now he sees it is their task to define and defend what they take to be living "in Christ" (13:5).

Finally, he responds to their wanting proof that Christ is speaking in him by conceding that Christ is not weak toward them but powerful in them while he and his colleagues are weak in Christ (13:3-4). Yet because Christ "was crucified from weakness but lives from God's power," so "we live with him from God's power toward you"—a power evident, apparently, in their speaking (13:4). In this way those who "speak in Christ" may be weak or powerful, but the power is God's and it binds together those who speak weakly and those who speak powerfully. Paul is no longer insisting that they imitate him in his weakness (see 1 Cor 4:16; 11:1) but that they recognize his weakness as a genuine "speaking in Christ" because, in his bringing word of God's power to Corinth, he "lives by the power of God toward them" (13:4).

On the Midrange Political, Social, and Economic Context

Immediately after announcing to the Corinthians that he is getting ready for the third time to come back to Corinth, Paul reverts to defending himself. He will not burden them with his expenses, will not deceive them for his own gain, will not seek his own good reputation but will work to strengthen them. Here he is contrasting himself not only to the Christian preachers he has been opposing in the previous argument (10:1–12:13) but more broadly to a Greco-Roman stereotype of the wily itinerant alien, an ancient form of the American snake-oil peddler (see sidebar: "A Swindler Satirized" on pp. 219–20).[8] Paul claims that he and his colleagues are not exploiting the vulnerable but are caring for congregations as parents do for their children, and he ties his string to Titus's kite, whom the Corinthians seem to find more reliable (12:14-15, 18-19). When Paul compares himself to a provident parent rather than to an anxious father as he had earlier (12:14; 11:2-3), it is not so much an authority claim as it is an effort to express his concern. Also, the word "parents" reminds us that he works with women colleagues whom he calls coworkers and fellow contenders in his other letters.[9]

In recent centuries when Western education was built on the classics, the Roman Empire was credited with the spread of Greek civilization across the Mediterranean world through its *Pax Romana*, which in turn allowed people like Paul to carry Christianity quickly from Asia to Europe and Africa. Almost a half century after Paul's letters, the Acts of the Apostles depicts Paul as this kind of hero of the Gospel's dissemination. Luke is writing Acts for the well-placed Theophilus and his friends decades after the brutal suppression of the Jewish revolt against Rome in 70 CE, and he shows the respect for the empire required from writers at that time. But Paul writes earlier, at mid-century, to small communities largely in Roman colonies and provincial capitals who faced suspicion as disruptive sectarians within Israel, itself a religious tradition only marginally recognized by Rome. Second Corinthians shows Paul depicting himself as an itinerant alien hounded from pillar to post.[10] He can hardly speak without defending himself against charges of extortion and manipulation. It is important to see in his defensiveness not only a perhaps oversensitive man experiencing violence for the first time as an adult but also an advocate of an alternate gospel to the imperial one. Now he finds himself under threat of losing the support of the community he founded in the key city of Corinth. There are reasons he keeps reverting to self-defense.

8. Hans Dieter Betz, *Der Apostel Paulus und die sokratische Tradition: Eine exegetische Untersuchung zu seiner "Apologie" 2 Korinther 10–13*, BHT 45 (Tübingen: J. C. B. Mohr [Paul Siebeck], 1972), 53–54, 104–7.

9. Rom 16:3; Phil 4:3. He also speaks of Corinthian households and the Corinthian community in Christ as a whole working together with him: 1 Cor 16:15-18; 2 Cor 1:24; 6:1.

10. 2 Cor 4:8-12; 6:4-10; 11:23-33; Timothy Luckritz Marquis, *Transient Apostle: Paul, Travel, and the Rhetoric of Empire* (New Haven: Yale University Press, 2013), 131–33, 155, n. 9.

When speaking of his concerns about returning to Corinth, Paul describes possible contention there with eight nouns, "quarreling, jealousy, anger, selfishness, slander, gossip, conceit, and disorder" (12:20). Does this depict the social life of the Corinthian community that Paul is addressing? At least it is not foreign to their ways. Paul began 1 Corinthians with the report from Chloe's people that some claim they belong to Apollos, some to Paul, and others to Peter (1 Cor 1:10-12). At the end of the first century Clement writes from Rome that the Corinthian church has deposed its elders (see sidebar: "Church Elders Dismissed" on pp. 254–55).[11] It was certainly the case in these Greek cities that private association members were prone to conflicts over leadership roles and financial support, as can be seen where one stone inscription records the decisions of opposing factions over ten years' time (see sidebar: "A Leadership Conflict in a Private Association Near Athens"). Yet 2 Corinthians itself does not dwell on contention within the community but on the community's contention with Paul. Or does he fear being humiliated when he comes (12:21) because he thinks some will oppose him and others support him, reflecting their internal conflicts?

A Leadership Conflict in a Private Association Near Athens

In the year that Hermogenes was civic leader (archon), in the month of Mounichion, at a regular assembly, Simon son of Simon of Poros made the following motion: . . . it has been agreed by the members that the one who happens to be chosen as priestess for the year following Hermogenes' civic leadership (archonship) shall, in accord with these and the other things, furnish two thrones of the finest quality, and give an ornament of silver to the cupbearers and those who attend the goddess for the collection of the contributions. If someone acts in violation of these rules, the sacrificing associates are empowered to fine the priestess who offends against any of these rules, up to fifty drachmas. . . . Whichever priestess has obtained the priesthood shall appoint an attendant from among those who have already been priestesses. But it is not permitted to appoint the same person twice until all have had their turn. Otherwise, the priestess will be liable to the same fines. The secretary (grammateus) shall inscribe the decree on a stone monument (stele) and set it up in the temple.

[some nine years later on the same stele] . . . [I]t has been resolved by the sacrificing associates to act in all matters that pertain to the decree that

11. *1 Clement* 44.1–45.3; 46.5–47.7.

2 Corinthians 12:14–13:13   277

was proposed by Simon of Poros and to appoint Metrodora as an attendant to the goddess for life, that she serve indefinitely those who happen to be priestesses and that she meets their needs in an honorable and appropriate manner. It was also resolved that they take care that all things pertaining to the goddess take place in a pious manner, just as her mother, Euaxis, continued to do these things. And let the secretary inscribe this decree on the monument (stele) of the sacrificing associates.[12]

An alternative explanation for Paul's warning against conflict than an existing conflict comes from a perennial practice in speech and letter writing of the time to counsel against strife and advocate concord (see sidebar: "Rhetoric Denouncing Civil Discord"). So Paul's list of eight kinds of conflict may simply be an appropriate way to round off a letter to a community and offend no one in an imperial setting. In fact, the first four nouns appear in the same order within Paul's list of the "works of the flesh" in Galatians 5:20. Therefore less can be said specifically about Corinthian conduct from their appearance here than about rhetoric in a Greek city in the Roman era.

Rhetoric Denouncing Civil Discord

Only by getting rid of the vices that excite and disturb men, the vices of envy, greed, contentiousness, the striving in each case to promote one's own welfare at the expense of both one's native land and the commonweal—only so, I repeat, is it possible ever to breathe the breath of harmony in full strength and vigour and to unite on a common policy. . . . [I]f one were to run through the entire list of citizens, I believe he would not discover even two men in Tarsus who think alike, but on the contrary, just as with certain incurable and distressing diseases which are accustomed to pervade the whole body, exempting no member of it from their inroads, so this state of discord, this almost complete estrangement of one from another, has invaded your entire body politic.[13]

12. Regulations of the Sacrificing Associates of the Mother of the Gods, Piraeus (Attica), 183–74, in *Associations of the Greco-Roman World: A Sourcebook*, ed. and trans. Richard S. Ascough, Philip A. Harland, and John S. Kloppenborg (Waco, TX: Baylor University Press and de Gruyter, 2012), 28–29.

13. Dio Chrysostom, *Thirty Fourth or Second Tarsic Discourse*, 19–20, Dio Chrysostom, *Discourses*, vol. 3: *31–36*, trans. J. W. Cohoon and H. Lamar Crosby, LCL (Cambridge, MA: Harvard University Press 1940), 355.

Much the same applies to the three sexual offenses named next—which the NRSV translates as impurity, sexual immorality, and licentiousness (12:20-21.) But the emphasis on sexuality is less characteristic of Greek speeches than of Jewish wisdom and apocalyptic literature in its critique of foreign conduct (see sidebar: "Rhetoric Denouncing Sexual Immorality"). Paul lists the same sexual offenses at the head of his Galatians 5:19 list of "works of the flesh." In 2 Corinthians he does point to certain people who had sinned earlier and not yet repented (12:21; 13:2) "and to all the rest"—one assumes those who sinned more recently—saying that he will not take this lightly when he comes. Yet this is the only explicit reference to sexual offenses in the letter and remains very general in nature. Contrast this with Paul's elaborate instructions about sexual conduct in 1 Corinthians 5–7.

> ### Rhetoric Denouncing Sexual Immorality
>
> All is in chaos . . . ingratitude, moral corruption, sexual perversion, breakdown of marriage, adultery, debauchery. For the worship of idols, whose names it is wrong even to mention, is the beginning, cause, and end of every evil. (Wis 14:25-27, NEB)[14]

Focusing on the Interaction between Paul and the Corinthians

Paul closes 2 Corinthians by announcing that he is ready for the third time to come to Corinth (12:14), probably referring back to an initial plan to come via Macedonia (1 Cor 16:5-7), a second plan to come on his way to Macedonia and on return to the east (2 Cor 1:16), and now, due to Titus's delay (2:13; 7:5), planning to come from Macedonia after all where he is writing this letter (2 Cor 7:5). He immediately reassures them that he will not burden them with his expenses nor deceive them as others have done (12:14-18; 11:13, 20). This makes him defensive about being defensive: "All along you are thinking that we have been defending ourselves! We are speaking in Christ before God, and everything, my loved ones, is for your construction!" (12:19).

---

14. See also 2 Macc 6:4; T. Reu. 3.10–6.4; T. Jos. passim; 1 Enoch 6–7; Rom 1:20-27.

He is probably right that they have heard more than enough of his vaunted financial independence and his sterling integrity, and, most of all, his not being defensive.[15] Now he admits his concern that they will not please him or he them when he comes. He fears that there will be every kind of conflict; that he will be humbled and grieving and shocked by those who were immoral and have not repented (12:20-21). What is striking here is that Paul lists many types of contention and indecency, using the same sequences of words he uses in Galatians 5:19-20, but specifies neither who is doing these things, nor in what way, nor what they should be doing. He simply announces, and I translate:

> This third time I am [indeed] coming to you [since] "any claim needs the confirmation of two or three statements." I have already spoken and I speak again—the second time as though present and now still absent—to those who sinned before and to all the others: if I come again I will spare no one. (13:1-2)

Clearly Paul is announcing that the time is up for sparing them and himself the pain of conflict by his staying away from Corinth (1:23–2:4; 13:10). Many interpreters also read Paul to be threatening judgment when he arrives, some think in reaction to a second visit he made in Corinth when he was humiliated (13:1-2).[16] But others, myself included, argue that Paul has never gone back to Corinth since hearing about their reaction to his instructions in 1 Corinthians. Instead, he sent Titus to get feedback, and now he is planning a third time to make it to Corinth (see introduction to this text above) and writes to prepare his way.[17] When he gives repeated initial stress in the Greek word order to the phrase "this third time" (12:14; 13:1), if it is not to refer to two previous visits, or surely to remind them how often he has vacillated in coming (1:17-20), it must be to highlight his patience in having twice spared them and

---

15. On his financial independence, see 1 Thess 2:9; 1 Cor 9:12, 15-18; 2 Cor 11:7-12; 12:16; on his integrity, see 1 Cor 4:4-5; 2 Cor 1:17; 4:2, 5; 8:20-21; 10:12-13; 12:6; on his not being defensive, see 2 Cor 3:1; 5:12; 12:19.

16. Victor Paul Furnish, *II Corinthians*, AB 32A (Garden City, NY: Doubleday, 1984), 575; Margaret E. Thrall, *A Critical and Exegetical Commentary on the Second Epistle to the Corinthians*, ICC (Edinburgh: T & T Clark, 1994), 872–76, but she follows John Chrysostom in taking Paul's "three statements/witnesses" to be the "three times" he has warned them he is coming, not to be three witnesses he will hear on arrival (*Homilies on Second Corinthians* 29.1).

17. Baur, "Die beiden Briefe," 337–43; Hyldahl, "Einheit des Zweiten Korintherbriefes," 303–6.

himself a bad visit and to convince them that the third and definitive time has arrived. He has spoken when present and in writing, and now he writes the third and final warning.

Is Paul then ready to deliver judgment? The NRSV and NEB translators assume as much, and this shapes the crucial translation of the next two verses (13:3-4). They take the repeated phrase εἰς ὑμᾶς not simply as "toward you" or "for you" but distinctively as "in dealing with you," so that Paul can claim to be the instrument of God's power in dealing with them. But, as a more literal translation shows, these lines contrast Paul's weakness with God's power toward them:

> If I come again I will spare no one since you are looking for proof that Christ is speaking in me, the Christ who is not weak toward you but is powerful in you. For he was indeed crucified out of weakness, but he lives from the power of God. So we are weak in him, but we will live with him from the power of God toward you.

If Paul had gone on to outline the standards by which he would judge them, this could yet possibly mean he would speak with God's power toward them. But Paul insists instead that they test themselves:

> Evaluate yourselves to see if you are in the faith. Test yourselves! Or do you not recognize that Jesus Christ is in you? If not, you are frauds!

The contrast of this to 1 Corinthians is striking. There Paul laid out instructions for each aspect of life and made his own practice of the weakness of Christ crucified into a model for them, his not exploiting even the rights given him in the Gospel.[18] Now after speaking only broadly against their conflicts with each other and their sexual immorality (12:20-21), he expects them to test themselves and determine what is a life of faith in Christ. To test "if you are in the faith" would have a different emphasis in each of Paul's letters. Faith always means trust in God, but in Romans and Galatians this trust is contrasted with seeking righteousness from works of the law, in 1 Corinthians with relying on human wisdom, in Philippians with fear in suffering. In 2 Corinthians we might say that faith is not yet sight, "for we walk by faith, not by sight" (5:7), but faith is in process toward sight—"being transformed into the same image [of the Lord] from one degree of glory to another" (3:18), becoming the new creation already being realized in Christ (5:17). Paul challenges the Corinthians to test whether they are "in the faith," whether "Jesus Christ is

---

18. 1 Cor 4:16-17; 9:11-18, 22-24; 10:23–11:1; 14:13-18.

in you. If not, you are frauds!" (13:5). Faith is then the opposite of being deceived and deceiving oneself. It is knowing and speaking: "We have faith and therefore we speak, knowing that the one who raised the Lord Jesus will also raise us with Jesus and present us with you" (4:14).

After a letter of self-defense, Paul has shifted from fielding the Corinthian judgment of him to challenging them to test whether their life in Christ is genuine or counterfeit. Yet this has implications for Paul since they are his letter of recommendation (3:1-2), and he quickly reverts to self-defense, claiming that he aims not for his own vindication but for theirs (13:6-9). Far from urging them to take on the weakness of Christ as he has in other letters,[19] he claims this weakness for himself and concedes to them the power that they claim in Christ as a power that can yet achieve their fulfillment, restoration, or perfecting (13:3-4, 9). This, he concludes, is the whole reason that he is writing them, so that when he comes, "I need not be severe in using the authority that the Lord gave me for construction and not destruction" (13:10).

The question remains whether he could in fact bring off on the ground the severe "speaking in Christ" that he seems to threaten, the kind of performative speech that is not blessing and continued engagement but cauterizing, curse, even separation. Or are his critics right all along that "his letters are weighty and strong, but his presence is weak and his speech worthless" (10:10)? He may realize that he cannot achieve reconciliation with them if he faces hostility on arrival, whether because his public speaking is that deficient and/or because he cannot keep his cool in face-to-face conflict. Paul's threatening here probably needs to be seen as a strategic move taken in order to avoid some calamity of destruction that violates his calling to construct communities of faith. Bärbel Bosenius argues this thesis in her study, *The Absence of the Apostle as a Theological Strategy: Second Corinthians as an Instance of the Epistolary Nature of Pauline Theology.*[20]

And how will this have played out when the letter was read aloud in Corinth? He has, after all, conceded that he recognizes in them Christ's life-giving power and asks them to recognize in him and his colleagues Christ's weakness that has brought them the news of God's new creation

---

19. 1 Cor 4:10-16; Phil 2:1-8; 3:17; Rom 15:1-3.

20. This is my translation of her title: *Die Abwesenheit des Apostels als theologisches Programm: Der zweite Korintherbrief als Beispiel für die Brieflichkeit der paulinischen Theologie* (Tübingen: Franke Verlag, 1994).

in Christ.[21] He has also conceded his inadequacy in public debate, although this undermines his threat to follow through against opposition on arrival.[22] He has not stipulated any specific conduct that he expects of them beyond overcoming contention and immorality, and he has left up to them when they test themselves to identify what characterizes collegiality and morality and what demonstrates living in the faith and speaking in Christ. Earlier parts of the letter show that the Corinthians had disciplined one person who offended Paul, perhaps the man who was living with his father's wife, and Titus told Paul that at least in this case they "repented" and disciplined someone that Paul challenged and they are ready to welcome Paul.[23]

Yet now the risk for the Corinthians of welcoming Paul on his own terms remains great, since he may not recognize their morality as moral and might see any opposition as contention. If they find a way to concede that Paul's weakness did have a powerful effect among them, it may come down to whether they can persuade Paul that they are indeed by their own lights "in the faith" and "speaking in Christ." Or they may reject Paul's advances altogether so that when he later writes to Rome from Corinth he finds only marginal support there among long-standing believers like Gaius or in outlying communities such as Cenchreae.[24]

Yet the very last lines of the letter do suggest Paul is confident that the letter will achieve his aim of a restored relationship with them (13:11-13). He encourages, greets, and blesses them. This is Paul's usual way of closing a letter, but several distinctive elements show he continues upbeat. He addresses them as ἀδελφοί (NRSV: brothers and sisters; NEB: my friends), a term used only three times in this letter compared to nineteen times in 1 Corinthians.[25] He tailors his words of encouragement for this setting: "Finally, brothers and sisters, be joyful, be restored, be

---

21. 2 Cor 3:2, 5; 4:7-14; 5:14-15; 11:30; 12:5-10; 13:3-5, 9.

22. 2 Cor 11:6, 30; 12:5, 9.

23. 1 Cor 5:1-6; 2 Cor 2:5-11; 7:8-12.

24. Rom 15:23, 26; 16:1-2; 23; 1 Cor 1:14.

25. This count is from Thrall, *Second Epistle*, 904–6, citing Alfred Plummer, *Second Epistle of St. Paul to the Corinthians* (Edinburgh: T & T Clark, 1915; repr., 1951), 380. It indicates that Paul has not been assuming an easy collegiality in this letter but feels able to assert the family bond in closing. The archaic King James Version reads "brethren," with the advantage of suggesting all in the community while retaining, as does the Greek, the masculine form that yet probably colors Paul's meaning. See p. 12, n. 20 above.

encouraged, be of one mind, be at peace, and the God of love and peace will be with you" (13:11).

Yet translators who read Paul's stance as monitory take χαίρετε, "rejoice," in its alternate meaning of "farewell" due to the closing location, turn the positive καταρτίζεσθε, "be restored/perfected," (13:11) toward a corrective sense such as "put things in order" (NRSV) or "mend your ways" (NEB), and read παρακαλεῖσθε, "be encouraged," (see 1:3-6; 1 Thess 4:18; 5:11) as "listen to my appeal" (NRSV) or "take our appeal to heart" (NEB). Yet Paul's greetings that follow (13:12) sustain his hopeful stance by calling the Corinthians to give each other a holy kiss and by sending them the greetings of "all the saints."

Paul's final blessing is performative speech, that is, speech expected to accomplish what it says. And whereas he normally closes his letters simply with "the grace of our Lord Jesus Christ be with you,"[26] here the blessing is extended with "the love of God and the communion of the Holy Spirit," making it the fullest benediction of any in Paul's letters (13:13). This blessing is as close as he comes to what was later called the trinitarian confession and is arguably the benediction most heard in American churches. This may be because it begins accessibly with the grace of Jesus, speaks from this of God's love rather than of God the creator or the father of a son, and culminates with the offer of participation in the life-giving Holy Spirit who animates the Corinthian community.[27] At the least, one can say that Paul's conclusion is not a curt ending. He sustains and brings to a climax an expression of his confidence that God can bring off the reconciliation God wants with these Corinthians, not for Paul's sake or finally even for theirs, but for God's own sake.[28] Or to put it the other way around, because God is reconciling the entire creation in Christ crucified whom Paul embodies and in Christ risen whom the Corinthians embody, what God does in them both is entirely for their sakes.[29]

26. 1 Thess 5:28; 1 Cor 16:23; Rom 16:20; Phil 4:23.
27. 1 Cor 2:9-16; 12:1-13; 14:1-12; 2 Cor 3:3, 6, 16-18.
28. 2 Cor 1:10-11; 4:13-15; 7:16; 9:11-15.
29. 2 Cor 3:17-18; 4:6, 11-15; 5:17-20; 12:9-10; 13:9.

Afterword

M y opening question—What happened to the Corinthian
women prophets that Paul restricted in 1 Corinthians?—
seems to be answered in 2 Corinthians. Not that he mentions them. Paul
is no longer talking about the Corinthians' conduct and giving cautionary
advice in response to their bold slogans. Now he is talking about his own
conduct and giving explanations in response to their critiques. The tables
have been turned. In 2 Corinthians his repeated claims of integrity before
God and goodwill toward them, his defense of himself not as singular
apostle but within a first-person plural of agents of good news, and his
recasting God as reconciler of the alienated all point to the Corinthians
having rejected his earlier instructions. Once we see the women prophets
among others in Corinth continuing their conduct that Paul proscribed
in 1 Corinthians we understand why Paul begins 2 Corinthians praising
God for his recent rescue to evoke the Corinthians' concern, excusing
his long absence as meant for their benefit, and defending his conduct
for five chapters before reporting that Titus did bring good news about
them. By then he has enough traction to plead for their reconciliation
with him and to challenge them to outshine Macedonia in their gift for
Jerusalem. Only in closing does he attack and ridicule rival preachers
of Christ who have exposed his deficiencies in appearance and speech.
He mocks the Corinthians for putting up with such arrogance, featuring himself as a fool for Christ and challenging the Corinthians to test
their own "speaking in Christ" as sharply as they have been testing his.

But all these labyrinths of Paul's rhetoric that have spawned partition
theories will not have brought the Corinthians around were it not for the

substantive concession that Paul makes within his self-defense. He does not mention his earlier restrictions—concerning women who prophesy: that they be open to marriage, cover their heads when speaking, and, finally, restrict their speech to their homes—and he affirms their experience of the resurrection life that he had once reserved for the dead. Whereas in 1 Corinthians he challenged the Corinthians at each point to imitate him and give up freedoms they had received in Christ to benefit others, in 2 Corinthians he takes them as the positive product of his harsh labors. They are the letter of Christ that he delivers, the treasure in his clay jar, the life that comes out of his death: "So death is active in us, but life in you" (4:12). The visible evidence of God's power and glory that they demand in him Paul finds realized through his labor in them, and they become his assurance that he will eventually share life with them as they together reflect Christ's image, dying and rising.

Yet this separating of roles could itself derail Paul's project if the Corinthians were to see themselves reduced to a product of Paul's agency. But he insists that God gave him authority only to build them up, not to tear them down, so his rivals will be checked only when "your agreement is complete" (10:6) and the good news will be extended in Achaia only when "your faithfulness grows" (10:15-16), claiming that it all depends on them.

When the letter ends and our sources run dry, the jury is still out. The Corinthians may have accepted Paul's terms and welcomed him back in their community at the expense of his stimulating rivals. Or they may have preferred his rivals, a prospect less fraught with possible reversions to Paul's earlier ways. I like to think that they satisfied neither Paul nor his rivals by welcoming both—not, one hopes, at the same time—testing for themselves what best would serve Christ living and speaking in them.

In addition to this primary question about the women prophets who heard Paul's letter, I have also explored the address of this letter to a Jewish messianic sect in a once-Greek city destroyed by Rome and reclaimed as a Roman colony and provincial capital. The impact of this letter on the multiple and conflicting identities of the people I call Corinthians is almost beyond tracing. But we can watch Paul counter the empire's claims to establish world peace and welfare by announcing the new creation of a worldwide assembly in the Roman-crucified and God-resurrected Jesus Christ. The message is revolutionary, yet the presentation, in contrast to that of the book of Revelation, is hardly countercultural. Paul travels on Roman roads as a Roman-style envoy to cultivate these new assemblies in Roman colonies and capital cities where Jewish synagogues and other

Greek associations were also proclaiming divine blessings and hearing words of present judgment and future hope. It seems that right under the nose of the "god of this world" is the place chosen for the nurture of a new world.

It is an interesting question whether Paul's readiness in 2 Corinthians to affirm Corinthian spiritual expression should be taken as a compromise with Greek culture and Roman hegemony at the expense of promoting in Corinth his own strict practice of God's power in weakness. I think this judgment ignores the radical difference between daily life in border provinces including Judea and Galilee occupied by the emperors' legions or vassals and the life in pacified internal provinces such as Italy and the Aegean cities where the flow of the world's wealth toward Rome came through them to make life possible. People from everywhere had migrated to Greek-speaking cities seeking bare survival and whatever group support and identity they could find. Is it a compromise with empire when women and men without name, education, or influence find through God's Spirit that they can speak to and for Christ about life in their new assemblies? It may be that Paul discovers through the women's persistence in prayer and prophecy that the losses he has taken in Christ as a free, educated male in a strong family are not laid on all, even that the visible glory of Christ that he cannot produce on demand is already being demonstrated in the Corinthians through expressing in their own idiom the good news he brought them.

A final comprehensive question I have been asking is what Paul's 2 Corinthians letter can contribute to our grasp of the eco-structure in which we live. In such a text can we step back before modern optimism about "man" controlling "nature" to find resources for seeing ourselves as agents among the myriad and interacting agencies of all animal, plant, and mineral life?[1] Paul's Greco-Roman city culture may be as blind as we are today to our dependence on farm, forest, and planet, but he shares with the Corinthians deep roots from their pasts in each one's tribal heritage where people and things were integrated within a spirit-given benevolence. So Paul attributes all good to God's Spirit that animates and transforms the world from within, liberating Moses from the veil, making inarticulate people like Paul into agents of good news, writing the "letter of Christ" that is the Corinthians, and giving them all participation and

---

1. See my "Human and Nonhuman Agency in Paul's Corinthian Letters," in *After the Corinthian Women Prophets: Rhetoric, Power, and Possibilities*, ed. Joseph A. Marchal, SemeiaSt (Atlanta: SBL Press, forthcoming).

communion in one Spirit. What God's Spirit does Paul also calls "grace." This is the boundless giving of God that fuels all God's creatures to give freely regardless of their own mortal limitations. What they then give is also called "grace," including their financial gifts. And in their living and speaking they in turn find themselves giving "grace" to God, which we translate weakly as "thanks."

The bottom line of Paul's good news is the report that God has raised a certain crucified Judean named Jesus from the dead. The evidence for this is less the recital of witnesses at the scene, which Paul gives only once in his letters (1 Cor 15:3-5). He claims rather the immediate evidence in Christ's transformation of people's lives—his own wake-up call to take the news to the nations, but equally the changed lives of those who have heard the news, as well as multiple and continuing occasions of life from death. I would say it is not a single event in the past that secures Paul's gospel but this repeated experience of the life-making God, from ancient Abraham and Sarah's receiving a child told in Romans 4 to his own recent rescue from a death sentence in Asia (2 Cor 1:8-11). And 2 Corinthians shows Paul discovering that the spiritual life of the Corinthians not only doesn't compete with God's Spirit but in fact demonstrates the life that has come out of dying. This is what Paul is celebrating: "All of us with unveiled faces that reflect the Lord's glory are being transformed into the same image from glory on to glory—this from the Lord, the Spirit!" (2 Cor 3:18). Reading 2 Corinthians in this way could open a door, at least for those of the Christian tribe, to join a new creation moving with ample grace through the deaths we face toward a wider life.

Works Cited

4 *Maccabees*. Translated by H. Anderson. Pages 561–62 in *Old Testament Pseudepigrapha*, edited by James H. Charlesworth. Vol. 2. Garden City, NY: Doubleday, 1985.

Aasgaard, Reidar. *My Beloved Brothers and Sisters! Christian Siblingship in Paul*. London: T & T Clark, 2004.

Acts of Paul and Thecla. Translated by R. McL. Wilson. Pages 330–33 and 353–64 in *New Testament Apocrypha*, edited by Edgar Hennecke and Wilhelm Schneemelcher. Vol. 2. Philadelphia: Westminster, 1964.

Adams, Edward. *Constructing the World: A Study of Paul's Cosmological Language*. Edinburgh: T & T Clark, 2000.

Adeyemo, Tokunboh. *Africa Bible Commentary*. Nairobi: World Alive Publishers, 2006.

Agamben, Giorgio. *The Time That Remains: A Commentary on the Letter to the Romans*. Stanford, CA: Stanford University Press, 2005.

Alcock, Susan E. *Graecea Capta: The Landscapes of Roman Greece*. Cambridge: Cambridge University Press, 1992.

———. "Regional Development in the Roman Empire: The Eastern Mediterranean." Pages 671–97 in *The Cambridge Economic History of the Greco-Roman World*, edited by Walter Scheidel, Jan Morris, and Richard Saller. Cambridge: Cambridge University Press, 2007.

Alkier, Stefan. *Wunder und Wirklichkeit in den Briefen des Apostel Paulus: Ein Beitrag zu einem Wunderverständnis jenseits von Entmythologisierung und Rehistorisierung*. WUNT 134. Tübingen: Mohr Siebeck, 2001.

Allen, Roland. *Missionary Methods: St. Paul's or Ours?* Chicago: Moody Press, 1959.

American Heritage Dictionary of the English Language. Edited by William Morris. Boston: Houghton Mifflin, 1969.

Apostolic Fathers. Edited by G. P. Goold. Translated by Kirsopp Lake. 2 vols. LCL. Cambridge, MA: Harvard University Press, 1975.

Aristophanes. Translated by Benjamin Bickley Rogers. 3 vols. LCL. Cambridge, MA: Harvard University Press, 1967.

Arrian. Translated by E. Iliff Robson. 2 vols. LCL. Cambridge, MA: Harvard University Press, 1966.

Arzt-Grabner, Peter. *2. Korinther. Unter Mitarbeit von Ruth E. Kritzer*. Vol. 4 of *Papyrologische Kommentare zum Neuen Testament*. Göttingen: Vandenhoeck & Ruprecht, 2014.

Ascough, Richard S., Philip A. Harland, and John S. Kloppenborg, eds. and trans. *Associations of the Greco-Roman World: A Sourcebook*. Waco, TX: Baylor University Press and de Gruyter, 2012.

Attridge, Harold W. "Making Scents of Paul: The Background and Sense of 2 Cor 2:14-17." Pages 71–88 in *Early Christianity and Classical Culture: Comparative Studies in Honor of Abraham J. Malherbe*, edited by John T. Fitzgerald, Thomas H. Olbricht, and L. Michael White. Leiden: Brill, 2003.

Bagnall, R. S., and R. C. Cribiore. *Women's Letters from Ancient Egypt, 300 BC–AD 800*. Ann Arbor: University of Michigan, 2006.

Barclay, John M. G. " 'Because He Was Rich He Became Poor': Translation, Exegesis and Hermeneutics in the Reading of 2 Cor 8–9." Pages 331–44 in *Theologizing in the Corinthian Conflict: Studies in the Exegesis and Theology of 2 Corinthians*, edited by Reimund Bieringer, Ma. Marilou S. Ibita, Dominika A. Kurek-Chomycz, and Thomas A. Vollmer. BTS 16. Leuven: Peeters, 2013.

———. *Paul and the Gift*. Grand Rapids, MI: Eerdmans, 2015.

———. *Pauline Churches and Diaspora Jews*. WUNT 275. Tübingen: Mohr Siebeck, 2011.

Barrett, C. K. *The New Testament Background: Selected Documents*. New York: Harper & Row, 1956.

———. "Ο ΑΔΙΚΗΣΑΣ (2 Cor. 7.12)." Pages 108–17 in his *Essays on Paul*. Philadelphia: Westminster, 1982.

Barrier, Jeremy W. "Two Visions of the Lord: A Comparison of Paul's Revelation to His Opponents' Revelation in 2 Corinthians 12:1-10." Pages 272–90 in *Finding a Woman's Place: Essays in Honor of Carolyn Osiek, R.S.C.J.*, edited by David L. Balch and Jason T. Lamoreaux. Eugene, OR: Wipf and Stock, 2011.

Baumert, N. *Täglich sterben und auferstehen. Der Literalsinn von 2 Kor 4,12–5,10*. Munich: Kösel Verlag, 1973.

Baur, Ferdinand Christian. "Die beiden Briefe an die Korinthier." Pages 337–43 in his *Paulus, Der Apostel Jesu Christi*. Vol 1. 2nd ed. Leipzig, 1866–67; repr., Osnabrück, 1968.

Beale, G. K. "The Background of ἐκκλησία Revisited." *JSNT* 38 (2015): 151–68.

Beard, Mary. "Ciceronian Correspondences." In *Classics in Progress*, edited by T. P. Wiseman. Oxford: Oxford University Press, 2002.

Becker, Eve-Marie. *Letter Hermeneutics in 2 Corinthians: Studies in* Literarkritik *and Communication Theory.* Translated by Helen S. Heron. London: T & T Clark, 2004.

———. "Paulus als weinender Briefschreiber (2 Kor 2,4): Epistolare *parousia* im Zeichen visualisierter Emotionalität." Pages 11–26 in *Der zweite Korintherbrief: Literarische Gestalt—historische Situation—theologische Argumentation. Festschrift zum 70. Geburtstag von Dietrich-Alex Koch,* edited by Dieter Sänger. Göttingen: Vandenhoeck & Ruprecht, 2012.

———. "Stellung und Funktion von 2. Korinther 8–9 im literarischen Endtext: Anmerkungen zum Stand der literarischen Diskussion." Pages 283–304 in *Theologizing in the Corinthian Conflict: Studies in the Exegesis and Theology of 2 Corinthians,* edited by Reimund Bieringer, Ma. Marilou S. Ibita, Dominika A. Kurek-Chomycz, and Thomas A. Vollmer. BTS 16. Leuven: Peeters, 2013.

Belleville, Linda. *Reflections of Glory: Paul's Polemical Use of the Moses-Doxa Tradition in 2 Corinthians 3:1-18.* Sheffield: Sheffield Academic, 1991.

———. "Scripture and Other Voices in Paul's Theology." Pages 233–61 in *Paul and Scripture: Extending the Conversation,* edited by Christopher D. Stanley. Atlanta: Society of Biblical Literature, 2012.

———. " 'Tradition or Creation'? Paul's Use of the Exodus 34 Tradition in 2 Corinthians 3:7-18." In *Paul and the Scriptures of Israel,* edited by Craig A. Evans and James A. Sanders. Sheffield: Sheffield Academic, 1993.

Bennett, Jane. *Vibrant Matter: A Political Ecology of Things.* Durham: Duke University Press, 2010.

Berge, Loïc P. M. *Faiblesse et force, présidence et collégialité chez Paul de Tarse: Recherche littéraire et théologique sur 2 Co 10–13 dans le contexte du genre épistolaire antique.* Leiden: Brill, 2015.

Betz, Hans Dieter. "2 Cor 6:14–7:1: An Anti-Pauline Fragment?" *JBL* 92 (1973): 88–108.

———. *2 Corinthians 8 and 9: A Commentary on Two Administrative Letters of the Apostle Paul.* Philadelphia: Fortress, 1985.

———. "Eine Christus-Aretalogie bei Paulus (2. Kor. 12,7-10)." *ZTK* 66 (1969): 288–305.

———. *Der Apostel Paulus in Rom.* Berlin: De Gruyter, 2013.

———. *Der Apostel Paulus und die sokratische Tradition: Eine exegetische Untersuchung zu seiner "Apologie" 2 Korinther 10–13.* BHT 45. Tübingen: J. C. B. Mohr (Paul Siebeck), 1972.

———. *Lukian von Samosata und das Neue Testament: Religionsgeschichtliche und paränetische Parallelen.* Berlin: Akademie-Verlag, 1961.

———. *Studies in Paul's Letter to the Philippians.* WUNT 343. Tübingen: Mohr Siebeck, 2015.

Bieringer, Reimund. "2 Korinther 6,14–7,1 im Kontext der 2. Korintherbriefes. Forschungsüberblick und Versuch eines eigenen Zugangs." Pages 567–70 in *Studies on 2 Corinthians,* edited by R. Bieringer and J. Lambrecht. BETL 112. Leuven: Leuven University Press, 1994.

————. " 'Reconcile Yourselves to God': An Unusual Interpretation of 2 Corinthians 5:20 in Its Context." Pages 28–38 in *Jesus, Paul, and Early Christianity: Studies in Honor of Henk Jan de Jonge*, edited by R. Buitenwerf, H. W. Hollander, and J. Tromp. Leiden: Brill, 2008.

Bieringer, R., and J. Lambrecht. *Studies on 2 Corinthians*. BETL 12. Leuven: Leuven University Press, 1994.

Bieringer, Reimund, Ma. Marilou S. Ibita, Dominika A. Kurek-Chomycz, and Thomas A. Vollmer, eds. *Theologizing in the Corinthian Conflict: Studies in the Exegesis and Theology of 2 Corinthians*. BTS 16. Leuven: Peeters, 2013.

Bolton, David. "Paul's Collection: Debt Theology Transformed into an Act of Love among Kin?" Pages 345–59 in *Theologizing in the Corinthian Conflict: Studies in the Exegesis and Theology of 2 Corinthians*, edited by Reimund Bieringer, Ma. Marilou S. Ibita, Dominika A. Kurek-Chomycz, and Thomas A. Vollmer. BTS 16. Leuven: Peeters, 2013.

Boobyer, George Henry. *"Thanksgiving" and the "Glory of God" in Paul*. Leipzig: Universitätsverlag von Robert Noske, 1929.

Bornkamm, Günter. "The History of the Origin of the So-Called Second Letter to the Corinthians." *NTS* 8 (1962): 258–63.

Bosenius, Bärbel. *Die Abwesenheit des Apostels als theologisches Programm: Der zweite Korintherbrief als Beispiel für die Brieflichkeit der paulinische Theologie*. Tübingen: Franke, 1994.

Botha, Pieter J. J. "Writing in the First Century." Pages 62–88 in *Orality and Literacy in Early Christianity*. Eugene, OR: Wipf and Stock, 2012.

Bouttier, Michel. *En Christ, Étude d'exégèse et de théologie pauliniennes*. Paris: Presses Universitaires de France, 1962.

————. "La souffrance de l'Apôtre: 2 Co 4, 7-18." Pages 29–49 in *The Diakonia of the Spirit (2 Co 4:7–7:4)*, edited by Lorenzo de Lorenzi. Rome: St. Paul's Abbey, 1989.

Breytenbach, Cilliers. *Grace, Reconciliation, Concord: The Death of Christ in Graeco-Roman Metaphors*. Leiden: Brill, 2010.

————. "Paul's Proclamation and God's 'Thriambos' (Notes on 2 Corinthians 2:14-16)." *Neot* 24 (1990): 262.

Bultmann, Rudolph. *The Second Letter to the Corinthians*. Minneapolis: Augsburg, 1985; German, 1976.

Calvin's Commentaries. Edited by David W. and Thomas F. Torrance. Translated by T. A. Small. Grand Rapids, MI: Eerdmans, 1964.

Carrez, Maurice. "Le 'Nous' en 2 Corinthiens." *NTS* 26 (1980): 474–86.

————. "Que représente la vie de Jésus pour l'apôtre Paul?" *RHPR* 68 (1988): 155–61.

Cartlidge, David R., and David L. Dungan. *Documents for the Study of the Gospels*. Cleveland: Collins, 1989.

Charlesworth, James H., ed. *Old Testament Pseudepigrapha*. 2 vols. Garden City, NY: Doubleday, 1983 and 1985.

Charlesworth, M. P. *Trade Routes and Commerce of the Roman Empire*. Chicago: Ares, 1974.

Chrysostom, John. *Homilies on Second Corinthians*. Vol. 12 in first series of *Nicene and Post-Nicene Fathers*. 14 vols. Edited by Philip Schaff. Peabody, MA: Hendrickson, 1995; repr. of Christian Literature Publishing Company, 1889.

Coakley, Sarah, ed. *Faith, Rationality and the Passions*. Chichester: Wiley-Blackwell, 2012.

Coakley, Sarah. "Sacrifice Regained: Reconsidering the Rationality of Religious Belief." An Inaugural Lecture by the Norris-Hulse Professor of Divinity. University of Cambridge, UK. October 13, 2009.

Cobb, John B., Jr. *Whitehead Word Book: A Glossary with Alphabetical Index to Technical Terms in* Process and Reality. Claremont: P & F Press, 2008.

Collange, J.-F. *Énigmes de la Deuxième épitre de Paul aux Corinthiens: Étude exégétique de 2 Cor. 2:14–7:4*. Cambridge: Cambridge University Press, 1972.

Collins, John N. *DIAKONIA: Reinterpreting the Ancient Sources*. New York: Oxford University Press, 1990.

———. *Diakonia Studies: Critical Issues in Ministry*. Oxford: Oxford Scholarship Online, 2014.

Conradie, Ernst. "The Road towards an Ecological Biblical and Theological Hermeneutics." *Scriptura: tsydskrif vir bybelkunde* 93 (2006): 305–14.

———. "Towards an Ecological Biblical Hermeneutics: A Review Essay on the Earth Bible Project." *Scriptura: tsydskrif vir bybelkunde* 85 (2004): 123–35.

Cook, John M. *The Troad: An Archaeological and Topographical Study*. Oxford: Clarendon, 1973.

Corley, Kathleen E. "Women's Inheritance Rights in Antiquity and Paul's Metaphor of Adoption." Pages 98–121 in *Feminist Companion to Paul*, edited by Amy-Jill Levine with Marianne Blickenstaff. FCNTECW 6. London: T & T Clark, 2004.

Crüsemann, Marlene. *2 Corinthians*. Stuttgart: Kohlhammer, forthcoming.

———. "2 Korintherbrief." Pages 2131–32 in *Bibel in gerechter Sprache*, edited by Ulrike Bail, Frank Crüsemann, Marlene Crüsemann, Erhard Domay, Jürgen Ebach, Claudia Janssen, Hanne Köhler, Helga Kuhlmann, Martin Jentzsch, and Luise Schottroff. Gütersloh: Gütersloher Verlagshaus, 2006.

———. "Das weite Herz und die Gemeinschaft der Heiligen: 2 Kor 6,11–7,4 im sozialgeschichtlichen Kontext." Pages 206–27 in *Gott ist Beziehung: Beiträge zur biblischen Rede von Gott*, edited by Claudia Janssen and Luise Schottroff. Gütersloh: Gütersloher Verlagshaus, 2014. Repr. of pages 351–75 in *Dem Tod nicht glauben: Sozialgeschichte der Bibel. Festschrift für Luise Schottroff zum 70. Geburtstag*, edited by Frank Crüsemann, Marlene Crüsemann, Claudia Janssen, Rainer Kessler, and Beate Wehn. Gütersloh: Güersloher Verlagshaus, 2004.

———. "Die Gegenwart des Verlorenen: Zur Rede vom 'Paradies' im Neuen Testament." Pages 228–49 in *Gott ist Beziehung: Beiträge zur biblischen Rede von Gott*, edited by Claudia Janssen and Luise Schottroff. Gütersloh: Gütersloher Verlagshaus, 2014. Repr. of pages 44–68 in *"Schau an der schönen Gärten Zier" Über irdische und himmlische Paradiese. Zu Kult und Kulturgeschichte des Gartens*. Jabboq 7. Gütersloh: Gütersloher Verlagshaus, 1999.

————. "Eine Christologie der Beziehung: Trost, *charis* und Kraft der Schwachen nach dem 2. Brief an die Gemeinde in Korinth." Pages 184–205 in *Gott ist Beziehung: Beiträge zur biblischen rede von Gott*, edited by Claudia Janssen and Luise Schottroff. Gütersloh: Gütersloher Verlagshaus, 2014. Repr. from *Christus und seine Geschwister. Christologie im Umfeld der* Bibel in gerechter Sprache, edited by Marlene Crüsemann and Carsten Jochum-Bortfeld. Gütersloh: Gütersloher Verlagshaus, 2009.

————. "Eine neue Perspektive auf Paulus." Pages 132–38 in *Gott ist Beziehung: Beiträge zur biblischen Rede von Gott*, edited by Claudia Janssen and Luise Schottroff. Gütersloh: Gütersloher Verlagshaus, 2014.

————. *Gott ist Beziehung: Beiträge zur biblischen Rede von Gott*. Edited by Claudia Janssen and Luise Schottroff. Gütersloh: Gütersloher Verlagshaus, 2014.

D'Angelo, Mary Rose. "Remembering Jesus: Women, Prophecy and Resistance." *Hor* 19 (1992): 199–218.

Dahl, Nils Alstrup. *Studies in Paul*. Minneapolis: Augsburg, 1977.

Danker, Frederick W., ed. *A Greek-English Lexicon of the New Testament and Other Early Christian Literature*. 3rd rev. Eng. ed. Original ed. Walter Bauer. Chicago: University of Chicago Press, 2000.

Dautzenberg, Gerhard. " 'Glaube' oder 'Hoffnung' in 2 Kor 4,13–5,10." Pages 75–104 in *The Diakonia of the Spirit (2 Co 4:7–7:4)*, edited by L. de Lorenzi. Rome: St. Paul's Abbey, 1989.

DeBaufre, Melanie Johnson, and Laura S. Nasrallah. "Beyond the Heroic Paul: Toward a Feminist Decolonizing Approach to the Letters of Paul." Pages 161–74 in *The Colonized Apostle: Paul through Postcolonial Eyes*, edited by Christopher Stanley. Minneapolis: Fortress, 2011.

Deichgräber, R. *Gotteshymnus und Christus-hymnus in der frühen Christenheit*. Göttingen: Vandenhoeck & Ruprecht, 1967.

Deissmann, G. Adolf. *Light from the Ancient East: The New Testament Illustrated by Recently Discovered Texts of the Graeco-Roman World*. New York: Hodder and Stoughton, 1910.

————. *Paul: A Study in Social and Religious History*. From the German 2nd ed. 1925. New York: Harper Brothers, 1957.

Derrida, Jacques. *Given Time: 1. Counterfeit Money*. Translated by P. Kamuf. Chicago: University of Chicago, 1992 (French 1991).

Dietzelbinger, Christian. *Die Berufung des Paulus als Ursprung seiner Theologie*. Neukirchen: Neukirchener Verlag, 1985.

Dinkler, Erich. "Die Taufterminologie in 2 Cor. 1:21f." Pages 173–91 in *Neotestamentica et Patristica*. Leiden: Brill, 1962.

Dio Chrysostom. Edited and translated by J. W. Cohoon and H. Lamar Crosby. 5 vols. LCL. Cambridge, MA: Harvard University Press, 1932–1951.

Downs, David J. *The Offering of the Gentiles*. Tübingen: Mohr Siebeck, 2008.

Dube, Musa W. *Postcolonial Feminist Interpretation of the Bible*. St. Louis: Chalice, 2000.

Dube Shomanah, Musa W., Andrew Mütüa Mbuvi, and Dora R. Mbuwayesango, eds. *Postcolonial Perspectives in African Biblical Interpretation*. Atlanta: Society of Biblical Literature, 2012.

Duff, Paul. "Metaphor, Motif, and Meaning: The Rhetorical Strategy behind the Image 'Led in Triumph' in 2 Corinthians 2:14." *CBQ* 53 (1991): 84–92.

———. "The Mind of the Redactor: 2 Cor 6:14–7:1 in Its Secondary Context." *NovT* 35 (1993): 60–80.

Dunn, James D. G. "2 Corinthians III. 17—'The Lord Is the Spirit.'" *JTS* 21 (1970): 309–20.

———. *Baptism in the Spirit*. Naperville, IL: Allenson, 1970.

———. *The Theology of Paul the Apostle*. Grand Rapids, MI: Eerdmans, 1998.

Elliott, Neil. *The Arrogance of Nations: Reading Romans in the Shadow of Empire*. Minneapolis: Fortress, 2008.

———. "Marxism and the Postcolonial Study of Paul." Pages 34–40 in *The Colonized Apostle: Paul through Postcolonial Eyes*, edited by Christopher Stanley. Minneapolis: Fortress, 2011.

Elliott, Neil, and Mark Reasoner, eds. *Documents and Images for the Study of Paul*. Minneapolis: Fortress, 2011.

Engels, Donald. *Roman Corinth: An Alternative Model for the Classical City*. Chicago: University of Chicago, 1990.

Fitzgerald, John T. *Cracks in an Earthen Vessel: An Examination of the Catalogues of Hardships in the Corinthian Correspondence*. Atlanta: Scholars Press, 1988.

———. "Paul and Paradigm Shifts: Reconciliation and Its Linkage Groups." Pages 241–62 in *Beyond the Judaism/Hellenism Divide*, edited by Troels Engberg-Pedersen. Louisville: Westminster John Knox, 2001.

Fitzmyer, Joseph A. "Qumran and the Interpolated Paragraph in 2 Cor 6:14–7:1." *CBQ* 23 (1961): 271–80.

Frank, Tenney. *A History of Rome*. New York: Henry Holt, 1923.

Frettlöh, Magdalene. "Der Charme der gerechten Gabe: Motive einer Theologie und Ethik der Gabe am Beispiel der paulinischen Kollekte für Jerusalem." Pages 105–62 in *"Leget Anmut in das Geben": Zum Verhältnis von Ökonomie und Theologie*, edited by Jürgen Ebach, Hans-Martin Gutmann, Magdalene Frettlöh, and Michael Weinrich. Gütersloh: Chr. Kaiser/Gütersloher Verlagshaus, 2001.

Fridrichsen, Anton. "Peristasenkatalog und Res Gestae. Nachtrag zu 2 Cor. 11:23ff." *Symbolae Osloensis* 8 (1929): 78–82.

———. "Zum Stil der paulinischen Peristasenkatalogs 2 Cor. 11:23ff." *Symbolae Osloensis* 7 (1928): 26–29.

Friesen, Steven. "The Cult of the Roman Emperors in Ephesos: Temple Wardens, City Titles, and the Interpretation of the Gospel of John." Pages 229–50 in *Ephesos: Metropolis of Asia: An Interdisciplinary Approach to its Archaeology, Religion, and Culture*, edited by Helmut Koester. Valley Forge, PA: Trinity Press International, 1995.

Frör, Hans. *You Wretched Corinthians! The Correspondence between the Church in Corinth and Paul.* London: SCM Press, 1995.

Furnish, Victor Paul. *II Corinthians.* AB 32A. Garden City, NY: Doubleday, 1984.

Gaventa, Beverley Roberts. *Our Mother, Saint Paul.* Louisville: Westminster John Knox, 2000.

——. "Our Mother, Saint Paul: Toward the Recovery of a Neglected Theme." Pages 85–97 in *A Feminist Companion to Paul,* edited by Amy-Jill Levine with Marianne Blickenstaff. FCNTECW 6. London: T & T Clark, 2004.

Georgi, Dieter. *The Opponents of Paul in Second Corinthians.* Philadelphia: Fortress, 1986; German, 1964.

——. *Remembering the Poor: The History of Paul's Collection for Jerusalem.* Nashville: Abingdon, 1992; German 1965, rev. 1994.

Gerber, Christine. "καυχᾶσθαι δεῖ, οὐ συμφέρον μέν . . . (2 Kor 12,1): Selbstlob bei Paulus vor dem Hintergrund der antiken Gepflogenheiten." Pages 213–34 in *Paul's Graeco-Roman Context,* edited by Cilliers Breytenbach. Leuven: Peeters, 2015.

——. *Paulus, Apostolat und Autorität, oder vom Lesen fremder Briefe.* Zürich: Theologischer Verlag Zürich, 2012.

——. *Paulus und seine "Kinder": Studien zur Beziehungsmetaphorik der paulinischen Briefe.* Berlin: de Gruyter, 2005.

Gorman, Michael J. *Becoming the Gospel: Paul, Participation, and Mission.* Grand Rapids, MI: Eerdmans, 2015.

Goulder, Michael. "2 Cor 6:14–7:1, an Integral Part of 2 Corinthians." *NovT* 36 (1994): 50–54.

Grant, F. C., ed. and trans. *Ancient Roman Religion.* New York: Liberal Arts Press, 1957.

Griffith-Jones, Robin. "Turning to the Lord: Vision, Transformation and Paul's Agenda in 2 Corinthians 1–8." Pages 255–79 in *Theologizing in the Corinthian Conflict: Studies in the Exegesis and Theology of 2 Corinthians,* edited by Reimund Bieringer, Ma. Marilou S. Ibita, Dominika A. Kurek-Chomycz, and Thomas A. Vollmer. BTS 16. Leuven: Peeters, 2013.

Guthrie, George H. "Paul's Triumphal Procession Imagery (2 Cor 2.14-16a): Neglected Points of Background." *NTS* 61 (2015): 79–91.

Hadley, Judith M. "From Goddess to Literary Construct: The Transformation of Asherah into Hokmah." Pages 360–99 in *A Feminist Companion to Reading the Bible: Approaches, Methods and Strategies,* edited by Athalya Brenner and Carole Fontaine. FCB 11. Sheffield: Sheffield Academic, 1997.

Hafemann, Scott J. *Paul, Moses, and the History of Israel: The Letter/Spirit Contrast and the Argument from Scripture in 2 Corinthians 3.* Tübingen: J. C. B. Mohr (Paul Siebeck), 1995.

——. *Suffering and Ministry in the Spirit: Paul's Defense of His Ministry in II Corinthians 2:14–3:3.* Grand Rapids, MI: Eerdmans, 1990.

Hardy, E. G. *Monumentum Ancyranum.* Oxford: Clarendon, 1923.

Harrill, J. Albert. *Paul the Apostle: His Life and Legacy in Their Roman Context.* Cambridge: Cambridge University Press, 2012.

Hays, Richard. *Echoes of Scripture in the Letters of Paul*. New Haven: Yale University Press, 1989.

Hearon, Holly E. "1 and 2 Corinthians." Pages 606–23 in *Queer Bible Commentary*, edited by Deryn Gaest, Robert E. Goss, Mona West, and Thomas Bohache. London: SCM, 2006.

Heckel, Ulrich. *Kraft in Schwachheit: Untersuchungen zu 2 Kor 10–13*. WUNT 2.56. Tübingen: J. C. B. Mohr (Paul Siebeck), 1993.

Heinemann, Joseph. *Prayer in the Talmud: Forms and Patterns*. Berlin: de Gruyter, 1977.

Heinrici, Georg. *Der zweite Brief an die Korinther*. Göttingen: Vandenhoeck & Ruprecht, 1887; rev. ed. 1900.

Heisinger, Bernhard. "Paulus und Philo als Mystiker? Himmelreisen im Vergleich (2 Kor 12,2-4; *Spec. Leg.* III 1-6)." Pages 189–204 in *Philo und das Neue Testament*, edited by R. Deiser and K.-W. Niebuhr. WUNT 172. Tübingen: Mohr Siebeck, 2004.

Hennecke, Edgar, and Wilhelm Schneemelcher, eds. *New Testament Apocrypha*. 2 vols. Philadelphia: Westminster, 1964.

Hock, Ronald F., and Edward N. O'Neil. *The* Chreia *in Ancient Rhetoric*. Vol. 1: *The Progymnasmata*. Atlanta: Scholars Press, 1986.

———. *The* Chreia *and Ancient Rhetoric*. Vol. 2: *Classroom Exercises*. Atlanta: Society of Biblical Literature, 2002.

Hodges, Robert. "Paul the Apostle and the First Century Tribulation Lists." *ZNW* 74 (1983): 59–80.

Horrell, David G. "Ecojustice in the Bible? Pauline Contributions to an Ecological Theology." Pages 164–72 in *Bible and Justice: Ancient Texts, Modern Challenges*, edited by Matthew J. M. Coomber. London: Equinox, 2011.

Horrell, David G., Cherryl Hunt, and Christopher Southgate. *Greening Paul: Reading Paul in a Time of Ecological Crisis*. Waco, TX: Baylor University Press, 2010.

Horsley, Richard A. "Rhetoric and Empire—and 1 Corinthians." Pages 72–102 in *Paul and Politics: Ekklesia, Israel, Imperium, Interpretation*, edited by Richard A. Horsley. Harrisburg, PA: Trinity Press International, 2000.

Horsley, Richard A. "1 and 2 Corinthians." Pages 237–44 in *A Postcolonial Commentary on the New Testament Writings*, edited by Fernando Segovia and R. S. Sugirtharajah. London: Bloomsbury, 2007.

Hughes, Philip Edgcumbe. *Paul's Second Epistle to the Corinthians*. Grand Rapids, MI: Eerdmans, 1962.

Humphrey, Edith M. *Joseph and Aseneth*. Sheffield: Sheffield Academic, 2000.

Hunt, Mary E. "Feminist Catholic Theology and Practice: From Kyriarchy to Discipleship of Equals." Pages 459–72 in *Toward a New Heaven and a New Earth: Essays in Honor of Elisabeth Schüssler Fiorenza*, edited by Fernando F. Segovia. Maryknoll, NY: Orbis Books, 1998.

Hyldahl, Niels. "Die Frage nach der literarischen Einheit des Zweiten Korintherbriefes." *ZNW* 64 (1973): 289–306.

Ibita, Ma. Marilou S. "Mending a Broken Relationship: The Social Relations and the Symbolic Universe of 2 Corinthians 1–7." Pages 43–68 in *Theologizing* in the Corinthian Conflict: Studies in the Exegesis and Theology of 2 Corinthians,* edited by Reimund Bieringer, Ma. Marilou S. Ibita, Dominika A. Kurek-Chomycz, and Thomas A. Vollmer. BTS 16. Leuven: Peeters, 2013.

Jackson, T. Ryan. *New Creation in Paul's Letters: A Study in the Historical and Social Setting of a Pauline Concept.* WUNT 2.272. Tübingen: Mohr Siebeck, 2010.

Janssen, Claudia. *Anders ist die Schönheit der Körper: Paulus und die Auferstehung in 1 Kor 15.* Gütersloh: Gütersloher Verlagshaus, 2005.

Jervell, Jacob. *IMĀGO DEI: Gen 1,26f. im Spätjudentum, in der Gnosis und in den paulinischen Briefen.* Göttingen: Vandenhoeck & Ruprecht, 1960.

Johnson, Lee A. "Paul's Letters as Artifacts: The Value of the Written Text among Non-Literate People." *BTB* 46 (2016): 25–34.

Joseph and Aseneth. Translated by C. Burchard. Pages 177–247 in *The Old Testament Pseudepigrapha,* edited by James H. Charlesworth. Vol. 2. Garden City, NY: Doubleday, 1985.

Josephus. *The Jewish War.* Translated by G. A. Williamson. Harmondsworth: Penguin, 1959.

Josephus. Translated by H. St. J. Thackeray, Ralph Marcus, Allen Wikgren, and Louis H. Feldman. 9 vols. LCL. Cambridge: Harvard University Press, 1966–1969.

Judge, E. A. "The Conflict of Educational Aims in New Testament Thought." *Journal of Christian Education* 9 (1966): 32–45.

Julian of Norwich. *Revelation of Love.* Edited and translated by John Skinner. New York: Image Books, 1996.

Kaithakottil, Joyce. " 'Death in Us, Life in You': Ministry and Suffering; A Study of 2 Cor 4:7-15." *BiBh* 28 (2002): 433–60.

Käsemann, Ernst. "Some Thoughts on the 'Doctrine of Reconciliation.' " Pages 52–57 in *The Future of Our Religious Past,* edited by J. M. Robinson. New York: Harper and Row, 1971.

Kittel, Gerhard, and Gerhard Friedrich, eds. *Theological Dictionary of the New Testament.* Translated by G. W. Bromiley. 10 vols. Grand Rapids, MI: Eerdmans, 1964–1976.

Kittredge, Cynthia Briggs. *Community and Authority: The Rhetoric of Obedience in the Pauline Tradition.* Harrisburg, PA: Trinity Press International, 1998.

Klein, Hans. "Die Begrundung für den Spendenaufruf für die Heiligen Jerusalems in 2 Kor 8 und 9." Pages 104–30 in *Der zweite Korintherbrief: Literarische Gestalt—historische Situation—theologische Argumentation. Festschrift zum 70. Geburtstag von Dietrich-Alex Koch,* edited by Dieter Sänger. Göttingen: Vandenhoeck & Ruprecht, 2012.

Kloppenborg, John S. "Greco-Roman *Thiasoi,* the *Ekklēsia* at Corinth and Conflict Management." Pages 187–218 in *Redescribing Paul and the Corinthians,* edited by Ron Cameron and Merrill P. Miller. Atlanta: Society of Biblical Literature, 2011.

Kloppenborg, John S., and Richard S. Ascough. *Greco-Roman Associations: Texts, Translations, and Commentary,* vol. 1: *Attica, Central Greece, Macedonia, Thrace.* Berlin: de Gruyter, 2011.

Koster, Severin. *Die Invektive in der griechischen und römischen Literatur.* Meisenheim am Glan: Anton Hain, 1980.

Kraemer, Ross Shepard. *When Aseneth Met Joseph: A Late Antique Tale of the Biblical Patriarch and His Egyptian Wife, Reconsidered.* New York: Oxford University Press, 1998.

Kraftchick, Steven J. "Death in Us, Life in You." Pages 169–78 in *Pauline Theology,* vol. 2: *1 and 2 Corinthians,* edited by David Mittay. Minnesota: Fortress, 1993.

Kurek-Chomycz, Dominika A. "The Scent of (Mediated) Revelations? Some Remarks on φανερόω with a Particular Focus on 2 Corinthians." Pages 90–95 in *Theologizing in the Corinthian Conflict: Studies in the Exegesis and Theology of 2 Corinthians,* edited by Reimund Bieringer, Ma. Marilou S. Ibita, Dominika A. Kurek-Chomycz, and Thomas A. Vollmer. BTS 16. Leuven: Peeters, 2013.

Lambrecht, Jan. "The nekrōsis of Jesus: Ministry and Suffering in 2 Cor 4,7-15." Pages 309–33 in *Studies on 2 Corinthians,* edited by Reimund Bieringer and Jan Lambrecht. BETL 112. Leuven: Leuven University Press, 1994.

———. *Second Corinthians.* SP 8. Collegeville, MN: Liturgical Press, 1999.

Land, Christopher. *The Integrity of 2 Corinthians and Paul's Aggravating Absence.* Sheffield: Sheffield Phoenix, 2015.

Lanier, Emilia. "Eve's Apology in Defense of Women." Page 103 in *Salve Deus Rex Judaeorum,* introduced by A. L. Rowse. Clarkson N. Potter, 1979.

Lapprenga, Benjamin. *Paul's Language of ζῆλος: Monosemy and the Rhetoric of Identity and Practice.* Leiden: Brill, 2015.

Larsen, J. A. O. "Roman Greece: Greece and Macedonia from Augustus to Gallienus." Pages 436–98 in *An Economic Survey of Ancient Rome,* edited by Tenney Frank. Baltimore: Johns Hopkins University Press, 1938.

The Letters of Alciphron, Aelian and Philosotratus. Translated by Allen Rogers Benner and Francis H. Forbes. LCL. Cambridge, MA: Harvard University Press, 1962.

Liddell, Henry George, and Robert Scott. *Greek-English Lexicon.* Oxford: Clarendon, 1968.

Lietzmann, Hans. *An die Korinther I II.* Enlarged by W. G. Kümmel. 5th ed. Tübingen: J. C. B. Mohr (Paul Siebeck), 1969.

Lindemann, Andreas. "'. . . an die Kirche in Korinth samt allen Heiligen in ganz Achaja': Zu Entstehung und Redaktion des '2. Korintherbriefes.'" Pages 131–59 in *Der zweite Korintherbrief: Literarische Gestalt—historische Situation—theologische Argumentation. Festschrift zum 70. Geburtstag von Dietrich-Alex Koch,* edited by Dieter Sänger. Göttingen: Vandenhoeck & Ruprecht, 2012.

Lindgård, Fredrik. *Paul's Line of Thought in 2 Corinthians 4:10–5:10.* Tübingen: Mohr-Siebeck, 2005.

Lohfink, Gerhard. "Kommentar als Gattung: Rudolf Schnackenburg zum 60. Geburtstag." *BibLeb* 15 (1974): 1–16.

Lohmeyer, Ernst. *Galiläa und Jerusalem.* Göttingen: Vandenhoeck & Ruprecht, 1936.

Lucian. Translated by A. M. Harmon, K. Kilburn, and M. D. Macloud. 8 vols. LCL. Cambridge, MA: Harvard University Press, 1913–1961.

Mack, Burton L. "Elaboration of the *Chreia* in the Hellenistic School." Pages 31–67 in *Patterns of Persuasion in the Gospels*, edited by Burton L. Mack and Vernon K. Robbins. Sonoma, CA: Polebridge Press, 1989.

Magie, David. *De Romanorum iuris publici sacrique vocabulis sollemnibus in Graecum sermonem conversis*. Leipzig: Tuebner, 1905.

Maher, Michael, ed. and trans. *Targum Pseudo-Jonathan: Exodus*. ArBib 2. Collegeville, MN: Liturgical Press, 1994.

Malter, Henry, ed. and trans. *The Treatise Ta'anit of the Babylonian Talmud*. Philadelphia: Jewish Publication Society of America, 1928.

Marquis, Timothy Luckritz. *Transient Apostle: Paul, Travel and the Rhetoric of Empire*. New Haven: Yale University Press, 2013.

Marsh, Frank Burr. *The Reign of Tiberius*. New York: Barnes & Noble, 1959.

Marshall, Peter. *Enmity in Corinth: Social Conventions in Paul's Relations with the Corinthians*. WUNT 2.23. Tübingen: J. C. B. Mohr (Paul Siebeck), 1987.

Martin, Ralph P. *2 Corinthians*. WBC 40. Waco, TX: Word Books, 1983.

Matthews, Shelly. "2 Corinthians." Pages 196–207 in *Searching the Scriptures*, edited by Elisabeth Schüssler Fiorenza. Vol. 2. New York: Crossroad, 1994.

Mauss, Marcell. *The Gift: The Form and Reason for Exchange in Archaic Societies*. Translated by W. D. Halls. London: Routledge, 1990 (French 1925).

McCarter, P. Kyle, Jr. *1 Samuel*. AB 8. Garden City, NY: Doubleday, 1980.

McNamara, Martin, ed., and Robert Hayward, notes. *Targum Neofiti 1: Exodus*. ArBib 2. Collegeville, MN: Liturgical Press, 1987.

McNamara, Martin. *Targum and Testament Revisited: Aramaic Paraphrases of the Hebrew Bible; A Light on the New Testament*. 2nd ed. Grand Rapids, MI: Eerdmans, 2010.

Mell, Ulrich. *Neue Schöpfung: Eine traditionsgeschichtliche und exegetische Studie zu einem soteriologischen Grundsatz paulinischer Theologie*. Berlin: de Gruyter, 1989.

Mell, Ulrich. "Paulus: scheiternder Gescheiter: Ein historischer und literarischer Einwurf." Pages 199–223 in *Der zweite Korintherbrief: Literarische Gestalt—historische Situation—theologische Argumentation. Festschrift zum 70. Geburtstag von Dietrich-Alex Koch*, edited by Dieter Sänger. Göttingen: Vandenhoeck & Ruprecht, 2012.

Merz, Annette. "Why Did the Pure Bride of Christ (2 Cor. 11.2) Become a Wedded Wife (Eph. 5.22-33)? Theses about the Intertextual Transformation of an Ecclesiological Metaphor." *JSNT* 79 (2000): 130–47; trans. Brian McNeil from pages 148–65 in *Paulus: Umstrittene Traditionen—lebendigen Theologie*, edited by Claudia Janssen, Luise Schottroff, and Beate Wehn. Gütersloh: Christian Kaiser/Gütersloher Verlagshaus, 2001.

Mesle, C. Robert. *Process Theology*. St. Louis: Chalice, 1993.

Miguez, Nestor. "Grace in Paul's Theology: Political and Economic Projections." *Neot* 46 (2012): 287–98.

Miller, Anna C. *Corinthian Democracy: Democratic Discourse in 1 Corinthians*. Eugene, OR: Pickwick Publications, 2015.

————. "Not with Eloquent Wisdom: Democratic *ekklēsia* Discourse in 1 Cor 1–4." *JSNT* 35 (2013): 323–64.

Mitchell, Margaret M. "The Corinthian Correspondence and the Birth of Pauline Hermeneutics." Pages 20–36 in *Paul and the Corinthians: Studies of a Community in Conflict*, edited by Trevor J. Burke and J. Keith Elliott. NovTSup 109. Leiden: Brill, 2003.

————. "New Testament Envoys in the Context of Greco-Roman Diplomatic and Epistolary Conventions: The Example of Timothy and Titus." *JBL* 111 (1992): 641–62.

————. *Paul, the Corinthians and the Birth of Christian Hermeneutics.* Cambridge: Cambridge University Press, 2010.

————. "Paul's Letters to Corinth: The Interpretive Intertwining of Literary and Historical Reconstruction." Pages 306–38 in *Urban Religion in Roman Corinth: Interdisciplinary Approaches*, edited by Daniel N. Schowalter and Steven J. Friesen. Cambridge: Harvard University Press, 2005.

Mommsen, Theodore. *The Provinces of the Roman Empire from Caesar to Diocletian.* Vol. 1. Chicago: Ares, 1909; repr., 1974.

Morray-Jones, C. R. A. "Paradise Revisited (2 Cor 12:1-12): The Jewish Mystical Backgrounds of Paul's Apostolate." *HTR* 86 (1993): 177–217, 265–92.

Morrison, Toni. *Beloved.* New York: Plume, 1987.

Müller, Markus. "Der sogenannte, 'schriftstellerische Plural'—neu betrachtet. Zur Frage der Mitarbeiter als Mitverfasser der Paulusbriefe." *BZ* 42 (1998): 181–201.

Munck, Johannes. *Paul and the Salvation of Mankind.* Richmond, VA: John Knox, 1959.

Murphy-O'Connor, Jerome. "The Date of Second Corinthians 10–13." Pages 149–69 in *Keys to Second Corinthians: Revisiting Major Issues.* Oxford: Oxford University Press, 2010.

————. "Relating 2 Corinthians 6:14–7:1 to Its Context." *NTS* 33 (1987): 272–75.

————. *St. Paul's Corinth: Texts and Archaeology.* Wilmington, DE: Michael Glazier, 1983.

Nasrallah, Laura Salah. *Archaeology and the Letters of Paul.* New York: Oxford University Press, 2019.

Nestle-Aland. *Novum Testamentum Graece.* 28th rev. ed. by Barbara and Kurt Aland, Johannes Karavidopouos, Carlo M. Martini, and Bruce M. Metzger. Stuttgart: Deutsche Bibelgesellschaft, 2012.

Niccum, Curt. "The Voice of the Manuscripts on the Silence of Women: The External Evidence for 1 Cor 14:34-35." *NTS* 43 (1997): 342–55.

Nickle, Keith F. *The Collection: A Study in Paul's Strategy.* Naperville, IL: Allenson, 1966.

Nilsson, Martin. *Greek Piety.* New York: Norton, 1969.

————. "The New Conception of the Universe in Greek Paganism." *Eranos* 44 (1946): 20–27.

Nongbri, Brent. "2 Corinthians and Possible Material Evidence for Composite Letters in Antiquity." Pages 54–67 in *Collecting Early Christian Letters: From the Apostle Paul to Late Antiquity,* edited by Bronwen Neil and Pauline Allen. Cambridge: Cambridge University Press, 2015.

Nowak, Martin A., and Sarah Coakley, eds. *Evolution, Games, and God: The Principle of Cooperation.* Cambridge, MA: Harvard University Press, 2013.

Oakes, Peter. *Reading Romans in Pompeii: Paul's Letter at Ground Level.* Minneapolis: Fortress, 2009.

Økland, Jorunn. "Paratexts: The 1 Cor 14 Gloss Theory Before and After *The Corinthian Women Prophets.*" In *After the Corinthian Women Prophets: Rhetoric, Power, and Possibilities,* edited by Joseph A. Marchal. SemeiaSt. Atlanta: SBL Press, forthcoming.

———. *Women in Their Place: Paul and the Corinthian Discourse of Gender and Sanctuary Space.* London: T & T Clark, 2004.

Oliveira, Anacleto de. *Die Diakonie der Gerechtigkeit und der Versöhnung in der Apologie des 2. Korintherbriefes: Analyse und Auslegung von 2 Cor 2,14–4,6; 5,11–6,10.* Münster: Aschendorf, 1990.

Olley, John W. "A Precursor of the NRSV? 'Sons and Daughters' in 2 Cor 6:18." *NTS* 44 (1998): 206–12.

Olson, Stanley Norris. "Confidence Expressions in Paul: Epistolary Conventions and the Purpose of 2 Corinthians." PhD diss., Yale University, 1976.

———. "Epistolary Uses of Expressions of Self-Confidence." *JBL* 103 (1984): 585–97.

Orr, Peter. *Christ Absent and Present: A Study in Pauline Christology.* Tübingen: Mohr Siebeck, 2014.

Perelman, Chaim, and L. Olbrechts-Tyteca. *The New Rhetoric: A Treatise on Argumentation.* Notre Dame: University of Notre Dame Press, 1969 (French, 1958).

Petersen, Norman. *Rediscovering Paul: Philemon and the Sociology of Paul's Narrative World.* Philadelphia: Fortress, 1985.

Philo. Translated by F. H. Colson and G. H. Whitaker. 9 vols. LCL. Cambridge, MA: Harvard University Press, 1929–1941.

Philonenko, Marc. *Joseph et Aseneth.* Leiden: Brill, 1968.

Pippin, Tina. *Death and Desire: The Rhetoric of Gender in the Apocalypse of John.* Louisville: Westminster John Knox, 1992.

Plummer, Alfred. *Second Epistle of St. Paul to the Corinthians.* Edinburgh: T & T Clark, 1915; repr., 1951.

Price, S. R. F. *Rituals and Power: The Roman Imperial Cult in Asia Minor.* Cambridge: Cambridge University Press, 1984.

Punt, Jeremy. "Paul and Postcolonial Hermeneutics: Marginality and/in Early Biblical Interpretation." Pages 261–90 in *As It Is Written: Studying Paul's Use of Scripture,* edited by Stanley E. Porter and Christopher D. Stanley. SymS 50. Leiden: Brill, 2008.

———. "Pauline Agency in Postcolonial Perspective: Subverter of or Agent for Empire." Pages 53–61 in *The Colonized Apostle: Paul through Postcolonial Eyes,* edited by Christopher Stanley. Minneapolis: Fortress, 2011.

Rabens, Volker. "Paul's Rhetoric of Demarcation: Separation from 'Unbelievers' (2 Cor 6:14–7:1) in the Corinthian Conflict." Pages 229–53 in *Theologizing in the Corinthian Conflict: Studies in the Exegesis and Theology of 2 Corinthians*, edited by Reimund Bieringer, Ma. Marilou S. Ibita, Dominika A. Kurek-Chomycz, and Thomas A. Vollmer. BTS 16. Leuven: Peeters, 2013.

Rajak, Tessa. "Benefactors in the Greco-Jewish Diaspora." Pages 372–91 in *The Jewish Dialogue with Greece and Rome: Studies in Cultural and Social Interaction.* Leiden: Brill, 2001.

Rebell, Walter. *Gehorsam und Unabhängigkeit. Eine sozialpsychologische Studie zu Paulus.* Münich: Christian Kaiser, 1986.

Reconciliation and Liberation—The Confession of 1967 (special issue). *Journal of Presbyterian History* 61 (1983).

Rehmann, Luzia Sutter. *Geh—Frage die Gebärerin: Feministisch-befreiungstheologische Untersuchungen zum Gebärmotiv in der Apokalyptik.* Gütersloh: Kaiser, Gütersloher Verlagshaus, 1995.

———. "Turning Groaning into Labor." Pages 74–84 in *Feminist Companion to Paul*, edited by Amy-Jill Levine with Marianne Blickenstaff. FCNTECW 6. London: T & T Clark, 2004.

Relihan, Joel C. *Ancient Menippean Satire.* Baltimore: Johns Hopkins University Press, 1993.

Rich, Adrienne. *Of Woman Born: Motherhood as Experience and Institution.* New York: Norton, 1976.

Richards, E. Randolf. *The Secretary in the Letters of Paul.* WUNT 2.42. Tübingen: Mohr Siebeck, 1991.

Rowe, C. Kavin. "New Testament Iconography? Situating Paul in the Absence of Material Evidence." Pages 293–306 in *Picturing the New Testament: Studies in Ancient Visual Images*, edited by Annette Weissenrieder, Friederike Wendt, and Petra von Gemünden. WUNT 2.193. Tübingen: Mohr Siebeck, 2005.

Rowland, Christopher. *The Open Heaven: A Study of Apocalyptic in Judaism and Early Christianity.* New York: Crossroad, 1982.

Safrai, S. "Relations between the Diaspora and the Land of Israel." Pages 184–215 in *The Jewish People in the First Century: Historical Geography, Political History, Social Cultural and Religious Life and Institutions*, edited by S. Safrai and M. Stern. Vol. 1. Philadelphia: Fortress, 1971.

Sandnes, Karl Olav. *Paul, One of the Prophets?* WUNT 2.43. Tübingen: J.C.B. Mohr (Paul Siebeck), 1991.

Särkiö, Riita. "Die Versöhnung mit Gott—und mit Paulus: Zur Bedeutung der Gemeindesituation in Korinth für 2 Kor 5,14-21." *ST* 52 (1998): 29–42.

Schadewaldt, Wolfgang. *Der Gott von Delphi und die Humanitätsidee.* 2nd ed. Stuttgart: Neske, 1965.

Schellenberg, Ryan S. "Paul, Samson Occom, and the Constraints of Boasting: A Comparative Reading of 2 Corinthians 10–13." *HTR* 109 (2016): 512–35.

Schmeller, Thomas. "Der ursprüngliche Kontext von 2 Kor 6,14-7,1. Zur Frage der Einheitlichkeit des 2 Korintherbriefes." *NTS* 52 (2006): 219-31.

———. *Der zweite Brief an die Korinther, Teilband 1: 2 Kor. 1:1–7:4.* Neukirchen-Vluyn: Neukirchener Verlag, 2010.

————. "No Bridge over Troubled Water? The Gap between 2 Corinthians 1–9 and 10–13 Revisited." *JSNT* 36 (2013): 73–84.

Schnelle, Udo. "Der 2. Korintherbrief und die Mission gegen Paulus." Pages 300–322 in *Der zweite Korintherbrief: Literarische Gestalt—historische Situation—theologische Argumentation. Festschrift zum 70. Geburtstag von Dietrich-Alex Koch*, edited by Dieter Sänger. Göttingen: Vandenhoeck & Ruprecht, 2012.

Schottroff, Luise. *Der erste Brief an die Gemeinde in Korinth.* Stuttgart: Kohlhammer, 2013.

Schubert, Paul. *Form and Function of the Pauline Thanksgivings.* BZNW 20. Berlin: Alfred Töpelmann, 1939.

Schüssler Fiorenza, Elisabeth. *The Book of Revelation: Justice and Judgment.* Philadelphia: Fortress, 1985.

————. *The Power of the Word: Scripture and the Rhetoric of Empire.* Minneapolis: Fortress, 2007.

————. *Revelation: Vision of a Just World.* Minneapolis: Fortress, 1991.

————. "Rhetoricity of Historical Knowledge: Pauline Discourse and its Contextualizations." Pages 443–69 in *Religious Propaganda and Missionary Competition in the New Testament World: Essays Honoring Dieter Georgi*, edited by Lukas Bormann, Kelly Del Tredici, and Angela Standhartinger. Leiden: Brill, 1994.

————, ed. *Searching the Scriptures.* 2 vols. With the assistance of Shelly Matthews and Ann Brock. New York: Crossroad, 1993–1994.

Schüssler Fiorenza, Elisabeth, Cynthia Briggs Kittredge, Sheila Briggs, and Antoinette Clark Wire. Responses to the editor Richard A. Horsley. Pages 40–57 and 103–29 in *Paul and Politics: Ekklesia, Israel, Imperium, Interpretation*, edited by Richard A. Horsley. Harrisburg, PA: Trinity Press International, 2000.

Scott, James M. "The Use of Scripture in 2 Corinthians 6.16c-18 and Paul's Restoration Theology." *JSNT* 56 (1994): 73–99.

Segal, A. F. *Paul the Convert: The Apostolate and Apostasy of Saul the Pharisee.* New Haven: Yale University Press, 1990.

Standhartinger, Angela. *Das Frauenbild im Judentum der hellenistischen Zeit.* Leiden: Brill, 1995.

————. "Letter from Prison as Hidden Transcript: What It Tells Us about the People at Philippi." Pages 114–24 in *The People Beside Paul: The Philippian Assembly and History from Below*, edited by Joseph A. Marchal. Atlanta: SBL Press, 2015.

Stanley, Christopher. *The Colonized Apostle: Paul through Postcolonial Eyes.* Minneapolis: Fortress, 2011.

————. *Paul and Scripture: Extending the Conversation.* Atlanta: Society of Biblical Literature, 2012.

————. "The Rhetoric of Quotations: An Essay on Method." Pages 18–27 in *Early Christian Interpretations of the Scriptures of Israel: Investigations and Proposals.* Sheffield: Sheffield Academic, 1997.

Starnitzke, Dierk. "Der Dienst des Paulus: Zur Interpretation von Ex 34 in 2 Korintherbrief 3." *WD* 25 (1999): 200–202.

Stegemann, Ekkehard. "Der Neue Bund im Alten: Zum Schriftverständnis des Paulus in II Kor 3." *TZ* 42 (1986): 112–13.

Sternberg, Meir. "Proteus in Quotation-Land: Mimesis and the Forms of Reported Discourse." *Poetics Today* 3 (1982): 107–10, 144–54.

Strabo. *Geography.* Vol. 4: *Books 8–9.* Translated by Horace Leonard Jones. LCL. Cambridge, MA: Harvard University Press, 1927; repr., 1968.

Sugirharajah, R. S. *The Bible and the Third World.* Cambridge: Cambridge University Press, 2001.

Sundermann, Hans-Georg. *Der schwache Apostel und die Kraft der Rede: Eine historische Analyse von 2 Kor 10–13.* Frankfurt am Main: Peter Lang, 1996.

Tabor, James D. *Things Unutterable: Paul's Ascent to Paradise in its Greco-Roman, Judaic, and Early Christian Contexts.* Lanham, MD: University Press of America, 1986.

Tannehill, Robert C. *Dying and Rising with Christ: A Study in Pauline Theology.* Berlin: Topelmann, 1967.

Thrall, Margaret E. *A Critical and Exegetical Commentary on the Second Epistle to the Corinthians.* ICC. Edinburgh: T & T Clark, 1994.

———. "The Offender and the Offence: A Problem of Detection in 2 Corinthians." Pages 65–78 in *Scripture: Meaning and Method*, edited by B. P. Thompson. Hull: Hull University Press, 1989.

———. "Paul's Journey to Paradise. Some Exegetical Issues in 2 Cor 12:2-4." Pages 347–63 in *The Corinthian Correspondence*, edited by Reimund Bieringer. Leuven: Leuven University Press, 1996.

———. " 'Putting on' or 'stripping off' in 2 Corinthians 5:3." Pages 221–35 in *New Testament Textual Criticism: Its Significance for Exegesis*, edited by Eldon Jay Epp and Gordon D. Fee. Oxford: Clarendon, 1981.

———. "The Pauline Use of ΣΥΝΕΙΔΗΣΙΣ." *NTS* 14 (1967): 118–25.

Traer, Robert. "Loving and Evolving Consciousness: A Bigger History." Pages 50–60 in *Gratitude and Hope: Doing Theology at Pilgrim Place*, edited by Paul Kitlass, Pat Patterson, and Connie Kimos. Vol. 10. Shelbyville, KY: Wasteland Press, 2015.

Trobisch, David. *Die Entstehung der Paulusbriefsammlung: Studien zu den Anfängen christlicher Publizistik.* Göttingen: Vandenhoeck & Ruprecht, 1989.

Uzukwu, Gesila Nneka. "The Poverty and Wealth of the Macedonians. A Grammatical and Rhetorical Analysis of 2 Corinthinas 8:1-5." Pages 319–30 in *Theologizing in the Corinthian Conflict: Studies in the Exegesis and Theology of 2 Corinthians*, edited by Reimund Bieringer, Ma. Marilou S. Ibita, Dominika A. Kurek-Chomycz, and Thomas A. Vollmer. BTS 16. Leuven: Peeters, 2013.

Vander Stichele, Caroline. "2 Corinthians." Pages 743–54 in *Feminist Biblical Interpretation: A Compendium of Critical Commentary on the Books of the Bible and Related Literature*, edited by Luise Schottroff and Marie-Theres Wacker.

Translated by Everett Kalin, Nancy Lukens, Linda M. Maloney, Barbara Rumscheidt, Martin Rumscheidt, and Tina Steiner. Grand Rapids, MI: Eerdmans, 2012; from German 2nd ed. 1999.

Vegge, Ivan. *2 Corinthians: A Letter about Reconciliation; A Psychagogical, Epistologographical and Rhetorical Analysis.* WUNT 2.239. Tübingen: Mohr Siebeck, 2008.

Verbrugge, Verlyn D. *Paul's Style of Church Leadership Illustrated by His Instructions to the Corinthians on the Collection.* San Francisco: Mellen Research University Press, 1992.

Virgil. Translation by H. Rushton Fairclough. 2 vols. LCL. Cambridge, MA: Harvard University Press, 1916.

Vouga, François. "Der Brief als Form der apostolischen Autorität." Pages 7–58 in *Studien und Texte zur Formgeschichte,* edited by Klaus Berger, Francois Vouga, Michael Wolter, and Dieter Zeller. Tübingen: Francke Verlag, 1992.

Wacker, Marie-Theres. *Von Göttinnen, Göttern und dem einzigen Gott: Studien zum biblischen Monotheismus aus feministisch-theologischer Sicht.* Münster: Literatur Verlag, 2004.

Waldenfels, Bernhard. *Antwortregister.* Frankfurt am Main: Suhrkamp, 1994.

———. "Un-ding der Gabe." Pages 385–409 in *Einsätze des Denkens, Zur Philosophie von Jacques Derrida,* edited by H.-D. Gondek and B. Waldenfels. Frankfurt am Main: Suhrkamp, 1997.

Watson, Frances. *Paul and the Hermeneutics of Faith.* London: T & T Clark, 2004.

Webb, William J. *Returning Home: New Covenant and Second Exodus as the Context for 2 Corinthians 6.14–7.1.* JSOTSup 85. Sheffield: Sheffield Academic, 1993.

———, "Who Are the Unbelievers (ἄπιστοι) in 2 Corinthians 7:14?" *BSac* 149 (1992): 27–44

Wedderburn, A. J. M. "2 Cor 5:14—A Key to Paul's Soteriology." Pages 267–83 in *Paul and the Corinthians: Studies of a Community in Conflict,* edited by Trevor J. Burke and J. Keith Elliott. NovTSup 109. Leiden: Brill, 2003.

Weiss, J. *Der erste Korintherbrief.* Göttingen: Vandenhoeck & Ruprecht, 1910; repr., 1977.

Welborn, L. L. "Paul's Appeal to the Emotions in 2 Corinthians 1.1–2.13; 7.5-16." *JSNT* 82 (2001): 31–60.

———. *The Young against the Old: Generational Conflict in First Clement.* Lanham, MD: Lexington/Fortress, 2018.

Wengst, Klaus. *"Freut euch, ihr Völker, mit Gottes Volk!" Israel und die Völker als Thema des Paulus.* Stuttgart: Kohlhammer, 2008.

White, John L. *Light from Ancient Letters.* Philadelphia: Fortress, 1986.

White, Peter. *Cicero in Letters.* Oxford: Oxford University Press, 2010.

Whitehead, Alfred North. *Process and Reality: An Essay in Cosmology.* New York: Harper, 1960; repr. of 1929.

Wickeri, Philip. *Seeking the Common Ground: Protestant Christianity, the Three-Self Movement, and China's United Front.* Maryknoll, NY: Orbis Books, 1988.

Windisch, Hans. *Der Zweite Korintherbrief.* Göttingen: Vandenhoeck & Ruprecht, 1924; repr., 1970.

Wire, Antoinette Clark. *The Corinthian Women Prophets: A Reconstruction through Paul's Rhetoric.* Minneapolis: Fortress, 1990; repr., Eugene, OR: Wipf and Stock, 2003.

———. "Human and Nonhuman Agency in Paul's Corinthian Letters." In *After the Corinthian Women Prophets: Rhetoric, Power, and Possibilities,* edited by Joseph A. Marchal. SemeiaSt. Atlanta: SBL Press, forthcoming.

———. *Holy Lives, Holy Deaths: A Close Hearing of Early Jewish Storytellers.* Atlanta: Society of Biblical Literature, 2002.

———. *Mark Composed in Performance.* Eugene, OR: Wipf and Stock, 2011.

———. "Reconciled to Glory in Corinth? 2 Cor 2:14–7:4." Pages 263–75 in *Antiquity and Humanity: Essays on Ancient Religion and Philosophy Presented to Hans Dieter Betz on His 70th Birthday,* edited by Adela Yarbro Collins and Margaret M. Mitchell. Tübingen: Mohr Siebeck, 2001.

———. "Women in Early Christian Stories: Serving and Served, Rural and Urban, in Occupied and Pacified Provinces." Pages 19–44 in *Bridges in New Testament Interpretation: Interdisciplinary Advances,* edited by Neil Elliott and Werner Kelber. Lanham, MD: Lexington Books/Fortress, 2018.

Wisemann, James. *The Land of the Ancient Corinthians.* Göteborg: Paul Aströms, 1978.

Wolff, Christian. *Der zweite Brief des Paulus an die Korinther.* Berlin: Evangelische Verlagsanstalt, 1989.

Wright, N. T. *Paul and the Faithfulness of God.* Minneapolis: Fortress, 2013.

Young, Frances, and David F. Ford. *Meaning and Truth in 2 Corinthians.* London: SPCK, 1987.

Zaleski, Carol. *Otherworld Journeys: Accounts of Near-Death Experience in Medieval and Modern Times.* New York: Oxford University Press, 1987.

Zanker, Paul. *The Power of Images in the Age of Augustus.* Ann Arbor: University of Michigan Press, 1988.

Zeilinger, Franz. "Die Echtheit von 2 Cor 6:14–7:1." *JBL* 112 (1993): 71–80.

Zmijewski, Josef. *Der Stil der paulinischen "Narrenrede:" Analyse der Sprachgestaltung in 2 Kor 11,1–12,10 als Beitrag zur Methodik von Stiluntersuchungen neutestamentlicher Texte.* Köln-Bonn: Hanstein, 1978.

Index of Scripture References and Other Ancient Writings

309

Index of Subjects

Barrett, C. K., 148 n. 36, 160 n. 3
Barrier, Jeremy W., 241 n. 16
Baumert, N., 81 n. 18
Baur, Ferdinand Christian, 166, 269 n. 1, 279 n. 17
Beale, G. K., 187 n. 37
Beard, Mary, lviii n. 24
Becker, Eve-Marie, lvi, lxvi n. 40, 16 n. 2, 32, 202, 210 n. 2
Belleville, Linda, 62 n. 15, 63 n. 16, 69 n. 39, 178 n. 10
Benner, Allen Rogers, 185 n. 32
Bennett, Jane, 58 n. 6
Berge, Loïc P. M., 263
Betz, Hans Dieter, li n. 7, 23 n. 18, 30 n. 34, 138 n. 3, 164 n. 8, 173, 176–78, 183 n. 23, 184 n. 30, 186 n. 33, 189 n. 49, 190 n. 53, 193 n. 65, 201–2, 203 n. 93, 218 n. 13, 219 n. 16, 222 n. 26, 239 n. 13, 240–41, 247 n. 39, 249, 261–62, 267 n. 91, 275 n. 8
Bieringer, Reimund, liii, lv, 116 n. 2, 127, 133, 139 n. 6, 140 n. 12, 145 n. 28, 165 n. 12, 210, 222 n. 26, 227, 294 n. 44, 247 n. 39
birth pains, xlvii, 107–9, 111, 116
blessing, 2, 4–6, 9–10, 12–13, 179, 236, 281, 283
boasting
    rivals accused of, 218, 221–22, 253
    Paul's as a fool/in weakness, 211, 226–227, 231–32, 234–35, 247, 250–54
Bolton, David, 189 n. 48, 192 n. 60
Boobyer, George Henry, 5 n. 12, 78 n. 5
Bornkamm, Günter, liv
Bosenius, Bärbel, liii n. 12, 216 n. 7, 223 n. 28, 239 n. 15
Botha, Pieter J. J., lvi n. 19
Bouttier, Michel, 83 n. 26, 86 n. 34, 87 n. 39, 90 n. 46, 95 n. 58, 129 n. 29

Breytenbach, Cilliers, 42 n. 16, 125 n. 21, 131, 134 n. 38, 253 n. 62
Briggs, Sheila, 82 n. 21
brothers
    carriers of collection, 198–201
    English translation, 12, 20, 145–56, 195–96
Bultmann, Rudolph, 42, 137 n. 1
Burchard, C., 72 n. 46, 93 n. 56

Calvin, John, 91
Carrez, Maurice, 38, 60
Cartlidge, David R., 124 n. 17
catalogue of hardships, 3–4, 82–83, 146–51, 233–40, 238 n. 12
Charlesworth, James H., 45 n. 27, 72 n. 46, 84 n. 29, 118 n. 7, 120 n. 11, 244 n. 32
Charlesworth, M. P., 42 n. 12
Chen, Kuanrong, xix, 7–8
Coakley, Sarah, 57
Cobb, John B., Jr., 58 n. 6
Cohoon, J. W., 41 n. 11, 149 n. 38, 277 n. 13
Collange, J. F., 131 n. 33, 132
colleagues, coworkers of Paul, 38, 50, 67, 90–91, 115, 214, 264
Collins, John N., 49 n. 35, 59 n. 9, 66 n. 31, 124 n. 17
Colson, F. H., 71 n. 44, 88 n. 40, 100 n. 5, 105 n. 15
comfort, courage, 2–4, 7
commentary, feminist
    at three ranges, xlvii–l, and developed in each chapter
competition
    between cities, provinces, 22, 24, 26–28, 163–64, 185–86, 194
    between Paul and his rivals, lvii, 214, 232, 235
confidence
    in face of death, lxii, 66, 83, 105–6, 283

Author

Antoinette Wire is professor emerita of New Testament at San Francisco Theological Seminary and the Graduate Theological Union. She lives in Claremont, California, in a community of activists retired from religious and nonprofit organizations. Her publications include *Holy Lives, Holy Deaths: A Close Hearing of Early Jewish Storytellers* (Atlanta: Society of Biblical Literature, 2002), *Mark Composed in Performance* (Eugene, OR: Wipf and Stock, 2012), and "Women in Early Christian Stories: Serving and Served, Rural and Urban, in Occupied and Pacified Provinces," in *Bridges in New Testament Interpretation*, ed. Neil Elliott and Werner Kelber (Lanham, MD: Lexington/Fortress, 2018).

Volume Editor

Mary Ann Beavis, editor of this volume, is professor of religion and culture at St. Thomas More College in Saskatoon, Canada. She is the co-author, with HyeRan Kim-Cragg, of two volumes in this Wisdom Commentary series, *Hebrews* (2014) and *1 and 2 Thessalonians* (2016), and has written *What Does the Bible Say? A Critical Conversation with Popular Culture in a Biblically Illiterate World* (Eugene, OR: Cascade, 2017). Her current research interest is in the area of slave religiosity in early Christianity.

Series Editor

Barbara E. Reid, OP, is a Dominican Sister of Grand Rapids, Michigan. She holds a PhD in biblical studies from The Catholic University of America and is professor of New Testament studies at Catholic Theological Union, Chicago. Her most recent publications are *Wisdom's Feast: An Invitation to Feminist Interpretation of the Scriptures* (2016) and *Abiding Word: Sunday Reflections on Year A, B, C* (3 vols.; 2011, 2012, 2013). She served as vice president and academic dean at CTU from 2009 to 2018 and as president of the Catholic Biblical Association in 2014–2015.